UNIFORM STANDARDS OF PROFESSIONAL APPRAISAL PRACTICE

2020-2021 EDITION

APPRAISAL STANDARDS BOARD

Published in the United States of America.

ISBN: 978-0-9985335-1-3

All Rights Reserved
Copyright © 2020, The Appraisal Foundation.

The Appraisal Foundation reserves all rights with respect to this material. No part of this publication may be reproduced, duplicated, altered or otherwise published in electronic or paper means or in any format or form without the express written permission of the publisher.

EFFECTIVE:

January 1, 2020 through December 31, 2021

APPRAISAL STANDARDS BOARD

The Appraisal Foundation has developed a series of courses related to the *Uniform Standards of Professional Appraisal Practice (USPAP)*. These courses are available for several appraisal disciplines: Business Valuation, Personal Property, Mass Appraisal and Real Property.

Please contact your educational provider for a schedule of course offerings.

15-HOUR USPAP COURSES

15-Hour National USPAP Course (Real Property)
15-Hour Personal Property USPAP Course
15-Hour Business Appraisal USPAP Course

7-HOUR USPAP COURSES

7-Hour National USPAP Update Course (Real Property)
7 Hour USPAP Update Course for Non-Residential Real Property
7-Hour Residential Review and Compliance Course (Real Property)
7-Hour USPAP Update Course for Mass Appraisal
7-Hour USPAP Update Course for Personal Property

YELLOW BOOK COURSES

Uniform Appraisal Standards for Federal Land Acquisitions (Yellow Book) Course
USPAP and the Yellow Book, A Guide to Understanding Their Relationship

ABOUT THE APPRAISAL FOUNDATION

The Appraisal Foundation is the nation's foremost authority on the valuation profession. The organization sets the Congressionally-authorized standards and qualifications for real estate appraisers, and provides voluntary guidance on recognized valuation methods and techniques for all valuation professionals. This work advances the profession by ensuring appraisals are independent, consistent, and objective. More information on The Appraisal Foundation is available at www.appraisalfoundation.org.

CONNECT WITH US

THE APPRAISAL FOUNDATION AND THE INTERNATIONAL VALUATION STANDARDS COUNCIL

The Appraisal Foundation is an Institutional Member and proud Sponsor of the International Valuation Standards Council (IVSC). In addition, the Foundation is an active participant of the IVSC Advisory Forum Work Group.

The IVSC is an independent, not-for-profit organization that acts as the global standard setter for valuation practice and the valuation profession, serving the public interest. The IVSC is the developer of the International Valuation Standards (IVS), the latest version of the global standards for valuation professionals. For more information on the IVSC and IVS visit **www.ivsc.org**.

The Foundation and the IVSC are working together to harmonize valuation standards. As part of this effort, both groups jointly released ***A Bridge from USPAP to IVS***. This document was developed to assist appraisers familiar with the *Uniform Standards of Professional Appraisal Practice* (USPAP) to produce a valuation that is also compliant with the IVS. While the document describes additional steps necessary to ensure that compliance, a full review of both sets standards is always encouraged. Both organizations note that this joint effort unveiled more commonalities than differences in the two sets of standards.

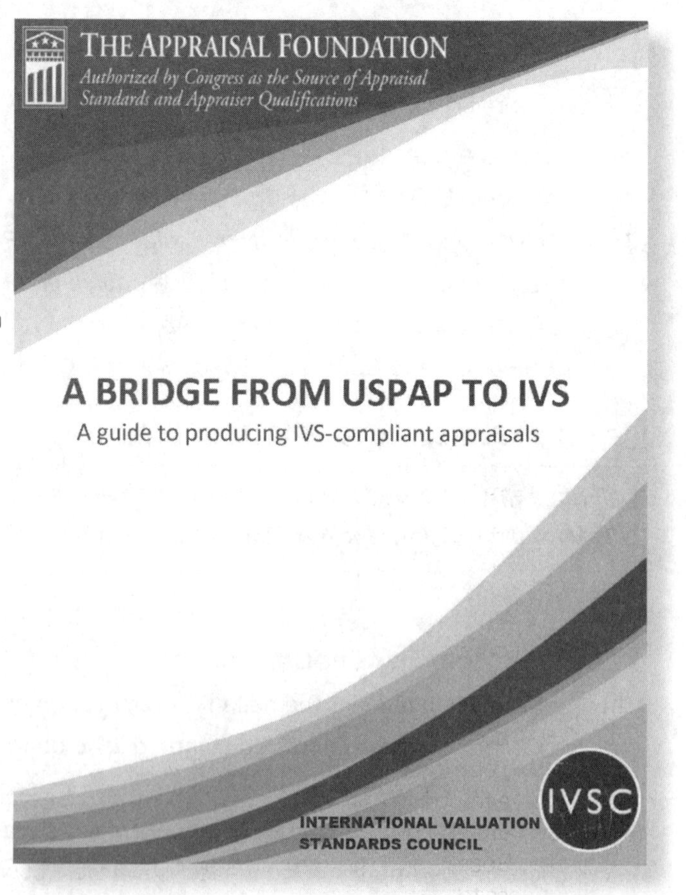

A Bridge from USPAP to IVS will be amended to be consistent with updates to IVS and USPAP as they occur.

For copies of ***A Bridge from USPAP to IVS***, visit **www.ivsc.org** or **www.appraisalfoundation.org**.

FOREWORD

The Appraisal Standards Board (ASB) of The Appraisal Foundation develops, interprets, and amends the *Uniform Standards of Professional Appraisal Practice* (USPAP) on behalf of appraisers and users of appraisal services. **The 2020-2021 Edition of USPAP (2020-2021 USPAP) is effective January 1, 2020 through December 31, 2021.**

USPAP has five sections: PREAMBLE, DEFINITIONS, Rules, Standards (including Standards Rules), and Statements on Appraisal Standards (there are currently no active Statements). For convenience of reference, USPAP is published with this Foreword and a Table of Contents. The publication also includes the Advisory Opinions and Frequently Asked Questions (FAQs) as additional reference materials. These reference materials are forms of "Other Communications" provided by the ASB for guidance only and are not part of USPAP.

It is important that individuals understand and adhere to changes that are adopted in each edition of USPAP. State and federal regulatory authorities enforce the content of the current or applicable edition of USPAP.

HISTORY OF USPAP

These Standards are based on the original *Uniform Standards of Professional Appraisal Practice* developed in 1986–87 by the Ad Hoc Committee on Uniform Standards and copyrighted in 1987 by The Appraisal Foundation. The effective date of the original Uniform Standards was April 27, 1987. Prior to the establishment of the ASB in 1989, USPAP had been adopted by major appraisal organizations in North America. USPAP represents the generally accepted and recognized standards of appraisal practice in the United States.

At its organizational meeting on January 30, 1989, the Appraisal Standards Board unanimously approved and adopted the original USPAP as the initial appraisal standards promulgated by the ASB. Portions of USPAP may be amended, interpreted, supplemented, or retired by the ASB after exposure to the appraisal profession, users of appraisal services, and the public in accordance with established rules of procedure.

CHANGES TO USPAP

Over the years, USPAP has evolved in response to changes in appraisal practice. The ASB has developed a process for developing both Standards and guidance based, in part, on written comments submitted in response to exposure drafts and oral testimony presented at public meetings.

GUIDANCE

The ASB issues guidance in the form of Advisory Opinions, *USPAP Frequently Asked Questions* (FAQ) and periodic "USPAP Q&A." These communications do not establish new Standards or interpret existing Standards and are not part of USPAP. They illustrate the applicability of Standards in specific situations and offer advice from the ASB for the resolution of specific appraisal issues and problems. Please note that the "See also FAQs" references shown in the margins of the Standards are in addition to already footnoted Advisory Opinions (AOs); the location of these references do not place greater importance of USPAP FAQs over AOs, they are simply another reference tool for the users of USPAP.

The USPAP Q&A is published periodically and available on The Appraisal Foundation website. These questions and responses are compiled and published in the *USPAP Frequently Asked Questions*.

INTERACTING WITH THE APPRAISAL STANDARDS BOARD

The ASB invites questions about USPAP, commentary on USPAP and proposed changes to USPAP from all interested parties, including appraisers, state enforcement agencies, users of appraisal services, and the public. The ASB is composed of five to nine members who are appointed by the Board of Trustees (BOT) and may serve up to eight years. Activities of the Board are directed by the Chair, who is appointed by the BOT for a one-year term. The current ASB consists of Board members who specialize in residential, commercial, personal, and mass property appraisal work. The process to become a Board member is competitive and transparent. The ASB issues Exposure Drafts on proposed changes to USPAP and obtains feedback at public meetings throughout the year in various regions of the country. To attend their meeting in-person, or watch them via a livestream, please check the Foundation's Events page for list of upcoming public meetings. Additionally, the ASB participates in speaking engagements on request and conducts live webinars. Please check the Webinars page on the Foundation's website to watch the recorded webinars, which are also posted on Foundation's YouTube channel.

© The Appraisal Foundation

If you have any comments, questions, or suggestions regarding USPAP, please contact the ASB.

Appraisal Standards Board
The Appraisal Foundation
1155 15th Street, NW, Suite 1111
Washington, DC 20005
Phone: 202-347-7722

E-Mail: info@appraisalfoundation.org

www.appraisalfoundation.org

2019 APPRAISAL STANDARDS BOARD MEMBERS

Wayne R. Miller – Chair
Patricia H. Atwood – Vice Chair
Michelle Czekalski Bradley
Lisa Desmarais
Roberta Ouellette
Robert P. Reardon

(The 2020-2021 USPAP was adopted by the 2019 Appraisal Standards Board on April 5, 2019.)

2018 APPRAISAL STANDARDS BOARD MEMBERS

Margaret A. Hambleton – Chair
Wayne R. Miller – Vice Chair
Patricia H. Atwood
Steven H. Berg
Michelle Czekalski Bradley
Lisa Desmarais
R. Lee Robinette

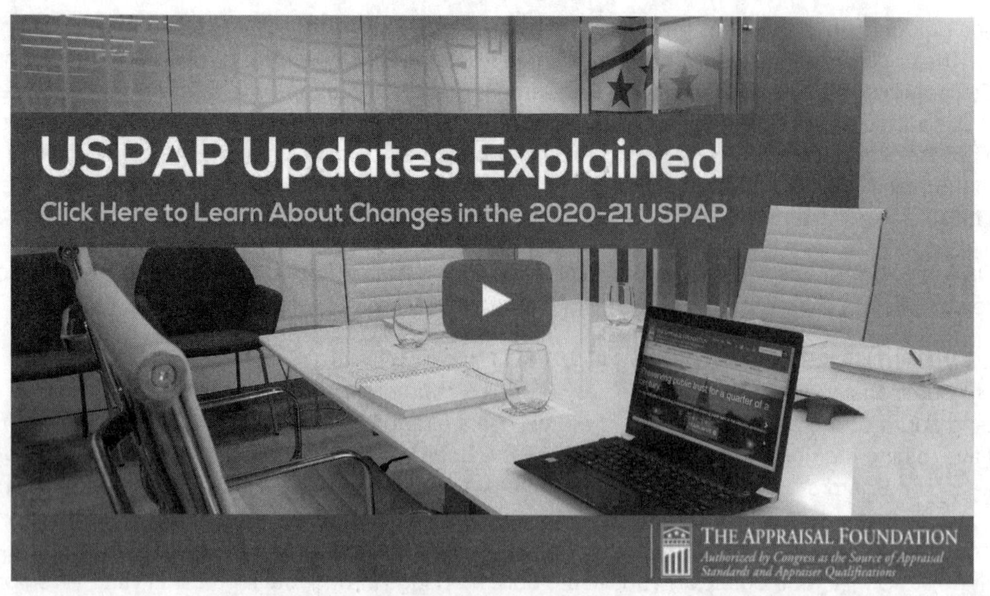

Learn about the new changes to 2020-21 edition of USPAP in the USPAP Updates Explained video on our Webinars page: www.appraisalfoundation.org.

© The Appraisal Foundation

REVISIONS TO USPAP AND USPAP ADVISORY OPINIONS

After the publication of the 2018-19 edition of USPAP, a series of one discussion and four exposure drafts were released to obtain feedback on possible modifications for the 2020-21 edition. On April 5, 2019, the Appraisal Standards Board (ASB) adopted modifications for the 2020-21 edition of the *Uniform Standards of Professional Appraisal Practice* (USPAP). These modifications include:

1. **Revisions to the Standards regarding reporting options and Comments in Standards Rules –** The Board adopted revisions to permit additional intended users besides the client for Restricted Appraisal Reports, as long as the other intended users are named in the report (i.e., not merely identified "by type"). The second adopted change for Restricted Appraisal Reports is a simplification of warning language that will no longer include a reference to the appraiser's workfile.

   The Board also adopted revisions to Standards Rules 2-3 and 4-3 to address situations where an assignment requires the use of a certification that does not include all of the certification elements in the respective Standards Rule. In such cases an appraiser is required to include a supplemental certification, which includes the remaining required certification elements. Notably, the Board is also clarifying that such supplemental certifications do not require signature by the appraiser(s). The Board also adopted revisions to enumerate and clarify the minimum level of reporting necessary under the reporting requirements for an Appraisal Report in STANDARDS 2, 8, and 10.

   The Board voted to delete some Comments that had redundant requirements clearly stated elsewhere, and to incorporate other Comments directly into the Standards Rules. In some cases, Comments were retained to provide interpretation and/or establish the context and conditions for the application of Standards Rules.

   The Board also adopted labels for each Standards Rule in order to make it easier for users to locate specific rule content in the document.

2. **Revision of SCOPE OF WORK RULE –** The Board adopted the proposed revisions in the Fourth Exposure Draft to add language to the Disclosure Obligations section of the SCOPE OF WORK RULE to address the flexibility afforded the appraiser in the disclosure of scope of work.

3. **Revisions to COMPETENCY RULE –** The Board moved the "Perfection is impossible to attain..." Comment from Standards Rules 1-1, 3-1, 5-1, 7-1, and 9-1, and added a slightly edited version to the COMPETENCY RULE. Moving the Comment into the COMPETENCY RULE reduces duplication and, at the same time, broadens the applicability since the COMPETENCY RULE applies to both development and reporting in all disciplines.

4. **Revising the DEFINITIONS –** The Board adopted some modifications and additions to the DEFINITIONS in order to help readers better understand USPAP. The Board adopted changes to the definitions of APPRAISAL, APPRAISAL PRACTICE, APPRAISAL REVIEW, APPRAISER, ASSIGNMENT CONDITIONS, ASSIGNMENT RESULTS, CLIENT, COST, EXPOSURE TIME, MARKET VALUE, PERSONAL PROPERTY, REAL PROPERTY, VALUATION SERVICE, VALUE and WORKFILE.

   The Board also adopted new definitions for the terms ASSIGNMENT ELEMENTS, EFFECTIVE DATE, MISLEADING, PERSONAL INSPECTION, PHYSICAL CHARACTERISTICS, and RELEVANT CHARACTERISTICS, to help clarify how each term is used in USPAP.

5. **Other Edits to Improve Clarity and Enforceability of USPAP –** The Board adopted changes related to the phrases "accept an assignment" and "intangible items." The edits are intended to improve clarity and consistency.

6. **Revisions to ADVISORY OPINION 1, *Sales History* –** The Board adopted revisions to Advisory Opinion 1, *Sales History*, to provide additional detail and illustrations related to an appraiser's obligation to analyze the listing, contract, and sales history of the subject property.

© The Appraisal Foundation

7. **Revisions to ADVISORY OPINION 2, *Inspection of Subject Property* –** The Board adopted revisions to Advisory Opinion 2, *Inspection of Subject Property*, to provide guidance and illustrations reflecting changes in the marketplace related to an appraiser's inspection of a property.

8. **Revisions to ADVISORY OPINION 3, *Update of a Prior Appraisal* –** The Board adopted revisions to Advisory Opinion 3, *Update of a Prior Appraisal*, to clarify an appraiser's obligations regarding confidentiality when performing an update of an appraisal using the "incorporate by reference" option.

9. **Revisions to ADVISORY OPINION 28, *Scope of Work Decision, Performance, and Disclosure* –** The Board adopted revisions to Advisory Opinion 28, *Scope of Work Decisions, Performance, and Disclosure*, including a new Illustration 2 regarding a scope of work problem related to tangible personal property, and adding an additional illustration regarding a scope of work problem related to real property.

10. **Revisions to ADVISORY OPINION 31, *Assignments Involving More than One Appraiser* –** The Board adopted revisions to Advisory Opinion 31, *Assignments Involving More than One Appraiser*, to help clarify guidance related to significant appraisal assistance and Standards Rules 2-3, 4-3, 6-3, 8-3, and 10-3.

11. **Revisions to ADVISORY OPINION 32, *Ad Valorem Property Tax Appraisal and Mass Appraisal Assignments* –** The Board adopted revisions to Advisory Opinion 32, *Ad Valorem Property Tax Appraisal and Mass Appraisal Assignments*, that adds a new Illustration 5 on the topic of an appraiser's obligations regarding the quantity and quality of factual data collected in a mass appraisal assignment.

12. **Revisions to ADVISORY OPINION 36, *Identification and Disclosure of Client, Intended Use, and Intended Users* –** The Board adopted revisions to Advisory Opinion 36, *Identification and Disclosure of Client, Intended Use, and Intended Users*, to clarify an appraiser's requirement to make a proper disclosure of the client and any other intended users in an Appraisal Report or Restricted Appraisal Report, particularly in cases where the client has requested anonymity in the report.

13. **Creation of ADVISORY OPINION 38, *Content of an Appraisal Report and Restricted Appraisal Report* –** The Board adopted newly-created Advisory Opinion 38, *Content of an Appraisal Report and Restricted Appraisal Report*. The new Advisory Opinion compares the reporting requirements under the revised Appraisal Report and Restricted Appraisal Report options, and replaces the prior guidance offered in Advisory Opinions 11 and 12.

14. **Retirement of ADVISORY OPINION 4, *Standards Rule 1-5(b)*; ADVISORY OPINION 11, *Content of the Appraisal Report Options of Standards Rules 2-2, 8-2, and 10-2*; and ADVISORY OPINION 12, *Use of the Appraisal Report Options of Standards Rules 2-2, 8-2, and 10-2* –** The Board adopted the retirement of Advisory Opinions 4, 11, and 12. Advisory Opinion 4 was narrowly-focused, and was more appropriately housed where it also currently exists in the USPAP *Frequently Asked Questions*. As stated above, Advisory Opinions 11 and 12 have been replaced with the newly-created Advisory Opinion 38, *Content of an Appraisal Report and Restricted Appraisal Report*.

Administrative edits were also made to USPAP and all guidance material, including the *USPAP Advisory Opinions* and *USPAP Frequently Asked Questions*, for conformity and consistency. The details of the changes to the 2020-21 edition of USPAP can be read on The Appraisal Foundation's website, www.appraisalfoundation.org in a document entitled *2019 Summary of Actions Related to Proposed USPAP Changes*.

© The Appraisal Foundation

TABLE OF CONTENTS

UNIFORM STANDARDS OF PROFESSIONAL APPRAISAL PRACTICE

STANDARDS AND STANDARD RULES

STATEMENTS ON APPRAISAL STANDARDS

Statements on Appraisal Standards (SMT) are authorized by the by-laws of The Appraisal Foundation and are specifically for the purposes of clarification, interpretation, explanation, or elaboration of the *Uniform Standards of Professional Appraisal Practice* (USPAP). Statements have the full weight of a Standards Rule and can be adopted by the Appraisal Standards Board only after exposure and comment. There are currently no active Statements.

© The Appraisal Foundation

PREAMBLE

The purpose of the *Uniform Standards of Professional Appraisal Practice* (USPAP) is to promote and maintain a high level of public trust in appraisal practice by establishing requirements for appraisers. It is essential that appraisers develop and communicate their analyses, opinions, and conclusions to intended users of their services in a manner that is meaningful and not misleading.

The Appraisal Standards Board promulgates USPAP for both appraisers and users of appraisal services. The appraiser's responsibility is to protect the overall public trust and it is the importance of the role of the appraiser that places ethical obligations on those who serve in this capacity. USPAP reflects the current standards of the appraisal profession.

USPAP addresses the ethical and performance obligations of appraisers through DEFINITIONS, Rules, Standards, Standards Rules, and Statements (there are currently no active Statements).

- The DEFINITIONS establish the application of certain terminology in USPAP.
- The ETHICS RULE sets forth the requirements for integrity, impartiality, objectivity, independent judgment, and ethical conduct.
- The RECORD KEEPING RULE establishes the workfile requirements for appraisal and appraisal review assignments.
- The COMPETENCY RULE presents pre-assignment and assignment conditions for knowledge and experience.
- The SCOPE OF WORK RULE presents obligations related to problem identification, research, and analyses.
- The JURISDICTIONAL EXCEPTION RULE preserves the balance of USPAP if a portion is contrary to law or public policy of a jurisdiction.
- The Standards establish the requirements for appraisal and appraisal review and the manner in which each is communicated.
  - STANDARDS 1 and 2 establish requirements for the development and communication of a real property appraisal.
  - STANDARDS 3 and 4 establish requirements for the development and communication of an appraisal review.
  - STANDARDS 5 and 6 establish requirements for the development and communication of a mass appraisal.
  - STANDARDS 7 and 8 establish requirements for the development and communication of a personal property appraisal.
  - STANDARDS 9 and 10 establish requirements for the development and communication of a business or intangible asset appraisal.
- There are currently no active Statements on Appraisal Standards.
- Comments are an integral part of USPAP and have the same weight as the component they address. These extensions of the DEFINITIONS, Rules, and Standards Rules provide interpretation and establish the context and conditions for application.

When Do USPAP Rules and Standards Apply?

USPAP does not establish who or which assignments must comply. Neither The Appraisal Foundation nor its Appraisal Standards Board is a government entity with the power to make, judge, or enforce law. An appraiser must comply with USPAP when either the service or the appraiser is required by law, regulation, or agreement with the client. Individuals may also choose to comply with USPAP any time that individual is performing the service as an appraiser. In order to comply with USPAP, an appraiser must meet the following obligations:

- An appraiser must act competently and in a manner that is independent, impartial, and objective.
- An appraiser must comply with the ETHICS RULE in all aspects of appraisal practice.
- An appraiser must maintain the data, information and analysis necessary to support his or her opinions for appraisal and appraisal review assignments in accordance with the RECORD KEEPING RULE.
- An appraiser must comply with the COMPETENCY RULE and the JURISDICTIONAL EXCEPTION RULE for all assignments.

© The Appraisal Foundation

46 • When an appraiser provides an opinion of value in an assignment, the appraiser must also comply with the
47 SCOPE OF WORK RULE, the RECORD KEEPING RULE, the applicable development and reporting Standards
48 and applicable Statements (there are currently no active Statements).
49 • When an appraiser provides an opinion about the quality of another appraiser's work that was performed as
50 part of an appraisal or appraisal review assignment, the appraiser must also comply with the SCOPE OF WORK
51 RULE, the RECORD KEEPING RULE, applicable portions of STANDARDS 3 and 4, and applicable Statements
52 (there are currently no active Statements).
53 • When preparing an appraisal or appraisal review that is a component of a larger assignment with additional
54 opinions, conclusions, or recommendations, the appraisal or appraisal review component must comply with
55 the applicable development and reporting Standards and applicable Statements (there are currently no
56 active Statements), and the remaining component of the assignment must comply with the ETHICS RULE, the
57 COMPETENCY RULE, and the JURISDICTIONAL EXCEPTION RULE.

© The Appraisal Foundation

DEFINITIONS

Defined terms are intended to clarify the meaning of words or phrases in USPAP that differ from or are not found in popular English dictionaries and, in a few instances, to indicate which popular dictionary definition is meant to be used if there are multiple definitions.

For the purpose of the *Uniform Standards of Professional Appraisal Practice* (USPAP), the following definitions apply:

APPRAISAL: (noun) the act or process of developing an opinion of value; an opinion of value.
(adjective) of or pertaining to appraising and related functions such as appraisal practice or appraisal services.

> Comment: An appraisal is numerically expressed as a specific amount, as a range of numbers, or as a relationship (e.g., not more than, not less than) to a previous value opinion or numerical benchmark (e.g., assessed value, collateral value).

APPRAISAL PRACTICE: valuation services performed by an individual acting as an appraiser, including but not limited to appraisal and appraisal review.

> Comment: *Appraisal practice* is provided only by appraisers, while *valuation services* are provided by a variety of professionals and others.[1] The terms *appraisal* and *appraisal review* are intentionally generic and are not mutually exclusive. For example, an opinion of value may be required as part of an appraisal review assignment.

APPRAISAL REVIEW: (noun) the act or process of developing an opinion about the quality of another appraiser's work (i.e., a report, part of a report, a workfile, or some combination of these), that was performed as part of an appraisal or appraisal review assignment; (adjective) of or pertaining to an opinion about the quality of another appraiser's work that was performed as part of an appraisal or appraisal review assignment.

APPRAISER: one who is expected to perform valuation services competently and in a manner that is independent, impartial, and objective.[2]

APPRAISER'S PEERS: other appraisers who have expertise and competency in a similar type of assignment.[3]

ASSIGNMENT: a valuation service that is provided by an appraiser as a consequence of an agreement with a client.

ASSIGNMENT CONDITIONS: Assumptions, extraordinary assumptions, hypothetical conditions, laws and regulations, jurisdictional exceptions, and other conditions that affect the scope of work.

ASSIGNMENT ELEMENTS: Specific information needed to identify the appraisal or appraisal review problem: client and any other intended users; intended use of the appraiser's opinions and conclusions; type and definition of value; effective date of the appraiser's opinions and conclusions; subject of the assignment and its relevant characteristics; and assignment conditions.

ASSIGNMENT RESULTS: An appraiser's opinions or conclusions, not limited to value, that were developed when performing an appraisal assignment, an appraisal review assignment, or a valuation service other than an appraisal or appraisal review.

> Comment: Physical characteristics are not assignment results.

BIAS: a preference or inclination that precludes an appraiser's impartiality, independence, or objectivity in an assignment.

BUSINESS ENTERPRISE: an entity pursuing an economic activity.

BUSINESS EQUITY: the interests, benefits, and rights inherent in the ownership of a business enterprise or a part thereof in any form (including, but not necessarily limited to, capital stock, partnership interests, cooperatives, sole proprietorships, options, and warrants).

1 See Advisory Opinion 21, *USPAP Compliance*.
2 See PREAMBLE and Advisory Opinion 21, *USPAP Compliance*.
3 See Advisory Opinion 29, *An Acceptable Scope of Work*.

© The Appraisal Foundation

96 **CLIENT:** the party or parties (i.e., individual, group, or entity) who engage an appraiser by employment or contract in a
97 specific assignment, whether directly or through an agent.

98 **CONFIDENTIAL INFORMATION:** information that is either:

99 • identified by the client as confidential when providing it to an appraiser and that is not available from any
100 other source;[4] or
101 • classified as confidential or private by applicable law or regulation.[5]

102 **COST:** the actual or estimated amount required to create, reproduce, replace, or obtain a property.

103 **CREDIBLE:** worthy of belief.

104 Comment: Credible assignment results require support, by relevant evidence and logic, to the degree
105 necessary for the intended use.

106 **EFFECTIVE DATE:** the date to which an appraiser's analyses, opinions, and conclusions apply; also referred to as date
107 of value.

108 **EXPOSURE TIME**: an opinion, based on supporting market data, of the length of time that the property interest being
109 appraised would have been offered on the market prior to the hypothetical consummation of a sale at market value
110 on the effective date of the appraisal.[6]

111 **EXTRAORDINARY ASSUMPTION:** an assignment-specific assumption as of the effective date regarding uncertain
112 information used in an analysis which, if found to be false, could alter the appraiser's opinions or conclusions.

113 Comment: Uncertain information might include physical, legal, or economic characteristics of the subject
114 property; or conditions external to the property, such as market conditions or trends; or the integrity of data
115 used in an analysis.

116 **FEASIBILITY ANALYSIS:** a study of the cost-benefit relationship of an economic endeavor.

117 **HYPOTHETICAL CONDITION:** a condition, directly related to a specific assignment, which is contrary to what is
118 known by the appraiser to exist on the effective date of the assignment results, but is used for the purpose of analysis.

119 Comment: Hypothetical conditions are contrary to known facts about physical, legal, or economic
120 characteristics of the subject property; or about conditions external to the property, such as market
121 conditions or trends; or about the integrity of data used in an analysis.

122 **INTANGIBLE PROPERTY (INTANGIBLE ASSETS):** nonphysical assets, including but not limited to franchises,
123 trademarks, patents, copyrights, goodwill, equities, securities, and contracts as distinguished from physical assets
124 such as facilities and equipment.

125 **INTENDED USE:** the use(s) of an appraiser's reported appraisal or appraisal review assignment results, as identified
126 by the appraiser based on communication with the client at the time of the assignment.[7]

127 **INTENDED USER:** the client and any other party as identified, by name or type, as users of the appraisal or
128 appraisal review report by the appraiser, based on communication with the client at the time of the assignment.[8]

129 **JURISDICTIONAL EXCEPTION:** an assignment condition established by applicable law or regulation, which precludes
130 an appraiser from complying with a part of USPAP.

---

4 See Confidentiality section of the ETHICS RULE.

5 For example, pursuant to the passage of the Gramm-Leach-Bliley Act in November 1999, some public agencies have adopted privacy regulations that affect appraisers. The Federal Trade Commission (FTC) issued two rules. The first rule (16 CFR 313) focuses on the protection of "non-public personal information" provided by consumers to those involved in financial activities "found to be closely related to banking or usual in connection with the transaction of banking." These activities include "appraising real or personal property." See GLB-Privacy. The second rule (16 CFR 314) requires appraisers to safeguard customer non-public personal information. See GLB-Safeguards-Rule. Significant liability exists for appraisers should they fail to comply with these FTC rules.

6 See Advisory Opinion 35, *Reasonable Exposure Time in Real and Personal Property Opinions of Value*.

7 See Advisory Opinion 36, *Identification and Disclosure of Client, Intended Use, and Intended Users* (AO-36).

8 See AO-36.

© The Appraisal Foundation

MARKET VALUE: a type of value, stated as an opinion, that presumes the transfer of a property (i.e., a right of ownership or a bundle of such rights), as of a certain date, under specific conditions set forth in the value definition that is identified by the appraiser as applicable in an appraisal.[9] 131 132 133

Comment: Appraisers are cautioned to identify the exact definition of market value, and its authority, applicable in each appraisal completed for the purpose of market value. 134 135

MASS APPRAISAL: the process of valuing a universe of properties as of a given date using standard methodology, employing common data, and allowing for statistical testing. 136 137

MASS APPRAISAL MODEL: a mathematical expression of how supply and demand factors interact in a market. 138

MISLEADING: Intentionally or unintentionally misrepresenting, misstating, or concealing relevant facts or conclusions. 139

PERSONAL INSPECTION: a physical observation performed to assist in identifying relevant property characteristics in a valuation service. 140 141

Comment: An appraiser's inspection is typically limited to those things readily observable without the use of special testing or equipment. Appraisals of some types of property, such as gems and jewelry, may require the use of specialized equipment. An inspection by an appraiser is not the equivalent of an inspection by an inspection professional (e.g., a structural engineer, home inspector, or art conservator).[10] 142 143 144 145

PERSONAL PROPERTY: any tangible or intangible article that is subject to ownership and not classified as real property, including identifiable tangible objects that are considered by the general public as being "personal," such as furnishings, artwork, antiques, gems and jewelry, collectibles, machinery and equipment; and intangible property that is created and stored electronically such as plans for installation art, choreography, emails, or designs for digital tokens. 146 147 148 149 150

PHYSICAL CHARACTERISTICS: attributes of a property that are observable or measurable as a matter of fact, as distinguished from opinions and conclusions, which are the result of some level of analysis or judgment. 151 152

PRICE: the amount asked, offered, or paid for a property. 153

Comment: Once stated, *price* is a fact, whether it is publicly disclosed or retained in private. Because of the financial capabilities, motivations, or special interests of a given buyer or seller, the price paid for a property may or may not have any relation to the *value* that might be ascribed to that property by others. 154 155 156

REAL ESTATE: an identified parcel or tract of land, including improvements, if any. 157

REAL PROPERTY: the interests, benefits, and rights inherent in the ownership of real estate. 158

RELEVANT CHARACTERISTICS: features that may affect a property's value or marketability such as legal, economic, or physical characteristics. 159 160

REPORT: any communication, written or oral, of an appraisal or appraisal review that is transmitted to the client or a party authorized by the client upon completion of an assignment. 161 162

SCOPE OF WORK: the type and extent of research and analyses in an appraisal or appraisal review assignment.[11] 163

SIGNATURE: personalized evidence indicating authentication of the work performed by the appraiser and the acceptance of the responsibility for content, analyses, and the conclusions in the report. 164 165

VALUATION SERVICE: a service pertaining to an aspect of property value, regardless of the type of service and whether it is performed by appraisers or by others. 166 167

VALUE: the monetary relationship between properties and those who buy, sell, or use those properties, expressed as an opinion of the worth of a property at a given time. 168 169

9 See General Comment on Market Value Definitions in Advisory Opinion 22, *Scope of Work in Market Value Appraisal Assignments for Real Property*.
10 See Advisory Opinion 2, *Inspection of Subject Property*.
11 See SCOPE OF WORK RULE.

© The Appraisal Foundation

170 Comment: In appraisal practice, value will always be qualified - for example, market value, liquidation value,
171 or investment value.

172 **WORKFILE:** data, information, and documentation necessary to support the appraiser's opinions and conclusions and
173 to show compliance with USPAP.[12]

12 See RECORD KEEPING RULE.

© The Appraisal Foundation

ETHICS RULE

An appraiser must promote and preserve the public trust inherent in appraisal practice by observing the highest standards of professional ethics. 174 175

An appraiser must comply with USPAP when obligated by law or regulation, or by agreement with the client or intended users. In addition to these requirements, an individual should comply any time that individual represents that he or she is performing the service as an appraiser. 176 177 178

Comment: This Rule specifies the personal obligations and responsibilities of the individual appraiser. An individual appraiser employed by a group or organization that conducts itself in a manner that does not conform to USPAP should take steps that are appropriate under the circumstances to ensure compliance with USPAP. 179 180 181

This ETHICS RULE is divided into three sections: **Conduct**, **Management**, and **Confidentiality**, which apply to all appraisal practice. 182 183

FAQ See also FAQ 10-33

CONDUCT: 184
An appraiser must perform assignments with impartiality, objectivity, and independence, and without accommodation of personal interests. 185 186

An appraiser: 187

- **must not perform an assignment with bias;** 188
- **must not advocate the cause or interest of any party or issue;** 189
- **must not agree to perform an assignment that includes the reporting of predetermined opinions and conclusions;** 190 191
- **must not misrepresent his or her role when providing valuation services that are outside of appraisal practice;**[13] 192
- **must not communicate assignment results with the intent to mislead or to defraud;** 193
- **must not use or communicate a report or assignment results known by the appraiser to be misleading or fraudulent;** 194 195
- **must not knowingly permit an employee or other person to communicate a report or assignment results that are misleading or fraudulent;** 196 197
- **must not use or rely on unsupported conclusions relating to characteristics such as race, color, religion, national origin, gender, marital status, familial status, age, receipt of public assistance income, handicap, or an unsupported conclusion that homogeneity of such characteristics is necessary to maximize value;** 198 199 200
- **must not engage in criminal conduct;** 201
- **must not willfully or knowingly violate the requirements of the RECORD KEEPING RULE; and** 202
- **must not perform an assignment in a grossly negligent manner.** 203

Comment: Development standards (1-1, 3-1, 5-1, 7-1 and 9-1) address the requirement that "an appraiser must not render appraisal services in a careless or negligent manner." The above requirement deals with an appraiser being grossly negligent in performing an assignment which would be a violation of the Conduct section of the ETHICS RULE. 204 205 206 207

If known prior to agreeing to perform an assignment, and/or if discovered at any time during the assignment, an appraiser must disclose to the client, and in each subsequent report certification: 208 209

- **any current or prospective interest in the subject property or parties involved; and** 210
- **any services regarding the subject property performed by the appraiser, as an appraiser or in any other capacity, within the three-year period immediately preceding the agreement to perform the assignment.** 211 212

13 See Advisory Opinion 21, *USPAP Compliance*.

© The Appraisal Foundation

213 Comment: Disclosing the fact that the appraiser has previously appraised the property is permitted except
214 in the case when an appraiser has agreed with the client to keep the mere occurrence of a prior assignment
215 confidential. If an appraiser has agreed with a client not to disclose that he or she has appraised a property,
216 the appraiser must decline all subsequent agreements to perform assignments that fall within the three-year
217 period.

218 In assignments in which there is no appraisal or appraisal review report, only the initial disclosure to the client
219 is required.

220 **MANAGEMENT:**
221 **An appraiser must disclose that he or she paid a fee or commission, or gave a thing of value in connection with**
222 **the procurement of an assignment.**

223 Comment: The disclosure must appear in the certification and in any transmittal letter in which conclusions
224 are stated; however, disclosure of the amount paid is not required. In groups or
225 organizations engaged in appraisal practice, intra-company payments to employees for
226 business development do not require disclosure.

FAQ **See also FAQ 34-52**

227 **An appraiser must not agree to perform an assignment, or have a compensation arrangement**
228 **for an assignment, that is contingent on any of the following:**

229 **1. the reporting of a predetermined result (e.g., opinion of value);**
230 **2. a direction in assignment results that favors the cause of the client;**
231 **3. the amount of a value opinion;**
232 **4. the attainment of a stipulated result (e.g., that the loan closes, or taxes are reduced); or**
233 **5. the occurrence of a subsequent event directly related to the appraiser's opinions and specific to the**
234 **assignment's purpose.**

235 **An appraiser must not advertise for or solicit assignments in a manner that is false, misleading, or exaggerated.**

236 **An appraiser must affix, or authorize the use of, his or her signature to certify recognition and acceptance of his or**
237 **her USPAP responsibilities in an appraisal or appraisal review assignment (see Standards Rules 2-3, 4-3, 6-3, 8-3,**
238 **and 10-3). An appraiser may authorize the use of his or her signature only on an assignment-by-assignment basis.**

239 **An appraiser must not affix the signature of another appraiser without his or her consent.**

240 Comment: An appraiser must exercise due care to prevent unauthorized use of his or her signature. An
241 appraiser exercising such care is not responsible for unauthorized use of his or her signature.

242 **CONFIDENTIALITY:**
243 **An appraiser must protect the confidential nature of the appraiser-client relationship.**[14]

244 **An appraiser must act in good faith with regard to the legitimate interests of the client in the use of confidential**
245 **information and in the communication of assignment results.**

246 **An appraiser must be aware of, and comply with, all confidentiality and privacy laws and regulations applicable**
247 **in an assignment.**[15]

14 See Advisory Opinion 27, *Appraising the Same Property for a New Client.*

15 For example, pursuant to the passage of the Gramm-Leach-Bliley Act in November 1999, some public agencies have adopted privacy regulations that affect appraisers. The Federal Trade Commission (FTC) issued two rules. The first rule (16 CFR 313) focuses on the protection of "non-public personal information" provided by consumers to those involved in financial activities "found to be closely related to banking or usual in connection with the transaction of banking." These activities include "appraising real or personal property." See GLB-Privacy. The second rule (16 CFR 314) requires appraisers to safeguard customer non-public personal information. See GLB-Safeguards-Rule. Significant liability exists for appraisers should they fail to comply with these FTC rules.

© The Appraisal Foundation

An appraiser must not disclose: (1) confidential information; or (2) assignment results to anyone other than:

FAQ See also FAQ 53-81

- **the client;**
- **parties specifically authorized by the client;**
- **state appraiser regulatory agencies;**
- **third parties as may be authorized by due process of law; or**
- **a duly authorized professional peer review committee except when such disclosure to a committee would violate applicable law or regulation.**

An appraiser must take reasonable steps to safeguard access to confidential information and assignment results by unauthorized individuals, whether such information or results are in physical or electronic form.

An appraiser must ensure that employees, co-workers, sub-contractors, or others who may have access to confidential information or assignment results, are aware of the prohibitions on disclosure of such information or results.

A member of a duly authorized professional peer review committee must not disclose confidential information presented to the committee.

Comment: When all confidential elements of confidential information, and assignment results are removed through redaction or the process of aggregation, client authorization is not required for the disclosure of the remaining information, as modified.

© The Appraisal Foundation

RECORD KEEPING RULE

265 An appraiser must prepare a workfile for each appraisal or appraisal review assignment. A
266 workfile must be in existence prior to the issuance of any report or other communication of
267 assignment results. A written summary of an oral report must be added to the workfile within a
268 reasonable time after the issuance of the oral report.

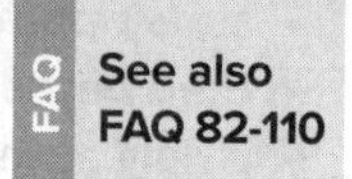

269 The workfile must include:

270 • the name of the client and the identity, by name or type, of any other intended users;
271 • true copies of all written reports, documented on any type of media. (A true copy is a replica of the report
272 transmitted to the client. A photocopy or an electronic copy of the entire report transmitted to the client
273 satisfies the requirement of a true copy.);
274 • summaries of all oral reports or testimony, or a transcript of testimony, including the appraiser's signed and
275 dated certification; and
276 • all other data, information, and documentation necessary to support the appraiser's opinions and
277 conclusions and to show compliance with USPAP, or references to the location(s) of such other data,
278 information, and documentation.

279 A workfile in support of a Restricted Appraisal Report or an oral appraisal report must be sufficient for the
280 appraiser to produce an Appraisal Report. A workfile in support of an oral appraisal review report must be
281 sufficient for the appraiser to produce an Appraisal Review Report.

282 An appraiser must retain the workfile for a period of at least five years after preparation or at least two years
283 after final disposition of any judicial proceeding in which the appraiser provided testimony related to the
284 assignment, whichever period expires last.

285 An appraiser must have custody of the workfile, or make appropriate workfile retention, access, and retrieval
286 arrangements with the party having custody of the workfile. This includes ensuring that a workfile is stored in a
287 medium that is retrievable by the appraiser throughout the prescribed record retention period.

288 An appraiser having custody of a workfile must allow other appraisers with workfile obligations related to an
289 assignment appropriate access and retrieval for the purpose of:

290 • submission to state appraiser regulatory agencies;
291 • compliance with due process of law;
292 • submission to a duly authorized professional peer review committee; or
293 • compliance with retrieval arrangements.

294 Comment: A workfile must be made available by the appraiser when required by a state appraiser regulatory
295 agency or due process of law.

296 An appraiser who willfully or knowingly fails to comply with the obligations of this RECORD KEEPING RULE is in
297 violation of the ETHICS RULE.

© The Appraisal Foundation

COMPETENCY RULE

An appraiser must: (1) be competent to perform the assignment; (2) acquire the necessary competency to perform the assignment; or (3) decline or withdraw from the assignment. In all cases, the appraiser must perform competently when completing the assignment.

FAQ See also FAQ 111-115

Perfection is impossible to attain, and competence does not require perfection. However, an appraiser must not render appraisal services in a careless or negligent manner. This Rule requires an appraiser to use due diligence and due care.

BEING COMPETENT

An appraiser must determine, prior to agreeing to perform an assignment, that he or she can perform the assignment competently. Competency requires:

1. **the ability to properly identify the problem to be addressed;**
2. **the knowledge and experience to complete the assignment competently; and**
3. **recognition of, and compliance with, laws and regulations that apply to the appraiser or to the assignment.**

Comment: Competency may apply to factors such as, but not limited to, an appraiser's familiarity with a specific type of property or asset, a market, a geographic area, an intended use, specific laws and regulations, or an analytical method. If such a factor is necessary for an appraiser to develop credible assignment results, the appraiser is responsible for having the competency to address that factor or for following the steps outlined below to satisfy this COMPETENCY RULE.

For assignments with retrospective opinions and conclusions, the appraiser must meet the requirements of this COMPETENCY RULE at the time the assignment is performed, rather than the effective date.

ACQUIRING COMPETENCY

If an appraiser determines he or she is not competent prior to agreeing to perform an assignment, the appraiser must:

1. **disclose the lack of knowledge and/or experience to the client before agreeing to perform the assignment;**
2. **take all steps necessary or appropriate to complete the assignment competently; and**
3. **describe, in the report, the lack of knowledge and/or experience and the steps taken to complete the assignment competently.**

Comment: Competency can be acquired in various ways, including, but not limited to, personal study by the appraiser, association with an appraiser reasonably believed to have the necessary knowledge and/or experience, or retention of others who possess the necessary knowledge and/or experience.

In an assignment where geographic competency is necessary, an appraiser who is not familiar with the relevant market characteristics must acquire an understanding necessary to produce credible assignment results for the specific property type and market involved.

© The Appraisal Foundation

COMPETENCY RULE

332 **When facts or conditions are discovered during the course of an assignment that cause an appraiser to**
333 **determine, at that time, that he or she lacks the required knowledge and experience to complete the**
334 **assignment competently, the appraiser must:**

335 **1. notify the client;**
336 **2. take all steps necessary or appropriate to complete the assignment competently; and**
337 **3. describe, in the report, the lack of knowledge and/or experience and the steps taken to complete the**
338 **assignment competently.**

339 **LACK OF COMPETENCY**

340 **If the assignment cannot be completed competently, the appraiser must decline or withdraw from the**
341 **assignment.**

© The Appraisal Foundation

SCOPE OF WORK RULE[16]

FAQ See also FAQ 163-331

342 **For each appraisal and appraisal review assignment, an appraiser must:**

343 1. **identify the problem to be solved;**
344 2. **determine and perform the scope of work necessary to develop credible assignment**
345 **results; and**
346 3. **disclose the scope of work in the report.**

347 **An appraiser must properly identify the problem to be solved in order to determine the appropriate scope of**
348 **work. The appraiser must be prepared to demonstrate that the scope of work is sufficient to produce credible**
349 **assignment results.**

350 Comment: Scope of work includes, but is not limited to:

351 • the extent to which the property is identified;
352 • the extent to which tangible property is inspected;
353 • the type and extent of data researched; and
354 • the type and extent of analyses applied to arrive at opinions or conclusions.

355 Appraisers have broad flexibility and significant responsibility in determining the appropriate scope of work
356 for an appraisal or appraisal review assignment.

357 Credible assignment results require support by relevant evidence and logic. The credibility of assignment
358 results is always measured in the context of the intended use.

359 **PROBLEM IDENTIFICATION**
360 **An appraiser must gather and analyze information about those assignment elements that are necessary to**
361 **properly identify the appraisal or appraisal review problem to be solved.**

362 Comment: The assignment elements necessary for problem identification are addressed in the applicable
363 Standards Rules (i.e., SR 1-2, SR 3-2, SR 5-2, SR 7-2, and SR 9-2). In an appraisal assignment, for example,
364 identification of the problem to be solved requires the appraiser to identify the following assignment
365 elements:

366 • client and any other intended users;
367 • intended use of the appraiser's opinions and conclusions;
368 • type and definition of value;
369 • effective date of the appraiser's opinions and conclusions;
370 • subject of the assignment and its relevant characteristics; and
371 • assignment conditions.

372 This information provides the appraiser with the basis for determining the type and extent of research
373 and analyses to include in the development of an appraisal. Similar information is necessary for problem
374 identification in appraisal review assignments.

375 Communication with the client is required to establish most of the information necessary for problem
376 identification. However, the identification of relevant characteristics is a judgment made by the appraiser that
377 requires competency in that type of assignment.

378 Assignment conditions include assumptions, extraordinary assumptions, hypothetical conditions, laws
379 and regulations, jurisdictional exceptions, and other conditions that affect the scope of work. Laws include
380 constitutions, legislative and court-made law, administrative rules, and ordinances. Regulations include rules
381 or orders, having legal force, issued by an administrative agency.

16 See Advisory Opinion 28, *Scope of Work Decision, Performance, and Disclosure* and Advisory Opinion 29, *An Acceptable Scope of Work*.

© The Appraisal Foundation

382 SCOPE OF WORK ACCEPTABILITY[17]

383 **The scope of work must include the research and analyses that are necessary to develop credible**
384 **assignment results.**

385 Comment: The scope of work is acceptable when it meets or exceeds:

386 • the expectations of parties who are regularly intended users for similar assignments; and
387 • what an appraiser's peers' actions would be in performing the same or a similar assignment.

388 Determining the scope of work is an ongoing process in an assignment. Information or conditions
389 discovered during the course of an assignment might cause the appraiser to reconsider the scope of work.

390 An appraiser must be prepared to support the decision to exclude any investigation, information, method, or
391 technique that would appear relevant to the client, another intended user, or the appraiser's peers.

392 **An appraiser must not allow assignment conditions to limit the scope of work to such a degree that the**
393 **assignment results are not credible in the context of the intended use.**

394 Comment: If relevant information is not available because of assignment conditions that limit research
395 opportunities (such as conditions that place limitations on inspection or information gathering), an appraiser
396 must withdraw from the assignment unless the appraiser can:

397 • modify the assignment conditions to expand the scope of work to include gathering the information; or
398 • use an extraordinary assumption about such information, if credible assignment results can still be
399 developed.

400 **An appraiser must not allow the intended use of an assignment or a client's objectives to cause the assignment**
401 **results to be biased.**

402 DISCLOSURE OBLIGATIONS

403 **The report must contain sufficient information to allow the client and other intended users to understand**
404 **the scope of work performed. The information disclosed must be appropriate for the intended use of the**
405 **assignment results.**

406 Comment: Proper disclosure is required because clients and other intended users rely on the assignment
407 results. Sufficient information includes disclosure of research and analyses performed and might also include
408 disclosure of research and analyses not performed.

409 The appraiser has broad flexibility and significant responsibility in the level of detail and manner of disclosing
410 the scope of work in the appraisal report or appraisal review report. The appraiser may, but is not required to,
411 consolidate the disclosure in a specific section or sections of the report, or use a particular label, heading or
412 subheading. An appraiser may choose to disclose the scope of work as necessary throughout the report.

17 See Advisory Opinion 29, *An Acceptable Scope of Work.*

© The Appraisal Foundation

JURISDICTIONAL EXCEPTION RULE

If any applicable law or regulation precludes compliance with any part of USPAP, only that part of USPAP becomes void for that assignment. 413 414

FAQ See also FAQ 116-126

Comment: When compliance with USPAP is required by federal law or regulation, no part of USPAP can be voided by a law or regulation of a state or local jurisdiction. 415 416

In an assignment involving a jurisdictional exception, an appraiser must: 417

1. **identify the law or regulation that precludes compliance with USPAP;** 418
2. **comply with that law or regulation;** 419
3. **clearly and conspicuously disclose in the report the part of USPAP that is voided by that law or regulation; and** 420 421
4. **cite in the report the law or regulation requiring this exception to USPAP compliance.** 422

Comment: The JURISDICTIONAL EXCEPTION RULE provides a saving or severability clause intended to preserve the balance of USPAP if compliance with one or more of its parts is precluded by the law or regulation of a jurisdiction. When an appraiser properly follows this Rule in disregarding a part of USPAP, there is no violation of USPAP. 423 424 425 426

Law includes constitutions, legislative and court-made law, and administrative rules and ordinances. Regulations include rules or orders having legal force, issued by an administrative agency. Instructions from a client or attorney do not establish a jurisdictional exception. 427 428 429

© The Appraisal Foundation

STANDARD 1: REAL PROPERTY APPRAISAL, DEVELOPMENT

430 **In developing a real property appraisal, an appraiser must identify the problem to be solved,**
431 **determine the scope of work necessary to solve the problem, and correctly complete research and**
432 **analyses necessary to produce a credible appraisal.**

FAQ **See also FAQ 127-264**

433 Comment: The requirements set forth in STANDARD 1 follow the appraisal development process in the order
434 of topics addressed and can be used by appraisers and the users of appraisal services as a checklist.

435 **STANDARDS RULE 1-1, GENERAL DEVELOPMENT REQUIREMENTS**
436 **In developing a real property appraisal, an appraiser must:**

437 **(a) be aware of, understand, and correctly employ those recognized methods and techniques that are**
438 **necessary to produce a credible appraisal;**

439 Comment: This Standards Rule recognizes that the principle of change continues to affect the manner in
440 which appraisers perform appraisal services. Changes and developments in the real estate field have a
441 substantial impact on the appraisal profession. Important changes in the cost and manner of constructing
442 and marketing commercial, industrial, and residential real estate as well as changes in the legal framework
443 in which real property rights and interests are created, conveyed, and mortgaged have resulted in
444 corresponding changes in appraisal theory and practice. Social change has also had an effect on appraisal
445 theory and practice. To keep abreast of these changes and developments, the appraisal profession is
446 constantly reviewing and revising appraisal methods and techniques and devising new methods and
447 techniques to meet new circumstances. For this reason, it is not sufficient for appraisers to simply maintain
448 the skills and the knowledge they possess when they become appraisers. Each appraiser must continuously
449 improve his or her skills to remain proficient in real property appraisal.

450 **(b) not commit a substantial error of omission or commission that significantly affects an appraisal; and**

451 Comment: An appraiser must use sufficient care to avoid errors that would significantly affect his or her
452 opinions and conclusions. Diligence is required to identify and analyze the factors, conditions, data, and other
453 information that would have a significant effect on the credibility of the assignment results.

454 **(c) not render appraisal services in a careless or negligent manner, such as by making a series of errors that,**
455 **although individually might not significantly affect the results of an appraisal, in the aggregate affects the**
456 **credibility of those results.**

457 **STANDARDS RULE 1-2, PROBLEM IDENTIFICATION**
458 **In developing a real property appraisal, an appraiser must:**

459 **(a) identify the client and other intended users;**[18]

460 **(b) identify the intended use of the appraiser's opinions and conclusions;**

461 Comment: An appraiser must not allow the intended use of an assignment or a client's objectives to cause
462 the assignment results to be biased.[19]

463 **(c) identify the type and definition of value, and ascertain whether the value is to be the most probable price:**

464 **(i) in terms of cash; or**

465 **(ii) in terms of financial arrangements equivalent to cash; or**

466 **(iii) in other precisely defined terms; and**

18 See Advisory Opinion 36, *Identification and Disclosure of Client, Intended Use, and Intended Users?* Also applicable to Standards Rule 1-2 (b).

19 See Advisory Opinion 19, *Unacceptable Assignment Conditions in Real Property Appraisal Assignments.*

© The Appraisal Foundation

(iv) **if the opinion of value is to be based on non-market financing or financing with unusual conditions or incentives, identify the terms of such financing and any influences on value;** 467 468

Comment: When reasonable exposure time is a component of the definition for the value opinion being developed, the appraiser must also develop an opinion of reasonable exposure time linked to that value opinion.[20] 469 470 471

(d) identify the effective date of the appraiser's opinions and conclusions;[21] 472

(e) identify, from sources the appraiser reasonably believes to be reliable, the characteristics of the property that are relevant to the type and definition of value and intended use of the appraisal,[22] **including:** 473 474

(i) **its location and physical, legal, and economic characteristics;** 475

(ii) **the real property interest to be valued;** 476

(iii) **any personal property, trade fixtures, or intangible assets that are not real property but are included in the appraisal;** 477 478

(iv) **any known easements, restrictions, encumbrances, leases, reservations, covenants, contracts, declarations, special assessments, ordinances, or other items of a similar nature; and** 479 480

(v) **whether the subject property is a fractional interest, physical segment, or partial holding;** 481

Comment on (i)–(v): An appraiser may use any combination of a property inspection, documents, such as a legal description, address, map reference, copy of a survey or map, property sketch, photographs, or other information to identify the relevant characteristics of the subject property. 482 483 484

When appraising proposed improvements, an appraiser must examine and have available for future examination, plans, specifications, or other documentation sufficient to identify the extent and character of the proposed improvements.[23] 485 486 487

Identification of the real property interest appraised can be based on a review of copies or summaries of title descriptions or other documents that set forth any known encumbrances. 488 489

An appraiser is not required to value the whole when the subject of the appraisal is a fractional interest, a physical segment, or a partial holding. 490 491

(f) identify any extraordinary assumptions necessary in the assignment. An extraordinary assumption may be used in an assignment only if: 492 493

(i) **the extraordinary assumption is required to properly develop credible opinions and conclusions;** 494

(ii) **the appraiser has a reasonable basis for the extraordinary assumption; and** 495

(iii) **use of the extraordinary assumption results in a credible analysis;** 496

(g) identify any hypothetical conditions necessary in the assignment. A hypothetical condition may be used in an assignment only if: 497 498

(i) **use of the hypothetical condition is clearly required for legal purposes, for purposes of reasonable analysis, or for purposes of comparison; and** 499 500

(ii) **use of the hypothetical condition results in a credible analysis; and** 501

20 See Advisory Opinion 35, *Reasonable Exposure Time in Real and Personal Property Opinions of Value*.
21 See Advisory Opinion 34, *Retrospective and Prospective Value Opinions*.
22 See Advisory Opinion 2, *Inspection of Subject Property*, and Advisory Opinion 23, *Identifying the Relevant Characteristics of the Subject Property of a Real Property Appraisal Assignment*.
23 See Advisory Opinion 17, *Appraisals of Real Property with Proposed Improvements*.

© The Appraisal Foundation

502 **(h) determine the scope of work necessary to produce credible assignment results in accordance with the**
503 **SCOPE OF WORK RULE.**[24]

504 **STANDARDS RULE 1-3, MARKET ANALYSIS, AND HIGHEST AND BEST USE**
505 **When necessary for credible assignment results in developing a market value opinion, an appraiser must:**

506 **(a) identify and analyze the effect on use and value of:**

507 **(i) existing land use regulations;**
508 **(ii) reasonably probable modifications of such land use regulations;**
509 **(iii) economic supply and demand;**
510 **(iv) the physical adaptability of the real estate; and**
511 **(v) market area trends; and**

512 Comment: An appraiser must avoid making an unsupported assumption or premise about market area
513 trends, effective age, and remaining life.

514 **(b) develop an opinion of the highest and best use of the real estate.**

515 Comment: An appraiser must analyze the relevant legal, physical, and economic factors to the extent necessary to
516 support the appraiser's highest and best use conclusion(s).

517 **STANDARDS RULE 1-4, APPROACHES TO VALUE**
518 **In developing a real property appraisal, an appraiser must collect, verify, and analyze all information necessary**
519 **for credible assignment results.**

520 **(a) When a sales comparison approach is necessary for credible assignment results, an appraiser must**
521 **analyze such comparable sales data as are available to indicate a value conclusion.**

522 **(b) When a cost approach is necessary for credible assignment results, an appraiser must:**

523 **(i) develop an opinion of site value by an appropriate appraisal method or technique;**
524 **(ii) analyze such comparable cost data as are available to estimate the cost new of the improvements**
525 **(if any); and**
526 **(iii) analyze such comparable data as are available to estimate the difference between the cost new**
527 **and the present worth of the improvements (depreciation).**

528 **(c) When an income approach is necessary for credible assignment results, an appraiser must:**

529 **(i) analyze such comparable rental data as are available and/or the potential earnings capacity of the**
530 **property to estimate the gross income potential of the property;**
531 **(ii) analyze such comparable operating expense data as are available to estimate the operating**
532 **expenses of the property;**
533 **(iii) analyze such comparable data as are available to estimate rates of capitalization and/or rates of**
534 **discount;**
535 **(iv) base projections of future rent and/or income potential and expenses on reasonably clear and**
536 **appropriate evidence;**[25] **and**
537 **(v) weigh historical information and trends, current supply and demand factors affecting such**
538 **trends, and anticipated events such as competition from developments under construction, when**
539 **developing income and expense statements and cash flow projections.**

24 See Advisory Opinion 28, *Scope of Work Decision, Performance, and Disclosure*, and Advisory Opinion 29, *An Acceptable Scope of Work*.
25 See Advisory Opinion 33, *Discounted Cash Flow Analysis*.

© The Appraisal Foundation

(d) When developing an opinion of the value of a leased fee estate or a leasehold estate, an appraiser must analyze the effect on value, if any, of the terms and conditions of the lease(s). 540 541

(e) When analyzing the assemblage of the various estates or component parts of a property, an appraiser must analyze the effect on value, if any, of the assemblage. An appraiser must refrain from valuing the whole solely by adding together the individual values of the various estates or component parts. 542 543 544

Comment: Although the value of the whole may be equal to the sum of the separate estates or parts, it also may be greater than or less than the sum of such estates or parts. 545 546

(f) When analyzing anticipated public or private improvements, located on or off the site, an appraiser must analyze the effect on value, if any, of such anticipated improvements to the extent they are reflected in market actions.[26] 547 548 549

(g) When personal property, trade fixtures, or intangible assets are included in the appraisal, the appraiser must analyze the effect on value of such non-real property assets. 550 551

Comment: When the scope of work includes an appraisal of personal property, trade fixtures, or intangible assets, competency in personal property appraisal (see STANDARD 7) or business appraisal (see STANDARD 9) is required. 552 553 554

STANDARDS RULE 1-5, SALE AGREEMENTS, OPTIONS, LISTINGS, AND PRIOR SALES 555

When the value opinion to be developed is market value, an appraiser must, if such information is available to the appraiser in the normal course of business:[27] 556 557

(a) analyze all agreements of sale, options, and listings of the subject property current as of the effective date of the appraisal; and 558 559

(b) analyze all sales of the subject property that occurred within the three (3) years prior to the effective date of the appraisal.[28] 560 561

STANDARDS RULE 1-6, RECONCILIATION 562

In developing a real property appraisal, an appraiser must: 563

(a) reconcile the quality and quantity of data available and analyzed within the approaches used; and 564

(b) reconcile the applicability and relevance of the approaches, methods and techniques used to arrive at the value conclusion(s). 565 566

26 See Advisory Opinion 17, *Appraisals of Real Property with Proposed Improvements.*
27 See Advisory Opinion 24, *Normal Course of Business.*
28 See Advisory Opinion 1, *Sales History.*

© The Appraisal Foundation

STANDARD 2: REAL PROPERTY APPRAISAL, REPORTING

567 **In reporting the results of a real property appraisal, an appraiser must communicate each analysis,**
568 **opinion, and conclusion in a manner that is not misleading.**

FAQ See also FAQ 265-334

569 Comment: STANDARD 2 addresses the content and level of information required in a report that
570 communicates the results of a real property appraisal.

571 STANDARD 2 does not dictate the form, format, or style of real property appraisal reports. The substantive
572 content of a report determines its compliance.

573 **STANDARDS RULE 2-1, GENERAL REPORTING REQUIREMENTS**
574 **Each written or oral real property appraisal report must:**

575 **(a) clearly and accurately set forth the appraisal in a manner that will not be misleading;**

576 **(b) contain sufficient information to enable the intended user(s) of the appraisal to understand the report**
577 **properly; and**

578 **(c) clearly and accurately disclose all assumptions, extraordinary assumptions, hypothetical conditions, and**
579 **limiting conditions used in the assignment.**

580 **STANDARDS RULE 2-2, CONTENT OF A REAL PROPERTY APPRAISAL REPORT**
581 **Each written real property appraisal report must be prepared under one of the following options and prominently**
582 **state which option is used: Appraisal Report or Restricted Appraisal Report.**[29]

583 **An appraiser may use any other label in addition to, but not in place of, the labels set forth in this Standards Rule**
584 **for the type of report provided. The use of additional labels such as analysis, consultation, evaluation, study, or**
585 **valuation does not exempt an appraiser from adherence to USPAP.**

586 **The report content and level of information requirements in this Standards Rule are minimums for each type of**
587 **report. An appraiser must supplement a report form, when necessary, to ensure that any intended user of the**
588 **appraisal is not misled and that the report complies with the applicable content requirements.**

589 **(a) The content of an Appraisal Report must be appropriate for the intended use of the appraisal and, at a**
590 **minimum:**

591 **(i) state the identity of the client; or if the client requested anonymity, state that the identity is**
592 **withheld at the client's request but is retained in the appraiser's workfile;**[30]

593 Comment: Because the client is an intended user, they must be identified in the report as such.
594 However, if the client has requested anonymity the appraiser must use care when identifying the client
595 to avoid violations of the Confidentiality section of the ETHICS RULE.

596 **(ii) state the identity of any other intended user(s) by name or type;**

597 Comment: A party receiving a copy of an Appraisal Report in order to satisfy disclosure requirements
598 does not become an intended user of the appraisal unless the appraiser identifies such party as an
599 intended user as part of the assignment.

600 **(iii) state the intended use of the appraisal;**

29 See Advisory Opinion 38, *Content of an Appraisal Report and Restricted Appraisal Report*.
30 See Advisory Opinion 25, *Clarification of the Client in a Federally Related Transaction*. See also Advisory Opinion 36, *Identification and Disclosure of Client, Intended Use, and Intended Users*. Also applicable to Standards Rules 2-2(a)(ii) and (iii).

© The Appraisal Foundation

(iv) contain information, documents, and/or exhibits sufficient to identify the real estate involved in the appraisal, including the physical, legal, and economic property characteristics relevant to the assignment;[31] 601 602 603

(v) state the real property interest appraised; 604

(vi) state the type and definition of value and cite the source of the definition; 605

Comment: Stating the definition of value also requires any comments needed to clearly indicate to the intended users how the definition is being applied. 606 607

When reporting an opinion of value, state whether the opinion is: 608

- in terms of cash or of financing terms equivalent to cash; or 609
- based on non-market financing or financing with unusual conditions or incentives. 610

When an opinion of value is based on non-market financing terms or financing with unusual conditions or incentives, summarize the terms of such financing and explain any influences on value. 611 612

When an opinion of reasonable exposure time has been developed in compliance with Standards Rule 1-2(c), the opinion must be stated in the report.[32] 613 614

(vii) state the effective date of the appraisal and the date of the report;[33] 615

(viii) summarize the scope of work used to develop the appraisal;[34] 616

Comment: Summarizing the scope of work includes disclosure of research and analyses performed and might also include disclosure of research and analyses not performed. 617 618

(ix) summarize the extent of any significant real property appraisal assistance; 619

(x) provide sufficient information to indicate that the appraiser complied with the requirements of STANDARD 1 by: 620 621

(1) summarizing the appraisal methods and techniques employed; 622

(2) stating the reasons for excluding the sales comparison, cost, or income approach(es) if any have not been developed; 623 624

(3) summarizing the results of analyzing the subject sales, agreements of sale, options, and listings in accordance with Standards Rule 1-5;[35] 625 626

Comment: If such information is unobtainable, a statement on the efforts undertaken by the appraiser to obtain the information is required. If such information is irrelevant, a statement acknowledging the existence of the information and citing its lack of relevance is required. 627 628 629

(4) stating the value opinion(s) and conclusion(s); and 630

(5) summarizing the information analyzed and the reasoning that supports the analyses, opinions, and conclusions, including reconciliation of the data and approaches; 631 632

(xi) state the use of the real estate existing as of the effective date and the use of the real estate reflected in the appraisal; 633 634

(xii) when an opinion of highest and best use was developed by the appraiser, state that opinion and 635

31 See Advisory Opinion 2, *Inspection of Subject Property*, and Advisory Opinion 23, *Identifying the Relevant Characteristics of the Subject Property of a Real Property Appraisal Assignment.*
32 See Advisory Opinion 35, *Reasonable Exposure Time in Real and Personal Property Opinions of Value.*
33 See Advisory Opinion 34, *Retrospective and Prospective Value Opinions.*
34 See Advisory Opinion 28, *Scope of Work Decision, Performance, and Disclosure*, and Advisory Opinion 29, *An Acceptable Scope of Work.*
35 See Advisory Opinion 1, *Sales History.*

© The Appraisal Foundation

636 **summarize the support and rationale for that opinion;**

637 **(xiii) clearly and conspicuously:**

638 - **state all extraordinary assumptions and hypothetical conditions; and**
639 - **state that their use might have affected the assignment results; and**

640 **(xiv) include a signed certification in accordance with Standards Rule 2-3.**

641 **(b) The content of a Restricted Appraisal Report must be appropriate for the intended use of the appraisal**
642 **and, at a minimum:**

643 **(i) state the identity of the client, or if the client requested anonymity, state that the identity is**
644 **withheld at the client's request but is retained in the appraiser's workfile;**[36]

645 Comment: Because the client is an intended user, they must be identified in the report as such.
646 However, if the client has requested anonymity the appraiser must use care when identifying the client
647 to avoid violations of the Confidentiality section of the ETHICS RULE.

648 **(ii) state the identity of any other intended user(s) by name;**

649 Comment: A Restricted Appraisal Report may be provided when the client is the only intended user; or,
650 when additional intended users are identified by name.

651 A party receiving a copy of a Restricted Appraisal Report in order to satisfy disclosure requirements
652 does not become an intended user of the appraisal unless the appraiser identifies such party as an
653 intended user as part of the assignment.

654 **(iii) clearly and conspicuously state a restriction that limits use of the report to the client and the named**
655 **intended user(s);**

656 **(iv) clearly and conspicuously warn that the report may not contain supporting rationale for all of the**
657 **opinions and conclusions set forth in the report;**

658 **(v) state the intended use of the appraisal;**

659 **(vi) state information sufficient to identify the real estate involved in the appraisal;**[37]

660 **(vii) state the real property interest appraised;**

661 **(viii) state the type of value and cite the source of its definition;**

662 Comment: When an opinion of reasonable exposure time has been developed in compliance with
663 Standards Rule 1-2(c), the opinion must be stated in the report.[38]

664 **(ix) state the effective date of the appraisal and the date of the report;**[39]

665 **(x) state the scope of work used to develop the appraisal;**[40]

666 Comment: Stating the scope of work includes disclosure of research and analyses performed and
667 might also include disclosure of research and analyses not performed.

668 **(xi) state the extent of any significant real property appraisal assistance;**[41]

---

36 See Advisory Opinion 36, *Identification and Disclosure of Client, Intended Use, and Intended Users*. Also applicable to Standards Rules 2-2(b)(ii) and (v).

37 See Advisory Opinion 2, *Inspection of Subject Property, and Advisory Opinion 23, Identifying the Relevant Characteristics of the Subject Property of a Real Property Appraisal Assignment.*

38 See Advisory Opinion 35, *Reasonable Exposure Time in Real Property and Personal Property Opinions of Value*.

39 See Advisory Opinion 34, *Retrospective and Prospective Value*.

40 See Advisory Opinions 28, *Scope of Work Decision, Performance, and Disclosure*, and Advisory Opinion 29, *An Acceptable Scope of Work*.

41 See Advisory Opinion 31, *Assignments Involving More than One Appraiser*.

© The Appraisal Foundation

(xii) provide sufficient information to indicate that the appraiser complied with the requirements of STANDARD 1 by: 669 670

(1) stating the appraisal methods and techniques employed; 671

(2) stating the reasons for excluding the sales comparison, cost, or income approach(es) if any have not been developed; 672 673

(3) summarizing the results of analyzing the subject sales, agreements of sale, options, and listings in accordance with Standards Rule 1-5;[42] and 674 675

Comment: If such information is unobtainable, a statement on the efforts undertaken by the appraiser to obtain the information is required. If such information is irrelevant, a statement acknowledging the existence of the information and citing its lack of relevance is required. 676 677 678

(4) stating the value opinion(s) and conclusion(s); 679

Comment: An appraiser must maintain a workfile that includes sufficient information to indicate that the appraiser complied with the requirements of STANDARD 1 and for the appraiser to produce an Appraisal Report.[43] 680 681 682

(xiii) state the use of the real estate existing as of the effective date and the use of the real estate reflected in the appraisal; 683 684

(xiv) when an opinion of highest and best use was developed by the appraiser, state that opinion; 685

(xv) clearly and conspicuously: 686

- **state all extraordinary assumptions and hypothetical conditions; and** 687
- **state that their use might have affected the assignment results; and** 688

(xvi) include a signed certification in accordance with Standards Rule 2-3. 689

STANDARDS RULE 2-3, CERTIFICATION 690

A signed certification is an integral part of the appraisal report. 691

(a) The wording of a certification does not have to match the following verbatim, but each of the elements must be addressed: 692 693

I certify that, to the best of my knowledge and belief: 694

— **the statements of fact contained in this report are true and correct.** 695

— **the reported analyses, opinions, and conclusions are limited only by the reported assumptions and limiting conditions and are my personal, impartial, and unbiased professional analyses, opinions, and conclusions.** 696 697 698

— **I have no (or the specified) present or prospective interest in the property that is the subject of this report and no (or the specified) personal interest with respect to the parties involved.** 699 700

— **I have performed no (or the specified) services, as an appraiser or in any other capacity, regarding the property that is the subject of this report within the three-year period immediately preceding the agreement to perform this assignment.** 701 702 703

— **I have no bias with respect to the property that is the subject of this report or to the parties involved with this assignment.** 704 705

— **my engagement in this assignment was not contingent upon developing or reporting predetermined results.** 706 707

42 See Advisory Opinion 1, *Sales History*.

43 See RECORD KEEPING RULE.

© The Appraisal Foundation

708 — **my compensation for completing this assignment is not contingent upon the development or**
709 **reporting of a predetermined value or direction in value that favors the cause of the client, the**
710 **amount of the value opinion, the attainment of a stipulated result, or the occurrence of a subsequent**
711 **event directly related to the intended use of this appraisal.**
712 — **my analyses, opinions, and conclusions were developed, and this report has been prepared, in**
713 **conformity with the *Uniform Standards of Professional Appraisal Practice*.**
714 — **I have (or have not) made a personal inspection of the property that is the subject of this report. (If**
715 **more than one person signs this certification, the certification must clearly specify which individuals**
716 **did and which individuals did not make a personal inspection of the appraised property.)**[44]
717 — **no one provided significant real property appraisal assistance to the person signing this certification.**
718 **(If there are exceptions, the name of each individual providing significant real property appraisal**
719 **assistance must be stated.)**[45]

720 **(b) An appraiser who signs any part of the appraisal report, including a letter of transmittal, must also sign a**
721 **certification.**

722 Comment: In an assignment that includes only assignment results developed by the real property
723 appraiser(s), any appraiser who signs a certification accepts full responsibility for all elements of the
724 certification, for the assignment results, and for the contents of the appraisal report. In an assignment that
725 includes personal property, business or intangible asset assignment results not developed by the real
726 property appraiser(s), any real property appraiser who signs a certification accepts full responsibility for the
727 real property elements of the certification, for the real property assignment results, and for the real property
728 contents of the appraisal report.

729 **(c) When a signing appraiser has relied on work done by appraisers and others who do not sign the**
730 **certification, the signing appraiser is responsible for the decision to rely on their work.**

731 **(i) The signing appraiser is required to have a reasonable basis for believing that those individuals**
732 **performing the work are competent; and**

733 **(ii) The signing appraiser must have no reason to doubt that the work of those individuals is credible.**

734 Comment: Although a certification must contain the names of individuals providing significant real
735 property appraisal assistance, it is not required that a summary of the extent of their assistance be
736 located in a certification. This disclosure may be in any part(s) of the report.

737 **(d) When an assignment requires the use of a certification that does not include all of the certification**
738 **elements in this Standards Rule, the appraisal report must contain a supplemental certification, which**
739 **includes the remaining required certification elements.**

740 **STANDARDS RULE 2-4, ORAL APPRAISAL REPORT**
741 **To the extent that it is both possible and appropriate, an oral real property appraisal report must address the**
742 **substantive matters set forth in Standards Rule 2-2(a).**

743 Comment: See the RECORD KEEPING RULE for corresponding requirements.

44 See Advisory Opinion 2, *Inspection of Subject Property*.
45 See Advisory Opinion 31, *Assignments Involving More than One Appraiser*.

© The Appraisal Foundation

STANDARD 3: APPRAISAL REVIEW, DEVELOPMENT

In developing an appraisal review, an appraiser must identify the problem to be solved, determine the scope of work necessary to solve the problem, and correctly complete research and analyses necessary to produce a credible appraisal review. 744 745 746

FAQ See also FAQ 335-364

Comment: The requirements set forth in STANDARD 3 generally follow the appraisal review development process in the order of topics addressed and can be used by appraisers and the users of appraisal services as a checklist. 747 748 749

In this Standard, the term "reviewer" is used to refer to an appraiser performing an appraisal review. 750

STANDARDS RULE 3-1, GENERAL DEVELOPMENT REQUIREMENTS 751

In developing an appraisal review, the reviewer must: 752

(a) be aware of, understand, and correctly employ those methods and techniques that are necessary to produce a credible appraisal review;. 753 754

Comment: Changes and developments in economics, finance, law, technology, and society can have a substantial impact on the appraisal profession. To keep abreast of these changes and developments, the appraisal profession is constantly reviewing and revising appraisal methods and techniques and devising new methods and techniques to meet new circumstances. Each appraiser must continuously improve his or her skills to remain proficient in appraisal review. 755 756 757 758 759

The reviewer must have the knowledge and experience needed to identify and perform the scope of work necessary to produce credible assignment results. Aspects of competency for an appraisal review, depending on the review assignment's scope of work, may include, without limitation, familiarity with the specific type of property or asset, market, geographic area, analytic method, and applicable laws, regulations and guidelines. 760 761 762 763 764

(b) not commit a substantial error of omission or commission that significantly affects an appraisal review; and 765 766

Comment: A reviewer must use sufficient care to avoid errors that would significantly affect his or her opinions and conclusions. Diligence is required to identify and analyze the factors, conditions, data, and other information that would have a significant effect on the credibility of the assignment results. 767 768 769

(c) not render appraisal review services in a careless or negligent manner, such as making a series of errors that, although individually might not significantly affect the results of an appraisal review, in the aggregate affects the credibility of those results. 770 771 772

STANDARDS RULE 3-2, PROBLEM IDENTIFICATION 773

In developing an appraisal review, the reviewer must: 774

(a) identify the client and other intended users;[46] 775

(b) identify the intended use of the reviewer's opinions and conclusions; 776

Comment: A reviewer must not allow the intended use of an assignment or a client's objectives to cause the assignment results to be biased. A reviewer must not advocate for a client's objectives. 777 778

The intended use refers to the use of the reviewer's opinions and conclusions by the client and other intended users; examples include, without limitation, quality control, audit, qualification, or confirmation. 779 780

46 See Advisory Opinion 36, *Identification and Disclosure of Client, Intended Use, and Intended Users*. Also applicable to Standards Rule 3-2(b).

© The Appraisal Foundation

781 **(c) identify the purpose of the appraisal review, including whether the assignment includes the development**
782 **of the reviewer's own opinion of value or review opinion related to the work under review;**[47]

783 Comment: The purpose of an appraisal review assignment relates to the reviewer's objective; examples
784 include, without limitation, to determine if the results of the work under review are credible for the intended
785 user's intended use, or to evaluate compliance with relevant USPAP requirements, client requirements, or
786 applicable regulations.

787 In the review of an appraisal assignment, the reviewer may provide an opinion of value for the property that
788 is the subject of the work under review.

789 In the review of an appraisal review assignment, the reviewer may provide an opinion of quality of the work
790 that is the subject of the appraisal review assignment.

791 **(d) identify the work under review and the characteristics of that work which are relevant to the intended use**
792 **and purpose of the appraisal review, including:**

793 **(i) any ownership interest in the property that is the subject of the work under review;**

794 **(ii) the date of the work under review and the effective date of the opinions or conclusions in the work**
795 **under review;**

796 **(iii) the appraiser(s) who completed the work under review, unless the identity is withheld by the client;**
797 **and**

798 **(iv) the physical, legal, and economic characteristics of the property, properties, property type(s), or**
799 **market area in the work under review;**

800 Comment: The subject of an appraisal review assignment may be all or part of a report, a workfile, or a
801 combination of these, and may be related to an appraisal or appraisal review assignment.

802 **(e) identify any extraordinary assumptions necessary in the review assignment. An extraordinary assumption**
803 **may be used in an assignment only if:**

804 **(i) the extraordinary assumption is required to properly develop credible opinions and conclusions;**

805 **(ii) the reviewer has a reasonable basis for the extraordinary assumption; and**

806 **(iii) use of the extraordinary assumption results in a credible analysis;**

807 **(f) identify any hypothetical conditions necessary in the review assignment. A hypothetical condition may be**
808 **used in an assignment only if:**

809 **(i) use of the hypothetical condition is clearly required for legal purposes, for purposes of reasonable**
810 **analysis, or for purposes of comparison; and**

811 **(ii) use of the hypothetical condition results in a credible analysis; and**

812 **(g) determine the scope of work necessary to produce credible assignment results in accordance with the**
813 **SCOPE OF WORK RULE.**[48]

814 Comment: Reviewers have broad flexibility and significant responsibility in determining the appropriate scope
815 of work in an appraisal review assignment.

816 Information that should have been considered by the original appraiser can be used by the reviewer in
817 developing an opinion as to the quality of the work under review.

47 See Advisory Opinion 20, *An Appraisal Review Assignment That Includes the Reviewer's Own Opinion of Value.*
48 See Advisory Opinion 28, *Scope of Work Decision, Performance, and Disclosure*, and Advisory Opinion 29, *An Acceptable Scope of Work.*

© The Appraisal Foundation

Information that was not available to the original appraiser in the normal course of business may also be used by the reviewer; however, the reviewer must not use such information in the reviewer's development of an opinion as to the quality of the work under review. 818 819 820

STANDARDS RULE 3-3, APPRAISAL REVIEW METHODS 821

In developing an appraisal review, a reviewer must apply the appraisal review methods and techniques that are necessary for credible assignment results. 822 823

(a) When necessary for credible assignment results in the review of analyses, opinions, and conclusions, the reviewer must: 824 825

(i) develop an opinion as to whether the analyses are appropriate within the context of the requirements applicable to that work; 826 827

(ii) develop an opinion as to whether the opinions and conclusions are credible within the context of the requirements applicable to that work; and 828 829

(iii) develop the reasons for any disagreement. 830

Comment: Consistent with the reviewer's scope of work, the reviewer is required to develop an opinion as to the completeness, accuracy, adequacy, relevance, and reasonableness of the analysis in the work under review, given law, regulations, or intended user requirements applicable to the work under review. 831 832 833

(b) When necessary for credible assignment results in the review of a report, the reviewer must: 834

(i) develop an opinion as to whether the report is appropriate and not misleading within the context of the requirements applicable to that work; and 835 836

(ii) develop the reasons for any disagreement. 837

Comment: Consistent with the reviewer's scope of work, the reviewer is required to develop an opinion as to the completeness, accuracy, adequacy, relevance, and reasonableness of the report, given law, regulations, or intended user requirements applicable to that work. 838 839 840

(c) When the assignment includes the reviewer developing his or her own opinion of value or review opinion, the following apply:[49] 841 842

(i) The requirements of STANDARDS 1, 5, 7, or 9 apply to the reviewer's opinion of value for the property that is the subject of the appraisal review assignment. 843 844

(ii) The requirements of STANDARD 3 apply to the reviewer's opinion of quality for the work that is the subject of the appraisal review assignment. 845 846

Comment: These requirements apply to: 847

- The reviewer's own opinion of value when the subject of the review is the product of an appraisal assignment; or 848 849
- The reviewer's own opinion regarding the work reviewed by another when the subject of the review is the product of an appraisal review assignment. 850 851

These requirements apply whether the reviewer's own opinion: 852

- concurs with the opinions and conclusions in the work under review; or 853
- differs from the opinions and conclusions in the work under review. 854

49 See Advisory Opinion 20, *An Appraisal Review Assignment That Includes the Reviewer's Own Opinion of Value.*

© The Appraisal Foundation

855 When the assignment includes the reviewer developing his or her own opinion of value or review
856 opinion, the following apply:

- 857 The reviewer's scope of work in developing his or her own opinion of value or review opinion may
858 be different from that of the work under review.
- 859 The effective date of the reviewer's opinion of value may be the same or different from the
860 effective date of the work under review.
- 861 The reviewer is not required to replicate the steps completed by the original appraiser. Those
862 items in the work under review that the reviewer concludes are credible can be extended to the
863 reviewer's development process on the basis of an extraordinary assumption. Those items not
864 deemed to be credible must be replaced with information or analysis developed in conformance
865 with STANDARD 1, 3, 5, 7, or 9, as applicable, to produce credible assignment results.

© The Appraisal Foundation

In reporting the results of an appraisal review, an appraiser must communicate each analysis, opinion, and conclusion in a manner that is not misleading.

FAQ See also FAQ 335-364

Comment: STANDARD 4 addresses the content and level of information required in a report that communicates the results of an appraisal review. STANDARD 4 does not dictate the form, format, or style of appraisal review reports. The substantive content of an appraisal review report determines its compliance.

STANDARDS RULE 4-1, GENERAL REPORTING REQUIREMENTS

Each written or oral appraisal review report must be separate from the work under review and must:

(a) clearly and accurately set forth the appraisal review in a manner that will not be misleading;

(b) contain sufficient information to enable the intended user(s) of the appraisal review to understand the report properly; and

(c) clearly and accurately disclose all assumptions, extraordinary assumptions, hypothetical conditions, and limiting conditions used in the assignment.

STANDARDS RULE 4-2, CONTENT OF AN APPRAISAL REVIEW REPORT

The content of an appraisal review report must be appropriate for the intended use of the appraisal review and, at a minimum:

(a) state the identity of the client, or if the client requested anonymity, state that the identity is withheld at the client's request but is retained in the appraiser's workfile; state the identity of any intended user(s) by name or type;[50]

Comment: Because the client is an intended user, they must be identified in the review report as such. However, if the client has requested anonymity the reviewer must use care when identifying the client to avoid violations of the Confidentiality section of the ETHICS RULE.

(b) state the intended use of the appraisal review;

(c) state the purpose of the appraisal review;

(d) state information sufficient to identify:

(i) the work under review, including any ownership interest in the property that is the subject of the work under review;

(ii) the date of the work under review;

(iii) the effective date of the opinions or conclusions in the work under review; and

(iv) the appraiser(s) who completed the work under review, or if the client has withheld their identity, state that the identity of the appraiser(s) has been withheld by the client;

(e) state the date of the appraisal review report;

(f) clearly and conspicuously:

- **state all extraordinary assumptions and hypothetical conditions; and**
- **state that their use might have affected the assignment results.**

50 See Advisory Opinion 36, *Identification and Disclosure of Client, Intended Use, and Intended Users.*

© The Appraisal Foundation

901 **(g) state the scope of work used to develop the appraisal review;**[51]

902 Comment: Stating the scope of work includes disclosure of research and analyses performed and might also
903 include disclosure of research and analyses not performed.

904 **(h) when any portion of the work involves significant appraisal or appraisal review assistance, state the**
905 **extent of that assistance;**[52]

906 **(i) state the reviewer's opinions and conclusions about the work under review, including the reasons for any**
907 **disagreement;**

908 Comment: The report must provide sufficient information to enable the client and intended users to understand the
909 rationale for the reviewer's opinions and conclusions.

910 **(j) when the scope of work includes the reviewer's development of an opinion of value or review opinion**
911 **related to the work under review, the reviewer must:**[53]

912 **(i) state which information, analyses, opinions, and conclusions in the work under review that the**
913 **reviewer accepted as credible and used in developing the reviewer's opinions and conclusions;**

914 **(ii) if applicable, state the effective date of the reviewer's opinion of value;**

915 **(iii) at a minimum, summarize any additional information relied on and the reasoning for the reviewer's**
916 **opinion of value or review opinion related to the work under review; and**

917 Comment: The reviewer may include his or her own opinion of value or review opinion related to
918 the work under review within the appraisal review report itself without preparing a separate report.
919 However, data and analyses provided by the reviewer to support a different opinion or conclusion must
920 match, at a minimum, except for the certification requirements, the reporting requirements for an:

921 - Appraisal Report for a real property appraisal (Standards Rule 2-2(a));
922 - Appraisal Report for a personal property appraisal (Standards Rule 8-2(a));
923 - Appraisal Review Report for an appraisal review (Standards Rule 4-2);
924 - Mass Appraisal Report for mass appraisal (Standards Rule 6-2); and
925 - Appraisal Report for business appraisal (Standards Rule 10-2(a)).

926 **(k) include a signed certification in accordance with Standards Rule 4-3.**

927 **STANDARDS RULE 4-3, CERTIFICATION**
928 **A signed certification is an integral part of the appraisal review report.**

929 **(a) The wording of a certification does not have to match the following verbatim, but each of the elements**
930 **must be addressed:**

931 **I certify that, to the best of my knowledge and belief:**

932 **— the statements of fact contained in this report are true and correct.**
933 **— the reported analyses, opinions, and conclusions are limited only by the reported assumptions and**
934 **limiting conditions and are my personal, impartial, and unbiased professional analyses, opinions, and**
935 **conclusions.**
936 **— I have no (or the specified) present or prospective interest in the property that is the subject of the**
937 **work under review and no (or the specified) personal interest with respect to the parties involved.**
938 **— I have performed no (or the specified) services, as an appraiser or in any other capacity, regarding**
939 **the property that is the subject of the work under review within the three-year period immediately**
940 **preceding the agreement to perform this assignment.**

51 See Advisory Opinion 28, *Scope of Work Decision, Performance, and Disclosure*, and Advisory Opinion 29, *An Acceptable Scope of Work*.
52 See Advisory Opinion 31, *Assignments Involving More than One Appraiser.*
53 See Advisory Opinion 20, *An Appraisal Review Assignment That Includes the Reviewer's Own Opinion of Value.*

© The Appraisal Foundation

- **I have no bias with respect to the property that is the subject of the work under review or to the parties involved with this assignment.** 941 942
- **my engagement in this assignment was not contingent upon developing or reporting predetermined results.** 943 944
- **my compensation is not contingent on an action or event resulting from the analyses, opinions, or conclusions in this review or from its use.** 945 946
- **my compensation for completing this assignment is not contingent upon the development or reporting of predetermined assignment results or assignment results that favors the cause of the client, the attainment of a stipulated result, or the occurrence of a subsequent event directly related to the intended use of this appraisal review.** 947 948 949 950
- **my analyses, opinions, and conclusions were developed and this review report was prepared in conformity with the *Uniform Standards of Professional Appraisal Practice*.** 951 952
- **I have (or have not) made a personal inspection of the subject of the work under review. (If more than one person signs this certification, the certification must clearly specify which individuals did and which individuals did not make a personal inspection of the subject of the work under review.) (For reviews of a business or intangible asset appraisal assignment, the inspection portion of the certification is not applicable.)**[54] 953 954 955 956 957
- **no one provided significant appraisal or appraisal review assistance to the person signing this certification. (If there are exceptions, the name of each individual providing appraisal or appraisal review assistance must be stated.)**[55] 958 959 960

(b) A reviewer who signs any part of the appraisal review report, including a letter of transmittal, must also sign a certification. 961 962

Comment: Any reviewer who signs a certification accepts responsibility for all elements of the certification, for the assignment results, and for the contents of the appraisal review report. 963 964

Appraisal review is distinctly different from the cosigning activity addressed in Standards Rules 2-3, 6-3, 8-3, and 10-3. To avoid confusion between these activities, a reviewer performing an appraisal review must not sign the work under review unless he or she intends to accept responsibility as a cosigner of that work. 965 966 967

(c) When a signing appraiser has relied on work done by appraisers and others who do not sign the certification, the signing appraiser is responsible for the decision to rely on their work. 968 969

(i) The signing appraiser is required to have a reasonable basis for believing that those individuals performing the work are competent; and 970 971

(ii) The signing appraiser must have no reason to doubt that the work of those individuals is credible. 972

Comment: Although a certification must contain the names of individuals providing significant appraisal or appraisal review assistance, it is not required that a summary of the extent of their assistance be located in a certification. This disclosure may be in any part(s) of the report. 973 974 975

(d) If the assignment requires the use of a certification that does not include all of the certification elements in this Standards Rule, the appraisal review report must contain a supplemental certification, which includes the remaining required certification elements. 976 977 978

STANDARDS RULE 4-4, ORAL APPRAISAL REVIEW REPORT 979

To the extent that it is both possible and appropriate, an oral appraisal review report must address the substantive matters set forth in Standards Rule 4-2. 980 981

Comment: See the RECORD KEEPING RULE for corresponding requirements. 982

54 See Advisory Opinion 2, *Inspection of Subject Property*.
55 See Advisory Opinion 31, *Assignments Involving More than One Appraiser*.

© The Appraisal Foundation

983 **In developing a mass appraisal, an appraiser must identify the problem to be solved, determine the**
984 **scope of work necessary to solve the problem, and correctly complete research and analyses necessary**
985 **to produce a credible mass appraisal.**

FAQ See also FAQ 127-264

986 Comment: STANDARD 5 applies to all mass appraisals of real or personal property regardless of the purpose
987 or use of such appraisals.[56] The reporting and jurisdictional exceptions applicable to public mass appraisals
988 prepared for ad valorem taxation do not apply to mass appraisals prepared for other purposes.

989 A mass appraisal includes:

990 1) identifying properties to be appraised;

991 2) defining market area of consistent behavior that applies to properties;

992 3) identifying characteristics (supply and demand) that affect the creation of value in that market area;

993 4) developing a model structure that reflects the relationship among the characteristics affecting value in
994 the market area;

995 5) calibrating the model structure to determine the contribution of the individual characteristics affecting value;

996 6) applying the conclusions reflected in the model to the characteristics of the property(ies) being
997 appraised; and

998 7) reviewing the mass appraisal results.

999 The JURISDICTIONAL EXCEPTION RULE may apply to several sections of STANDARD 5 because ad valorem
1000 tax administration is subject to various state, county, and municipal laws.

1001 **STANDARDS RULE 5-1, GENERAL DEVELOPMENT REQUIREMENTS**
1002 **In developing a mass appraisal, an appraiser must:**

1003 **(a) be aware of, understand, and correctly employ those recognized methods and techniques necessary to**
1004 **produce a credible mass appraisal;**

1005 Comment: Mass appraisal provides for a systematic approach and uniform application of appraisal
1006 methods and techniques to obtain estimates of value that allow for statistical review and analysis of results.

1007 This requirement recognizes that the principle of change continues to affect the manner in which appraisers
1008 perform mass appraisals. Changes and developments in the real property and personal property fields have
1009 a substantial impact on the appraisal profession.

1010 To keep abreast of these changes and developments, the appraisal profession is constantly reviewing
1011 and revising appraisal methods and techniques and devising new methods and techniques to meet
1012 new circumstances. For this reason it is not sufficient for appraisers to simply maintain the skills and the
1013 knowledge they possess when they become appraisers. Each appraiser must continuously improve his or her
1014 skills to remain proficient in mass appraisal.

1015 **(b) not commit a substantial error of omission or commission that significantly affects a mass appraisal; and**

1016 Comment: An appraiser must use sufficient care to avoid errors that would significantly affect his or her
1017 opinions and conclusions. Diligence is required to identify and analyze the factors, conditions, data, and other
1018 information that would have a significant effect on the credibility of the assignment results.

1019 **(c) not render a mass appraisal in a careless or negligent manner.**

56 See Advisory Opinion 32, *Ad Valorem Property Tax Appraisal and Mass Appraisal Assignments.*

© The Appraisal Foundation

STANDARDS RULE 5-2, PROBLEM IDENTIFICATION

In developing a mass appraisal, an appraiser must:

(a) identify the client and other intended users;[57]

Comment: In ad valorem mass appraisal, the assessor, or party responsible for certification of the assessment or tax roll is required to apply the relevant law or statute and identify the clients and other intended users (if any).

(b) identify the intended use of the appraisal;

Comment: An appraiser must not allow the intended use of an assignment or a client's objectives to cause the assignment results to be biased.

(c) identify the type and definition of value, and ascertain whether the value is to be the most probable price:

(i) in terms of cash; or

(ii) in terms of financial arrangements equivalent to cash; or

(iii) in such other terms as may be precisely defined; and

(iv) if the opinion of value is to be based on non-market financing or financing with unusual conditions or incentives, identify the terms of such financing and any influences on value;

(d) identify the effective date of the appraisal;[58]

(e) identify, from sources the appraiser reasonably believes to be reliable, the characteristics of the properties that are relevant to the type and definition of value and intended use,[59] **including:**

(i) the group with which a property is identified according to similar market influence;

(ii) the appropriate market area and time frame relative to the property being valued; and

(iii) their location and physical, legal, and economic characteristics;

Comment: The properties must be identified in general terms, and each individual property in the universe must be identified, with the information on its identity stored or referenced in its property record.

When appraising proposed improvements, an appraiser must examine and have available for future examination, plans, specifications, or other documentation sufficient to identify the extent and character of the proposed improvements.[60]

Ordinarily, proposed improvements are not appraised for ad valorem tax purposes. Appraisers, however, are sometimes asked to provide opinions of value of proposed improvements so that developers can estimate future property tax burdens. Sometimes units in condominiums and planned unit developments are sold with an interest in un-built community property, the pro rata value of which, if any, must be considered in the analysis of sales data.

(f) identify the characteristics of the market that are relevant to the purpose and intended use of the mass appraisal including:

(i) location of the market area;

(ii) physical, legal, and economic characteristics;

(iii) time frame of market activity; and

(iv) property interests reflected in the market;

57 See Advisory Opinion 36, *Identification and Disclosure of Client, Intended Use, and Intended Users.* Also applicable to Standards Rule 5-2(b).
58 See Advisory Opinion 34, *Retrospective and Prospective Value Opinions.*
59 See Advisory Opinion 23, *Identifying the Relevant Characteristics of the Subject Property of a Real Property Appraisal Assignment*, if applicable.
60 See Advisory Opinion 17, *Appraisals of Real Property with Proposed Improvements*, if applicable.

© The Appraisal Foundation

1057 **(g) in appraising real property or personal property:**

1058 **(i) identify the appropriate market area and time frame relative to the property being valued;**

1059 **(ii) when the subject is real property, identify and consider any personal property, trade fixtures, or**
1060 **intangible assets that are not real property but are included in the appraisal;**

1061 **(iii) when the subject is personal property, identify and consider any real property or intangible assets**
1062 **that are not personal property but are included in the appraisal;**

1063 **(iv) identify known easements, restrictions, encumbrances, leases, reservations, covenants, contracts,**
1064 **declarations, special assessments, ordinances, or other items of similar nature; and**

1065 **(v) identify and analyze whether an appraised fractional interest, physical segment or partial holding**
1066 **contributes pro rata to the value of the whole;**

1067 Comment: The above requirements do not obligate the appraiser to value the whole when the subject
1068 of the appraisal is a fractional interest, physical segment, or a partial holding. However, if the value
1069 of the whole is not identified, the appraisal must clearly reflect that the value of the property being
1070 appraised cannot be used to develop the value opinion of the whole by mathematical extension.

1071 **(h) analyze the relevant economic conditions at the time of the valuation, including market acceptability of**
1072 **the property and supply, demand, scarcity, or rarity;**

1073 **(i) identify any extraordinary assumptions necessary in the assignment. An extraordinary assumption may**
1074 **be used in an assignment only if:**

1075 **(i) the extraordinary assumption is required to properly develop credible opinions and conclusions;**

1076 **(ii) the appraiser has a reasonable basis for the extraordinary assumption; and**

1077 **(iii) use of the extraordinary assumption results in a credible analysis;**

1078 **(j) identify any hypothetical conditions necessary in the assignment. A hypothetical condition may be used**
1079 **in an assignment only if:**

1080 **(i) use of the hypothetical condition is clearly required for legal purposes, for purposes of reasonable**
1081 **analysis, or for purposes of comparison; and**

1082 **(ii) use of the hypothetical condition results in a credible analysis; and**

1083 **(k) determine the scope of work necessary to produce credible assignment results in accordance with the**
1084 **SCOPE OF WORK RULE.**[61]

1085 **STANDARDS RULE 5-3, PROPERTY'S USE AND APPROPRIATE MARKET**
1086 **When necessary for credible assignment results, an appraiser must:**

1087 **(a) in appraising real property, identify and analyze the effect on use and value of the following factors:**

1088 **(i) existing land use regulations;**

1089 **(ii) reasonably probable modifications of such regulations;**

1090 **(iii) economic supply and demand;**

1091 **(iv) the physical adaptability of the real estate;**

1092 **(v) neighborhood trends; and**

1093 **(vi) highest and best use of the real estate; and**

61 See Advisory Opinion 28, *Scope of Work Decision, Performance, and Disclosure*, and Advisory Opinion 29, *An Acceptable Scope of Work.*

USPAP 2020-2021 Edition
© The Appraisal Foundation

Comment: This requirement sets forth a list of factors that affect use and value. In considering neighborhood trends, an appraiser must avoid stereotyped or biased assumptions relating to race, age, color, gender, or national origin or an assumption that race, ethnic, or religious homogeneity is necessary to maximize value in a neighborhood. Further, an appraiser must avoid making an unsupported assumption or premise about neighborhood decline, effective age, and remaining life. In considering highest and best use, an appraiser must develop the concept to the extent required for a proper solution to the appraisal problem. 1094–1100

(b) in appraising personal property, identify and analyze the effects on use and value of industry trends, value-in-use, and trade level of personal property. Where applicable, analyze the current use and alternative uses to encompass what is profitable, legal, and physically possible, as relevant to the type and definition of value and intended use of the appraisal. Personal property has several measurable marketplaces; therefore, the appraiser must define and analyze the appropriate market consistent with the type and definition of value. 1101–1106

STANDARDS RULE 5-4, APPRAISAL METHODS 1107

In developing a mass appraisal, an appraiser must: 1108

(a) identify the appropriate procedures and market information required to perform the appraisal, including all physical, functional, and external market factors as they may affect the appraisal; 1109–1110

Comment: Such efforts customarily include the development of standardized data collection forms, procedures, and training materials that are used uniformly on the universe of properties under consideration. 1111–1113

(b) employ recognized techniques for specifying property valuation models; and 1114

Comment: The formal development of a model in a statement or equation is called model specification. Mass appraisers must develop mathematical models that, with reasonable accuracy, represent the relationship between property value and supply and demand factors, as represented by quantitative and qualitative property characteristics. The models may be specified using the cost, sales comparison, or income approaches to value. The specification format may be tabular, mathematical, linear, nonlinear, or any other structure suitable for representing the observable property characteristics. Appropriate approaches must be used in appraising a class of properties. The concept of recognized techniques applies to both real and personal property valuation models. 1115–1122

(c) employ recognized techniques for calibrating mass appraisal models. 1123

Comment: Calibration refers to the process of analyzing sets of property and market data to determine the specific parameters of a model. The table entries in a cost manual are examples of calibrated parameters, as well as the coefficients in a linear or nonlinear model. Models must be calibrated using recognized techniques, including, but not limited to, multiple linear regression, nonlinear regression, and adaptive estimation. 1124–1127

STANDARDS RULE 5-5, APPROACHES TO VALUE 1128

In developing a mass appraisal, when necessary for credible assignment results, an appraiser must: 1129

(a) collect, verify, and analyze such data as are necessary and appropriate to develop: 1130

- **(i) the cost new of the improvements;** 1131
- **(ii) depreciation;** 1132
- **(iii) value of the land by sales of comparable properties;** 1133
- **(iv) value of the property by sales of comparable properties;** 1134
- **(v) value by capitalization of income or potential earnings (i.e., rentals, expenses, interest rates, capitalization rates, and vacancy data);** 1135–1136

© The Appraisal Foundation

1137 Comment: This Standards Rule requires appraisers engaged in mass appraisal to take reasonable
1138 steps to ensure that the quantity and quality of the factual data that are collected are sufficient to
1139 produce credible mass appraisals.

1140 **(b) base estimates of capitalization rates and projections of future rental rates and/or potential earnings**
1141 **capacity, expenses, interest rates, and vacancy rates on reasonable and appropriate evidence;**[62]

1142 Comment: This requirement calls for an appraiser, in developing income and expense statements and cash
1143 flow projections, to weigh historical information and trends, current market factors affecting such trends, and
1144 reasonably anticipated events, such as competition from developments either planned or under construction.

1145 **(c) identify and, as applicable, analyze terms and conditions of any available leases; and**

1146 **(d) identify the need for and extent of any physical inspection.**[63]

1147 **STANDARDS RULE 5-6, CALIBRATED MASS APPRAISAL MODEL APPLICATION**
1148 **When necessary for credible assignment results in applying a calibrated mass appraisal model an appraiser must:**

1149 **(a) value improved parcels by recognized methods or techniques based on the cost approach, the sales**
1150 **comparison approach, and income approach;**

1151 **(b) value sites by recognized methods or techniques; such techniques include but are not limited to the sales**
1152 **comparison approach, allocation method, abstraction method, capitalization of ground rent, and land**
1153 **residual technique;**

1154 **(c) when developing the value of a leased fee estate or a leasehold estate, analyze the effect on value, if any,**
1155 **of the terms and conditions of the lease;**

1156 Comment: In ad valorem taxation the appraiser may be required by rules or law to appraise the property as if
1157 in fee simple, as though unencumbered by existing leases. In such cases, market rent would be used in the
1158 appraisal, ignoring the effect of the individual, actual contract rents.

1159 **(d) analyze the effect on value, if any, of the assemblage of the various parcels, divided interests, or**
1160 **component parts of a property; the value of the whole must not be developed by adding together the**
1161 **individual values of the various parcels, divided interests, or component parts; and**

1162 Comment: Although the value of the whole may be equal to the sum of the separate estates or parts, it also
1163 may be greater than or less than the sum of such estates or parts.

1164 **(e) when analyzing anticipated public or private improvements, located on or off the site, analyze the effect on**
1165 **value, if any, of such anticipated improvements to the extent they are reflected in market actions.**

1166 **STANDARDS RULE 5-7, RECONCILIATION**
1167 **In developing a mass appraisal an appraiser must:**

1168 **(a) reconcile the quality and quantity of data available and analyzed within the approaches used and the**
1169 **applicability and relevance of the approaches, methods and techniques used; and**

1170 **(b) employ recognized mass appraisal testing procedures and techniques to ensure that standards of**
1171 **accuracy are maintained.**

---

62 See Advisory Opinion 33, *Discounted Cash Flow Analysis.*
63 See Advisory Opinion 2, *Inspection of Subject Property.*

USPAP 2020-2021 Edition
© The Appraisal Foundation

Comment: It is implicit in mass appraisal that, even when properly specified and calibrated mass appraisal models are used, some individual value conclusions will not meet standards of reasonableness, consistency, and accuracy. However, appraisers engaged in mass appraisal have a professional responsibility to ensure that, on an overall basis, models produce value conclusions that meet attainable standards of accuracy. This responsibility requires appraisers to evaluate the performance of models, using techniques that may include but are not limited to, goodness-of-fit statistics, and model performance statistics such as appraisal-to-sale ratio studies, evaluation of hold-out samples, or analysis of residuals. 1172 1173 1174 1175 1176 1177 1178

© The Appraisal Foundation

1179 **In reporting the results of a mass appraisal, an appraiser must communicate each analysis, opinion,**
1180 **and conclusion in a manner that is not misleading.**

FAQ See also FAQ 265-334

1181 Comment: STANDARD 6 addresses the content and level of information required in a report that
1182 communicates the results of a mass appraisal.

1183 STANDARD 6 does not dictate the form, format, or style of mass appraisal reports. The substantive content of
1184 a report determines its compliance.

1185 **STANDARDS RULE 6-1, GENERAL REPORTING REQUIREMENTS**
1186 **Each written report of a mass appraisal must:**

1187 **(a) clearly and accurately set forth the appraisal in a manner that will not be misleading;**

1188 **(b) contain sufficient information to enable the intended user(s) of the appraisal to understand the report**
1189 **properly; and**

1190 Comment: Documentation for a mass appraisal for ad valorem taxation may be in the form of (1) property
1191 records, (2) sales ratios and other statistical studies, (3) appraisal manuals and documentation, (4) market
1192 studies, (5) model building documentation, (6) regulations, (7) statutes, and (8) other acceptable forms.

1193 **(c) clearly and accurately disclose all assumptions, extraordinary assumptions, hypothetical conditions, and**
1194 **limiting conditions used in the assignment.**

1195 **STANDARDS RULE 6-2, CONTENT OF A MASS APPRAISAL REPORT**
1196 **The content of a mass appraisal report must be appropriate for the intended use of the appraisal and, at a**
1197 **minimum:**

1198 **(a) state the identity of the client, or if the client has requested anonymity, state that the identity is withheld**
1199 **at the client's request but is retained in the appraiser's workfile; state the identity of any intended user(s)**
1200 **by name or type;**[64]

1201 Comment: Because the client is an intended user, they must be identified in the report as such. However, if the
1202 client has requested anonymity the appraiser must use care when identifying the client to avoid violations of the
1203 Confidentiality section of the ETHICS RULE.

1204 **(b) state the intended use of the appraisal;**

1205 **(c) disclose any assumptions or limiting conditions that result in deviation from recognized methods and**
1206 **techniques or that affect analyses, opinions, and conclusions;**

1207 **(d) state the effective date of the appraisal and the date of the report;**

1208 Comment: In ad valorem taxation the effective date of the appraisal may be prescribed by law. If no
1209 effective date is prescribed by law, the effective date of the appraisal, if not stated, is presumed to be
1210 contemporaneous with the data and appraisal conclusions.[65]

1211 **(e) state the type and definition of value and cite the source of the definition;**

1212 Comment: Stating the type and definition of value also requires any comments needed to clearly indicate to
1213 intended users how the definition is being applied.

64 See Advisory Opinion 36, *Identification and Disclosure of Client, Intended Use, and Intended Users.* Also applicable to Standards Rules 6-2(b).

65 See Advisory Opinion 34, *Retrospective and Prospective Value Opinions.*

© The Appraisal Foundation

When reporting an opinion of value, state whether the opinion is: 1214

- In terms of cash or of financing terms equivalent to cash; or 1215
- Based on non-market financing with unusual conditions or incentives. 1216

When an opinion of value is based on non-market financing terms or financing with unusual conditions or incentives, summarize the terms of such financing and any influences on value. 1217 1218

(f) state the properties appraised including the property rights; and, when the property rights to be appraised are specified in a statute or court ruling, reference the law; 1219 1220

Comment: The report documents the sources for location, describing and listing the property. When applicable, include references to legal descriptions, addresses, parcel identifiers, photos, and building sketches. In mass appraisal this information is often included in property records. 1221 1222 1223

(g) summarize the scope of work used to develop the appraisal,[66] and explain the exclusion of the sales comparison approach, cost approach, or income approach; 1224 1225

Comment: Summarizing the scope of work includes disclosure of research and analyses performed and might also include disclosure of research and analyses not performed. 1226 1227

(h) when any portion of the work involves significant mass appraisal assistance, summarize the extent of that assistance;[67] 1228 1229

(i) summarize and support the model specification(s) considered, data requirements, and the model(s) chosen; provide sufficient information to enable the client and intended users to have confidence that the process and procedures used conform to accepted methods and result in credible value conclusions; and include a summary of the rationale for each model, the calibration techniques to be used, and the performance measures to be used; 1230 1231 1232 1233 1234

Comment: In the case of mass appraisal for ad valorem taxation, stability and accuracy are important to the credibility of value opinions. 1235 1236

(j) summarize the procedure for collecting, validating, and reporting data; and summarize the sources of data and the data collection and validation processes; 1237 1238

Comment: Reference to detailed data collection manuals or electronic records must be made, as appropriate, including where they may be found for inspection. 1239 1240

(k) summarize calibration methods considered and chosen, including the mathematical form of the final model(s); summarize how value conclusions were reviewed; and, if necessary, state the availability and location of individual value conclusions; 1241 1242 1243

(l) when an opinion of highest and best use, or the appropriate market or market level was developed, summarize how that opinion was determined, and reference case law, statute, or public policy that describes highest and best use requirements; 1244 1245 1246

Comment: When actual use is the requirement, the report must summarize how use-value opinions were developed. The appraiser's reasoning in support of the highest and best use opinion must be provided in the depth and detail required by its significance to the appraisal. 1247 1248 1249

(m) identify the appraisal performance tests used and the performance measures attained; 1250

(n) summarize the reconciliation performed, in accordance with Standards Rule 5-7; and 1251

(o) include a signed certification in accordance with Standards Rule 6-3. 1252

66 See Advisory Opinion 28, *Scope of Work Decision, Performance, and Disclosure* and Advisory Opinion 29, *An Acceptable Scope of Work.*
67 See Advisory Opinion 31, *Assignments Involving More than One Appraiser.*

© The Appraisal Foundation

1253 **STANDARDS RULE 6-3, CERTIFICATION**

1254 **A signed certification is an integral part of the appraisal report.**

1255 **(a) The wording of a certification does not have to match the following verbatim, but each of the elements**
1256 **must be addressed:**

1257 **I certify that, to the best of my knowledge and belief:**

1258 **— the statements of fact contained in this report are true and correct.**
1259 **— the reported analyses, opinions, and conclusions are limited only by the reported assumptions and**
1260 **limiting conditions, and are my personal, impartial, and unbiased professional analyses, opinions, and**
1261 **conclusions.**
1262 **— I have no (or the specified) present or prospective interest in the property that is the subject of this**
1263 **report, and no (or the specified) personal interest with respect to the parties involved.**
1264 **— I have performed no (or the specified) services, as an appraiser or in any other capacity, regarding**
1265 **the property that is the subject of this report within the three-year period immediately preceding the**
1266 **agreement to perform this assignment.**
1267 **— I have no bias with respect to the property that is the subject of this report or to the parties involved**
1268 **with this assignment.**
1269 **— my engagement in this assignment was not contingent upon developing or reporting predetermined**
1270 **results.**
1271 **— my compensation for completing this assignment is not contingent upon the reporting of a**
1272 **predetermined value or direction in value that favors the cause of the client, the amount of the value**
1273 **opinion, the attainment of a stipulated result, or the occurrence of a subsequent event directly related**
1274 **to the intended use of this appraisal.**
1275 **— my analyses, opinions, and conclusions were developed, and this report has been prepared, in**
1276 **conformity with the *Uniform Standards of Professional Appraisal Practice*.**
1277 **— I have (or have not) made a personal inspection of the properties that are the subject of this report. (If**
1278 **more than one person signs this certification, the certification must clearly specify which individuals**
1279 **did and which individuals did not make a personal inspection of the appraised property.)**[68]
1280 **— no one provided significant mass appraisal assistance to the person signing this certification. (If there**
1281 **are exceptions, the name of each individual providing significant mass appraisal assistance must be**
1282 **stated.)**[69]

1283 Comment: The above certification is not intended to disturb an elected or appointed assessor's work
1284 plans or oaths of office.

1285 **(b) An appraiser who signs any part of the appraisal report, including a letter of transmittal, must also sign a**
1286 **certification.**

1287 Comment: In an assignment that includes only assignment results developed by the real property appraiser,
1288 any appraiser who signs a certification accepts full responsibility for all elements of the certification, for the
1289 assignment results, and for the contents of the appraisal report. In an assignment that includes personal
1290 property assignment results not developed by the real property appraiser(s), any real property appraiser who
1291 signs a certification accepts full responsibility for the real property elements of the certification, for the real
1292 property assignment results, and for the real property contents of the appraisal report.

68 See Advisory Opinion 2, *Inspection of Subject Property.*
69 See Advisory Opinion 31, *Assignments Involving More than One Appraiser.*

© The Appraisal Foundation

In an assignment that includes only assignment results developed by the personal property appraiser(s), any appraiser who signs a certification accepts full responsibility for all elements of the certification, for the assignment results, and for the contents of the appraisal report. In an assignment that includes real property assignment results not developed by the personal property appraiser(s), any personal property appraiser who signs a certification accepts full responsibility for the personal property elements of the certification, for the personal property assignment results, and for the personal property contents of the appraisal report. 1293–1298

(c) When a signing appraiser has relied on work done by appraisers and others who do not sign the certification, the signing appraiser is responsible for the decision to rely on their work. 1299–1300

(i) The signing appraiser is required to have a reasonable basis for believing that those individuals performing the work are competent; and 1301–1302

(ii) The signing appraiser must have no reason to doubt that the work of those individuals is credible. 1303

Comment: Although a certification must contain the names of individuals providing significant mass appraisal assistance, it is not required that a summary of the extent of their assistance be located in a certification. This disclosure may be in any part(s) of the report. 1304–1306

© The Appraisal Foundation

STANDARD 7: PERSONAL PROPERTY APPRAISAL, DEVELOPMENT

1307 **In developing a personal property appraisal, an appraiser must identify the problem to be solved,**
1308 **determine the scope of work necessary to solve the problem, and correctly complete research**
1309 **and analyses necessary to produce a credible appraisal.**

FAQ See also FAQ 265-334

1310 Comment: The requirements set forth in STANDARD 7 follow the appraisal development process in the order
1311 of topics addressed and can be used by appraisers and the users of appraisal services as a checklist.

1312 **STANDARDS RULE 7-1, GENERAL DEVELOPMENT REQUIREMENTS**
1313 **In developing a personal property appraisal, an appraiser must:**

1314 **(a) be aware of, understand, and correctly employ those recognized methods and techniques that are**
1315 **necessary to produce a credible appraisal;**

1316 Comment: This Standards Rule recognizes that the principle of change continues to affect the manner in
1317 which appraisers perform appraisal services. Changes and developments in personal property practice have
1318 a substantial impact on the appraisal profession. Important changes in the cost and manner of acquiring,
1319 producing, and marketing personal property and changes in the legal framework in which appraisers perform
1320 their assignments result in the need for corresponding changes in personal property appraisal theory and
1321 practice. Social change has also had an effect on appraisal theory and practice. The appraisal profession
1322 responds to changing circumstances with revised and new appraisal methods and techniques. Therefore,
1323 it is not sufficient for appraisers to maintain the skills and the knowledge they possess when they become
1324 appraisers. Each appraiser must improve and update his or her skills and knowledge to remain proficient in
1325 the appraisal of personal property.

1326 **(b) not commit a substantial error of omission or commission that significantly affects an appraisal; and**

1327 Comment: An appraiser must use sufficient care to avoid errors that would significantly affect his or her
1328 opinions and conclusions. Diligence is required to identify and analyze the factors, conditions, data, and other
1329 information that would have a significant effect on the credibility of the assignment results.

1330 **(c) not render appraisal services in a careless or negligent manner, such as by making a series of errors that,**
1331 **although individually might not significantly affect the results of an appraisal, in the aggregate affect the**
1332 **credibility of those results.**

1333 **STANDARDS RULE 7-2, PROBLEM IDENTIFICATION**
1334 **In developing a personal property appraisal, an appraiser must:**

1335 **(a) identify the client and other intended users;**[70]

1336 **(b) identify the intended use of the appraiser's opinions and conclusions;**

1337 Comment: An appraiser must not allow the intended use of an assignment or a client's objectives to cause
1338 the assignment results to be biased.

1339 **(c) identify the type and definition of value; and ascertain whether the value is to be:**

1340 **(i) in terms of cash; or**

1341 **(ii) in terms of financial arrangements equivalent to cash; or**

1342 **(iii) in other precisely defined terms; and**

1343 **(iv) if the opinion of value is to be based on non-market financing or financing with unusual conditions or**
1344 **incentives, identify the terms of such financing and any influences on value;**

70 See Advisory Opinion 36, *Identification and Disclosure of Client, Intended Use, and Intended Users*. Also applicable to Standards Rule 7-2(b).

© The Appraisal Foundation

Comment: When reasonable exposure time is a component of the definition for the value opinion being developed, the appraiser must also develop an opinion of reasonable exposure time linked to that value opinion.[71] 1345 1346 1347

(d) identify the effective date of the appraiser's opinions and conclusions;[72] 1348

(e) identify, from sources the appraiser reasonably believes to be reliable, the characteristics of the property that are relevant to the type and definition of value and intended use of the appraisal, including: 1349 1350

(i) sufficient characteristics to establish the identity of the item including the method of identification;[73] 1351 1352

(ii) sufficient characteristics to establish the relative quality of the item (and its component parts, where applicable) within its type; 1353 1354

(iii) all other physical and economic characteristics with a material effect on value; 1355

Comment: Some examples of physical and economic characteristics include condition, style, size, quality, manufacturer, author, materials, origin, age, provenance, alterations, restorations, and obsolescence. The type of property, the type and definition of value, and intended use of the appraisal determine which characteristics have a material effect on value. 1356 1357 1358 1359

(iv) the ownership interest to be valued; 1360

(v) any known restrictions, encumbrances, leases, covenants, contracts, declarations, special assessments, ordinances, or other items of a similar nature if relevant to the assignment; and 1361 1362

(vi) any real property or intangible assets that are not personal property but which are included in the appraisal; 1363 1364

Comment on (i)–(vi): An appraiser may use any combination of a property inspection, documents, or other information to identify the relevant characteristics of the subject property. 1365 1366

When appraising proposed modifications, an appraiser must examine and have available for future examination, documentation sufficient to identify the extent and character of the proposed modifications. 1367 1368

An appraiser may not be required to value the whole when the subject of the appraisal is a fractional interest, a physical segment, or a partial holding. 1369 1370

(f) identify any extraordinary assumptions necessary in the assignment. An extraordinary assumption may be used in an assignment only if: 1371 1372

(i) the extraordinary assumption is required to properly develop credible opinions and conclusions; 1373

(ii) the appraiser has a reasonable basis for the extraordinary assumption; and 1374

(iii) use of the extraordinary assumption results in a credible analysis; 1375

(g) identify any hypothetical conditions necessary in the assignment. A hypothetical condition may be used in an assignment only if: 1376 1377

(i) use of the hypothetical condition is clearly required for legal purposes, for purposes of reasonable analysis, or for purposes of comparison; and 1378 1379

(ii) use of the hypothetical condition results in a credible analysis; and 1380

(h) determine the scope of work necessary to produce credible assignment results in accordance with the SCOPE OF WORK RULE.[74] 1381 1382

71 See Advisory Opinion 35, *Reasonable Exposure Time in Real Property and Personal Property Opinions of Value.*

72 See Advisory Opinion 34, Retrospective and Prospective Value.

73 See Advisory Opinion 2, *Inspection of Subject Property.*

74 See Advisory Opinion 34, *Retrospective and Prospective Value.*

© The Appraisal Foundation

1383 **STANDARD RULE 7-3, PROPERTY'S USE, MARKET, AND RELEVANT ECONOMIC CONDITIONS**
1384 **In developing a personal property appraisal, when necessary for credible assignment results, an appraiser**
1385 **must:**

1386 **(a) analyze the property's current use and alternative uses as relevant to the type and definition of value and**
1387 **intended use of the appraisal;**

1388 Comment: In the context of personal property, value can be a function of the choice of the appropriate
1389 market or, in some cases, market level for the type of item, the type and definition of value, and the intended
1390 use of the appraisal.

1391 The appraiser must consider the various uses of the property when viable alternative uses exist and when
1392 those alternative uses may result in a different value.

1393 **(b) define and analyze the appropriate market consistent with the type and definition of value; and**

1394 Comment: The appraiser must recognize that there are distinct levels of trade (measureable marketplaces),
1395 and each may generate its own data. For example, a property may have a different value at a wholesale level
1396 of trade, retail level of trade, or under various auction conditions. Therefore, the appraiser must analyze the
1397 subject property within the correct market context.

1398 **(c) analyze the relevant economic conditions that exist on the effective date of the valuation, including**
1399 **market acceptability of the property and supply, demand, scarcity or rarity.**

1400 **STANDARDS RULE 7-4, APPROACHES TO VALUE**
1401 **In developing a personal property appraisal, an appraiser must collect, verify, and analyze all information**
1402 **necessary for credible assignment results.**

1403 **(a) When a sales comparison approach is necessary for credible assignment results, an appraiser must**
1404 **analyze such comparable sales data as are available to indicate a value conclusion.**

1405 **(b) When a cost approach is necessary for credible assignment results, an appraiser must:**

1406 **(i) analyze such comparable cost data as are available to estimate the cost new of the property; and**

1407 **(ii) analyze such comparable data as are available to estimate the difference between cost new and**
1408 **the present worth of the property (depreciation).**

1409 **(c) When an income approach is necessary for credible assignment results, an appraiser must:**

1410 **(i) analyze such comparable data as are available to estimate the market income of the property;**

1411 **(ii) analyze such comparable operating expense data as are available to estimate the operating**
1412 **expenses of the property;**

1413 **(iii) analyze such comparable data as are available to estimate rates of capitalization and/or rates of**
1414 **discount; and**

1415 **(iv) base projections of future income and expenses on reasonably clear and appropriate evidence.**

1416 Comment: An appraiser must, in developing income and expense statements and cash flow
1417 projections, weigh historical information and trends, current supply and demand factors affecting such
1418 trends, and competition.

1419 **(d) When developing an opinion of the value of a lease, leased, or encumbered property, an appraiser must**
1420 **analyze the effect on value, if any, of the terms and conditions of the lease(s) or encumbrances.**

1421 **(e) When appraising multiple objects, the appraiser must consider the significance of the value of the**
1422 **individual assets to the assignment results. Those objects which are more significant to the assignment**
1423 **results should be the focus of the analysis and analyzed in appropriate detail.**

© The Appraisal Foundation

Comment: A group of objects may have a mix of high and low value items. Those objects that are more significant to the assignment results should be subject to a greater and appropriate depth of analysis. 1424 1425

(f) **When analyzing the assemblage of the various component parts of a property, an appraiser must analyze the effect on value, if any, of the assemblage. An appraiser must refrain from valuing the whole solely by adding together the individual values of the various component parts.** 1426 1427 1428

Comment: Although the value of the whole may be equal to the sum of the separate parts, it also may be greater than or less than the sum of such parts. 1429 1430

(g) **When analyzing anticipated modifications to the subject property, an appraiser must analyze the effect on value, if any, of such modifications to the extent they are reflected in market actions.** 1431 1432

(h) **When real property or intangible assets are included in the appraisal, the appraiser must analyze the effect on value of such non-personal property assets.** 1433 1434

Comment: When the scope of work includes an appraisal of real property or intangible assets, competency in real property appraisal (see STANDARD 1) or business appraisal (see STANDARD 9) is required. In addition, competency in other types of personal property outside of the appraiser's specialty area may be necessary (see the COMPETENCY RULE). 1435 1436 1437 1438

STANDARDS RULE 7-5, SALE AGREEMENTS, OPTIONS, LISTINGS, AND PRIOR SALES 1439

When necessary for credible assignment results, an appraiser must, if such information is available to the appraiser in the normal course of business:[75] 1440 1441

(a) **analyze all agreements of sale, validated offers or third-party offers to sell, options, and listings of the subject property current as of the effective date of the appraisal if warranted by the intended use of the appraisal; and** 1442 1443 1444

(b) **analyze all prior sales of the subject property that occurred within a reasonable and applicable time period if relevant given the intended use of the appraisal and property type.** 1445 1446

STANDARDS RULE 7-6, RECONCILIATION 1447

In developing a personal property appraisal, an appraiser must: 1448

(a) **reconcile the quality and quantity of data available and analyzed within the approach or approaches used; and** 1449 1450

(b) **reconcile the applicability and relevance of the approach or approaches, methods and techniques used to arrive at the value conclusion(s).** 1451 1452

75 See Advisory Opinion 24, *Normal Course of Business*.

© The Appraisal Foundation

STANDARD 8: PERSONAL PROPERTY APPRAISAL, REPORTING

FAQ See also FAQ 127-264

1453 **In reporting the results of a personal property appraisal, an appraiser must communicate each**
1454 **analysis, opinion, and conclusion in a manner that is not misleading.**

1455 Comment: STANDARD 8 addresses the content and level of information required in a report that
1456 communicates the results of a personal property appraisal.

1457 STANDARD 8 does not dictate the form, format, or style of personal property appraisal reports. The
1458 substantive content of a report determines its compliance.

1459 **STANDARDS RULE 8-1, GENERAL REPORTING REQUIREMENTS**
1460 **Each written or oral personal property appraisal report must:**

1461 **(a) clearly and accurately set forth the appraisal in a manner that will not be misleading;**

1462 **(b) contain sufficient information to enable the intended user(s) of the appraisal to understand the report**
1463 **properly; and**

1464 **(c) clearly and accurately disclose all assumptions, extraordinary assumptions, hypothetical conditions, and**
1465 **limiting conditions used in the assignment.**

1466 **STANDARDS RULE 8-2, CONTENT OF A PERSONAL PROPERTY APPRAISAL REPORT**
1467 **Each written personal property appraisal report must be prepared under one of the following options and**
1468 **prominently state which option is used: Appraisal Report or Restricted Appraisal Report.[76]**

1469 **An appraiser may use any other label in addition to, but not in place of, the labels set forth in this Standards Rule**
1470 **for the type of report provided. The use of additional labels such as analysis, consultation, evaluation, study, or**
1471 **valuation does not exempt an appraiser from adherence to USPAP.**

1472 **The report content and level of information requirements in this Standards Rule are minimums for each type of**
1473 **report.**

1474 **(a) The content of an Appraisal Report must be appropriate for the intended use of the appraisal and, at a**
1475 **minimum:**

1476 **(i) state the identity of the client, or if the client requested anonymity, state that the client's identity is**
1477 **withheld at the client's request but is retained in the appraiser's workfile;[77]**

1478 Comment: Because the client is an intended user, they must be identified in the report as such.
1479 However, if the client has requested anonymity the appraiser must use care when identifying the client
1480 to avoid violations of the Confidentiality section of the ETHICS RULE.

1481 **(ii) state the identity of any other intended user(s) by name or type;**

1482 Comment: A party receiving a copy of an Appraisal Report in order to satisfy disclosure requirements
1483 does not become an intended user of the appraisal unless the appraiser identifies such party as an
1484 intended user as part of the assignment.

1485 **(iii) state the intended use of the appraisal;**

1486 **(iv) summarize information sufficient to identify the property involved in the appraisal, including the**
1487 **physical and economic property characteristics relevant to the assignment;**

1488 **(v) state the property interest appraised;**

76 See Advisory Opinion 38, *Content of an Appraisal Report and Restricted Appraisal Report.*
77 See Advisory Opinion 36, *Identification and Disclosure of Client, Intended Use, and Intended Users.* Also applicable to Standards Rules 8-2(a)(ii) and (iii).

© The Appraisal Foundation

(vi) state the type and definition of value and cite the source of the definition; 1489

Comment: Stating the definition of value also requires any comments needed to clearly indicate to the intended users how the definition is being applied. 1490 1491

When reporting an opinion of value, state whether the opinion is: 1492

- in terms of cash or of financing terms equivalent to cash; or 1493
- based on non-market financing or financing with unusual conditions or incentives. 1494

When an opinion of value is based on non-market financing terms or financing with unusual conditions or incentives, summarize the terms of such financing and any influences on value. 1495 1496

When an opinion of reasonable exposure time has been developed in compliance with Standards Rule 7-2(c), the opinion must be stated in the report.[78] 1497 1498

(vii) state the effective date of the appraisal and the date of the report;[79] 1499

(viii) summarize the scope of work used to develop the appraisal;[80] 1500

Comment: Summarizing the scope of work includes disclosure of research and analyses performed and might also include disclosure of research and analyses not performed. 1501 1502

(ix) summarize the extent of any significant personal property appraisal assistance and, in an assignment involving appraisers with expertise in different specialties (e.g., antiques, fine art, or machinery and equipment), disclose the role of each appraiser signing the certification;[81] 1503 1504 1505

(x) provide sufficient information to indicate that the appraiser complied with the requirements of STANDARD 7 by: 1506 1507

(1) summarizing the appraisal methods or techniques employed; 1508

(2) stating the reasons for excluding the sales comparison, cost, or income approach(es) if any have not been developed; 1509 1510

(3) summarizing the results of analyzing the subject property's sales, agreements of sale, options, and listings when, in accordance with Standards Rule 7-5, it was necessary for credible assignment results and if such information was available to the appraiser in the normal course of business;[82] 1511 1512 1513 1514

Comment: If such information is unobtainable, a statement on the efforts undertaken by the appraiser to obtain the information is required. If such information is irrelevant, a statement acknowledging the existence of the information and citing its lack of relevance is required. 1515 1516 1517

(4) stating the value opinion(s) and conclusion(s); and 1518

(5) summarizing the information analyzed and the reasoning that supports the analyses, opinions, and conclusions, including reconciliation of the data and approaches; 1519 1520

(xi) state, as appropriate to the class of personal property involved, the use of the property existing as of the effective date and the use of the property reflected in the appraisal; 1521 1522

Comment: In the context of personal property, value can be a function of the current and alternative use of the subject property, the choice of the appropriate market or market level for the type of item, the type and definition of value, and intended use of the report. 1523 1524 1525

78 See Advisory Opinion 35, *Reasonable Exposure Time in Real and Personal Property Opinions of Value*.
79 See Advisory Opinion 34, *Retrospective and Prospective Value Opinions*.
80 See Advisory Opinion 28, *Scope of Work Decision, Performance, and Disclosure* and Advisory Opinion 29, *An Acceptable Scope of Work*.
81 See Advisory Opinion 31, *Assignments Involving More than One Appraiser*.
82 See Advisory Opinion 24, *Normal Course of Business*.

© The Appraisal Foundation

1526 **(xii) when, in compliance with Standards Rule 7-3, an opinion of the appropriate market or market level**
1527 **was developed by the appraiser, state that opinion and summarize the support and rationale for**
1528 **that opinion;**

1529 **(xiii) clearly and conspicuously:**

1530 - **state all extraordinary assumptions and hypothetical conditions; and**
1531 - **state that their use might have affected the assignment results; and**

1532 **(xiv) include a signed certification in accordance with Standards Rule 8-3.**

1533 **(b) The content of a Restricted Appraisal Report must be appropriate for the intended use of the appraisal**
1534 **and, at a minimum:**

1535 **(i) state the identity of the client, or if the client requested anonymity, state that the identity is**
1536 **withheld at the client's request but is retained in the appraiser's workfile;**[83]

1537 Comment: Because the client is an intended user, they must be identified in the report as such.
1538 However, if the client has requested anonymity the appraiser must use care when identifying the client
1539 to avoid violations of the Confidentiality section of the ETHICS RULE.

1540 **(ii) state the identity of any other intended user(s) by name;**

1541 Comment: A Restricted Appraisal Report may be provided when the client is the only intended user; or,
1542 when additional intended users are identified by name.

1543 A party receiving a copy of a Restricted Appraisal Report in order to satisfy disclosure requirements
1544 does not become an intended user of the appraisal unless the appraiser identifies such party as an
1545 intended user as part of the assignment.

1546 **(iii) clearly and conspicuously state a restriction that limits use of the report to the client and the named**
1547 **intended user(s);**

1548 **(iv) clearly and conspicuously warn that the report may not contain supporting rationale for all of the**
1549 **opinions and conclusions set forth in the report;**

1550 **(v) state the intended use of the appraisal;**

1551 **(vi) state information sufficient to identify the property involved in the appraisal;**

1552 **(vii) state the property interest appraised;**

1553 **(viii) state the type of value and cite the source of its definition;**

1554 Comment: When an opinion of reasonable exposure time has been developed in compliance with
1555 Standards Rule 7-2(c), the opinion must be stated in the report.[84]

1556 **(ix) state the effective date of the appraisal and the date of the report;**[85]

1557 **(x) state the scope of work used to develop the appraisal;**[86]

1558 Comment: Stating the scope of work includes disclosure of research and analyses performed and
1559 might also include disclosure of research and analyses not performed.

1560 **(xi) state the extent of any significant personal property appraisal assistance;** [87]

83 See Advisory Opinion 36, *Identification and Disclosure of Client, Intended Use, and Intended Users.* Also applicable to Standards Rules 8-2(b)(ii) and (v).
84 See Advisory Opinion 35, *Reasonable Exposure Time in Real and Personal Property Opinions of Value.*
85 See Advisory Opinion 34, *Retrospective and Prospective Value Opinions.*
86 See Advisory Opinion 28, *Scope of Work Decision, Performance, and Disclosure* and Advisory Opinion 29, *An Acceptable Scope of Work.*
87 See Advisory Opinion 2, *Inspection of Subject Property.*

© The Appraisal Foundation

(xii) provide sufficient information to indicate that the appraiser complied with the requirements of STANDARD 7 by: 1561 1562

(1) stating the appraisal methods and techniques employed; 1563

(2) stating the reasons for excluding the sales comparison, cost, or income approach(es) if any have not been developed; 1564 1565

(3) summarizing the results of analyzing the subject sales, agreements of sale, options, and listings in accordance with Standards Rule 7-5; and 1566 1567

Comment: If such information is unobtainable, a statement on the efforts undertaken by the appraiser to obtain the information is required. If such information is irrelevant, a statement acknowledging the existence of the information and citing its lack of relevance is required. 1568 1569 1570

(4) stating the value opinion(s) and conclusion(s); 1571

Comment: An appraiser must maintain a workfile that includes sufficient information to indicate that the appraiser complied with the requirements of STANDARD 7 and for the appraiser to produce an Appraisal Report.[88] 1572 1573 1574

(xiii) state, as appropriate to the class of personal property involved, the use of the property existing as of the effective date and the use of the property reflected in the appraisal; 1575 1576

Comment: In the context of personal property, value can be a function of the current and alternative use of the subject property, the choice of the appropriate market or market level for the type of item, the type and definition of value, and intended use of the report. 1577 1578 1579

(xiv) when an opinion of the appropriate market or market level was developed by the appraiser, state that opinion; 1580 1581

(xv) clearly and conspicuously: 1582

- **state all extraordinary assumptions and hypothetical conditions; and** 1583
- **state that their use might have affected the assignment results; and** 1584

(xvi) include a signed certification in accordance with Standards Rule 8-3. 1585

STANDARDS RULE 8-3, CERTIFICATION 1586

A signed certification is an integral part of the appraisal report. 1587

(a) The wording of a certification does not have to match the following verbatim, but each of the elements must be addressed: 1588 1589

I certify that, to the best of my knowledge and belief: 1590

— the statements of fact contained in this report are true and correct. 1591

— the reported analyses, opinions, and conclusions are limited only by the reported assumptions and limiting conditions and are my personal, impartial, and unbiased professional analyses, opinions, and conclusions. 1592 1593 1594

— I have no (or the specified) present or prospective interest in the property that is the subject of this report and no (or the specified) personal interest with respect to the parties involved. 1595 1596

— I have performed no (or the specified) services, as an appraiser or in any other capacity, regarding the property that is the subject of this report within the three-year period immediately preceding the agreement to perform this assignment. 1597 1598 1599

— I have no bias with respect to the property that is the subject of this report or to the parties involved with this assignment. 1600 1601

88 See RECORD KEEPING RULE.

© The Appraisal Foundation

1602 — **my engagement in this assignment was not contingent upon developing or reporting predetermined**
1603 **results.**
1604 — **my compensation for completing this assignment is not contingent upon the development or**
1605 **reporting of a predetermined value or direction in value that favors the cause of the client, the**
1606 **amount of the value opinion, the attainment of a stipulated result, or the occurrence of a subsequent**
1607 **event directly related to the intended use of this appraisal.**
1608 — **my analyses, opinions, and conclusions were developed, and this report has been prepared, in**
1609 **conformity with the *Uniform Standards of Professional Appraisal Practice*.**
1610 — **I have (or have not) made a personal inspection of the property that is the subject of this report. (If**
1611 **more than one person signs this certification, the certification must clearly specify which individuals**
1612 **did and which individuals did not make a personal inspection of the appraised property.)**[89]
1613 — **no one provided significant personal property appraisal assistance to the person signing this**
1614 **certification. (If there are exceptions, the name of each individual providing significant personal**
1615 **property appraisal assistance must be stated.)**[90]

1616 **(b) An appraiser who signs any part of the appraisal report, including a letter of transmittal, must also sign a**
1617 **certification.**

1618 Comment: In an assignment that includes only assignment results developed by the personal property
1619 appraiser(s) from the same personal property specialty, any appraiser who signs a certification accepts full
1620 responsibility for all elements of the certification, for the assignment results, and for the contents of the
1621 appraisal report. In an assignment involving appraisers with expertise in different specialties (e.g., antiques,
1622 fine art, or machinery and equipment), an appraiser who signs a certification may accept responsibility only
1623 for the elements of the certification, assignment results, and report contents specific to the appraiser's
1624 specialty. The role of each appraiser signing a certification must be disclosed in the report.

1625 In an assignment that includes real property, business or intangible asset assignment results not developed
1626 by the personal property appraiser(s), any personal property appraiser who signs a certification accepts full
1627 responsibility for the personal property elements of the certification, for the personal property assignment
1628 results, and for the personal property contents of the appraisal report.

1629 **(c) When a signing appraiser has relied on work done by appraisers and others who do not sign the**
1630 **certification, the signing appraiser is responsible for the decision to rely on their work.**

1631 **(i) The signing appraiser is required to have a reasonable basis for believing that those individuals**
1632 **performing the work are competent; and**

1633 **(ii) The signing appraiser must have no reason to doubt that the work of those individuals is credible.**

1634 Comment: Although a certification must contain the names of individuals providing significant personal
1635 property appraisal assistance, it is not required that a summary of the extent of their assistance be
1636 located in a certification. This disclosure may be in any part(s) of the report.

1637 **STANDARDS RULE 8-4, ORAL APPRAISAL REPORT**
1638 **To the extent that it is both possible and appropriate, an oral personal property appraisal report must address**
1639 **the substantive matters set forth in Standards Rule 8-2(a).**

1640 Comment: See the RECORD KEEPING RULE for corresponding requirements.

89 See Advisory Opinion 2, *Inspection of Subject Property*.
90 See Advisory Opinion 31, *Assignments Involving More than One Appraiser.*

© The Appraisal Foundation

STANDARD 9: BUSINESS APPRAISAL, DEVELOPMENT

In developing an appraisal of an interest in a business enterprise or intangible asset, an appraiser must identify the problem to be solved, determine the scope of work necessary to solve the problem, and correctly complete the research and analyses necessary to produce a credible appraisal. 1641–1644

FAQ See also FAQ 265-334

STANDARDS RULE 9-1, GENERAL DEVELOPMENT REQUIREMENTS 1645

In developing an appraisal of an interest in a business enterprise or intangible asset, an appraiser must: 1646

(a) be aware of, understand, and correctly employ those recognized approaches, methods and procedures that are necessary to produce a credible appraisal; 1647–1648

Comment: Changes and developments in the economy and in investment theory have a substantial impact on the business and intangible asset appraisal profession. Important changes in the financial arena, securities regulation, financial reporting requirements, and law may result in corresponding changes in appraisal theory and practice. 1649–1652

(b) not commit a substantial error of omission or commission that significantly affects an appraisal; and 1653

Comment: An appraiser must use sufficient care to avoid errors that would significantly affect his or her opinions and conclusions. Diligence is required to identify and analyze the factors, conditions, data, and other information that would have a significant effect on the credibility of the assignment results. 1654–1656

(c) not render appraisal services in a careless or negligent manner, such as by making a series of errors that, although individually might not significantly affect the results of an appraisal, in the aggregate affect the credibility of those results. 1657–1659

STANDARDS RULE 9-2, PROBLEM IDENTIFICATION 1660

In developing an appraisal of an interest in a business enterprise or intangible asset, an appraiser must: 1661

(a) identify the client and other intended users;[91] 1662

(b) identify the intended use of the appraiser's opinions and conclusions; 1663

Comment: An appraiser must not allow the intended use of an assignment or a client's objectives to cause the assignment results to be biased. 1664–1665

(c) identify the standard (type) and definition of value and the premise of value; 1666

(d) identify the effective date of the appraisal; 1667

(e) identify, from sources the appraiser reasonably believes to be reliable, the characteristics of the subject property that are relevant to the standard (type) and definition of value and intended use of the appraisal, including: 1668–1670

(i) the subject business enterprise or intangible asset, if applicable; 1671

(ii) the interest in the business enterprise, equity, asset, or liability to be valued; and the attributes of the interest being appraised, including the rights and benefits of ownership; 1672–1673

Comment: The interest to be valued may represent all ownership rights or a subset of those rights, such as a specific right to use the asset. 1674–1675

91 See Advisory Opinion 36, *Identification and Disclosure of Client, Intended Use, and Intended Users*. Also applicable to Standards Rule 9-2(b).

© The Appraisal Foundation

1676 **(iii) all buy-sell and option agreements, investment letter stock restrictions, restrictive corporate charter or**
1677 **partnership agreement clauses, and similar features or factors that may have an influence on value;**

1678 **(iv) the extent to which the interest contains elements of ownership control; and**

1679 Comment: The elements of control in a given situation may be affected by law, distribution of
1680 ownership interests, contractual relationships, and many other factors.

1681 **(v) the extent to which the interest is marketable and/or liquid;**

1682 **(f) identify any extraordinary assumptions necessary in the assignment. An extraordinary assumption may**
1683 **be used in an assignment only if:**

1684 **(i) the extraordinary assumption is required to properly develop credible opinions and conclusions;**

1685 **(ii) the appraiser has a reasonable basis for the extraordinary assumption; and**

1686 **(iii) use of the extraordinary assumption results in a credible analysis;**

1687 **(g) identify any hypothetical conditions necessary in the assignment. A hypothetical condition may be used**
1688 **in an assignment only if:**

1689 **(i) use of the hypothetical condition is clearly required for legal purposes, for purposes of reasonable**
1690 **analysis, or for purposes of comparison; and**

1691 **(ii) use of the hypothetical condition results in a credible analysis; and**

1692 **(h) determine the scope of work necessary to produce credible assignment results in accordance with the**
1693 **SCOPE OF WORK RULE.**[92]

1694 **STANDARDS RULE 9-3, PREMISE OF VALUE**
1695 **In developing an appraisal of an interest in a business enterprise with the ability to cause liquidation, an appraiser**
1696 **must investigate the possibility that the business enterprise may have a higher value by liquidation of all or part of**
1697 **the enterprise than by continued operation as is. If liquidation of all or part of the enterprise is the indicated premise**
1698 **of value, an appraisal of any real property or personal property to be liquidated may be appropriate.**

1699 Comment: This Standards Rule requires the appraiser to recognize that continued operation of a business
1700 is not always the best premise of value because liquidation of all or part of the enterprise may result in a
1701 higher value. However, this typically applies only when the business interest being appraised is in a position
1702 to cause liquidation. If liquidation of all or part of the enterprise is the appropriate premise of value, the scope
1703 of work may include an appraisal of real property or personal property. If so, competency in real property
1704 appraisal (STANDARD 1) or personal property appraisal (STANDARD 7) is required.

1705 **STANDARDS RULE 9-4, APPROACHES TO VALUE**
1706 **In developing an appraisal of an interest in a business enterprise or intangible asset, an appraiser must collect**
1707 **and analyze all information necessary for credible assignment results.**

1708 **(a) An appraiser must develop value opinion(s) and conclusion(s) by use of one or more approaches that are**
1709 **necessary for credible assignment results.**

1710 **(b) An appraiser must, when necessary for credible assignment results, analyze the effect on value, if any, of:**

1711 **(i) the nature and history of the business enterprise or intangible asset;**

1712 **(ii) financial and economic conditions affecting the business enterprise or intangible asset, its industry,**
1713 **and the general economy;**

1714 **(iii) past results, current operations, and future prospects of the business enterprise;**

92 See Advisory Opinion 28, *Scope of Work Decision, Performance, and Disclosure,* and Advisory Opinion 29, *An Acceptable Scope of Work.*

© The Appraisal Foundation

(iv) **past sales of capital stock or other ownership interests in the business enterprise or intangible asset being appraised;** 1715 1716

(v) **sales of capital stock or other ownership interests in similar business enterprises;** 1717

(vi) **prices, terms, and conditions affecting past sales of similar ownership interests in the asset being appraised or a similar asset; and** 1718 1719

(vii) **economic benefit of tangible and intangible assets.** 1720

Comment on (i)-(vii): This Standards Rule directs the appraiser to study the prospective and retrospective aspects of the business enterprise in terms of the economic and industry environment within which it operates. 1721 1722

(c) **An appraiser must, when necessary for credible assignment results, analyze the effect on value, if any, of buy-sell and option agreements, investment letter stock restrictions, restrictive corporate charter or partnership agreement clauses, and similar features or factors that may influence value.** 1723 1724 1725

(d) **An appraiser must, when necessary for credible assignment results, analyze the effect on value, if any, of the extent to which the interest appraised contains elements of ownership control and is marketable and/or liquid. An appraiser must analyze factors such as holding period, interim benefits, and the difficulty of marketing the subject interest.** 1726 1727 1728 1729

Comment: Equity interests in a business enterprise are not necessarily worth the pro rata share of the business enterprise interest value as a whole. Also, the value of the business enterprise is not necessarily a direct mathematical extension of the value of the fractional interests. The degree of control, marketability and/or liquidity or lack thereof depends on a broad variety of facts and circumstances that must be analyzed when applicable. 1730 1731 1732 1733 1734

STANDARDS RULE 9-5, RECONCILIATION 1735

In developing an appraisal of an interest in a business enterprise or intangible asset, an appraiser must: 1736

(a) **reconcile the quality and quantity of data available and analyzed within the approaches, methods, and procedures used; and** 1737 1738

(b) **reconcile the applicability and relevance of the approaches, methods and procedures used to arrive at the value conclusion(s).** 1739 1740

© The Appraisal Foundation

STANDARD 10: BUSINESS APPRAISAL, REPORTING

1741 **In reporting the results of an appraisal of an interest in a business enterprise or intangible asset,**
1742 **an appraiser must communicate each analysis, opinion, and conclusion in a manner that is not**
1743 **misleading.**

FAQ See also FAQ 265-334

1744 Comment: STANDARD 10 addresses the content and level of information required in a report that
1745 communicates the results of an appraisal of an interest in a business enterprise or intangible asset developed
1746 under STANDARD 9.

1747 STANDARD 10 does not dictate the form, format, or style of business or intangible asset appraisal reports.
1748 The substantive content of a report determines its compliance.

1749 **STANDARDS RULE 10-1, GENERAL REPORTING REQUIREMENTS**
1750 **Each written or oral appraisal report for an interest in a business enterprise or intangible asset must:**

1751 **(a) clearly and accurately set forth the appraisal in a manner that will not be misleading;**

1752 **(b) contain sufficient information to enable the intended user(s) of the appraisal to understand the report**
1753 **properly; and**

1754 **(c) clearly and accurately disclose all assumptions, extraordinary assumptions, hypothetical conditions, and**
1755 **limiting conditions used in the assignment.**

1756 **STANDARDS RULE 10-2, CONTENT OF A BUSINESS APPRAISAL REPORT**
1757 **Each written appraisal report for an interest in a business enterprise or intangible asset must be prepared in**
1758 **accordance with one of the following options and prominently state which option is used: Appraisal Report or**
1759 **Restricted Appraisal Report.**[93]

1760 **An appraiser may use any other label in addition to, but not in place of, the labels set forth in this Standards**
1761 **Rule for the type of report provided. The use of additional labels such as analysis, consultation, evaluation,**
1762 **study, or valuation does not exempt an appraiser from adherence to USPAP.**

1763 **The report content and level of information requirements in this Standards Rule are minimums for both types of**
1764 **report.**

1765 **(a) The content of an Appraisal Report must be appropriate for the intended use of the appraisal and, at a**
1766 **minimum:**

1767 **(i) state the identity of the client, or if the client requested anonymity, state that the identity is**
1768 **withheld at the client's request but is retained in the appraiser's workfile;**[94]

1769 Comment: Because the client is an intended user, they must be identified in the report as such.
1770 However, if the client has requested anonymity the appraiser must use care when identifying the client
1771 to avoid violations of the Confidentiality section of the ETHICS RULE.

1772 **(ii) state the identity of any other intended user(s) by name or type;**

1773 Comment: A party receiving a copy of an Appraisal Report does not become an intended user of the
1774 appraisal unless the appraiser identifies such party as an intended user as part of the assignment.

1775 **(iii) state the intended use of the appraisal;**

93 See Advisory Opinion 38, *Content of an Appraisal Report and Restricted Appraisal Report.*
94 See Advisory Opinion 36, *Identification and Disclosure of Client, Intended Use, and Intended Users.* Also applicable to Standards Rules 10-2(a)(ii) and (iii).

© The Appraisal Foundation

(iv) contain information sufficient to identify the business or intangible asset and the interest appraised, including property characteristics relevant to the type and definition of value and intended use of the appraisal; 1776 1777 1778

(v) state the extent to which the interest appraised contains elements of ownership control, including the basis for that determination; 1779 1780

(vi) state the extent to which the interest appraised lacks elements of marketability and/or liquidity, including the basis for that determination; 1781 1782

(vii) state the standard (type) and definition of value and the premise of value and cite the source of the definition; 1783 1784

Comment: Stating the definition of value also requires any comments needed to clearly indicate to the intended users how the definition is being applied. 1785 1786

(viii) state the effective date of the appraisal and the date of the report; 1787

(ix) summarize the scope of work used to develop the appraisal;[95] 1788

Comment: Summarizing the scope of work includes disclosure of research and analyses performed and might also include disclosure of research and analyses not performed. 1789 1790

(x) when any portion of the work involves significant business and/or intangible asset appraisal assistance, summarize the extent of that assistance;[96] 1791 1792

(xi) provide sufficient information to indicate that the appraiser complied with the requirements of STANDARD 9 by: 1793 1794

(1) summarizing the appraisal procedures followed; 1795

(2) stating the reason(s) for excluding the market, asset-based (cost), or income approach(es) if any have not been developed; 1796 1797

(3) stating the value opinions and conclusions; and 1798

(4) summarizing the information analyzed and the reasoning that supports the analyses, opinions, and conclusions, including reconciliation of the data and approaches; 1799 1800

(xii) clearly and conspicuously: 1801

- **state all extraordinary assumptions and hypothetical conditions; and** 1802
- **state that their use might have affected the assignment results; and** 1803

(xiii) include a signed certification in accordance with Standards Rule 10-3. 1804

(b) The content of a Restricted Appraisal Report must be appropriate for the intended use of the appraisal and, at a minimum: 1805 1806

(i) state the identity of the client, or if the client requested anonymity, state that the identity is withheld at the client's request but is retained in the appraiser's workfile;[97] 1807 1808

Comment: Because the client is an intended user, they must be identified in the report as such. However, if the client has requested anonymity the appraiser must use care when identifying the client to avoid violations of the Confidentiality section of the ETHICS RULE. 1809 1810 1811

(ii) state the identity of any other intended user(s) by name; 1812

95 See Advisory Opinion 28, *Scope of Work Decision, Performance, and Disclosure*, and Advisory Opinion 29, *An Acceptable Scope of Work.*
96 See Advisory Opinion 31, *Assignments Involving More than One Appraiser*.
97 See Advisory Opinion 36, *Identification and Disclosure of Client, Intended Use, and Intended Users*. Also applicable to Standards Rules 10-2(b)(ii) and (v).

© The Appraisal Foundation

1813 Comment: A Restricted Appraisal Report may be provided when the client is the only intended user; or,
1814 when additional intended users are identified by name.

1815 A party receiving a copy of a Restricted Appraisal Report does not become an intended user of the
1816 appraisal unless the appraiser identifies such party as an intended user as part of the assignment.

1817 **(iii) clearly and conspicuously state a restriction that limits use of the report to the client and the named**
1818 **intended user(s);**

1819 **(iv) clearly and conspicuously warn that the report may not contain supporting rationale for all of the**
1820 **opinions and conclusions set forth in the report;**

1821 **(v) state the intended use of the appraisal;**

1822 **(vi) state information sufficient to identify the business or intangible asset and the interest appraised;**

1823 **(vii) state the extent to which the interest appraised contains elements of ownership control, including**
1824 **the basis for that determination;**

1825 **(viii) state the extent to which the interest appraised lacks elements of marketability and/or liquidity,**
1826 **including the basis for that determination;**

1827 **(ix) state the standard (type) of value and the premise of value, and cite the source of its definition;**

1828 **(x) state the effective date of the appraisal and the date of the report;**

1829 **(xi) state the scope of work used to develop the appraisal;**[98]

1830 Comment: Stating the scope of work includes disclosure of research and analyses performed and
1831 might also include disclosure of research and analyses not performed.

1832 **(xii) state the extent of any significant business and/or intangible asset appraisal assistance;**

1833 **(xiii) provide sufficient information to indicate that the appraiser complied with the requirements of**
1834 **STANDARD 9 by:**

1835 **(1) stating the appraisal procedures followed;**

1836 **(2) stating the reason(s) for excluding the market, asset-based (cost), or income approach(es) if**
1837 **any have not been developed; and**

1838 **(3) stating the value opinions and conclusions;**

1839 Comment: An appraiser must maintain a workfile that includes sufficient information to indicate
1840 that the appraiser complied with the requirements of STANDARD 9 and for the appraiser to
1841 produce an Appraisal Report.

1842 **(xiv) clearly and conspicuously:**

1843 - **state all extraordinary assumptions and hypothetical conditions; and**
1844 - **state that their use might have affected the assignment results; and**

1845 **(xv) include a signed certification in accordance with Standards Rule 10-3.**

98 See Advisory Opinion 28, *Scope of Work Decision, Performance, and Disclosure* and Advisory Opinion 29, *An Acceptable Scope of Work.*

© The Appraisal Foundation

STANDARDS RULE 10-3, CERTIFICATION 1846

A signed certification is an integral part of the appraisal report. 1847

(a) The wording of a certification does not have to match the following verbatim, but each of the elements must be addressed: 1848 1849

I certify that, to the best of my knowledge and belief: 1850

- **the statements of fact contained in this report are true and correct.** 1851
- **the reported analyses, opinions, and conclusions are limited only by the reported assumptions and limiting conditions and are my personal, impartial, and unbiased professional analyses, opinions, and conclusions.** 1852 1853 1854
- **I have no (or the specified) present or prospective interest in the property that is the subject of this report, and I have no (or the specified) personal interest with respect to the parties involved.** 1855 1856
- **I have performed no (or the specified) services, as an appraiser or in any other capacity, regarding the property that is the subject of this report within the three-year period immediately preceding the agreement to perform this assignment.** 1857 1858 1859
- **I have no bias with respect to the property that is the subject of this report or to the parties involved with this assignment.** 1860 1861
- **my engagement in this assignment was not contingent upon developing or reporting predetermined results.** 1862 1863
- **my compensation for completing this assignment is not contingent upon the development or reporting of a predetermined value or direction in value that favors the cause of the client, the amount of the value opinion, the attainment of a stipulated result, or the occurrence of a subsequent event directly related to the intended use of this appraisal.** 1864 1865 1866 1867
- **my analyses, opinions, and conclusions were developed, and this report has been prepared, in conformity with the *Uniform Standards of Professional Appraisal Practice*.** 1868 1869
- **no one provided significant business and/or intangible asset appraisal assistance to the person signing this certification. (If there are exceptions, the name of each individual providing significant business and/or intangible asset appraisal assistance must be stated.)**[99] 1870 1871 1872

(b) An appraiser who signs any part of the appraisal report, including a letter of transmittal, must also sign a certification. 1873 1874

Comment: In an assignment that includes only assignment results developed by the business and/or intangible asset appraiser(s), any appraiser who signs a certification accepts full responsibility for all elements of the certification, for the assignment results, and for the contents of the appraisal report. In an assignment that includes real property or personal property assignment results not developed by the business and/or intangible asset appraiser(s), any business and/or intangible asset appraiser who signs a certification accepts full responsibility for the business and/or intangible asset elements of the certification, for the business and/or intangible asset assignment results, and for the business and/or intangible asset contents of the appraisal report. 1875 1876 1877 1878 1879 1880 1881 1882

(c) When a signing appraiser has relied on work done by appraisers and others who do not sign the certification, the signing appraiser is responsible for the decision to rely on their work. 1883 1884

(i) The signing appraiser is required to have a reasonable basis for believing that those individuals performing the work are competent; and 1885 1886

(ii) The signing appraiser must have no reason to doubt that the work of those individuals is credible. 1887

99 See Advisory Opinion 31, *Assignments Involving More than One Appraiser.*

© The Appraisal Foundation

1888 Comment: Although a certification must contain the names of individuals providing significant business
1889 and/or intangible asset appraisal assistance, it is not required that a summary of the extent of their
1890 assistance be located in a certification. This disclosure may be in any part(s) of the report.

1891 **STANDARDS RULE 10-4, ORAL APPRAISAL REPORT**

1892 **To the extent that it is both possible and appropriate, an oral appraisal report for an interest in a business**
1893 **enterprise or intangible asset must address the substantive matters set forth in Standards Rule 10-2(a).**

1894 Comment: See the RECORD KEEPING RULE for corresponding requirements.

© The Appraisal Foundation

2020-2021 EDITION

USPAP ADVISORY OPINIONS

APPRAISAL STANDARDS BOARD

USPAP ADVISORY OPINIONS

APPRAISAL STANDARDS BOARD

Published in the United States of America.

All Rights Reserved
Copyright © 2020, The Appraisal Foundation.

The Appraisal Foundation reserves all rights with respect to this material. No part of this publication may be reproduced, duplicated, altered or otherwise published in electronic or paper means or in any format or form without the express written permission of the publisher.

EFFECTIVE:

January 1, 2020 through December 31, 2021

FOREWORD

The Appraisal Standards Board (ASB) of The Appraisal Foundation develops, interprets, and amends the *Uniform Standards of Professional Appraisal Practice* (USPAP) on behalf of appraisers and users of appraisal services. **The 2020-2021 edition of USPAP is effective January 1, 2020 through December 31, 2021.** It is important that individuals understand and adhere to changes in each edition of USPAP. State and federal authorities enforce the content of the current or applicable edition of USPAP.

Advisory Opinions are a form of guidance issued by the ASB to illustrate the applicability of USPAP in specific situations and to offer advice from the ASB for the resolution of appraisal issues and problems. Advisory Opinions do not establish new standards or interpret existing standards. Advisory Opinions are not part of USPAP and can be approved by the ASB without public exposure and comment.

Advisory Opinions are based on presumed conditions without investigation or verification of actual circumstances. Guidance provided in the Advisory Opinions does not represent the only possible solution to the issues discussed and the advice provided may not be applied equally to seemingly similar situations.

The *USPAP Advisory Opinions* are a reference for appraisers, enforcement officials, users of appraisal services, and the public. The use of this edition of the *USPAP Advisory Opinions* is intended to be in conjunction with the 2018-2019 edition of USPAP.

Each Advisory Opinion applies to one or more appraisal disciplines as identified both in the Advisory Opinion and Table of Contents. However, there may be cases where the guidance in a particular Advisory Opinion could be helpful to an appraiser working in an appraisal discipline that is not specified. As the Advisory Opinions are not part of USPAP and do not establish new standards or interpret existing standards, their use is not limited solely to the appraisal discipline(s) specified.

Contacting the Appraisal Standards Board

The ASB invites questions about USPAP, commentary on USPAP and proposed changes to USPAP from all interested parties, including appraisers, state enforcement agencies, users of appraisal services, and the public.

If you have any comments, questions, or suggestions regarding USPAP, please contact the ASB.

Appraisal Standards Board
The Appraisal Foundation
1155 15th Street, NW, Suite 1111
Washington, DC 20005
Phone: 202-347-7722
E-Mail: info@appraisalfoundation.org
www.appraisalfoundation.org

© The Appraisal Foundation

TABLE OF CONTENTS

USPAP ADVISORY OPINIONS

Each Advisory Opinion is labeled as to its applicability to the various appraisal disciplines. The abbreviations are:

- Real Property – RP
- Personal Property – PP
- Intangible Property – IP (includes business interests)
- All disciplines – ALL

Advisory Opinions 4, 11 and 12 have been retired by the Appraisal Standards Board for the 2020-21 edition of USPAP. These three join other Advisory Opinions that have been retired in the past in response to the evolving appraisal profession. Advisory Opinions are not renumbered when a prior Advisory Opinion is retired.

© The Appraisal Foundation

ADVISORY OPINION 1 (AO-1)

This communication by the Appraisal Standards Board (ASB) does not establish new standards or interpret existing standards. Advisory Opinions are issued to illustrate the applicability of appraisal standards in specific situations and to offer advice from the ASB for the resolution of appraisal issues and problems. 1 2 3

SUBJECT: Sales History 4

APPLICATION: Real Property 5

THE ISSUE: 6
The *Uniform Standards of Professional Appraisal Practice* (USPAP) contain sales history requirements that obligate appraisers of real property to analyze and report pending and recent agreements, options, listings, and sales involving the property being appraised. Because of differences in federal law and regulations, state laws and operating practices relating to the disclosure and confidentiality of real property sales data, the ways in which appraisers comply with the sales history requirements vary according to the jurisdiction and the availability of information. This lack of consistency has raised questions regarding the applicability and relevance of the sales history requirements. 7 8 9 10 11 12

How can the appraiser best comply with the sales history provisions of the applicable appraisal standards in the face of obstacles that are beyond the control of the appraiser? 13 14

ADVICE FROM THE ASB ON THE ISSUE: 15
Relevant USPAP & Advisory References 16

- Advisory Opinion 24 which addresses the "normal course of business" 17

Analysis and Reporting Requirements 18
This Advisory Opinion offers advice and guidance for compliance with the requirements to analyze and report sales history and related information in the appraisal of real property. 19 20

USPAP Standards Rules 1-5(a) and (b) require an appraiser, when the value opinion to be developed is market value, and if such information is available to the appraiser in the normal course of business, to analyze all agreements of sale, options, or listings of the subject property current as of the effective date of the appraisal, and to analyze all sales of the subject property that occurred within three (3) years prior to the effective date of the appraisal. USPAP Standards Rules 2-2(a)(x)(3) and (b)(xii)(3) call for the written appraisal report to contain a summary of the results of those analyses. It should be noted that even in a Restricted Appraisal Report, it is necessary to include a "summary," not just a statement. If sales history information is unobtainable, the written appraisal report must include a commentary on the efforts taken by the appraiser to obtain the information. 21 22 23 24 25 26 27 28

Laws, regulations and guidelines issued by government agencies, or government sponsored enterprises, also contain requirements that require the appraiser to analyze and report sales history information, and these requirements vary according to jurisdiction. Some clients might also require analyses beyond what is required by USPAP. For example, while USPAP does not specifically require that a report include an affirmative statement regarding the lack of prior sales, it is often a client requirement to do so. 29 30 31 32 33

The requirement for the appraiser to analyze and report sales history and related information is fundamental to the appraisal process. Just as the appraiser must analyze the details of pending and recent sales of comparable properties, the appraiser must also take into account the various factors associated with all pending and recent sales of the subject property itself. This is not to say that the agreed price in a pending or recent sale of the subject property is necessarily representative of value as defined in the report, but the appraiser's failure to analyze and report these facts may exclude important information from the sales comparison approach. Information pertaining to the current market status and the sales history of the subject property may also be useful information for the determination of highest and best use or the analysis of market trends. 34 35 36 37 38 39 40 41

Analysis of sales, offerings, etc., as referenced in Standards Rule 1-5, requires more than just stating the known facts about the transaction. Each pertinent factor should be examined individually, methodically, and in detail, to ascertain whether it has relevance to, or potential impact on, the transaction and potentially other assignment results, including the opinion of market value (if applicable). By examining (or evaluating) the specific details of all agreements of 42 43 44 45

© The Appraisal Foundation

46 sale, options, or current listings on the subject property, and all sales that occurred within the prior three years, the
47 appraiser gains valuable (or important) insights into market trends, property and buyer characteristics.

48 **Illustrations**

49 Following are examples that might be included in an appraisal report in compliance with the applicable standards.

50 1. For a property that is not under agreement or option, that is not offered for sale on the open market and that has
51 not changed hands within the past three years, the sales history might be shown in the appraisal report as follows:

52 Research of the applicable public records, private data services and an interview of the current owner,
53 revealed that the subject property is not under current agreement or option and is not offered for sale on the
54 open market. Additionally, according to these sources, the subject property has not been transferred during
55 the past three years.

56 2. For a property that is currently offered for sale (a current listing) wording similar to one of the following examples
57 might be used in the appraisal report, if relevant and if appropriate data exists for comparison. Comparing
58 competitive listings to the subject property's list price helps to give a perspective of what might be a reasonable
59 marketing time in situations where this is an assignment condition, for example:

60 A. As of the effective date, the subject property has been listed for sale for 112 days. Originally listed at
61 $369,900, the price was reduced to the current amount of $350,000 after 60 days on the market. Since the
62 current list prices of comparable properties range from $342,000 to $359,900, and the average marketing
63 time is 90 days, the subject property appears to be competitively priced.

64 B. As of the effective date, the subject property has been listed for sale for 174 days. Originally listed at $199,900,
65 the price was reduced to the current level of $179,000 after 50 days on the market. Superior properties have
66 list prices under $179,000, and the average marketing time is 40 days. Therefore, the subject property may
67 experience a longer marketing period and further reductions in list price.

68 C. The subject property is listed for sale at $339,000. As of the effective date it had been listed for 4 days.
69 Based on a comparison with other current listings, the subject appears to be superior to similarly priced
70 properties. These differences may result in a quicker sale or buyers bidding the price up beyond the list price.

71 According to the public records, there have been no other transfers of the subject property within the past
72 three years.

73 3. For a property that is currently under contract (a pending sale) reporting the summary of the analysis might be
74 similar to one of the following examples:

75 A. The subject property is under contract to sell for $525,000. It had been listed for sale at $535,000 for 107
76 days prior to the contract. The contract provided to the appraiser contains no atypical terms or conditions.
77 There are no reported seller concessions. This appears to be an arm's-length transaction.

78 B. The subject property is under contract to sell for $525,000. It had been listed for sale at $535,000 for
79 107 days prior to the contract. The contract provided to the appraiser includes a provision for the seller to
80 retain possession of the premises for 30 days after the closing. In effect, the buyer is making a concession
81 approximately equivalent to one month's rent. Otherwise, there are no atypical terms or conditions. There are no
82 reported seller concessions. This appears to be an arm's-length transaction, and assuming that the parties were
83 acting in their own best interests (per definition of market value), the price was likely affected by the concession.

84 C. The subject property is under contract to sell for $525,000. It had been listed for sale at $535,000 for 107
85 days prior to the contract. The contract provided to the appraiser contains no atypical terms or conditions.
86 The contract states that the seller will pay 2% of the sale price ($10,500) toward the buyer's closing costs.
87 This appears to be an arm's-length transaction, and assuming that the parties were acting in their own best
88 interests (per definition of market value), the price was likely affected by the concession.

© The Appraisal Foundation

4. For a property that is not for sale but was acquired by the current owner during the past three years, the summary to be included in the appraisal report might appear as follows:

   A. The subject property previously sold for $400,000 on (insert sale date). Based on discussions with the owner and a review of MLS and public records, the prior sale appears to have been an arm's-length transaction and was not impacted by any concessions.

   B. The subject property (land only) previously sold for $100,000 on (insert sale date) prior to construction of the now existing improvements. Based on discussions with the owner and a review of MLS and public records, the prior sale appears to have been an arm's-length transaction and was not impacted by any concessions.

   C. The subject property previously sold for $250,000 on (insert sale date). Based on discussions with the owner and a review of MLS and public records, the prior sale was a bank-owned (REO) property. In this market, REO properties are typically marketed for a quick sale and usually sell at a discount. The prior sale is not considered to be a market value transaction.

Special Circumstances

In cases where pertinent information is not available to the appraiser in the normal course of business, wording in the sales histories would likely differ from the examples shown above. The following examples are offered for purposes of illustration only.

Illustrations

5. In cases where the property being appraised is known to be the subject of a pending transaction, but the appraiser is not privy to the terms of the pending transaction and the parties to the transaction have declined to disclose the terms of the transaction to the appraiser, the summary to be included in the appraisal report might include wording similar to the following:

   The property being appraised is known to be the subject of a pending purchase and sale agreement, but the appraiser was unable to obtain the terms of the contract. The current owner confirmed that the property is under contract for sale but declined to disclose the details of the agreement.

6. In jurisdictions where reliable price information cannot be found in the public records and where the appraiser is unable to obtain complete information regarding a prior sale in the normal course of business, it would be appropriate to include in the appraisal report a comment similar to the following:

   The subject property was sold by John Jones to the current owner on June 1, 20XX, for an unknown price. Sale prices are not a matter of public record in this state. The appraiser attempted to obtain the purchase price and other terms of the transaction without success. The parties to the transaction declined to discuss the terms or conditions of the sale.

   According to the public records, there have been no other transfers of the subject property within the past three years.

In many cases, a property may require analyses of multiple items under Standards Rule 1-5 (e.g., both a prior sale and a current listing) and in those cases, each of the analyses must be summarized in the report.

© The Appraisal Foundation

ADVISORY OPINION 2 (AO-2)

This communication by the Appraisal Standards Board (ASB) does not establish new standards or interpret existing standards. Advisory Opinions are issued to illustrate the applicability of appraisal standards in specific situations and to offer advice from the ASB for the resolution of appraisal issues and problems.

SUBJECT: Inspection of Subject Property

APPLICATION: Real Property, Personal Property

THE ISSUE:

For real property and personal property appraisal assignments, USPAP requires the report to contain a certification indicating whether the subject property was personally inspected by the appraiser(s).

- What is the purpose of inspecting the subject property?
- What constitutes a personal inspection?
- Does USPAP mandate a minimum level of property inspection?
- What are my obligations if I rely upon an inspection of the property performed by someone else?
- What are the disclosure obligations relating to inspection?

ADVICE FROM THE ASB ON THE ISSUE:

Relevant USPAP & Advisory References:

- DEFINITIONS, specifically the following:
  - PERSONAL INSPECTION: a physical observation performed to assist in identifying relevant property characteristics in a valuation service.

    Comment: An appraiser's inspection is typically limited to those things readily observable without the use of special testing or equipment. Appraisals of some types of property, such as gems and jewelry, may require the use of specialized equipment. An inspection by an appraiser is not the equivalent of an inspection by an inspection professional (e.g., a structural engineer, home inspector, or art conservator).
  - RELEVANT CHARACTERISTICS: features that may affect a property's value or marketability such as legal, economic, or physical characteristics.
- Standards Rules 1-2(e) and 7-2(e)
- Standards Rules 2-3 and 8-3
- SCOPE OF WORK RULE
- Advisory Opinion 23, *Identifying the Relevant Characteristics of the Subject Property in a Real Property Appraisal Assignment*

Purpose of an Inspection

The primary reason for inspecting the subject property is to gather information about the characteristics of the property that are *relevant* to its value.[1]

What is a Personal Inspection?

While there are other ways to gather information on the subject property's relevant characteristics, in many cases the personal observations of the appraiser are the primary source of information regarding the subject property.

These personal observations can be assisted by tools, and as technology evolves, so too will the tools available to an appraiser. For example, the use of unmanned aerial vehicles, or drones, now allows appraisers to view much more of the subject or comparables and with greater detail. Drones are tools that can be used to amplify vision like binoculars or a jeweler's loupe.

1 See Advisory Opinion 23, *Identifying the Relevant Characteristics of the Subject Property of a Real Property Appraisal Assignment.*

© The Appraisal Foundation

The use of a drone may be a critical tool for some appraisers who, for example, value large acreage properties. However, just as viewing photographs of a house does not constitute a personal inspection by the appraiser, neither does viewing recordings of aerial photography. In order for a real property appraiser to include the statement, "I have made a personal inspection of the subject property" in the certification, the appraiser must have physically visited the subject property.

Minimum Level of Inspection

An inspection is not required by USPAP, but one is often conducted. While an inspection is not required, appraisal reports for real and personal property must contain a signed certification that clearly states whether the appraiser has or has not personally inspected the subject property. This is further discussed under the Disclosure Requirements section which follows.

The extent of the inspection process is an aspect of the scope of work, and may vary based on assignment conditions and the intended use of the assignment results.[2] It is the appraiser's responsibility to determine the appropriate scope of work, including the degree of inspection necessary to produce credible assignment results given the intended use.

Every assignment is subject to assignment conditions that may limit the inspection of the subject property. Regardless of the level of detail, it is always possible to perform an inspection that is more thorough. The appraiser's inspection commonly is limited to those things readily observable without the use of special testing or equipment.

An inspection conducted by an appraiser is usually not the equivalent of an inspection by an inspection professional (e.g., a structural engineer, home inspector, or art conservator).

Regardless of how the information is gathered, it must be sufficient for the development of relevant analyses, such as highest and best use, the application of the approaches, etc.

An appraiser may use any combination of a property inspection, documents, such as a legal description, address, map reference, copy of a survey or map, property sketch, photographs, or other information to identify the relevant characteristics of the subject property. For some assignments, it may be necessary to rely on information provided by other professionals. In such cases the appraiser must comply with USPAP requirements related to reliance on work done by others.

There are many circumstances that influence the extent of the appraiser's property inspection. In some assignments, the client may request that the appraiser perform an exterior-only inspection from the street or perform no inspection of the subject property (i.e., a "desktop appraisal"). There are situations where inspection of the subject property is not possible; for example, if the improvements have been destroyed, removed, or not yet built. In some cases the appraiser is denied access to the property for legal, personal safety, or other reasons. In such cases, the appraiser must use other means to gather information about the relevant characteristics of the subject property in order to provide credible assignment results.

Relying on an Inspection Performed by Someone Else

In some cases, the client may provide the appraiser with the results of an inspection performed by a third party, or the appraiser may hire a third party to perform the inspection.

Whether the inspection is performed by the appraiser, another appraiser, or a third-party inspector, an appraiser must ensure that the degree of inspection is sufficient for the appraiser to understand the subject property's relevant characteristics, so the appraiser can develop a credible appraisal. Therefore, in cases when the appraiser relies upon a third-party inspector's report, it may be necessary to obtain additional information and/or examine other documents in order to understand the relevant characteristics of the property.

In all cases, when adequate information about relevant characteristics is not available through a personal inspection or from sources the appraiser reasonably believes are reliable, the appraiser must:

- modify the assignment conditions to expand the scope of work to include gathering the necessary information;
- use an extraordinary assumption about such uncertain information, if credible assignment results can still be developed; or
- withdraw from the assignment.

2 See Advisory Opinion 28, *Scope of Work Decision, Performance, and Disclosure.*

© The Appraisal Foundation

Disclosure Requirements

Appraisal reports for real and personal property must contain a signed certification indicating whether the appraiser has or has not personally inspected the subject property. All appraisal reports must also contain sufficient information to enable the intended users to understand the extent of the inspection that was performed.

If the appraiser relies on inspection information from another appraiser (e.g., photographs, aerial footage, inventory, etc.), and the information constitutes significant appraisal assistance, the inspector must be identified in the Certification as having provided significant appraisal assistance. Further, the extent of the assistance must be indicated within the report.

Because of the variability of inspections, the appraisal report should clearly communicate the degree of the inspection for the report to be meaningful.[3]

Illustrations

1. I have been asked to appraise a single-unit property based on an exterior-only inspection from the street. What are my development and reporting obligations?

   If an appraiser's observations are limited to an exterior-only inspection from the street, then the appraiser must gather information on relevant characteristics from other data sources and/or use extraordinary assumptions.[4] The data sources used are often the same sources used to gather information on comparable sales. For example, the size of the property might be obtained from public records, and other information might be obtained from interior photographs included in a listing of the property for sale, or information from the appraiser's own files.

   The report must disclose the extent of the property inspection in a manner that is clear to the intended users. For example, in this case it would probably be insufficient to merely state that the property was inspected. The report must make clear that the appraisal was based on an "exterior only" inspection from the street and state the sources used to identify the relevant characteristics other than those observed during the inspection.

2. A client has asked me to appraise a Rolex wristwatch. I will not be provided access to the watch. However, I have been given the serial number, a copy of a certificate of authenticity, and several recent photographs. Can I develop an appraisal based solely on this information?

   The key question is whether the information provided will enable the appraiser to comply with Standards Rule 7-2(e), which requires the appraiser to "identify, from sources the appraiser reasonably believes to be reliable, the characteristics of the property that are relevant to the type and definition of value and intended use of the appraisal." It is up to the appraiser to know whether the serial number, certificate of authenticity, and recent photographs are sufficient to identify these characteristics or if an in-person and/or professional specialist inspection is needed. In some cases, the answer may depend upon the assignment conditions.

   For example, if the intended use is an insurance claim after a client's house has burned down –damaging or destroying the Rolex watch, then this limited information may be all that is available. In that scenario, the question becomes whether the provided information can be presumed to accurately identify the relevant characteristics of the watch. If there is a reasonable basis for this assumption and if the appraiser judges that credible assignment results can be developed, the appraiser may decide to make an extraordinary assumption. The extraordinary assumption will require proper disclosure.

   For other intended uses and under less dire assignment conditions, the appraiser will need more information to develop a credible appraisal when appraising a Rolex watch. This is because certificates of authenticity and photographs of Rolex watches are often misleading.

3. A client has asked me to perform an appraisal, but instead of requiring me to physically inspect the subject, they will provide me with the results of an inspection of the property done by someone else. Does USPAP allow this?

---

3 See Standards Rules 2-2(a)(viii), 2-2(b)(x), 8-2(a)(viii), and 8-2(b)(x).
4 See Standards Rules 2-2(a)(xiii), 2-2(b)(xv), 8-2(a)(xiii), and 8-2(b)(xv).

© The Appraisal Foundation

Yes. USPAP does not require an appraiser to inspect the subject per the SCOPE OF WORK RULE. However, while an inspection is not required, appraisal reports for real and personal property must contain a signed certification that clearly states whether the appraiser personally inspected the subject. 132 133 134

Standards Rules 1-2(e) and 7-2(e) require an appraiser to identify, from sources the appraiser reasonably believes to be reliable, the characteristics of the property that are relevant to the type and definition of value and the intended use of the appraisal, including its legal and economic characteristics. In a real property appraisal assignment, an appraiser may use any combination of a property inspection, documents, such as a legal description, address, map reference, copy of a survey or map, property sketch, photographs, or other information to identify the relevant characteristics of the subject property. In a personal property appraisal, an appraiser may use any combination of a property inspection, documents, or other information to identify the relevant characteristics of the subject property. 135 136 137 138 139 140 141 142

Standards Rules 1-1(b) and 7-1(b) require that an appraiser not commit a substantial error of omission or commission that significantly affects an appraisal. Therefore, the appraiser has to have a reasonable basis to believe the information contained in the inspection report provided by the client is credible, or must seek additional information, which could include interviewing the inspector or gathering data from other sources. If uncertainties remain, but the appraiser can still develop credible assignment results, the appraiser may need to use an extraordinary assumption regarding the decision to rely on the information contained in the third-party inspection report. An appraiser must not allow assignment conditions to limit the scope of work to such a degree that the assignment results are not credible in the context of the intended use. If an appraiser determines that the only way to meet these criteria is by personally inspecting the property, he or she must either discuss changing the scope of work with the client, or withdraw from the assignment.[5] 143 144 145 146 147 148 149 150 151 152

4. I have been contacted by a property owner who is being transferred by his company to another city. The owner indicated that while he might want a "detailed appraisal" later, right now he only needs a rough idea of the value of the residence to begin negotiations related to the relocation. The owner has asked me to perform a "desktop" appraisal (i.e., an appraisal with no inspection of the property). I believe that, given this intended use, credible assignment results can be developed without an inspection. Is this permitted under USPAP? 153 154 155 156 157

   Yes, this is permitted if sufficient information regarding the relevant characteristics of the property is available. Such information could be obtained from public records, previous listings of the property for sale, appraiser's files, etc. If use of extraordinary assumptions related to various relevant characteristics is necessary, then one must comply with the requirements for their use. 158 159 160 161

5 See SCOPE OF WORK RULE.

© The Appraisal Foundation

ADVISORY OPINION 3 (AO-3)

1 *This communication by the Appraisal Standards Board (ASB) does not establish new standards or interpret existing*
2 *standards. Advisory Opinions are issued to illustrate the applicability of appraisal standards in specific situations and*
3 *to offer advice from the ASB for the resolution of appraisal issues and problems.*

4 **SUBJECT: Update of a Prior Appraisal**

5 **APPLICATION: Real Property, Personal Property, Intangible Property**

6 **THE ISSUE:**
7 Once an appraisal of a property has been completed, there are many cases in which a client may need a subsequent
8 appraisal involving the same property. Examples include:

9 • In the appraisal of real property, a current value is commonly required by lenders and secondary market
10 participants when the time frame between the effective date of a prior appraisal and the closing of a loan
11 exceeds certain limits. A current value is also required by agencies in eminent domain cases when time has
12 elapsed between a prior appraisal and the date of taking.
13 • In the appraisal of business equity of privately held companies held by Employee Stock Ownership Trusts,
14 current values are required at least annually.
15 • In the appraisal of personal property, it may be necessary to appraise equipment every two years for financing
16 purposes.

17 Clients sometimes label such requests as "updates," "reappraisals," or "recertifications." Does USPAP address these
18 and how can an appraiser comply with USPAP for such assignments?

19 **ADVICE FROM THE ASB ON THE ISSUE:**
20 **Clarification of Terminology**
21 Various terms have been developed by clients and client groups for certain appraisal assignments, including
22 "updates" and "recertifications." While such terms may be convenient for use in a business setting, they do not
23 necessarily impart the same meaning in every situation.

24 The term "Update" is often used by clients when they are seeking a current appraisal of a property that was the
25 subject of a prior assignment. This practice is addressed in this Advisory Opinion.

26 The term "Recertification of Value" is often mistakenly used by some clients in lieu of the term "Update." A
27 Recertification of Value is performed to confirm whether or not the conditions of a prior appraisal have been met.
28 A Recertification of Value does not change the effective date of the value opinion. If a client uses this term in an
29 assignment request that includes an updated value opinion, then it constitutes a new appraisal assignment that must
30 be completed as discussed in this Advisory Opinion.

31 **A New Assignment of a Prior Assignment**
32 Regardless of the nomenclature used, when a client seeks a more current value or analysis of a property that was
33 the subject of a prior assignment, this is not an *extension* of that prior assignment that was already completed – it is
34 simply a new assignment. An "assignment" is defined in USPAP as:

35 *a valuation service that is provided by an appraiser as a consequence of an agreement with a client.*

36 The same USPAP requirements apply when appraising or analyzing a property that was the subject of a prior
37 assignment. There are no restrictions on who the appraiser is in such a circumstance, who the client is,[1] what length
38 of time may have elapsed between the prior and current assignments, or whether the characteristics of the subject
39 property are unchanged or significantly different than in the prior assignment.

1 See Advisory Opinion 27, *Appraising the Same Property for a New Client*.

© The Appraisal Foundation

Development Requirements 40

For all assignments, the development of the assignment results must be in accordance with the requirements contained in the applicable STANDARD (1, 3, 5, 7, or 9). When developing an opinion regarding a property that was the subject of a previous assignment, the scope of work in the new assignment may be different from the scope of work in the prior one. In addition, rather than duplicating steps in the appraisal process, the appraiser can elect to incorporate some of the analyses from the previous assignment (those items that the appraiser concludes are credible and in compliance with the applicable development Standard) into the new assignment through the use of an extraordinary assumption. 41 42 43 44 45 46

Reporting Requirements 47

For all assignments, the results must be reported in accordance with the requirements of STANDARDS 2, 4, 6, 8, or 10, as applicable. The new report is not required to have the same level of detail as the original report. However, the new report must contain sufficient information to be meaningful and not misleading to the intended users. There are three ways that the reporting requirements can be satisfied for these types of assignments: 48 49 50 51

1. Provide a new report that contains all the necessary information/analysis to satisfy the applicable reporting requirements, *without incorporation* of the prior report by either attachment or reference. 52 53
2. Provide a new report that *incorporates by attachment* specified information/analysis from the prior report so that, in combination, the attached portions and the new information/analysis added satisfies the applicable reporting requirements. 54 55 56
3. Provide a new report that *incorporates by reference* specified information/analysis from the prior report so that, in combination, the referenced portions and the new information/analysis added satisfies the applicable reporting requirements. When this incorporation by reference option is used, the following items from that prior report should be specifically identified in the new report to avoid being misleading: 57 58 59 60

   - subject property 61
   - client and any other intended users 62
   - intended use 63
   - appraiser(s) 64
   - effective date of value or assignment results 65
   - date of report, and 66
   - interest(s) appraised 67

When information is being extended to the report by use of an extraordinary assumption, the requirements in USPAP for use of an extraordinary assumption must be met. 68 69

Confidentiality 70

In all assignments the appraiser must comply with the Confidentiality section of the ETHICS RULE with respect to the handling of confidential information – i.e., if the prior appraisal or appraisal review report included any confidential information, its disclosure in a new report to a different client or intended user might violate the ETHICS RULE. This includes the requirement to comply with *all confidentiality and privacy laws and regulations.* 71 72 73 74

Assignment results and confidential information from a prior appraisal or appraisal review may only be disclosed to the client or parties authorized by the client. Thus, when incorporating a prior report by reference or attachment, if completing the report for a different client, the appraiser must receive authorization from the original client. 75 76 77

Record Keeping 78

If the assignment includes use of, or reliance upon, all or part of a prior report, that report (or the portions used or relied upon) must be retained in the workfile for the new assignment, or its location must be properly referenced in the workfile. Refer to the RECORD KEEPING RULE for more information. 79 80 81

© The Appraisal Foundation

ADVISORY OPINION 7 (AO-7)

This communication by the Appraisal Standards Board (ASB) does not establish new standards or interpret existing standards. Advisory Opinions are issued to illustrate the applicability of appraisal standards in specific situations and to offer advice from the ASB for the resolution of appraisal issues and problems.

SUBJECT: Marketing Time Opinions

APPLICATION: Real Property, Personal Property

THE ISSUE:

The *Uniform Standards of Professional Appraisal Practice* recognizes that some assignment conditions require the appraiser to analyze and report a reasonable marketing period (also referred to as marketing time) for the subject property when developing and reporting an opinion of market value of real or personal property.

How is this reasonable marketing period opinion developed, and what is the relationship of this opinion of marketing time to the appraisal process?

ADVICE FROM THE ASB ON THE ISSUE:

The reasonable marketing time is an opinion of the amount of time it might take to sell a real or personal property interest at the concluded market value or at a benchmark price during the period immediately after the effective date of an appraisal.

Stakeholders often confuse exposure time and marketing time. Marketing time is a forecast that is made looking forward from the effective date. Marketing time differs from exposure time, which is always presumed to precede the effective date of an appraisal.[1]

Rationale and Method for Developing a Marketing Time Opinion

The development of a marketing time opinion uses some of the same data analyzed in the process of developing a reasonable exposure time opinion as part of the appraisal process and is not intended to be a prediction of a date of sale or a one-line statement. It is an integral part of the analyses conducted during the appraisal assignment. The opinion may be expressed as a range or a number. An Appraisal Report should include a summary of the analysis upon which that opinion is based. The opinion can be based on one or more of the following:

- statistical information about days on market,
- information from data collection services,
- information gathered through sales verification,
- interviews of market participants, and
- anticipated changes in market conditions.

Related information garnered through this process includes other market conditions that may affect marketing time, such as the identification of typical buyers and sellers for the type of real or personal property involved and typical equity investment levels and/or financing terms. The reasonable marketing time is a function of price, time, use, and anticipated market conditions, such as changes in the cost and availability of funds, and is not an isolated opinion of time alone.

Appraisers should not simply use the estimate of reasonable exposure time as their forecast of the marketing period. A key difference in the analysis of marketing time is that the appraiser must also research and consider anticipated changes in market conditions. For example, while conducting research, the appraiser observes signs of strengthening in the market place. Signs could include shortening exposure periods, rising prices, lowering interest rates, increases in the ratio of listing price to sale price or reductions in inventory. An improving market place suggests property may be selling faster than it has in the past. The opposite is also true.

1 See Advisory Opinion 35, *Reasonable Exposure Time in Real and Personal Property Opinions of Value.*

© The Appraisal Foundation

Discussion of Marketing Time in the Appraisal Report 40

Marketing time occurs after the effective date of the market value opinion and the marketing time opinion is related to, 41
yet apart from, the appraisal process. Therefore, it is appropriate for the section of the appraisal report that discusses 42
marketing time and its implications to appear toward the end of the report after the market value conclusion. The 43
request to provide a reasonable marketing time opinion exceeds the normal information required for the appraisal 44
process and should be treated separately from that process. 45

It is also appropriate for the appraiser to discuss the impact of price/value relationships on marketing time and to 46
contrast different potential prices and their associated marketing times with an appraiser's market value opinion for 47
the subject property. 48

Applications of Client Conditions on an Appraisal 49

Clients concerned with marketing real or personal properties who obtain a market value appraisal as part of their 50
decision-making process should be aware that it may be inappropriate to assume that the value remains stable during 51
the marketing period. Therefore, it is technically incorrect for the user of an appraisal to take a current value opinion, 52
carry it forward to the end of a concluded marketing period, and then discount back to the present. 53

Some clients attempt to solve their problem by ordering a "120-day market value," a "six-month market value," or a 54
"one-year market value" from the appraiser. Unless the opinion of reasonable exposure time made by the appraiser 55
in the course of such an assignment coincides with the precondition imposed by the client, the answer to this 56
assignment will not necessarily be market value under a typical definition of the term. In such situations, the appraiser 57
must clearly distinguish between a market value opinion allowing for reasonable exposure time and any alternative, 58
appropriately defined, value opinion(s) subject to a special limiting condition resulting from the client-imposed 59
marketing time. 60

Whether or not the appraiser and client define the appraisal problem to include more than one opinion of value, the 61
roles of the parties must be kept clear. The appraiser provides the client with a supported opinion of defined value in 62
an appropriately documented report that includes a section on reasonable marketing time and any inherent price/value 63
implications. The ultimate decision on issues such as what price to ask, when to accept a particular offering price, and 64
how to account for the asset during the interim rests with the client. 65

SUMMARY: 66

- An estimate of marketing time is often an assignment condition but it is not a requirement of USPAP. 67
- The appraiser's opinion of marketing time is a forecast of time that begins as of the effective date of the 68
appraisal. 69
- Marketing time is different for various types of property and under various market conditions. 70
- Marketing time may be expressed as a single point in time or a range. 71
- The answer to the question "what is a reasonable forecast of marketing time," should always incorporate the 72
answer to the question "for what kind of property at what price range," rather than appear as a statement of an 73
isolated time period. 74
- When value is predicated on a marketing time that differs from the subject's reasonable exposure time the 75
resulting value will not necessarily be market value. 76

© The Appraisal Foundation

ADVISORY OPINION 9 (AO-9)

This communication by the Appraisal Standards Board (ASB) does not establish new standards or interpret existing standards. Advisory Opinions are issued to illustrate the applicability of appraisal standards in specific situations and to offer advice from the ASB for the resolution of appraisal issues and problems.

SUBJECT: The Appraisal of Real Property That May Be Impacted by Environmental Contamination

APPLICATION: Real Property

THE ISSUE:
Appraisals of contaminated properties, or properties suspected of being contaminated, are sometimes developed using either a hypothetical condition or an extraordinary assumption that the property is free of the contamination. While this is acceptable practice under certain conditions and for certain intended uses, there are assignments that require an appraisal of the "as-is" condition of the property, with full consideration of the effects of environmental contamination. In these assignments, the appraiser is asked to analyze the effects of known environmental contamination on the value of the subject property.

How does an appraiser comply with USPAP when appraising properties that may be impacted by environmental contamination?

ADVICE FROM THE ASB ON THE ISSUE:
Relevant USPAP & Advisory References

- DEFINITIONS, specifically the definitions of

  - *EXTRAORDINARY ASSUMPTION: an assignment-specific assumption as of the effective date regarding uncertain information used in an analysis which, if found to be false, could alter the appraiser's opinions or conclusions.*

    Comment: Uncertain information might include physical, legal, or economic characteristics of the subject property; or conditions external to the property, such as market conditions or trends; or the integrity of data used in an analysis.

  - *HYPOTHETICAL CONDITION: a condition, directly related to a specific assignment, which is contrary to what is known by the appraiser to exist on the effective date of the assignment results, but is used for the purpose of analysis.*

    Comment: Hypothetical conditions are contrary to known facts about physical, legal, or economic characteristics of the subject property; or about conditions external to the property, such as market conditions or trends; or about the integrity of data used in an analysis.

- ETHICS RULE, particularly:

  Conduct: *An appraiser must perform assignments with impartiality, objectivity, and independence, and without accommodation of personal interests .... An appraiser must not communicate assignment results with the intent to mislead or to defraud.*

- COMPETENCY RULE:
  An appraiser must: (1) be competent to perform the assignment; (2) acquire the necessary competency to perform the assignment; or (3) decline or withdraw from the assignment. In all cases, the appraiser must perform competently when completing the assignment.
- Standards Rule 1-1(a):
  In developing a real property appraisal, an appraiser must: (a) be aware of, understand, and correctly employ those recognized methods and techniques that are necessary to produce a credible appraisal;
- Standards Rule 1-2(e):
  In developing a real property appraisal, an appraiser must: (e) identify, from sources the appraiser reasonably believes to be reliable, the characteristics of the property that are relevant to the type and definition of value and intended use of the appraisal....

© The Appraisal Foundation

- Standards Rule 1-2(f) and (g):
  In developing a real property appraisal, an appraiser must: (f) identify any extraordinary assumptions necessary in the assignment; and (g) identify any hypothetical conditions necessary in the assignment.
- Standards Rule 1-3(b):
  When necessary for credible assignment results in developing a market value opinion, an appraiser must: (b) develop an opinion of the highest and best use of the real estate.
- Standards Rule 1-4:
  In developing a real property appraisal, an appraiser must collect, verify, and analyze all information necessary for credible assignment results.

Competency and Related Issues

Consistent with Standards Rule 1-1(a): in the appraisal of a property as impacted by environmental contamination, an appraiser must *be aware of, understand, and correctly employ those recognized methods and techniques necessary to produce a credible appraisal*. Accordingly, an appraiser must have the requisite knowledge about appropriate methods, and be able to assemble the required information. An appraiser who lacks knowledge and experience in analyzing the impact of environmental contamination on the value of real property must take the steps necessary to complete the assignment competently, as required by the COMPETENCY RULE. However, an appraiser need not be an expert on the scientific aspects of environmental contamination, and in most situations the appraiser will utilize scientific and other technical data prepared by others, such as environmental engineers. In these situations, the appraiser should utilize an extraordinary assumption regarding the information obtained from other experts that is used in the appraisal.[1] Examples of such information include items (1) to (10) under the header titled "Relevant Property Characteristics" later in this Advisory Opinion. This is especially important in situations where there is conflicting information about such information.

Specialized Terms and Definitions

The appraisal of properties that may be impacted by environmental contamination involves specialized terms and definitions that might not be used in an appraisal assignment in which the effect of the property's environmental condition is not analyzed, or when the property is not contaminated. Though it is recognized that there are other valid definitions of these and similar terms, for purposes of this Advisory Opinion, the following definitions apply:

Diminution in Value (Property Value Diminution): The difference between the unimpaired and impaired values of the property being appraised. This difference can be due to the increased risk and/or costs attributable to the property's environmental condition.

Environmental Contamination: Adverse environmental conditions resulting from the release of hazardous substances into the air, surface water, groundwater or soil. Generally, the concentrations of these substances would exceed regulatory limits established by the appropriate federal, state, and/or local agencies.

Environmental Risk: The additional or incremental risk of investing in, financing, buying and/or owning property attributable to its environmental condition. This risk is derived from perceived uncertainties concerning:

1) the nature and extent of the contamination;
2) estimates of future remediation costs and their timing;
3) potential for changes in regulatory requirements;
4) liabilities for cleanup (buyer, seller, third party);
5) potential for off-site impacts; and
6) other environmental risk factors, as may be relevant.

Environmental Stigma: An adverse effect on property value produced by the market's perception of increased environmental risk due to contamination. (See Environmental Risk.)

Impaired Value: The market value of the property being appraised with full consideration of the effects of its environmental condition and the presence of environmental contamination on, adjacent to, or proximate to the property. Conceptually, this could be considered the "as-is" value of a contaminated property.

1 See Standards Rule 1-2(f).

© The Appraisal Foundation

90 **Remediation Cost:** The cost to cleanup (or remediate) a contaminated property to the appropriate regulatory
91 standards. These costs can be for the cleanup of on-site contamination as well as mitigation of off-site impacts due to
92 migrating contamination.

93 **Remediation Lifecycle:** A cycle consisting of three stages of cleanup of a contaminated site: before remediation
94 or cleanup; during remediation; and after remediation. A contaminated property's remediation lifecycle stage is an
95 important determinant of the risk associated with environmental contamination. Environmental risk can be expected to
96 vary with the remediation lifecycle stage of the property.

97 **Source, Non-source, Adjacent and Proximate Sites:** Source sites are the sites on which contamination is, or has been,
98 generated. Non-source sites are sites onto which contamination, generated from a source site, has migrated. An adjacent
99 site is not contaminated, but shares a common property line with a source site. Proximate sites are not contaminated and
100 not adjacent to a source site, but are in close proximity to the source site.

101 **Unimpaired Value:** The market value of a contaminated property developed under the hypothetical condition that the
102 property is not contaminated.

103 **Relevant Property Characteristics**
104 The appraisal of a property that includes the effects of environmental contamination on its value usually requires data
105 not typically used in an appraisal of an otherwise similar but uncontaminated property or an appraisal of a potentially
106 impacted property using either a hypothetical condition or an extraordinary assumption that it is uncontaminated or
107 not impacted. The inclusion of these additional relevant property characteristics is consistent with Standards Rule
108 1-2(e). The relevant property characteristics may include, but are not limited to:

109 1) whether the contamination discharge was accidental or permitted;
110 2) the status of the property with respect to regulatory compliance requirements;
111 3) the remediation lifecycle stage (before, during or after cleanup) of the property as of the appraisal date;
112 4) the contamination constituents (petroleum hydrocarbons, chlorinated solvents, etc.);
113 5) the contamination conveyance (air, groundwater, soil, etc.);
114 6) whether the property is a source, non-source, adjacent or proximate site;
115 7) the cost and timing of any site remediation plans;
116 8) liabilities and potential liabilities for site cleanup;
117 9) potential limitations on the use of the property due to the contamination and its remediation; and
118 10) potential or actual off-site impacts due to contaminant migration (for source sites).

119 Since the appraiser is usually not an expert on the scientific aspects of contamination, experts from other fields
120 will typically provide this information. Appropriate regulatory authorities should also be consulted to confirm the
121 presence or absence of contamination. The appraiser should consider the use of extraordinary assumptions when this
122 information serves as a basis for an opinion of value. The appraiser should also collect similar data for any comparable
123 sales used in the analysis.

124 **Valuation Issues – As If Unimpaired**
125 In some assignments, the appraiser may be asked to appraise a property known to be contaminated under
126 the *hypothetical condition* that the real estate is free of contamination. In these assignments, an appraiser may
127 appraise interests in real estate that is known to be contaminated under the hypothetical condition that the real
128 estate is free of contamination when:

129 1) the resulting appraisal report is not misleading,
130 2) the client has been advised of the limitation, and
131 3) all the requirements of the ETHICS RULE have been satisfied.

132 To avoid confusion in the marketplace, the appraiser should disclose available information about the contamination
133 problem, explain the purpose of the hypothetical condition that the real estate is not contaminated, and state that
134 the use of the hypothetical condition might have affected the assignment results in accordance with Standards Rule
135 2-2(a)(xiii) and (b)(xv).

136 In other situations, the appraiser may be asked to appraise a property believed to be free of contamination or for
137 which the environmental status is uncertain due to the lack of information or conflicting information. For these

© The Appraisal Foundation

assignments, the property may be appraised under the *extraordinary assumption* concerning assumed factual information about its environmental condition and status. Indeed, since an appraiser is usually not an expert in detecting contamination, or confirming its absence, extraordinary assumptions regarding environmental condition may be necessary in many assignments.

Valuation Issues - As Impaired

Highest and Best Use Issues: The appraisal of properties that may be impacted by environmental contamination usually involves extensive highest and best use analysis. In accordance with Standards Rules 1-2(e) and 1-3(b), the appraiser must consider relevant factors in developing an opinion of the highest and best use of the property in its impaired condition. The valuation of properties impacted by environmental contamination usually involves the estimate of two values: the unimpaired value and the impaired. As such, two highest and best use analyses are typically required. The first does not consider any limitations on the property due to the environmental contamination. The second does consider any limitations due to the contamination, its remediation, and any legal use restrictions associated with the cleanup of the contamination source. Environmental contamination and its remediation to appropriate regulatory standards may affect the feasibility of site development or redevelopment, use of the site during remediation, use of the site after remediation, marketability of the site, and other economic and physical characteristics of a contaminated property. The appraiser should consider the possibility that site remediation and any remaining limitations on the use of the site following remediation may alter or limit its highest and best use in the impaired condition. In addition, excessive environmental risk and stigma may deter site development or redevelopment and thereby limit the highest and best use until the property's environmental risk is reduced to levels acceptable to the relevant market participants.

Satisfying Standards Rule 1-4 Requirements: When the appraiser addresses the diminution in value of a contaminated property and/or its impaired value, the appraiser must recognize that the value of an interest in impacted or contaminated real estate may not be measurable simply by deducting the remediation or compliance cost estimate from the opinion of the value as if unaffected (unimpaired value). Rather, *cost, use* and *risk* effects can potentially impact the value of contaminated property. *Cost effects* primarily represent deductions for costs to remediate a contaminated property. These costs are usually estimated by someone other than the appraiser, and should include consideration of any increased operating costs due to property remediation. The appraiser should also be aware that the market might not recognize all estimated costs as having an effect on value. *Use effects* reflect impacts on the utility of the site as a result of the contamination. If the contamination and/or its cleanup rendered a portion of the site unusable, or limited the future highest and best use of the property, then there could be a use effect on value. *Risk effects* are typically estimated by the appraiser and often represent the most challenging part of the appraisal assignment. These effects are derived from the market's perception of increased environmental risk and uncertainty. The analysis of the effects of increased environmental risk and uncertainty on property value (environmental stigma) must be based on market data, rather than unsupported opinion or judgment.

In general, an opinion of the subject property's unimpaired value can be developed using the sales comparison approach [Standards Rule 1-4(a)], cost approach [Standards Rule 1-4(b)], and income approach [Standards Rule 1-4(c)]. Estimating the effects of environmental contamination on real property value usually involves the application of one or more specialized valuation methods. These methods should be consistent with the requirements related to the valuation approaches in USPAP.

© The Appraisal Foundation

ADVISORY OPINION 13 (AO-13)

1 *This communication by the Appraisal Standards Board (ASB) does not establish new standards or interpret existing*
2 *standards. Advisory Opinions are issued to illustrate the applicability of appraisal standards in specific situations and*
3 *to offer advice from the ASB for the resolution of appraisal issues and problems.*

4 **SUBJECT: Performing Evaluations of Real Property Collateral to Conform with USPAP**

5 **APPLICATION: Real Property**

6 **THE ISSUE:**
7 How can an appraiser operating under the *Uniform Standards of Professional Appraisal Practice* (USPAP) develop
8 and communicate a valuation of real property collateral that complies with the *Interagency Appraisal and Evaluation*
9 *Guidelines*?[1]

10 **ADVICE FROM THE ASB ON THE ISSUE:**
11 **Relevant USPAP & Advisory References**

12 • The DEFINITIONS in USPAP include the following: *APPRAISAL: (noun) the act or process of developing an*
13 *opinion of value; an opinion of value.*
14 • Also included in the DEFINITIONS is the following: *APPRAISER: one who is expected to perform valuation*
15 *services competently and in a manner that is independent, impartial, and objective.*
16 • The SCOPE OF WORK RULE states in part, *Appraisers have broad flexibility and significant responsibility in*
17 *determining the appropriate scope of work for an appraisal or appraisal review assignment.*
18 • Under STANDARD 1, in developing a real property appraisal, an appraiser must *be aware of, understand,*
19 *and correctly employ those recognized methods and techniques that are necessary to produce a credible*
20 *appraisal.*
21 • STANDARD 2 requires that a real property appraisal report *contain sufficient information to enable intended*
22 *user(s) of the appraisal to understand the report properly.*

23 **Background**
24 The terms "appraisal" and "evaluation" have specific meanings and uses for institutions regulated by and under
25 the rules and published guidelines of the Office of the Comptroller of the Currency (OCC), the Board of Governors
26 of the Federal Reserve System (FRS), the Federal Deposit Insurance Corporation (FDIC), and the National Credit
27 Union Administration (NCUA) (Agencies). The federal regulators require that an appraisal must conform to generally
28 accepted appraisal standards as evidenced by USPAP, but that an evaluation need not conform to USPAP. The Glossary
29 (Appendix D) to the December 2010, *Interagency Appraisal and Evaluation Guidelines* (Agencies' Guidelines) defines
30 "evaluation" as: *A valuation permitted by the Agencies' appraisal regulations for transactions that qualify for the*
31 *appraisal threshold exemption, business loan exemption, or subsequent transaction exemption*. However, appraisers
32 who are bound by USPAP must recognize that an evaluation meets the USPAP definition of appraisal and appraisers
33 must comply with USPAP when providing such a service.

34 Appraisers must be aware that each lender may have its own internal policies and requirements regarding the format
35 and content of an evaluation. Those policies and requirements supplement the requirements stated in the Agencies'
36 Guidelines. It is critical that the appraiser and the client have a mutual understanding of the intended use and the
37 scope of work for the assignment. One way to enhance this mutual understanding is for the appraiser to request
38 copies of the institution's evaluation standards or requirements pertinent to the assignment.

39 **ASB Opinion on Evaluations of Real Property Collateral**

40 USPAP defines an appraisal as:

41 *(noun) the act or process of developing an opinion of value; an opinion of value.*

1 *Interagency Appraisal and Evaluation Guidelines*, 75 *Federal Register* 77449 (December 2010)

© The Appraisal Foundation

An evaluation, per the Agencies' Guidelines, provides an estimate of market value. When that estimate of market value is the opinion of an individual who is required to comply with USPAP, that opinion (i.e., the evaluation) is, per USPAP, an appraisal. Therefore, an appraiser who is required to comply with USPAP must meet both the Agencies' requirements for an evaluation and the requirements of STANDARDS 1 and 2 and other applicable parts of USPAP.

Any request for an opinion of value of real property requires compliance with the SCOPE OF WORK RULE, which states in part:

> *The scope of work must include the research and analyses that are necessary to develop credible assignment results.*
>
> *An appraiser must be prepared to support the decision to exclude any investigation, information, method, or technique that would appear relevant to the client, another intended user, or the appraiser's peers.*
>
> *An appraiser must not allow assignment conditions to limit the scope of work to such a degree that the assignment results are not credible in the context of the intended use.*

Under the SCOPE OF WORK RULE, any development requirements imposed on an assignment for evaluation of real property collateral would be considered assignment conditions.

If an individual is engaged to provide information or analysis that does not include an opinion of value, the assignment is neither an appraisal (per USPAP), nor an evaluation (per Agencies' Guidelines). However, if the individual providing that service is acting as an appraiser (as defined in USPAP), the assignment would be appraisal practice and the appraiser would be obligated to comply with the ETHICS RULE, the COMPETENCY RULE, and the JURISDICTIONAL EXCEPTION RULE.

Examples of requests for services that do not require a value conclusion include, but are not limited to:

- providing sales and rent data, listings, assessments and other similar information, without adjustments or determination of comparability to indicate or suggest the value of a specific property; and
- providing data describing a neighborhood, community, or any other real estate market segment and analyses on real estate market trends.

Appraisers who believe certain requests for evaluations of real property collateral are inconsistent with USPAP or contrary to law or regulation should explain their concerns to the potential client. If necessary, additional information and advice may be obtained from the appropriate federal regulator regarding the Agencies' Guidelines. If the client does not agree to an assignment that allows the appraiser to comply with USPAP and applicable law or regulation, the appraiser must decline or withdraw from the assignment.

Illustration

A potential client requests evaluations of real property collateral for two properties from an appraiser who is required to comply with USPAP. The client wants to know the market value of the fee simple interest in the properties presented in very brief and concise reports. The client is knowledgeable about the market for the types of property involved.

In an assignment to appraise either property, the appraiser must determine the appropriate scope of work to develop credible assignment results based on the problem to be solved before considering the reporting requirements of STANDARD 2.

One evaluation is for an existing single-family residential fee simple property in connection with a real estate loan amount of less than $250,000. The client requests only the sales comparison approach for this residential evaluation.

If the appraiser determines that the sales comparison approach alone is sufficient to produce credible assignment results in the appraisal of the residential property, an evaluation (i.e., an appraisal) based solely on this approach can be performed in compliance with USPAP.

The other evaluation is for an existing office building, occupied by the owner (without a lease). The lender is considering a business loan amount of $1,000,000 or less that is not dependent on the sale of, or rental income

© The Appraisal Foundation

85 derived from, real estate as the primary source of repayment.[2] The client requests only the income capitalization
86 approach for this office building evaluation.

87 If the appraiser determines that the income capitalization approach alone is sufficient to produce credible assignment
88 results in the appraisal of the office building property, an evaluation of this property based solely on the income
89 approach can be performed. However, if the sales comparison approach is necessary for credible results, the
90 appraiser should discuss the necessity of developing and reporting it with the client. The appraiser is ultimately
91 responsible and must include whatever research and analysis is necessary for credible results in the scope of work.

92 **Reporting the Results of an Evaluation**

93 When reporting evaluations, appraisers need to be aware that the evaluation content, described in the Agencies'
94 Guidelines, may differ from the content required for appraisal reports under STANDARD 2. It is important that the
95 contents of all appraisal reports satisfy the requirements of STANDARD 2 as well as all applicable assignment
96 conditions. In many cases, an Appraisal Report may be required, but in other cases, a Restricted Appraisal Report may
97 be sufficient if expanded to include all of the content requirements for an evaluation.[3]

98 In addition to the requirements in USPAP, an appraisal report used in an evaluation assignment must also comply with
99 the *Interagency Appraisal and Evaluation Guidelines*. The December 2010 Agencies' Guidelines include the following
100 report requirements:

101 ***XIII. Evaluation Content***

102 *An evaluation should contain sufficient information detailing the analysis, assumptions, and conclusions to*
103 *support the credit decision. An evaluation's content should be documented in the credit file or reproducible. The*
104 *evaluation should, at a minimum:*

105 • *Identify the location of the property.*
106 • *Provide a description of the property and its current and projected use.*
107 • *Provide an estimate of the property's market value in its actual physical condition, use and zoning*
108 *designation as of the effective date of the evaluation (that is, the date that the analysis was completed),*
109 *with any limiting conditions.*
110 • *Describe the method(s) the institution used to confirm the property's actual physical condition and the*
111 *extent to which an inspection was performed.*
112 • *Describe the analysis that was performed and the supporting information that was used in valuing the*
113 *property.*
114 • *Describe the supplemental information that was considered when using an analytical method or*
115 *technological tool.*
116 • *Indicate all source(s) of information used in the analysis, as applicable, to value the property, including:*
117 - *External data sources (such as market sales databases and public tax and land records);*
118 - *Property-specific data (such as previous sales data for the subject property, tax assessment data, and*
119 *comparable sales information);*
120 - *Evidence of a property inspection;*
121 - *Photos of the property;*
122 - *Description of the neighborhood; or*
123 - *Local market conditions.*
124 • *Include information on the preparer when an evaluation is performed by a person, such as the name and*
125 *contact information, and signature (electronic or other legally permissible signature) of the preparer.*

126 **Conclusion**

127 An evaluation, when performed by an individual acting as an appraiser, is an appraisal. In addition to complying
128 with USPAP, the appraiser must be aware of and comply with any additional assignment conditions and reporting
129 requirements imposed on the assignment.

2 National Credit Union Administration regulations do not contain an exemption from the appraisal requirements specific to member business loans.

3 See Advisory Opinion 38, *Content of an Appraisal Report and Restricted Appraisal Report*.

© The Appraisal Foundation

ADVISORY OPINION 14 (AO-14)

This communication by the Appraisal Standards Board (ASB) does not establish new standards or interpret existing standards. Advisory Opinions are issued to illustrate the applicability of appraisal standards in specific situations and to offer advice from the ASB for the resolution of appraisal issues and problems. 1 2 3

SUBJECT: Appraisals for Subsidized Housing 4

APPLICATION: Real Property 5

THE ISSUE: 6
Preparation of appraisals for subsidized housing in compliance with the *Uniform Standards of Professional Appraisal Practice* (USPAP) requires knowledge and experience that goes beyond typical residential appraisal competency. What guidance does USPAP provide for the appraisal of subsidized housing? 7 8 9

ADVICE FROM THE ASB ON THE ISSUE: 10
Relevant USPAP & Advisory References 11

- The COMPETENCY RULE states, in part: 12

  Competency requires: 13
  1. the ability to identify the problem to be addressed; and 14
  2. the knowledge and experience to complete the assignment competently. 15

- The COMPETENCY RULE also requires: 16

  recognition of, and compliance with, laws and regulations that apply to the appraiser or to the assignment. 17

- The Comment to Standards Rule 1-1(a) states, in part: 18

  Important changes in the cost and manner of constructing and marketing commercial, industrial, and residential real estate as well as changes in the legal framework in which real property rights and interests are created, conveyed, and mortgaged have resulted in corresponding changes in appraisal theory and practice. Social change has also had an effect... 19 20 21 22

- Standards Rule 1-2, particularly (a), (b), (c)(iv), (e) and (h); Standards Rule 1-3(a) and (b); and Standards Rule 1-4(g) 23

Identification of Subsidized Housing 24
Subsidized housing may be defined as single- or multifamily residential real estate targeted for ownership or occupancy by low- or moderate-income households as a result of public programs and other financial tools that assist or subsidize the developer, purchaser, or tenant in exchange for restrictions on use and occupancy. The United States Department of Housing and Urban Development (HUD) provides the primary definition of income and asset eligibility standards for low- and moderate-income households. Other federal, state, and local agencies define income eligibility standards for specific programs and developments under their jurisdictions. 25 26 27 28 29 30

Competency Issues 31
Appraisers should be aware that the competency required to appraise subsidized housing extends beyond typical residential appraisal competency. Subsidized housing appraisals require the appraiser to understand the various programs, definitions, and pertinent tax considerations involved in the particular assignment applicable to the location and development. An appraiser should be capable of analyzing the impact of the programs and definitions in the local subsidized housing submarket, as well as in the general market that is unaffected by subsidized housing programs. Appraisers should also be aware of possible political changes that will affect the durability of the benefits and restrictions to subsidized housing projects and fully understand interpretation and enforcement of subsidy programs. An appraiser's lack of knowledge and understanding of the impact of the various influences that affect subsidized housing projects could lead to misleading conclusions. For example, subsidized housing projects may have differences in income, expenses, and rates of returns when compared with nonsubsidized housing projects. Appraisers should reflect the actions of the participants in the market and avoid any stereotyped or biased assumptions. 32 33 34 35 36 37 38 39 40 41 42

© The Appraisal Foundation

43 **Property Rights Issues**
44 Subsidies and incentives that encourage housing for low- and moderate-income households may create intangible property
45 rights in addition to real property rights and may also create restrictions that modify real property rights. The appraiser
46 should demonstrate the ability to discern the differences between the real and intangible property rights and value the
47 various rights involved. Low-Income Housing Tax Credits (LIHTCs) are an example of an incentive that results in intangible
48 property rights that are not real property but might be included in the appraisal. Project-based rent subsidies are an
49 example of a subsidy accompanied by restrictions that modify real property rights. Appraisers should be aware that tenant-
50 based rent subsidies do not automatically result in a property right to the owner or developer of subsidized housing.

51 Standards Rule 1-2(e) allows the inclusion of intangible assets that are not real property in the appraisal. *When*
52 *personal property, trade fixtures, or intangible assets are included in the appraisal, the appraiser must analyze the*
53 *effect on value of such non-real property assets*, as required by Standards Rule 1-4(g).

54 A critical factor in all subsidized housing appraisals is the analysis of whether or not the various subsidies, incentives,
55 and restrictions remain with the real property following a sale or foreclosure and thus are marketable property rights
56 to be included in the appraisal.

57 **Value Definition Issues**
58 The value definition in any appraisal is a controlling factor of the bundle of rights to be considered in the appraisal.
59 Standards Rule 1-2(c) requires an appraiser to identify the type and definition of value. Standards Rule 1-2(c) further
60 required an appraiser to *ascertain whether the value is to be the most probable price:*

61 *(i) in terms of cash; or*
62 *(ii) in terms of financial arrangements equivalent to cash; or*
63 *(iii) in other precisely defined terms; and*
64 *(iv) if the opinion of value is to be based on non-market financing or financing with unusual conditions or*
65 *incentives, identify the terms of such financing and any influences on value.*

66 The appraiser must determine if requirement (i), (ii), (iii), or (iv) above applies to the specific definition selected
67 or required by the client. The appraiser can then determine if the programs and intangible assets created by
68 the programs affecting the subject property qualify under the selected or required market value definition. This
69 determination requires competent knowledge of the programs and whether the programs qualify under (i), (ii), (iii), or
70 (iv) above.

71 USPAP does not mandate market value appraisals, but it does require that the type and definition of value be
72 identified.

73 In appraisal of subsidized housing, the value definition selected or required by the client and the reporting techniques
74 used should be discussed with the client prior agreeing to perform the assignment because the analyses may be
75 based on general market terms, subsidized housing submarket financing with unusual conditions or incentives, both,
76 or some other defined premise.

77 Subsidies and incentives should be explained in the appraisal report, and their effect on value, if any, needs to be
78 reported in conformity with STANDARD 2.

79 **Market Analysis Issues**
80 Certain specific steps should be taken when appraising subsidized property. Research with housing organizations
81 and public agencies should be completed to find appropriate data on financing, rental and occupancy restrictions,
82 resale restrictions, and sales of comparably subsidized or restricted properties. Knowledge of the general markets
83 and the subsidized housing submarkets should be evident in all analyses. The market analyses should also address
84 the subject's ability to attract a sufficient number of subsidized tenants. Reversion projections should be based on
85 interviews with market participants; any factual information from developments that have reached the expiration of
86 their subsidies, incentives, and restrictions; and other relevant information.

© The Appraisal Foundation

ADVISORY OPINION 16 (AO-16)

This communication by the Appraisal Standards Board (ASB) does not establish new standards or interpret existing standards. Advisory Opinions are issued to illustrate the applicability of appraisal standards in specific situations and to offer advice from the ASB for the resolution of appraisal issues and problems. 1 2 3

SUBJECT: Fair Housing Laws and Appraisal Report Content 4

APPLICATION: Real Property 5

THE ISSUE: 6
In developing and reporting an appraisal or appraisal review assignment, what should an appraiser consider to comply with current fair housing laws? 7 8

BACKGROUND: 9
Fair housing law(s) preclude the use of certain specific information or supported conclusions related to protected group(s) in some assignments. Accordingly, an appraiser should be knowledgeable about the laws that affect the subject property of an assignment. Laws and regulations on fair lending and fair housing (such as the Fair Housing Act; the Equal Credit Opportunity Act (ECOA), and the laws and regulations of applicable federal, state, and local jurisdictions) continue to evolve. Further, appraisers must continue to provide appraisals that do not illegally discriminate or contribute to illegal discrimination. The Conduct section of the ETHICS RULE states in part, *An appraiser must not use or rely on **unsupported** conclusions relating to characteristics such as race, color, religion, national origin, gender, marital status, familial status, age, receipt of public assistance income, handicap, or an **unsupported** conclusion that homogeneity of such characteristics is necessary to maximize value* (bold added for emphasis). 10 11 12 13 14 15 16 17 18

In some cases, even **supported** conclusions in assignments relating to characteristics such as race, color, religion, national origin, gender, marital status, familial status, age, receipt of public assistance income, handicap, or group homogeneity cannot be used because they are precluded by applicable law. 19 20 21

ADVICE FROM THE ASB ON THE ISSUE: 22
Relevant USPAP & Advisory References 23

- The PREAMBLE states, in part: 24
  It is essential that appraisers develop and communicate their analyses, opinions, and conclusions to intended users of their services in a manner that is meaningful and not misleading. 25 26
- The Conduct section of the ETHICS RULE states, in part: 27
  An appraiser must not engage in criminal conduct. 28
  An appraiser must perform assignments with impartiality, objectivity, and independence, and without accommodation of personal interests. 29 30
- The COMPETENCY RULE states, in part: 31
  An appraiser must: (1) be competent to perform the assignment; (2) acquire the necessary competency to perform the assignment; or (3) decline or withdraw from the assignment. In all cases, the appraiser must perform competently when completing the assignment. 32 33 34
- *Competency requires:* 35
  (1) the ability to properly identify the problem to be addressed; and (2) the knowledge and experience to complete the assignment competently; and (3) recognition of, and compliance with, laws and regulations that apply to the appraiser or to the assignment. 36 37 38
- The Comment to the COMPETENCY RULE states, in part: 39
  Competency may apply to factors such as, but not limited to, an appraiser's familiarity with a specific type of property or asset, a market, a geographic area, an intended use, specific laws and regulations, or an analytical method. 40 41
- The Comment to Standards Rule 1-1(a) states, in part: 42
  Social change has also had an effect on appraisal theory and practice. To keep abreast of these changes and developments, the appraisal profession is constantly reviewing and revising appraisal methods and techniques and developing new methods and techniques to meet new circumstances. For this reason, it is not sufficient for appraisers to simply maintain the skills and the knowledge they possess when they become appraisers. Each appraiser must continuously improve his or her skills to remain proficient in real property appraisal. 43 44 45 46 47

© The Appraisal Foundation

48 • Standards Rule 2-1(a) states, in part:
49 *Each written or oral real property appraisal report must clearly and accurately set forth the appraisal in a*
50 *manner that will not be misleading.*
51 • The content of the certification in Standards Rules 2-3(a), 4-3(a), and 6-3(a) requires the following disclosures:
52 *I certify that, to best of my knowledge and belief, ... the reported analyses, opinions, and conclusions are*
53 *my personal, impartial, and unbiased professional analyses, opinions, and conclusions ...[and] my analyses,*
54 *opinions, and conclusions were developed, and this report has been prepared, in conformity with the*
55 *Uniform Standards of Professional Appraisal Practice.*
56 • The Conduct section of the ETHICS RULE states, in part:
57 *An appraiser must not use or rely on unsupported conclusions relating to characteristics such as race, color,*
58 *religion, national origin, gender, marital status, familial status, age, receipt of public assistance income, handicap,*
59 *or an unsupported conclusion that homogeneity of such characteristics is necessary to maximize value.*

60 **Appraisal Report Content**
61 Appraisers must ensure that their appraisal or appraisal review opinions and conclusions are impartial and
62 objective and do not illegally discriminate or contribute to illegal discrimination through subjective or stereotypical
63 assumptions.

64 The use of terms or descriptive phrases in place of factual information in a report imposes particular obligations on
65 an appraiser to ensure that the user properly understands the report and is not misled. An appraiser needs to have,
66 and should report wherever possible and appropriate, factual information to support the use of terms or descriptive
67 phrases that reflect a scale or rating of a market or property that affects value or marketability conclusions. If
68 such factual information is absent, an appraiser should clearly disclose that the rating or descriptive phrase is the
69 appraiser's opinion but that no factual information was available to support that rating or descriptive phrase and
70 ensure that the use of the term or descriptive phrase is not illegally discriminatory.

71 An appraiser should research the actions of participants in the subject's market to identify factors having a direct
72 favorable or unfavorable influence on marketability or value. Failure to extract pertinent market information (e.g., sales,
73 rents, occupancy rates, expense ratios, capitalization or discount rates, construction costs, depreciation, or exposure
74 times) from the subject's market could produce conclusions that are misleading and/or illegally discriminatory.

75 Appraisers should exercise care that comments made in a report will not be perceived as illegally biased or
76 discriminatory. Factual descriptions, rather than subjective phrases, allow users of a report to draw their own
77 conclusions. The use of terms that reflect a scale such as "high," "low," "good," "fair," "poor," "strong," "weak,"
78 "rapid," "slow," "average," or the like should also provide contextual information that properly explains the frame
79 of reference and the relative position of the subject property on the scale. For example, if absorption is stated as
80 "rapid," the context of the rating should be cited as well ("rapid" relative to what?).

81 **Competency**
82 Situations such as those listed below require specific research and competency to avoid the use of unsupported
83 conclusions:

84 • the property is designed to suit the needs of a protected group;
85 • there is little or no transaction information available on similar properties;
86 • the property is in a market setting where similar properties have not previously existed;
87 • market conditions are not similar to the conditions prevailing during the time frame in which previous market
88 transactions occurred; or
89 • there are financially subsidized rental or ownership programs.

90 **Illustrations:**
91 1. An appraiser is completing an assignment in an area where crime activity has recently been publicized. The
92 appraiser considers the use of the term "high-crime area."

93 This is a subjective term that may be understood by the appraiser but may mislead the client. This term does
94 not provide the evidence that the appraiser used in making the observation. The appraiser may provide a
95 specific reference that is factual and objective (e.g., one crime per 100 people or one crime per 1,000,000
96 people) but may still mislead the client. If the appraiser is to be competent with these types of statistics, the

© The Appraisal Foundation

crime ratio should be correlated to the actions of the market in reflecting a valuation adjustment or other indication of property demand. If all of the comparables used by the appraiser are from a market sharing the same crime characteristic, the appraiser should question whether the term and/or the statistic(s) are relevant to the appraisal assignment. 97 98 99 100

2. A religious organization requests an appraiser to determine if a facility offering unique services to specific religious members is feasible. The appraiser must research a geographic market and identify concentrations of individuals that are members of that specific religion. Is the appraiser permitted to complete the assignment under USPAP? 101 102 103 104

   The assignment is not covered by ECOA or the Fair Housing Act. Under USPAP, the appraiser must comply with the ETHICS RULE concerning discrimination. 105 106

   The key in this case is not to use or rely on unsupported conclusions. If the appraiser can identify the market behavior of the religious members and relate that behavior to the assignment, the appraiser is not in violation of USPAP. 107 108 109

3. An appraiser is requested to review a portfolio of apartment appraisal reports in a market area where apartments with public rent subsidies also exist. How does the Conduct section of the ETHICS RULE affect the appraisal reviewer's actions? 110 111 112

   The review and conclusion of acceptance or rejection of the reports should not rely on the appraisal reviewer's unsupported conclusions regarding public assistance projects. 113 114

4. An appraiser is requested to appraise a house with specific features (e.g., ramps, wider doorways, and special plumbing fixtures) designed to accommodate disabled individuals. How does the appraiser analyze the unique improvements? 115 116 117

   The appraiser should reflect market preferences for the components of the structure. However, the appraiser should not draw an unsupported conclusion that the fixtures either enhance or diminish value. 118 119

© The Appraisal Foundation

ADVISORY OPINION 17 (AO-17)

This communication by the Appraisal Standards Board (ASB) does not establish new standards or interpret existing standards. Advisory Opinions are issued to illustrate the applicability of appraisal standards in specific situations and to offer advice from the ASB for the resolution of appraisal issues and problems.

SUBJECT: Appraisals of Real Property with Proposed Improvements

APPLICATION: Real Property

THE ISSUE:
Can either a current or a prospective value opinion for a property subject to completion of proposed improvements be provided in compliance with the *Uniform Standards of Professional Appraisal Practice* (USPAP)?

BACKGROUND:
An appraisal of real property with proposed improvements presents complex analysis and reporting issues because some portion of the property appraised does not exist at the time of the appraisal. Consequently, an appraiser must use particular care when performing an appraisal of such property to ensure that the results are credible and the appraisal report is not misleading.

A client may have a legitimate need for either a current or a prospective opinion of value (or both) concerning proposed improvements to real property. This kind of appraisal may be performed for a variety of client types, such as lenders, developers, private investors, trusts, attorneys, government agencies, or insurance companies. Further, such an appraisal may be for purposes other than providing an opinion of market value.

Many real property appraisers have been uncertain whether a current value opinion, rather than a prospective value opinion, may be provided in compliance with USPAP for a property subject to completion of proposed improvements and, if so, which portions of USPAP are most relevant to the assignment.

Advisory Opinion 34 addresses how an appraiser may provide a prospective value opinion in a manner that is not misleading. This Advisory Opinion provides guidance in performing an assignment involving proposed improvements to real property, whether the purpose of the assignment is to develop a current value opinion or to develop a prospective value opinion.

The value opinion in an appraisal assignment involving proposed improvements is developed on the basis of one or more extraordinary assumptions. Using an extraordinary assumption always requires specific reporting steps. An appraiser must properly address the requirements set forth in Standards Rule 1-2(f) related to use of an extraordinary assumption in developing an appraisal and must address Standards Rules 2-2(a)(xiii) and (b)(xv) in reporting the appraisal opinions and conclusions so as to ensure that the results are credible and not misleading.

ADVICE FROM THE ASB ON THE ISSUE:
<u>Relevant USPAP & Advisory References</u>
The following USPAP references are applicable when completing an assignment involving proposed improvements to real property:

- COMPETENCY RULE, as it relates to the complexity of an appraisal assignment involving proposed improvements;
- SCOPE OF WORK RULE particularly regarding laws, regulations, or guidelines which may augment USPAP;
- JURISDICTIONAL EXCEPTION RULE;
- STANDARD 1, particularly Standards Rules 1-1(a), 1-2(d), 1-2(e), 1-2(h), 1-3(a); and
- STANDARD 2, particularly Standards Rules 2-1(a), 2-1(c), and Standards Rule 2-2.

Additional guidance appears in the following Advisory Opinions:
- AO-7, *Marketing Time Opinions;*
- AO-30, *Appraisals for Use by a Federally Regulated Financial Institution;*
- AO-33, *Discounted Cash Flow Analysis;*

© The Appraisal Foundation

- AO-34, *Retrospective and Prospective Value Opinions;* 44
- AO-35, *Reasonable Exposure Time in Real and Personal Property Opinions of Value.* 45

Additional guidance appears in Advisory Opinion 7, which addresses marketing time opinions. AO-30, *Appraisals for* 46
Use by a Federally Regulated Financial Institution addresses when other requirements may augment USPAP. 47

General Comments 48
Both current and prospective value appraisals subject to completion of proposed improvements to real property are 49
permitted under USPAP. As noted in Advisory Opinion 34, a current value appraisal occurs when the effective date of 50
appraisal is contemporaneous with the date of the report, and a prospective value appraisal occurs when the effective 51
date of appraisal is after the date of the report. 52

Development of a value opinion(s) for a subject property with proposed improvements in a current value appraisal 53
involves at least one hypothetical condition, specifically that the described improvements have been completed as 54
of the effective date. The use of a hypothetical condition, in turn, imposes additional reporting requirements as set 55
forth in Standards Rule 1-2(g) and Standards Rules 2-2(a)(xiii) and (b)(xv). The additional reporting requirements are to 56
ensure that an intended user understands that: 57

(a) the improved subject property does not yet, in fact, exist as of the date of appraisal; 58
(b) the analyses performed to develop the opinion of value are based on a hypothesis, specifically that the 59
improved subject property is assumed to exist when in fact it does not exist; 60
(c) certain events need to occur, as disclosed in the report, before the property appraised with the proposed 61
improvements will in fact exist; and 62
(d) the appraisal does not address unforeseeable events that could alter the proposed property improvements 63
and/or the market conditions reflected in the analyses. 64

Development of a value opinion based on a hypothetical condition is addressed in Standards Rule 1-2(g). Use of a 65
hypothetical condition is permitted when it is clearly required for legal purposes, for purposes of reasonable analysis, 66
or for purposes of comparison. An analysis based on a hypothetical condition must not result in an appraisal or 67
appraisal review report that is misleading. The hypothetical condition must be clearly and conspicuously disclosed 68
in the report with a description of the hypothetical condition and a statement that its use might have affected the 69
assignment results. 70

There may be laws, regulations or guidelines that affect how and when a hypothetical condition may be used in an 71
appraisal assignment. Appraisers should consider these assignment conditions, but they must make certain that 72
developing and reporting a current value opinion under a hypothetical condition in accordance with the assignment 73
conditions still results in an appraisal that complies with USPAP. 74

Assignment Considerations 75
An appraiser asked to complete an assignment involving proposed improvements to real property should consider 76
and discuss with the client: 77

- the intended use of the appraisal report; 78
- the effective date of the appraisal and the date when the proposed improvements are expected to be 79
complete; 80
- the physical and economic changes to the existing property and changes in the market for the property that 81
may result from completion of the proposed improvement; and 82
- the possible change in market competition from other properties over the time frame of the improvement 83
project. 84

It is important for an appraiser to ensure that the client knows that the differences in the information considered in 85
the two types of analyses can result in significant differences between a current and a prospective value opinion 86
concerning the same subject property. 87

Taken together, these factors and the client's needs determine whether it is most appropriate to develop: 88

- a current value opinion on the basis of a hypothetical condition that the proposed improvements already have 89
been completed, or 90

© The Appraisal Foundation

91 • a prospective value opinion on the basis of an extraordinary assumption that the property will be improved as
92 of a future date, as proposed.

93 If a prospective value opinion is the most appropriate, the appraiser should review and follow the guidance in
94 Advisory Opinion 34 in the course of completing the assignment.

95 As stated in "General Comments" above, an appraisal of a property subject to completion of proposed improvements
96 with a current effective date always involves use of at least one hypothetical condition (i.e., the proposed improvements
97 have been completed as of the effective date), and this always requires reporting that the proposed improvements are
98 appraised as if completed as described in the report, as of the effective date.

99 In an appraisal with a prospective effective date, the extraordinary assumption that the proposed improvements are
100 complete as of that future date must be disclosed clearly and conspicuously. The appraiser also should report that the
101 extraordinary assumption might have affected the assignment results.

102 An appraiser should carefully review Standards Rule 1-2(e) and determine whether the information available for
103 analysis is sufficient to identify the extent and character of the proposed improvements. If sufficient information is
104 not available, an appraiser may use an extraordinary assumption about the extent and character of the proposed
105 improvements, if credible assignment results can still be developed. In an appraisal with a prospective effective date,
106 the extraordinary assumption about the extent and character of the improvements is in addition to the extraordinary
107 assumption about those improvements being completed on the future effective date.

108 A current value opinion assignment does not require an appraiser to provide a prospective value opinion. However,
109 so as to not be misleading the appraisal report should clearly indicate the fact that the value of the property that
110 actually exists as of the date of the report would be different from the value concluded for the property with the
111 proposed improvements completed as described in the hypothetical condition(s) used in the appraisal.

112 **Illustrations:**

113 1. A client is considering financing the construction of a single-family residence. Construction is expected to be
114 complete in six to eight months from the date of the appraisal report. No significant changes in market conditions
115 are foreseeable during the construction period. The client requests a current value opinion based on the
116 hypothetical condition that the improvements are complete as of the current date. Can such an appraisal be
117 provided in compliance with USPAP?

118 Yes, provided sufficient information about the extent and character of the proposed improvements is available
119 or can be reasonably assumed under a hypothetical condition used for purposes of reasonable analysis in
120 this case. Given the intended use of the appraisal (construction financing) and the lack of significant change
121 in the market conditions during the construction period, in this case, a current value appraisal would not
122 be misleading solely on the basis of the hypothetical condition that the improvements are complete as of a
123 current date.

124 2. A client requests an appraisal to assist in establishing contract rent in a build-to-suit agreement. The agreement
125 stipulates that contract rent will be based on a stated percentage of the market value of the property as if it
126 were completed as of a current date. The client requests a current value opinion based on the hypothetical
127 condition that the improvements are complete as of the current date. Can such an appraisal be provided in
128 compliance with USPAP?

129 Yes. Given the intended use of the appraisal, the use of the hypothetical condition is necessary for purposes
130 of reasonable analysis and would not in itself result in a misleading appraisal.

131 3. A client is considering making a current loan on a hotel and requests an opinion of the current value. The
132 current occupancy levels are below 60% and are not expected to improve for at least two years. The client has
133 requested the appraiser to utilize a hypothetical condition which assumes that the occupancy level of the hotel is
134 70%. Can such an appraisal be provided in compliance with USPAP?

135 No. The resulting appraisal would be misleading because of the combination of the intended use of the
136 appraisal to make a current loan and the market conditions that are expected to affect the subject property.

© The Appraisal Foundation

4. A client is considering construction of a large apartment complex. The client expects construction to be complete in about two years. Currently, demand for similar apartment units is strong, but because of the amount of new construction under way or planned in the near future, vacancy levels are expected to rise from the current level (below 1 percent) to about 20 percent in two years. 137 138 139 140

   A. The client requests an appraisal with a current value opinion for use in obtaining financing from a non-regulated financial institution, based on the hypothetical condition that the apartment complex is complete and at stabilized occupancy. Can such an appraisal be provided in compliance with USPAP? 141 142 143

      No, because given the intended use and the foreseeable changes in market competition during the course of construction, a current value opinion for the property, as if complete, would most likely be misleading. A prospective value opinion, with an effective date as of the expected completion date, would more realistically reflect market conditions affecting the subject property as proposed. 144 145 146 147

   B. The client requests an appraisal with a current value opinion for use in testing project feasibility or investment alternatives, based on the hypothetical condition that the apartment complex is complete and at stabilized occupancy. Can such an appraisal be provided in compliance with USPAP? 148 149 150

      Yes, because the intended use of the appraisal and the hypothesis, in this type of assignment, is for purposes of reasonable analysis and comparison. However, so as not to be misleading, the appraisal analyses should reflect the market risk resulting from the foreseeable trend in vacancy and its probable impact on cash flow and market competition, and the appraisal report must clearly indicate the intended use of the appraisal. 151 152 153 154 155

© The Appraisal Foundation

ADVISORY OPINION 18 (AO-18)

This communication by the Appraisal Standards Board (ASB) does not establish new standards or interpret existing standards. Advisory Opinions are issued to illustrate the applicability of appraisal standards in specific situations and to offer advice from the ASB for the resolution of appraisal issues and problems.

SUBJECT: Use of an Automated Valuation Model (AVM)

APPLICATION: Real Property, Personal Property, Intangible Property

THE ISSUE:
What steps should an appraiser take when using an AVM as a tool in the development of an appraisal or appraisal review concerning an individual property?

In addition, what steps should appraisers take when they are using an AVM only to process information and communicate the AVM's output but is not performing an appraisal or appraisal review assignment?

BACKGROUND:
This Advisory Opinion addresses how an appraiser may use an AVM.

An AVM is a computer software program that analyzes data using an automated process. For example, AVMs may use regression, adaptive estimation, neural network, expert reasoning, and artificial intelligence programs.

The output of an AVM is not, by itself, an appraisal. An AVM's output may become a basis for appraisal or appraisal review if the appraiser believes the output to be credible for use in a specific assignment.

An appraiser can use an AVM as a tool in the development of an appraisal or appraisal review. However, the appropriate use of an AVM is, like any tool, dependent upon the skill of the user and the tool's suitability to the task at hand.

This Advisory Opinion applies when an appraiser uses an AVM in connection with an individual property. This Advisory Opinion does not apply to mass appraising.

An appraiser needs to know, before using an AVM, whether it is to be used:

1. to perform an appraisal or appraisal review or
2. solely to provide the client with AVM output.

When appraisers use an AVM to develop their own opinions or conclusions in an appraisal or appraisal review assignment, all of the USPAP rules governing that assignment apply and all of this Advisory Opinion is relevant.

Appraisers are not performing an appraisal or appraisal review assignment when they simply run an AVM by using information provided by the client and:

1. do not alter the input or affect the output of the AVM, and
2. do not communicate their own appraisal or appraisal review regarding the AVM's output.

If the appraiser uses an AVM only to provide the client with the AVM output, the references to the Conduct section of the ETHICS RULE and the "Communicating the AVM Output" section in this Advisory Opinion are relevant.

ADVICE FROM THE ASB ON THE ISSUE:
Relevant USPAP References

- Conduct section of the ETHICS RULE:

    An appraiser must not engage in criminal conduct.
    An appraiser must perform assignments with impartiality, objectivity, and independence, and without accommodation of personal interests.

    Further,

© The Appraisal Foundation

An appraiser must not communicate assignment results with the intent to mislead or to defraud. An appraiser must not use or communicate a report that is known by the appraiser *to be misleading or fraudulent.*

- The COMPETENCY RULE states, in part:

  ... Competency requires: (1) the ability to properly identify the problem to be addressed; and (2) the knowledge and experience to complete the assignment competently; and (3) recognition of, and compliance with, laws and regulations that apply to the appraiser or to the assignment.

- The Comment to the COMPETENCY RULE states, in part:

  Competency may apply to factors such as, but not limited to, an appraiser's familiarity with a specific type of property or asset, a market, a geographic area, an intended use, specific laws and regulations, or an analytical method.

- SCOPE OF WORK RULE:
  The scope of work must include the research and analyses that are necessary to develop credible assignment results... Appraisers have broad flexibility and significant responsibility in determining the appropriate scope of work for an appraisal or appraisal review assignment. The appraiser must be prepared to demonstrate that the scope of work is sufficient to produce credible assignment results... An appraiser must not allow the intended use of an assignment or a client's objectives to cause the assignment results to be biased.
- Standards Rule 1-1(a):
  An appraiser must *be aware of, understand, and correctly employ those recognized methods and techniques that are necessary to produce a credible appraisal.*
- Standards Rule 1-1(b):
  An appraiser must *not commit a substantial error of omission or commission that significantly affects an appraisal.*
- Standards Rule 1-1(c):
  An appraiser must *not render appraisal services in a careless or negligent manner, such as by making a series of errors that, although individually might not significantly affect the results of an appraisal, in the aggregate affect the credibility of those results.*
- Standards Rule 1-6(b):
  An appraiser must *reconcile the applicability and relevance of the approaches, methods and techniques used to arrive at the value conclusion(s).*
- STANDARD 2:
  In reporting the results of a real property appraisal, an appraiser must communicate each analysis, opinion, and conclusion in a manner that is not misleading.
- STANDARD 3:
  In developing an appraisal review assignment, an appraiser acting as a reviewer must identify the problem to be solved, determine the scope of work necessary to solve the problem, and correctly complete research and analyses necessary to produce a credible appraisal review.
- STANDARD 4:
  In reporting the results of an appraisal review assignment, an appraiser acting as a reviewer must communicate each analysis, opinion, and conclusion in a manner that is not misleading.
- Advisory Opinion 37, *Computer Assisted Valuation Tools.*

Competency

When appraisers are asked to use an AVM in an assignment, the appraisers must ensure that they can comply with the requirements of the COMPETENCY RULE both prior to agreeing to perform the assignment and in the course of performing it.

In an appraisal assignment, an appraiser must have a basic understanding of how the AVM works in order to reasonably determine that:

© The Appraisal Foundation

86 1. use of the AVM is appropriate for the assignment;
87 2. the output of the AVM is credible for use in the assignment; and
88 3. the AVM does not exclude relevant market measures or factual information necessary for a credible calculation.

89 A client may suggest or request the use of an AVM in an appraisal or appraisal review assignment, but ultimately
90 the appraiser is responsible for the decision to use or not use the AVM and its output. The appraiser must be able to
91 reasonably conclude that the AVM's output is credible before deciding to use the AVM or rely on its output. For example,
92 in an appraisal assignment, the credibility of the AVM output may be established by comparison to the subject market. If
93 the appraiser concludes that using the AVM output in an assignment would be misleading, the appraiser should either use
94 other tools to perform the analysis or decline or withdraw from the assignment.

95 **Under What Conditions May AVMs Be Used?**
96 There are five critical questions to which the appraiser should answer "yes" before deciding to use an AVM in an
97 appraisal or appraisal review assignment:

98 1. Does the appraiser have a basic understanding of how the AVM works?
99 2. Can the appraiser use the AVM properly?
100 3. Are the AVM and the data it uses appropriate given the intended use of assignment results?
101 4. Is the AVM output credible?
102 5. Is the AVM output sufficiently reliable for use in the assignment?

103 The answers to these questions may be affected by the degree to which the appraiser can interact with the AVM. The
104 decision to use an AVM may also be affected by support information supplied by the AVM's developer, the appraiser's
105 previous experience in using the AVM, or other available information.

106 **Database**
107 Credibility of the AVM output depends on the quality of its database and how well the AVM is designed to analyze
108 that database. When using an AVM in an appraisal or appraisal review assignment, the appraiser must have reason to
109 believe the AVM appropriately uses data that are relevant.

110 **Understanding and Control of the AVM**
111 When using an AVM in an appraisal or appraisal review assignment, an appraiser should have a basic understanding
112 of how the AVM analyzes data to determine whether the AVM measures and reflects market activity for the subject
113 property. The appraiser does not need to know, or be able to explain, the AVM's algorithm or intricacies of its statistical
114 or mathematical formulae. However, the appraiser should be able to describe the AVM's overall process and verify that
115 the AVM is consistent in producing results that accurately reflect prevailing market behavior for the subject property.

116 AVMs differ in the number and type of data characteristics as well as in the volume of data analyzed. The appraiser
117 should know which characteristics (e.g., size, location, quality) are analyzed and how the analysis is tested for
118 accuracy and reasonableness. The appraiser should ascertain that the characteristics analyzed are those to which the
119 market responds.

120 Some AVMs allow the appraiser to select the data analyzed on the basis of, for example, distance from subject,
121 size, or age of the improvements. An appraiser's ability to change the AVM's selection parameters may affect the
122 appraiser's decision to use or rely on the AVM output.

123 The appraiser should be aware that the AVM may not perform consistently given the same input criteria. The appraiser
124 should be confident of the AVM's credibility when applied to a specific property. The appraiser decides whether to rely
125 on the AVM output, regardless of the AVM's overall test performance. In some cases, the appraiser may accept the AVM's
126 output, while in other cases that same AVM's output would not be acceptable.

127 **Communicating the AVM Output**
128 Appraisers must ensure that their communication of an AVM's output is not misleading.

129 An AVM's output is not, by itself, an appraisal, and communication of an AVM's output is not, in itself, an appraisal
130 report. When an AVM is used in an appraisal or appraisal review assignment, information furnished about an AVM
131 in the appraiser's report must satisfy the reporting requirements applicable to the type of report provided (e.g., in
132 the case of a real property appraisal, an Appraisal Report or Restricted Appraisal Report). The appraiser should cite
133 the name and version of the AVM software and provide a brief description of its methods, assumptions, and level

© The Appraisal Foundation

of allowed user intervention. The report should, to the extent possible, identify the database (e.g., Multiple Listing Services) and the data analyzed. 134 135

An appraiser bound by USPAP may be asked to run an AVM and communicate its output without performing an appraisal or appraisal review assignment. For example, an appraiser may be asked to simply enter property characteristics provided by the client but not alter the input or affect the AVM's output. In this specific instance, the appraiser is not acting in the capacity of an appraiser but rather is functioning only as an AVM operator. In such a situation, an appraiser must carefully avoid any action that could be considered misleading or fraudulent. The appraiser should take steps to ensure that communication of the AVM's output is not misconstrued as an appraisal or appraisal review report. For example, appraisers should: 136 137 138 139 140 141 142

1. not communicate their opinions or conclusions as an appraiser regarding the credibility or reliability of the AVM's output; 143 144
2. not provide an appraiser's certification or statement of limiting conditions in connection with the AVM's output; and 145 146
3. ensure that their role as only an AVM operator is clearly indicated if their signature or other identification marks appear on document(s) used to communicate the AVM's output. 147 148

Analyzing an AVM's Effectiveness 149

An appraiser bound by law, regulation, or an agreement to comply with USPAP may be asked to analyze and comment on the effectiveness of an AVM for a stated intended use. Such a request involves an aspect of value and thereby this would be an appraisal practice service, but one for which USPAP has no specific performance standards. Before agreeing to perform such an assignment, an appraiser bound to comply with USPAP must ensure compliance with the ETHICS RULE, the COMPETENCY RULE, and the JURISDICTIONAL EXCEPTION RULE. To meet the COMPETENCY RULE, at a minimum, the appraiser should also have a basic understanding of how the AVM works. 150 151 152 153 154 155

Review of the Output of an AVM 156

An appraiser bound by law, regulation, or an agreement to comply with USPAP may be asked if the output of an AVM is credible for a specific property, given the intended use of the AVM's output. Such a request involves an aspect of value and thereby making this determination is an appraisal practice service, but one for which USPAP has no specific performance standards. The appraiser must ensure compliance with the ETHICS RULE, the COMPETENCY RULE, and the JURISDICTIONAL EXCEPTION RULE. 157 158 159 160 161

Review of an Appraisal Report Containing Output of an AVM 162

An appraiser may be asked to review an appraisal report that includes an opinion of value based on the output of an AVM. This is an appraisal review assignment under USPAP which must follow the requirements of STANDARDS 3 and 4. This kind of appraisal review assignment may be performed if the appraiser conducting the review understands how the AVM works and can form an opinion as to the adequacy and relevancy of the data and the appropriateness of the analysis, based on the information provided in the report under review. 163 164 165 166 167

Use of an AVM in an Appraisal Review Assignment 168

An AVM may be used in the process of reviewing a real property appraisal report. The appraisal reviewer may use the AVM to test the reasonableness of the value conclusion in the report under review if the appraisal reviewer has a basic understanding of how the AVM works, can use the AVM properly, determines that use of the AVM is appropriate for the appraisal review assignment, and believes the AVM output is credible and sufficient for the appraisal review assignment. 169 170 171 172

Illustrations: 173

1(a). Staff Appraiser D, who has access to market databases, is asked to use an AVM to process information. When Appraiser D runs the AVM, she has done no other appraisal research. Appraiser D does not apply any of her appraisal knowledge or judgment in operating the AVM. Appraiser D has entered only property characteristics provided by the client and does not know how the AVM analyzes the data. Is the AVM output an appraisal? 174 175 176 177

No. The AVM output by itself is not an appraisal. Appraiser D did not apply her appraisal knowledge, judgment, or expertise, nor did she represent that the output was her own opinion of value. 178 179

Appraiser D must be very careful in communicating the AVM output to ensure that there is no misunderstanding as to her role in operating the AVM or communicating its output. For example, Appraiser D should: 180 181 182

© The Appraisal Foundation

183 1. not communicate her opinions or conclusions as an appraiser regarding the credibility or reliability of the
184 AVM's output;
185 2. not provide an appraiser's certification or statement of limiting conditions in connection with the AVM's
186 output; and
187 3. ensure that her role as only an AVM operator is clearly indicated if her signature or other identification
188 mark appears on documents used to communicate the AVM's output.

189 1(b). Staff Appraiser D receives AVM output from a coworker who is not an appraiser. Appraiser D is requested to
190 determine if the AVM output is credible, given the intended use. What can Appraiser D do?

191 Appraiser D should not express an opinion regarding value. However, the request involves an aspect of
192 value and, therefore, Appraiser D can indicate if the AVM output is credible. USPAP includes no specific
193 performance standards for this kind of service. However, because performing the service requires an appraiser
194 to consider an aspect of property value, it is part of appraisal practice. Appraiser D must, therefore, ensure
195 compliance with the ETHICS RULE, the COMPETENCY RULE, and the JURISDICTIONAL EXCEPTION RULE.

196 1(c). After staff Appraiser D has received the AVM output, can she incorporate the information into the appraisal
197 process?

198 Yes. However, Appraiser D must be able to understand how the AVM works and determine that the
199 information analyzed is credible and reliable.

200 2. Appraiser V provides residential appraisals to Client A, whose intended use is to document security for equity
201 lines of credit. Appraiser V has determined that Orange Box AVM is sufficiently reliable to use as a tool in
202 these appraisals. Orange Box AVM was recently used by Appraiser V on a house in a suburban single-family
203 residential subdivision.

204 Client B requests Appraiser V to use Orange Box AVM, alone, for a relocation appraisal assignment on an
205 identical house in the same subdivision. Can Appraiser V use Orange Box AVM alone in this relocation appraisal
206 assignment?

207 AVM itself and the AVM output for Client A's needs may not be appropriate for Client B's needs.

208 Client A's intended use of the appraisal is to document security for an equity line of credit. Typically, Client A's
209 lending decision is based primarily on the homeowner's capacity to pay the debt and only secondarily on the
210 value of the house. The reliability expectation of the value opinion needed by Client A is relatively low.

211 The intended use of the relocation appraisal for Client B is to develop an opinion of a sale price of the house
212 under very specific conditions. Typically, the reliability expectation of the opinion needed by Client B is
213 relatively high because their intended use involves a near-term transfer of the house, with immediate financial
214 implications. Appraiser V must determine if Orange Box AVM's output is sufficiently reliable to meet Client B's
215 stated expectations.

216 3(a). Appraiser A developed a regression analysis model that suggests a relationship between the size of a residence and
217 the price per square foot of similar residences in a specific market. This relationship has been confirmed by market
218 behavior, and the database used is believed to be reliable. Can the appraiser use the regression analysis model in
219 other appraisal assignments of similar properties in the same market?

220 Yes, because the appraiser knows how the regression analysis model works, has independently tested the
221 conclusions it provides, and believes the database is reliable. However, the appraiser must consider whether
222 the AVM output is credible and reliable for each assignment on a case by case basis.

223 3(b). Appraiser A's friend, Appraiser B, works in a different market area. Appraiser B is impressed with Appraiser A's
224 model and wants to use the model in Appraiser B's market area. Can Appraiser B use Appraiser A's model?

225 Yes, if Appraiser B understands how Appraiser A's model works and verifies by independent testing that the
226 model produces reliable results in Appraiser B's market area and that the database used by Appraiser B
227 reflects behavior in Appraiser B's market area. However, the appraiser must consider whether the AVM output
228 is credible and reliable for each assignment on a case-by-case basis.

© The Appraisal Foundation

4(a). A client of Appraiser A requests that Appraiser A use Blue Box AVM. The client says, "Since we are only doing residential appraisals, you can skip the cost and income approach. To lower the cost of the appraisal just use the Blue Box AVM results as the basis for your value conclusion." The client also says, "Blue Box AVM makes thirteen adjustments, and that is all that the appraiser needs to be concerned with." The Blue Box AVM developer feels that appraisers cannot understand this new technology and that appraisers do not need to know how the thirteen adjustments are made. What should Appraiser A do? 229 230 231 232 233 234

Appraiser A should: 235

1. learn how the Blue Box AVM works; 236
2. determine if he can use the AVM properly; and, 237
3. given the intended use, determine if the output of Blue Box AVM is credible and sufficiently reliable for use in the assignment. 238 239

If Appraiser A cannot understand how the Blue Box AVM works or concludes that the results are not credible, given the intended use, Appraiser A should discuss the issue with the client. This discussion may result in a modified scope of work or in the appraiser declining the assignment. 240 241 242

4(b). Another client requests that Appraiser A consider Green Box AVM. The client indicates that Appraiser A can modify six of the thirteen items analyzed in Green Box AVM, such as the distance within which the comparables are selected and the size range (square footage) of the comparables. The developer of Green Box AVM will also describe how the AVM works and provide the results of test data, which indicate that the model is reliable. What should Appraiser A do? 243 244 245 246 247

Appraiser A should follow the same steps described in 4(a). 248

© The Appraisal Foundation

ADVISORY OPINION 19 (AO-19)

This communication by the Appraisal Standards Board (ASB) does not establish new standards or interpret existing standards. Advisory Opinions are issued to illustrate the applicability of appraisal standards in specific situations and to offer advice from the ASB for the resolution of appraisal issues and problems.

SUBJECT: Unacceptable Assignment Conditions in Real Property Appraisal Assignments

APPLICATION: Real Property

ISSUE:
All real property appraisal assignments involve conditions that affect the appraiser's scope of work and the type of report. What types of assignment conditions are unacceptable?

BACKGROUND:
Many residential property appraisers report requests for service where the caller includes statements or information in the request similar to the following:

1. We need comps for (property description) that will support a loan of $____________; can you provide them?
2. Sales Price: ____________
3. Approximate (or minimum) value needed: ____________
4. Amount needed: ____________
5. Owner's estimate of value: ____________
6. If this property will not appraise for at least ____________, stop and call us immediately.
7. Please call and notify if it is NOT possible to support a value at or above ____________ BEFORE YOU PROCEED!!!!

Appraisers report that the caller usually makes it clear that they do not want the appraiser to do any fieldwork. Some callers refer to the service requested as a "comp check" while others refer to it as a "preliminary appraisal" or use some terms other than appraisal (such as preliminary evaluation, study, analysis, etc.). Some callers indicate that if the numbers will not work, the appraiser can send a bill for research services or a "preliminary" inspection. Other callers promise future assignments if the appraiser can make the present deal work.

Appraisers ask, "Can I respond to such requests without violating USPAP and, if so, how?"

ADVICE FROM THE ASB ON THE ISSUE:
<u>Relevant USPAP & Advisory References</u>
Appraisers receiving requests for services that include the kind of information and situations described in the Background section of this Advisory Opinion should carefully review:

- The <u>Conduct</u> and <u>Management</u> sections of the ETHICS RULE, particularly in regard to assignments offered under condition of "predetermined opinions or conclusions" or compensation conditioned on the reporting of a predetermined value result, a direction in assignment results that favors the cause of the client, the amount of a value opinion, the attainment of a stipulated result, or the occurrence of a subsequent event directly related to the appraiser's opinions and specific to the assignment's purpose.
- The definitions of "Appraisal," "Appraisal Practice," "Assignment" and "Scope of Work" in the DEFINITIONS section of USPAP.
- Standards Rule 1-1(b), particularly as it relates to diligence in the level of research and analysis necessary to develop credible opinions and conclusions.
- Standards Rules 1-2(f), (g), and (h), regarding identification of the scope of work necessary to complete an assignment and any extraordinary assumptions or hypothetical conditions necessary in an assignment.
- Standards Rules 1-5(a) and (b), regarding the analysis of current or historical market activity regarding the property appraised.
- The SCOPE OF WORK RULE, with particular attention to the appraiser's responsibility in connection with the scope of work decision and disclosure obligations

© The Appraisal Foundation

- As guidance, Advisory Opinions 13 and 38. 45

Unacceptable Conditions 46

Certain types of conditions are unacceptable in any assignment because performing an assignment under such 47
conditions violates USPAP. Specifically, an assignment condition is unacceptable when it: 48

- precludes an appraiser's impartiality, because such a condition destroys the objectivity and independence 49
required for the development and communication of credible results; 50
- limits the scope of work to such a degree that the assignment results are not credible, given the intended use 51
of the assignment; or 52
- limits the content of a report in a way that results in the report being misleading. 53

Acceptable Assignment Conditions 54

The intended use of the assignment results affect whether assignment conditions are acceptable. Some assignment 55
conditions may be acceptable in one type of assignment but not in another. An appraiser should carefully consider 56
the information provided by the client in a prospective assignment before agreeing to perform or declining the 57
assignment. (See Advisory Opinion 36.) 58

In the highly competitive financial services market, cost versus benefit is always an issue. Residential appraisers, 59
particularly, have seen an increase in the use of sophisticated loan application screening tools by their lender-clients. 60
Many lenders believe an appraiser can enhance their screening efforts by doing "preliminary work" that they do not 61
view as an "appraisal." 62

Other client groups also ask appraisers to provide services under conditions that limit the appraiser's scope of work. 63
Investors, trust administrators, and portfolio account managers often require opinions and data from appraisers in 64
order to make decisions. Attorneys often rely on appraisers in counseling their clients and in preparing for litigation. 65

When considering a request for service, appraisers should ascertain: 66

- whether the service involves an appraisal, 67
- what levels of risk are associated with the service, and 68
- whether there are any unacceptable conditions attached to the assignment. 69

Appraisers should take care to communicate with prospective clients to reach a common understanding about 70
assignment conditions. Further, the appraiser and client need to recognize that: 71

**1) the type of assignment in each request described in the Background section of this Advisory Opinion is 72
an appraisal.** 73

If an appraiser is asked whether a specific property has a value (a point, a range, or a relationship to some 74
benchmark), that request is for an opinion of value (an appraisal). Appraisers, obligated to comply with USPAP, 75
must develop a real property appraisal in accordance with STANDARD 1. Reporting that value opinion must be 76
accomplished in accordance with STANDARD 2. 77

Appraisers, like other professionals, must ensure that those who use their services recognize the amount of work 78
required - and the expertise needed - to develop a credible value conclusion about a property. 79

However, this does not mean that the appraiser cannot provide an economic and competitive service. Indeed, the 80
Uniform Standards of Professional Appraisal Practice recognize the need for different kinds of appraisals. A competent 81
appraiser can vary the scope of work in an assignment, in accordance with the type and definition of value and 82
intended use of the appraiser's opinions and conclusions in the assignment, and remain in compliance with USPAP. 83

2) assignment limitations affect the level of risk accepted by each party in an assignment; 84

Appraisers and users of appraisals should recognize that assignment limitations affect the reliability of an appraiser's 85
opinions and conclusions. In some assignments, an appraiser can reasonably apply extraordinary assumptions to 86
compensate for assignment limitations. In other situations, the use of the same assumptions may not be acceptable. 87

© The Appraisal Foundation

88 When the intended use is to screen a potential business for feasibility, the use of assumptions or extraordinary
89 assumptions is more appropriate than when the intended use is for loan documentation or loan settlement. Because
90 intended users' reliance on an appraisal may be affected by the scope of work, the report must enable them to be
91 properly informed and not misled.

92 **3) assignment conditions that compromise an appraiser's impartiality and objectivity in an assignment are**
93 **unacceptable.**

94 While a client may feel that offering preference in current or future assignments on the basis of "making the
95 numbers work" in a specific assignment is appropriate, attaching such a condition to an assignment compromises an
96 appraiser's impartiality and destroys the appraiser's credibility.

97 The *Uniform Standards of Professional Appraisal Practice* is explicit about such matters. Agreeing to perform an
98 appraisal assignment under such a condition violates the Conduct section of the ETHICS RULE in USPAP, which
99 states, in part:

100 *An appraiser must perform assignments with impartiality, objectivity, and independence, and without*
101 *accommodation of personal interests.*

102 *An appraiser must not agree to perform an assignment that includes the reporting of predetermined opinions*
103 *and conclusions.*

104 Furthermore, accepting compensation for completing an appraisal assignment under such a condition violates the
105 Management section of the ETHICS RULE in USPAP, which states:

106 *An appraiser must not agree to perform an assignment, or have a compensation arrangement for an*
107 *assignment, that is contingent on any of the following:*

108 *1. the reporting of a predetermined result (e.g., opinion of value);*
109 *2. a direction in assignment results that favors the cause of the client;*
110 *3. the amount of a value opinion;*
111 *4. the attainment of a stipulated result (e.g., that the loan closes or taxes are reduced); or*
112 *5. the occurrence of a subsequent event directly related to the appraiser's opinions and specific to the*
113 *assignment's purpose.*

114 **Illustrations:**
115 Some of the requests shown in the Background section of this Advisory Opinion share common characteristics.
116 Possible responses to each common group of requests could be:

117 1. *We need comps for (a specific property) that will support a loan of ____________; can you provide them?*

118 "Maybe, but I'll need to research the market to know whether the 'comps' will support a value range relative
119 to the loan amount. In doing this, I will be deciding which sales are 'comps' and what those 'comps' mean.
120 Those decisions will result in a range of value for your prospective borrower's property, which is an appraisal.

121 You also need to recognize that there are risks in this kind of assignment. You should realize that my value
122 conclusion could change if I subsequently perform an appraisal. Under the research and analysis limitations
123 you suggest, I would not have verified some of the data and would have to use extraordinary assumptions
124 about the market data and your borrower's property information. I would not have performed some of the
125 analyses steps I might complete in an appraisal assignment without those limitations. If all of that is agreeable
126 to you, we can proceed."

127 2. *Sales Price: ____________*

128 "As long as the amount is only to inform me of the pending contract [or of the sale price] and is not a
129 condition for your placement of this assignment with me, we can proceed. However, if that amount is a
130 condition of this assignment, agreeing to perform an assignment under that condition violates professional
131 ethics."

132 Note: A sale price (in a pending or a settled transaction) is part of the information an appraiser is required
133 to ascertain in accordance with Standards Rules 1-5(a) and (b). Receiving this information with a request for

© The Appraisal Foundation

service is appropriate. However, it is a violation of USPAP to agree to perform an assignment if the price in an agreement of sale, option, or listing or a sale price in a settled transaction is given as a predetermined value. 134 135

3. *Approximate (or minimum) value needed: ___________* 136

4. *Amount needed: _______________* 137

5. *Owner's estimate of value: ____________* 138

"As long as the amount is only to inform me of your objectives or someone else's opinion and is not a condition for your placement of this assignment with me, we can proceed. However, if that amount is a condition of this assignment, agreeing to perform an assignment under that condition violates professional ethics." 139 140 141

6. *If this property will not appraise for at least ____________, stop and call us immediately.* 142

7. *Please call and notify if it is NOT possible to support a value at or above ___________ BEFORE YOU PROCEED!!!!* 143 144

"Your request is acknowledged, but it is important for you to be aware that I must develop an appraisal before I can tell you whether the property will support the value indicated. It is also important for you to be aware that your statement of that amount with this request for service does not, in my view, establish a 'condition' for my performing the appraisal. If you intend it to be a condition for performing the assignment, I cannot agree to perform the assignment because it violates professional ethics." 145 146 147 148 149

Research Illustration: 150

The foregoing illustrations all include an appraisal assignment. In some situations, a client will request a service that is not an appraisal or appraisal review assignment as defined in USPAP. The service to be performed by the appraiser in the following illustration is: 151 152 153

- not an appraisal assignment (the appraiser does not develop a value opinion); and 154
- not a real property appraisal review (there is no appraisal to review). 155

The caller in this illustration is usually in the process of making a business decision and needs impartial and objective information but has not yet decided whether to pursue the matter at hand. The caller knows there is the potential for needing an appraisal, depending, in part, on what the sales data shows. The caller also believes that, if the data indicates that an appraisal is worthwhile, having that work completed by the appraiser in that subsequent assignment will lessen the time required to perform an appraisal. The prospective client may ask: 156 157 158 159 160

"We want you to check your data resources to see if there are sales within the past six months that are within one mile of [address]. If you find some, we may order an appraisal from you." 161 162

One possible response would be: 163

"If what you want is only the sales of properties shown in the databases available to me with the criteria you specified, I can do that research and send you the result. Then you can decide what you think your client's property is worth. If I do only that, it is just research and is not an appraisal. 164 165 166

However, you need to recognize that there are risks if you decide to have the research done that way. If you decide to limit my work to just gathering the sales data using the research criteria you set, you are taking the risk that those criteria are both adequate and appropriate to find all of the market data relevant to your client's property. You also take the risk that any appraiser's analysis of that data would result in a value conclusion within the price range suggested by the sales data assembled using your criteria. There is no assurance that such would be the case." 167 168 169 170 171

Staff or Multi-Appraiser Firm Context 172

The foregoing illustrations reflect communications between a client and an appraiser in the context of the appraiser as an independent contractor (fee appraiser). 173 174

In a staff context, such as where the appraisal function is established as a business or agency unit, the part of the entity that uses the appraiser's opinions and conclusions represents the "client" (intended user) and the part that completes the assignment represents the "appraiser." 175 176 177

© The Appraisal Foundation

178 In that context, the "assignment" originates from the "intended user" part of the entity. The appraisal unit's response to
179 an "intended user" in situations like those in the foregoing illustrations reasonably could be similar because imposing
180 assignment conditions that compromise an appraiser's impartiality and objectivity is unacceptable, whatever the setting.

181 However, the example responses in the illustrations do not apply to the customary interaction and dialogue that
182 occurs between appraisers within organizations or peers in multi-appraiser firms. Such interaction and dialogue within
183 the unit or group that develops the opinions and conclusions in an assignment is not the same as communicating
184 opinions and conclusions to an intended user.

© The Appraisal Foundation

ADVISORY OPINION 20 (AO-20)

This communication by the Appraisal Standards Board (ASB) does not establish new standards or interpret existing standards. Advisory Opinions are issued to illustrate the applicability of appraisal standards in specific situations and to offer advice from the ASB for the resolution of appraisal issues and problems.

SUBJECT: An Appraisal Review Assignment That Includes the Reviewer's Own Opinion of Value

APPLICATION: Real Property, Personal Property, Intangible Property

THE ISSUE:
A client may want appraisers, who are functioning as a reviewer, to develop and report their own opinion of value (i.e., an appraisal) within an appraisal review assignment. This leads to two questions:

How does the assignment change when the reviewer's scope of work includes the development of the reviewer's own opinion of value?

What language in appraisal review reports indicates when the reviewer did or did not develop an opinion of value?

BACKGROUND:
Appraisal review is a specialized area of appraisal practice. Appraisal reviews are used in a variety of business, governmental, and legal situations and also have an important role in the enforcement of professional standards.

STANDARDS 3 and 4 allow the reviewer to address all or part of the work under review (also referred to in this Advisory Opinion as the "original work"). In every appraisal review assignment, the reviewer is required to *"...identify the problem to be solved, determine the scope of work necessary to solve the problem, and correctly complete research and analyses necessary to produce a credible appraisal review."* The reviewer's opinion about the quality of the work under review can include addressing its completeness, relevance, appropriateness, and reasonableness, all in the context of the requirements applicable to that work.

However, a client may also want the reviewer to develop and report the reviewer's own opinion of value (an appraisal) within an appraisal review assignment. In this instance, the appraisal review assignment is actually a two-stage assignment: an appraisal review *plus* a value opinion by the reviewer.

The purpose and intended use together, of an appraisal review assignment, affect the scope of work in an assignment. Therefore, it is essential that reviewers clearly identify the purpose and intended use of the appraisal review and establish a well-defined scope of work with their client to ensure a clear understanding of what steps are and are not necessary in an appraisal review assignment.

This Advisory Opinion applies to both STANDARDS 3 and 4, and provides guidance to help appraisers, clients, and other users or readers of an appraisal review report:

A. recognize how terminology used in STANDARDS 3 and 4, and in this Advisory Opinion prevents confusion as to the function the reviewer is fulfilling in an appraisal review assignment;
B. understand how the purpose of the appraisal review and the intended use of the appraisal review results affect the scope of work in an appraisal review assignment;
C. recognize how the scope of work changes when an appraisal review assignment includes a requirement for the reviewer to develop (STANDARD 3) and report (STANDARD 4) an opinion of value concerning the subject property of the work under review; and
D. understand how the language in an appraisal review report can be used to indicate whether a value opinion was or was not developed by the reviewer.

© The Appraisal Foundation

39 **ADVICE FROM THE ASB ON THE ISSUE:**

40 **Relevant USPAP & Advisory References**

41 • DEFINITIONS section, specifically the definition of "Appraisal," "Appraisal Review," and "Assignment"
42 • STANDARD 3, Appraisal Review, Development
43 • STANDARD 4, Appraisal Review, Reporting

44 Portions of the referenced material are cited in this Advisory Opinion. An appraiser performing an appraisal review
45 assignment should carefully study the complete text to ensure a proper understanding of the requirements and the
46 text in STANDARDS 1, 5, 7, or 9, as applicable, as well as those in STANDARDS 3 and 4.

47 **A. TERMINOLOGY**

48 When reading the references cited above, appraisers performing appraisal review assignments (referred to as
49 "reviewers" in USPAP) should note that the terminology used in STANDARDS 3 and 4 have very specific meanings.

50 The term "Appraisal Review" is used in USPAP to identify the activity of a reviewer in an appraisal review
51 assignment. Appraisers sometimes use such terms as "Desk Review," "Field Review," "Complete Review,"
52 "Limited Review," "Technical Review," and "Administrative Review." However, without appropriate explanation,
53 these terms and phrases can result in misunderstanding about the function being performed by a reviewer.
54 While such terms may be convenient labels for use in a business setting, they do not necessarily impart the
55 same meaning in every situation.

56 Rather than simply using labels, reviewers should also accurately define the scope of work — in fact, Standards
57 Rule 3-2(g) requires the reviewer to *"...determine the scope of work necessary to produce credible assignment*
58 *results in accordance with the SCOPE OF WORK RULE"* and Standards Rule 4-2(g) requires the reviewer to *"state*
59 *the scope of work used to develop the appraisal review..."* These requirements are designed to ensure that an
60 intended user of appraisal review results is not misled as to the reviewer's scope of work and the basis for his or
61 her opinions and conclusions.

62 The terms "Review Appraisal" and "Review Appraiser" are also sometimes used in practice, primarily to refer to
63 the marketing of services or to an appraiser's functional status in employment. These phrases are not used in
64 STANDARDS 3 and 4, in part to avoid giving confusing implications, such as, for example, the impression that an
65 appraisal is always part of a review.

66 **B. HOW PURPOSE AND INTENDED USE AFFECT SCOPE OF WORK**

67 A reviewer's scope of work in an appraisal review assignment is determined primarily by the purpose(s) of the
68 assignment and the intended use of the assignment results. Standards Rule 3-2(b) requires, in part, that the
69 reviewer must ***"identify the intended use of the reviewer's opinions and conclusions."*** In addition, Standards
70 Rule 3-2(c) states the reviewer must "***identify the purpose of the appraisal review, including whether the***
71 ***assignment includes the development of the reviewer's own opinion of value or review opinion related to the***
72 ***work under review."***

73 Examples of intended use include (without limitation) quality control, audit, qualification, or confirmation. Each type
74 of intended use affects the scope of work that may be appropriate for a particular appraisal review assignment.

75 As examples, a client may want the reviewer to develop (STANDARD 3) and report (STANDARD 4) an opinion as
76 to the quality of another appraiser's work, *and*:

77 1. only state the corrective action to be taken by the appraiser with regard to curing any deficiency, leaving
78 the client to decide whether to interact with the appraiser to accomplish the correction; or
79 2. act on behalf of the client to interact with the appraiser who prepared the original work to ensure any
80 deficiency is appropriately corrected by that appraiser; or
81 3. make corrections to cure an error, such as a mathematical miscalculation, by showing what the
82 calculation would have been if correct but without expressing the result as the reviewer's own opinion of
83 value; or
84 4. make corrections to cure a deficiency, expressing the result as the reviewer's own opinion of value,
85 which is to be developed within the same scope of work as was applicable in the assignment that
86 generated the original work; or

© The Appraisal Foundation

5. make corrections to cure a deficiency, expressing the result as the reviewer's own opinion of value, which is to be developed using a different scope of work than was applicable in the assignment that generated the original work; or
6. regardless of the appraisal review result, develop an opinion of value using the same scope of work as was applicable in the assignment that generated the original work; or
7. regardless of the appraisal review result, develop an opinion of value using a different scope of work than was applicable in the assignment that generated the original work.

In Examples 1, 2, and 3 the reviewer has not taken any steps to offer an opinion of value, and therefore, has not bridged over into the appraisal stage.

In Examples 4, 5, 6, and 7, the appraisal review assignment is actually a two stage assignment—an appraisal review *plus* a value opinion by the reviewer. It is also important to note that this second stage occurs even if the reviewer concurs with the value opinion in the original work. This is because a reviewer's concurrence in a value opinion developed by another appraiser converts it to the reviewer's *own* opinion of value—in effect, the reviewer is taking ownership of that value by concurring with it. As such, it constitutes a value opinion (i.e., appraisal) by the reviewer.

In Examples 6 and 7, the client might, alternatively, engage the reviewer (as an appraiser) in a separate assignment to perform an appraisal outside the context of the appraisal review assignment.

In any case, the reviewer must carefully develop the scope of work as required by Standards Rule 3-2(g) and state the scope of work in the report as required by Standards Rule 4-2(g). The concluding language used (see illustrations to follow) should also be consistent with the scope of work decision.

C. SCOPE OF WORK AND THE REVIEWER'S OPINION OF VALUE

An appraisal review assignment that includes a requirement for the reviewer to develop the reviewer's own opinion of value imposes on the reviewer an expanded scope of work. This additional scope of work requirement is set forth in the Comment to Standards Rule 3-2(g), which states, in part:

> ***Determine the scope of work necessary to produce credible assignment results in accordance with the SCOPE OF WORK RULE.***
>
> Comment: *Reviewers have broad flexibility and significant responsibility in determining the appropriate scope of work in an appraisal review assignment. Information that should have been considered by the original appraiser can be used by the reviewer in developing an opinion as to the quality of the work under review. Information that was not available to the original appraiser in the normal course of business may also be used by the reviewer; however, the reviewer must not use such information in the reviewer's development of an opinion as to the quality of the work under review.*

Compliance with STANDARD 1, 5, 7, or 9 through the Use of Extraordinary Assumption(s)—The development of the reviewer's opinion of value requires compliance with STANDARD 1, 5, 7, or 9 as applicable. The reviewer's use of those items from the work under review that the reviewer concludes are credible and in compliance with the applicable development standard is based on an extraordinary assumption. This is because, unless the reviewer actually replicates the steps necessary to develop those items, the reviewer is assuming the integrity of that work without personal verification. If those assumptions were found to be false, the reviewer's appraisal-related opinions and conclusions would be affected. As such, this situation constitutes an extraordinary assumption (refer to requirements for proper application in Standards Rule 1-2(f), 5-2(i), 7-2(f), or 9-2(f) as applicable). Those items not deemed to be credible or in compliance must be replaced with information or analysis by the reviewer, developed in conformance with STANDARD 1, 5, 7, or 9, as applicable, to produce a credible value opinion.

Altering the Scope of Work in Developing the Reviewer's Opinion of Value—In some appraisal review assignments, the client needs a reviewer's opinion of value to be developed under a different scope of work than in the original appraisal.

If the reviewer's assignment has a different scope of work than does the original work, or if the reviewer relies on different information not available to, or not used by, the original appraiser, then it is possible that the two appraisal results could also differ. This does not mean that either set of results is "wrong" per se; in any event, the reviewer should not use information unavailable to the original appraiser as the basis to discredit the original appraiser's opinion of value.

© The Appraisal Foundation

136 If there is a difference between the appraiser's opinion of value and the reviewer's opinion of value, the reviewer
137 should use care to ensure correct identification of the cause of that difference in the appraisal review process.
138 The reviewer should also use care to not mislead an intended user when providing support for the reviewer's
139 conclusions in the appraisal review report. This is critical from an enforcement perspective as well as in a
140 business setting. Incorrectly characterizing the cause of a deficiency can erode the credibility of appraisal review
141 conclusions and of the reviewer's value opinion.

142 **D. APPRAISAL REVIEW REPORT CONTENT**

143 The reviewer's opinions and conclusions stated in compliance with Standards Rule 4-2(i) can vary significantly,
144 depending on the purpose and intended use of the appraisal review. Reviewers should carefully compose the
145 particular language stating their opinions and conclusions to avoid misleading the user of the appraisal review
146 report as to the scope of work completed in the assignment and the meaning of the reviewer's stated opinions
147 and conclusions. Note that any additional information relied upon and the reasoning and basis for the reviewer's
148 opinion of value must be summarized, in contrast to the other requirements in this section that must only be
149 stated. Additionally, changes to the report content by the reviewer to support a different value conclusion must
150 match, at a minimum, the reporting requirements for an Appraisal Report.

151 **An Appraisal Review Assignment WITHOUT an Opinion of Value**—If the assignment is only to develop an
152 opinion as to the quality of another appraiser's work, the appraisal review report content must include:

153 1. the information set forth in Standards Rules 4-2; and
154 2. the reviewer's certification in accordance with Standards Rule 4-3.

155 When the appraisal review is only for ascertaining quality, the reviewer should use extreme care to ensure the
156 appraisal review report does not include language that implies the reviewer developed an opinion of value
157 concerning the subject property of the original work. When the reviewer uses language to signify concurrence with
158 the value or a different value opinion, the reviewer has additional appraisal development and reporting obligations.

159 **Illustrations of the Language in an Appraisal Review Report WITHOUT an Opinion of Value**

160 The following are examples of language that might be used in an appraisal review report that does not express an
161 opinion of value and thus does not constitute evidence of an appraisal by the reviewer:

162 • "the value opinion stated in the appraisal report is (or is not) adequately supported;"
163 • "the value conclusion is (or is not) appropriate and reasonable given the data and analyses presented;"
164 • "the value opinion stated in the report under review was (or was not) developed in compliance with
165 applicable standards and requirements;"
166 • "the content, analyses, and conclusions stated in the report under review are (or are not) in compliance
167 with applicable standards and requirements;"
168 • "I reject the value conclusion as lacking credibility due to the errors and/or inconsistencies found;"
169 • "the value conclusion is not appropriate due to (for example) a significant math error in the Sales Comparison
170 Approach—if calculated properly, the value conclusion would change to $XXX; however, the reader is
171 cautioned that this solely represents a recalculation and not a different opinion of value by the reviewer;"
172 • "I accept (or approve) the appraisal report for use by XYZ bank (or agency)."

173 Such language, or language that conveys similar meanings to the intended users of the appraisal review report,
174 relates to the quality of the work under review, including the opinion of value stated in that work, but does not
175 suggest either concurrence or a different opinion of value by the reviewer. It is also important that this language be
176 consistent with the scope of work described in the appraisal review report.

177 **An Appraisal Review Assignment WITH an Opinion of Value**—When the appraisal reviewer develops an opinion
178 as to the quality of another appraiser's work PLUS the reviewer's own opinion of value, the appraisal review report
179 content must include:

180 1. the information set forth in Standards Rules 4-2; and
181 2. the reviewer's certification in accordance with Standards Rule 4-3.

© The Appraisal Foundation

The appraisal-related content of the appraisal review report, in combination with the content of the original work under review that the reviewer concludes is in compliance with the Standards applicable to that work, must at least match the report content required for an Appraisal Report.

The reviewer is not required to replicate or duplicate in the appraisal review report the material in the work under review that the reviewer concludes is in compliance with the Standards applicable to that work. The reviewer can incorporate by reference those portions of the work under review that the reviewer concludes are in compliance with the applicable Standards by use of an extraordinary assumption.

Illustrations of the Language in an Appraisal Review Report WITH an Opinion of Value

The following are examples of language that signify a value opinion (i.e., either by concurrence or by indication of a numeric point, a range, or a relationship to a numeric benchmark). These examples DO constitute evidence of a value opinion (i.e., appraisal) by the reviewer, thereby making the appraisal review one that includes an appraisal.

- "I concur (or do not concur) with the value."
- "I agree (or disagree) with the value."
- "In my opinion, the value is (the same)."
- "In my opinion, the value is incorrect and should be $XXX."
- "In my opinion, the value is too high (or too low)."

Such language, or language that conveys similar meanings to the intended users of the report, represents that the reviewer has completed the steps required to develop a value opinion. Such language indicates the reviewer has either concurred with the appraiser's value opinion in the underlying work, and thus has adopted that value opinion as the reviewer's own, or has developed a different opinion of value. It is important that this language be consistent with the scope of work described in the appraisal review report.

Note that if reviewers reject the value, they should use care in how that result is stated. If the language of such rejection is based on errors or inconsistencies in the original work and does not include any qualifiers that would relate to a direction in value, it does not imply an appraisal by the reviewer.

However, if such rejection is stated in relation to a value or value range, such as indicating a direction in value (i.e., more than, less than) or to an established benchmark, that language indicates the appraisal review has taken on the "opinion of value" characteristic of an appraisal. This is an important distinction that must be kept in mind by the reviewer when composing any language regarding the original appraiser's opinions or conclusions. In addition, whichever category such language may fall under, it must also be consistent with the purpose, scope of work, and intended use of the appraisal review assignment results.

The following list summarizes the requirements in a real property appraisal review assignment with the reviewer's opinion of value. The sequence of steps completed in this type of assignment is presented in order.

1. The reviewer develops **opinions and conclusions about the quality** of the work under review.
2. The reviewer develops **an opinion of value for the subject property** of the work under review.
3. The reviewer then **communicates the opinions and conclusions** developed in the first two steps in the report.

© The Appraisal Foundation

ADVISORY OPINION 21 (AO-21)

1 *This communication by the Appraisal Standards Board (ASB) does not establish new standards or interpret existing*
2 *standards. Advisory Opinions are issued to illustrate the applicability of appraisal standards in specific situations and*
3 *to offer advice from the ASB for the resolution of appraisal issues and problems.*

4 **SUBJECT: USPAP Compliance**

5 **APPLICATION: Real Property, Personal Property, Intangible Property**

6 **THE ISSUE:**
7 Individuals perform numerous roles within the broad realm of valuation services. Examples include appraisal,
8 brokerage, auctioning, property management, consulting, appraisal review and collecting market data. Some
9 valuation services are part of appraisal practice and require compliance with USPAP. What are the USPAP compliance
10 requirements for these various services? More specifically:

11 1. When should an individual comply with USPAP?
12 2. What is the relationship between Valuation Services and Appraisal Practice?
13 3. What does acting "as an appraiser" or performing a service "as an appraiser" mean?
14 4. Why does an expectation for an individual to act as an appraiser indicate an obligation to comply with USPAP?
15 5. What are the responsibilities of an appraiser regarding intended user expectations?
16 6. What are the USPAP obligations for appraisal practice outside of appraisal and appraisal review?
17 7. What are the USPAP obligations for valuation services outside of appraisal practice?

18 **ADVICE FROM THE ASB ON THE ISSUE:**
19 **1. <u>When should an individual comply with USPAP?</u>**

20 The PREAMBLE states that *compliance with USPAP is required when either the service or the appraiser is*
21 *obligated to comply by law or regulation, or by agreement with the client or intended users.* An obligation to
22 comply with USPAP is created by law, regulation, or agreement with intended users.[1] In such cases an appraiser
23 must follow USPAP. The PREAMBLE also states that *when not obligated, individuals may still choose to comply*
24 with USPAP. The ETHICS RULE states that *an individual should comply any time that individual represents that*
25 *he or she is performing the service as an appraiser.*[2] An ethical obligation to comply with USPAP is created by
26 choice, that is, by choosing to represent oneself as an appraiser.

27 Therefore,

28 • When required by law, regulation, or agreement, an individual <u>must</u> comply with USPAP.
29 • When choosing to represent oneself as an appraiser, an individual <u>should</u> comply with USPAP.

30 **2. <u>What is the relationship between Valuation Services and Appraisal Practice?</u>**
31 A key to distinguishing an appraiser's obligations is understanding the relationship between a "valuation service"
32 and "appraisal practice" in USPAP. Appraisal practice is a subset of valuation services.

33 A "valuation service" is a service pertaining to an aspect of property value – regardless of the type of service and
34 whether it is performed by appraisers or by others. Appraisers and others for whom value is an issue provide
35 valuation services. Examples include appraisal, brokerage, auctioning, property management, consulting,
36 appraisal review and collecting market data.

37 "Appraisal practice" is defined as *valuation services performed by an individual acting as an appraiser, including*
38 *but not limited to appraisal and appraisal review.* Only appraisers may offer services that are considered appraisal
39 practice. Examples include appraisal, appraisal review and collecting market data (acting as an appraiser).

---

1 USPAP gains legal authority through adoption by the various state and federal jurisdictions. Consequently, the legal requirement to follow USPAP is rooted in federal and state laws or regulations.

2 The PREAMBLE states that the appraiser's responsibility is to protect the overall public trust and it is the importance of the role of the appraiser that places ethical obligations on those who serve in this capacity. However, the PREAMBLE also states that USPAP does not establish who or which assignments must comply. Neither The Appraisal Foundation nor its Appraisal Standards Board is a government entity with the power to make, judge, or enforce law.

© The Appraisal Foundation

Since USPAP obligations apply to those who are acting as appraisers, USPAP applies to appraisal practice. 40

3. **What does acting "as an appraiser" or performing a service "as an appraiser" mean?** 41
An "appraiser" is defined as *one who is expected to perform valuation services* ***competently*** *and in a manner* 42
that is ***independent, impartial, and objective*** (bold added for emphasis). Therefore, an individual "acting as an 43
appraiser" is expected, in part, to be competent in the service being provided. Also, an individual "acting as an 44
appraiser" is expected to provide the service in a manner that is independent, impartial, and objective. Performing 45
a service in a manner that is independent, impartial, and objective is an ethical requirement within USPAP. 46

"Acting as an appraiser" means representing oneself as an appraiser. Many individuals have other professional 47
roles in addition to their appraiser role. For example, some appraisers are also brokers, consultants, or leasing 48
agents. Individuals who have appraiser roles as well as other professional roles must be careful to explain their 49
role in performing a given valuation service (see question #7 below). 50

Law, regulation, agreement, or representation (choice) each prescribes when a valuation service is to be provided 51
by an appraiser as part of appraisal practice. Emphasizing another portion of the definition of an "appraiser" is *one* 52
who is ***expected*** *to perform valuation services competently and in a manner that is independent, impartial, and* 53
objective (bold added for emphasis). Expectation is the crucial element in determining when one is acting as an 54
appraiser. 55

4. **Why does an expectation for an individual to act as an appraiser indicate an obligation to comply with USPAP?** 56
Public trust requires that when individuals are expected to perform with the ethics and competency of an 57
appraiser, they will do so. An individual who agrees to perform a valuation service as an appraiser has a duty to 58
comply with the ethics and competency that the public expects from an appraiser. This obligates the individual to 59
comply with USPAP in performing the service. 60

The definition of an appraiser in conjunction with the need for public trust establishes the "expectation" as the 61
basis for the obligation to comply with USPAP. 62

Intended user expectations for valuation services performed in compliance with USPAP are created when 63
individuals represent that they are acting as an appraiser in a service. For example, these expectations can arise 64
when an individual advertises or solicits as an appraiser (such as telephone listings, professional directories, 65
business cards, stationery, or office signage), holds appraiser accreditation from a licensing agency, or maintains 66
membership in a professional appraiser organization. An individual's identification as an appraiser in a given 67
valuation service establishes a justifiable expectation that the valuation service will be performed in compliance 68
with USPAP. 69

In summary, expectation is the basis for determining when an individual providing a valuation service is acting as an 70
appraiser. Because of the need to preserve public trust and confidence in appraisal practice, the expectations of the 71
client and other intended users for ethical and competent performance create an obligation to comply with USPAP. 72

5. **What are the responsibilities of an appraiser regarding intended user expectations?** 73
Appraisers have a professional responsibility to recognize the capacity in which they are performing. The 74
responsibility includes inquiry about, and recognition of, the intended users' expectations. When an individual's 75
appraisal expertise and reputation for providing services without bias induce the client or other intended users 76
to select the individual to provide a valuation service, there is a justifiable expectation that the valuation service 77
will be performed in compliance with USPAP. When individuals who act as an appraiser in some circumstances 78
choose to provide a valuation service in some other capacity (i.e., not as an appraiser and outside of appraisal 79
practice), they must not represent themselves to be acting in the capacity of an appraiser. Since choice is an 80
instrument to create USPAP obligations it follows that when individuals have an opportunity to choose the 81
capacity in which they will provide a valuation service, they are free to provide the valuation service as an 82
appraiser or in some other capacity. However, an individual who is recognized as an appraiser must use great 83
care not to violate the public trust 84

6. **What are the USPAP compliance obligations for appraisal practice outside of appraisal and appraisal review?** 85

Within appraisal practice, there are some assignments that are addressed by the Standards. The Standards 86
describe the requirements for appraisal or appraisal review assignments. 87

© The Appraisal Foundation

88 However, the Standards do not apply in the performance of all appraisal practice services. Examples include
89 assignments (performed as an appraiser) to teach appraisal courses, provide sales data, collect market data,
90 analyze specific elements of value (e.g., reproduction cost or functional utility), and develop educational texts. As
91 defined in USPAP, assignments are performed by an individual acting as an appraiser. Therefore, all assignments
92 fall within appraisal practice.

93 The PREAMBLE, the DEFINITIONS, the ETHICS RULE, the COMPETENCY RULE, and the JURISDICTIONAL
94 EXCEPTION RULE apply generally to all appraisal practice. As a result, assignments to which the Standards do not
95 apply must be provided without bias or accommodation of personal interest by competent appraisers.

96 The RECORD KEEPING RULE applies to appraisal and appraisal review assignments. For other assignments,
97 there are no workfile or record keeping requirements in USPAP. The SCOPE OF WORK RULE also applies only to
98 appraisal and appraisal review assignments.

99 Some assignments may include appraisal or appraisal review as well as other analyses that lead to additional
100 opinions or recommendations. In these assignments, the appraiser must comply with the USPAP requirements
101 that apply to appraisal or appraisal review in the appraisal or appraisal review portion of the assignment and, at a
102 minimum comply with the ETHICS RULE, the COMPETENCY RULE and the JURISDICTIONAL EXCEPTION RULE
103 for the rest of the assignment.

104 7. **What are the USPAP obligations for valuation services outside of appraisal practice?**
105 As previously stated, many individuals have other professional roles in addition to their appraiser role. For
106 example, some appraisers are also attorneys, accountants, brokers, or consultants. USPAP also places an
107 obligation on individuals who sometimes act as an appraiser even when they provide a valuation service in
108 some other capacity – that obligation being not to mislead the users of the valuation service about the capacity
109 in which they are acting. The ETHICS RULE states that *an appraiser must not misrepresent his or her role when*
110 *providing valuation services that are outside of appraisal practice.* If a valuation service is premised on advocacy
111 or compensation arrangements that are contrary to the ETHICS RULE, the valuation service is not consistent with
112 the objectives of USPAP and cannot be performed by the individual acting as an appraiser.

113 An individual who sometimes provides services as an appraiser, but who is currently acting in another role,
114 must ensure that intended users are not misled as to the individual's role in providing that valuation service.
115 This can be accomplished through such means as disclosure, notification, or careful distinction when providing
116 the valuation service as to the individual's role. Additionally, clear representation of the valuation services to be
117 rendered in the engagement communication, scope of work description, or contract, as well as in written and oral
118 correspondence with the client should assist in ensuring intended users are not misled.

© The Appraisal Foundation

Relationships and Application 119

The relationship between valuation services and appraisal practice can be illustrated as follows: 120

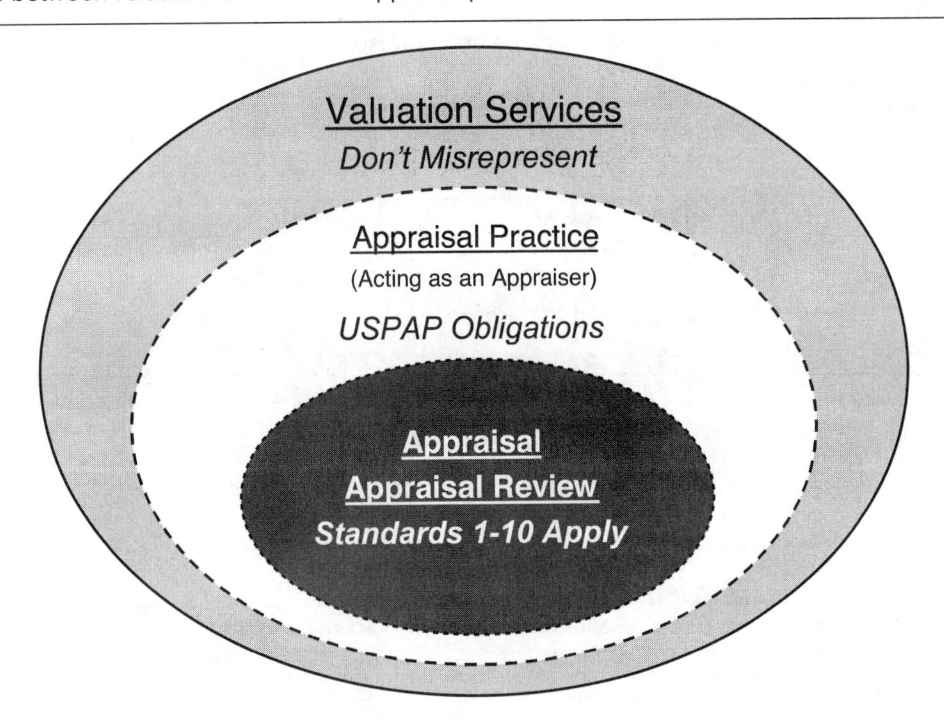

Valuation Services (large light-shaded oval): When providing valuation services, the obligation for an individual recognized in some circumstances as an appraiser is not to misrepresent his or her role.

Appraisal Practice (dotted-line oval): Within valuation services is appraisal practice (i.e., valuation services provided by an individual acting as an appraiser). All services performed as part of appraisal practice must comply with USPAP. The portions of USPAP that apply generally to appraisal practice include the PREAMBLE, the DEFINITIONS, the ETHICS RULE, the COMPETENCY RULE, and the JURISDICTIONAL EXCEPTION RULE.

Appraisal and Appraisal Review (dark-shaded oval within Appraisal Practice oval): Within appraisal practice, there are requirements that apply to developing and reporting appraisal or appraisal review assignments in addition to those that apply to all appraisal practice. These requirements are described by the Standards, the SCOPE OF WORK RULE, and the RECORD KEEPING RULE.

© The Appraisal Foundation

← Valuation Services →

Appraisal Practice Valuation services performed by an individual acting as an appraiser		Valuation services when **not** acting as an appraiser
Appraisal and Appraisal Review (Development and Reporting)	Other valuation services when acting as an appraiser	
All Rules apply. Standards apply. Which ones apply varies by assignment.	Three Rules apply: ETHICS RULE COMPETENCY RULE JURISDICTIONAL EXCEPTION RULE No Standards apply in these assignments. Compliance with the RECORD KEEPING RULE and SCOPE OF WORK RULE is not required in these assignments.	When performing these services, do not misrepresent your role: i.e., clearly communicate that you are **not** acting as an appraiser.

Examples

Appraisal and Appraisal Review (Development and Reporting)	Other valuation services when acting as an appraiser	Valuation services when not acting as an appraiser
Appraisal with Appraisal Report	Researching market data (when acting as appraiser)	Brokerage
Appraisal with Restricted Appraisal Report	Teaching appraisal courses	Consulting (when acting as an advocate)
Appraisal with oral appraisal report	Analyzing specific elements of value (e.g., reproduction cost of functional utility)	Ad valorem tax consulting (when acting as an advocate)
Expert witness testimony	Consulting (when acting as an appraiser)	Auctioning
Appraisal Review with report	Mechanical computation	Litigation support (when acting as an advocate)
Selecting comparable sales data	Developing educational texts	Property management
*Calculation engagement *Limited scope appraisal *Evaluation	Ad valorem tax consulting (when acting as an appraiser)	Mortgage underwriting
Purchase price allocation	Providing raw sales data	Leasing (agent)
Valuation engagement	Litigation support (when acting as an appraiser)	

* **Note:** These terms are commonly used by appraisers to describe appraisals with a narrow scope of work. Regardless of the label used in the assignment, these opinions of value are appraisals as defined in USPAP. An appraiser may perform these assignments under USPAP by complying with the Rules and applicable Standards.

121 **SUMMARY:**

122 • An individual must comply with USPAP when required by law, regulation, or agreement.
123 • An individual should comply with USPAP when choosing to represent oneself as an appraiser.
124 • Appraisal practice is a subset of valuation services. Since USPAP obligations apply to those who act as
125 appraisers, USPAP applies to appraisal practice.
126 • The definition of appraiser and need for public trust establish the factor of "expectation" as the basis for the
127 obligation to comply with USPAP.
128 • An individual's public identification as an appraiser establishes a justifiable expectation that valuation services
129 will be performed in compliance with USPAP. Because of the need to preserve public trust and confidence

© The Appraisal Foundation

in appraisal practice, the expectations of the client and other intended users for ethical and competent performance create an obligation to comply with USPAP. 130 131

- Appraisers have a professional responsibility to recognize the capacity in which they are performing. The responsibility includes inquiry about, and recognition of, the client's expectations. 132 133
- When individuals have has an opportunity to choose the capacity in which they will provide a valuation service, they are free to provide the valuation service as an appraiser or in some other capacity. 134 135
- An individual who is recognized as an appraiser must use great care not to violate the public trust. An appraiser acting in another role must ensure that intended users are not misled as to the individual's role in providing that valuation service. 136 137 138
- USPAP also places an obligation on appraisers even when they provide a valuation service in some other capacity – that obligation being to not mislead the intended users of the valuation service about the capacity in which they are acting. 139 140 141
- If a valuation service is premised on advocacy, or compensation arrangements that are contrary to the ETHICS RULE, an individual acting as an appraiser cannot perform the valuation service. 142 143
- Within appraisal practice, there are Standards that describe the requirements for developing and communicating appraisal or appraisal review assignments. Appraisers who provide valuation services for which there are no Standards must comply with the portions of USPAP that apply generally to appraisal practice. 144 145 146
- The RECORD KEEPING RULE applies to appraisal or appraisal review assignments. For other assignments, there are no USPAP record keeping or workfile requirements. 147 148
- The SCOPE OF WORK RULE applies only to appraisal and appraisal review assignments. 149

Illustrations: 150

Brokerage and Appraisal 151

1. Robert Agent is an individual who provides both brokerage and appraisal services. What are Robert's obligations under USPAP when preparing a broker's price opinion (BPO)? 152 153

   Answer: Many states' brokerage and appraiser licensing laws have specific provisions for appraisers who are also brokers. In the absence of such laws, USPAP provides flexibility for brokers/appraisers and others who have multiple professional roles. 154 155 156

   If providing the service as an agent or broker, USPAP requires only that appraisers must not misrepresent their role. In others words, if Robert was contacted by his client because he is an agent or broker and signing his report as an agent or broker, then Robert need not comply with USPAP except to not misrepresent his role. If Robert is contacted by the client because he is known as an appraiser and is signing his report as an appraiser, then USPAP applies. 157 158 159 160 161

Appraisal Review 162

2. Dan Williams is an appraiser. He was asked by a client to perform an "administrative screening review" of an appraisal report to determine if a more thorough review is warranted. The client would like Dan to check the math calculations and determine whether the appraisal report complies with the client's basic content specifications. What are Dan's obligations under USPAP? 163 164 165 166

   Answer: The client has engaged Dan because of his identification as an appraiser; this clearly creates an expectation by the client that the service will be provided in compliance with USPAP. Therefore, this service is part of appraisal practice; *at a minimum* Dan must comply with the portions of USPAP that apply generally to appraisal practice (i.e., the PREAMBLE, the DEFINITIONS, the ETHICS RULE, the COMPETENCY RULE, and the JURISDICTIONAL EXCEPTION RULE). 167 168 169 170 171

   Dan must next decide if compliance with STANDARDS 3 and 4 is required. To do this, Dan must consider the intended use, intended user, and type and definition of value for the assignment. These factors are the basis of Dan's scope of work decision. If the appropriate scope of work includes *developing or communicating an opinion about the quality of another appraiser's work that was performed as part of an appraisal or appraisal review assignment*, then that assignment is by definition an appraisal review. The label placed on the service cannot support acting outside of STANDARDS 3 and 4. The client may call the assignment an "administrative screening review," but it is the extent of the service that defines it. Dan must decide, based on the problem to be solved and scope of work, if the assignment is an *appraisal review* as defined by USPAP. If the 172 173 174 175 176 177 178 179

© The Appraisal Foundation

180 assignment is an *appraisal review*, then Dan must comply with the development and reporting requirements of
181 STANDARDS 3 and 4.

182 There may be circumstances when Dan is not acting as an appraiser. If Dan acts in other roles, say as a mortgage
183 underwriter, then Dan may be in a position to provide the valuation service outside of appraisal practice. If Dan acts
184 outside of appraisal practice, he must ensure that he does not misrepresent his role and that the client and any
185 other intended users do not expect him to act as an appraiser.

186 *Rent Survey*

187 3. A client has asked Mike Black to perform a rent survey. The client owns the Acme Office Building and wants to
188 know if he is charging enough rent. The client asked Mike to perform this work because he knows Mike is an
189 appraiser; therefore, this valuation service is included in appraisal practice and USPAP applies. How can Mike
190 provide this service in compliance with USPAP?

191 Answer: Mike should fully investigate the client's expectations before determining the scope of work for this
192 assignment. Does the client want only to know what rental rates are being charged for other office buildings
193 in the area? If so, this is likely a service for which USPAP has no Standards (i.e., STANDARDS 1 and 2 when
194 providing real property appraisals). Mike would then be obligated to comply with the portions of USPAP
195 that apply generally to appraisal practice (i.e., the PREAMBLE, the DEFINITIONS, the ETHICS RULE, the
196 COMPETENCY RULE, and the JURISDICTIONAL EXCEPTION RULE). The development and reporting of the
197 assignment results would be entirely at his discretion, and a workfile would not be required.

198 However, if the client expects Mike to collect rental rate and lease term information and to analyze them to
199 conclude the market rental terms for the Acme Building, this is an appraisal. This assignment is an appraisal
200 because it includes a specific subject property (i.e., the right to use space in the building) and the problem
201 to be solved in the assignment is a value opinion (i.e., the market rental terms for that space). The appraisal
202 assignment should then be completed in compliance with STANDARDS 1 and 2.

203 *Litigation Services*

204 4. Marie Vaughn has a diverse practice with a specialization in litigation services. She commonly aids attorneys in
205 developing cross-examination strategies for expert witness testimony from appraisers. How does USPAP apply to
206 Marie's "litigation services?"

207 Answer: In order to determine Marie's obligation, it is necessary to understand the nature of her role. If she is
208 acting as an appraiser, her litigation services are part of appraisal practice. The PREAMBLE, the DEFINITIONS,
209 the ETHICS RULE, the COMPETENCY RULE, and the JURISDICTIONAL EXCEPTION RULE will apply to the
210 assignment. As an appraiser, Marie cannot act as an advocate for any party or issue.

211 If Marie's services include providing an opinion of value, she must also comply with the appropriate appraisal
212 standards (STANDARDS 1 and 2, 7 and 8, or 9 and 10). If Marie's services include providing an opinion about
213 the quality of another appraiser's work, the appraisal review requirements of STANDARDS 3 and 4 apply.
214 If the service includes providing analysis, recommendation, or an opinion to solve a problem where an
215 opinion of value is a component of the analysis leading to the assignment results, then Marie must comply
216 with the ETHICS RULE, the COMPETENCY RULE and the JURISDICTIONAL EXCEPTION RULE for the entire
217 assignment; and she must also comply with any applicable Rules and Standards if she performs an appraisal
218 or appraisal review as part of the assignment.

219 On the other hand, if Marie provides litigation services as an advocate, then she is providing a valuation service
220 outside of appraisal practice. When performing services outside of appraisal practice, Marie can act as an
221 advocate and accept contingent compensation. The only USPAP obligation is that she not misrepresent her role.
222 She must use care to distinguish her role from other roles that would carry an expectation of being impartial,
223 objective, and independent, i.e., acting as an appraiser.

224 Marie may provide litigation services by either acting as an appraiser **or** acting as an advocate for the client's
225 cause; however, she must not perform both roles in the same case.

226 *Assignments with Services Other Than Appraisal or Appraisal Review*

227 5a. Jane Doe, an appraiser, agrees to perform an assignment to perform a feasibility analysis for a proposed real
228 estate subdivision. In order to complete the assignment, she develops prospective market value opinions for the

© The Appraisal Foundation

potential lots in the subdivision given several different possible configurations. Each configuration may also have different absorption rates and/or absorption periods. The objective of the assignment is to recommend the optimal configuration. With which parts of USPAP must Jane comply in this assignment? 229 230 231

Answer: Jane must comply with the ETHICS RULE, the COMPETENCY RULE, and the JURISDICTIONAL EXCEPTION RULE for the entire assignment. 232 233

Because the value opinions are appraisals, the SCOPE OF WORK RULE and the RECORD KEEPING RULE apply to the appraisal portion of the assignment. In addition, she must develop each value opinion in compliance with STANDARD 1 and report the opinions in compliance with STANDARD 2. 234 235 236

5b. John Doe, an appraiser, agrees to perform to advise a client regarding the feasibility of replacing existing manufacturing equipment with newer, more efficient pieces. In order to complete the assignment, he uses a liquidation value appraisal of the existing machinery. That appraisal was prepared by another appraiser and will be reviewed by John. The objective of the assignment is to recommend whether to replace the equipment now, or to wait. With which parts of USPAP must John comply in this assignment? 237 238 239 240 241

Answer: John must comply with the ETHICS RULE, the COMPETENCY RULE, and the JURISDICTIONAL EXCEPTION RULE for the entire assignment. 242 243

Since John is doing an appraisal review, the SCOPE OF WORK RULE and the RECORD KEEPING RULE apply to the appraisal review portion of the assignment. He must also develop and report the review opinion in compliance with STANDARDS 3 and 4. 244 245 246

5c. Chris Filo is an appraiser who has an assignment to advise a corporation regarding a potential stock offering. The corporate officers have provided Chris with a value for the existing stock. Chris has made the extraordinary assumption that the value provided is credible and will use that value as part of the analysis before making final recommendations. Which parts of USPAP apply to this assignment? 247 248 249 250

Answer: Chris must comply with the ETHICS RULE, the COMPETENCY RULE, and the JURISDICTIONAL EXCEPTION RULE for this assignment. 251 252

Because this assignment does not include an appraisal or appraisal review, neither the SCOPE OF WORK RULE nor the RECORD KEEPING RULE applies. In addition, there are no development or reporting standards applicable to this assignment. 253 254 255

5d. Jane Doe is a real estate practitioner who offers a variety of services to her clients. She is a licensed real estate broker and is also a certified appraiser. Jane has been asked by a client to perform a service that is viewed by Jane and her client as a consulting service that relates to value, but is to be undertaken by her in the role of a broker/consultant, not as an appraiser. Which parts of USPAP apply to Jane in this assignment? 256 257 258 259

Answer: Individuals may fulfill different roles in different assignments. In general, USPAP applies only when an individual is acting as an appraiser. As long as it is clear that Jane is not performing as an appraiser, Jane's only obligation when acting as a broker/consultant is stated in Conduct section of the ETHICS RULE, which states: 260 261 262

an appraiser: 263

must not misrepresent his or her role when providing valuation services that are outside of appraisal practice; 264 265

© The Appraisal Foundation

ADVISORY OPINION 22 (AO-22)

1 *This communication by the Appraisal Standards Board (ASB) does not establish new standards or interpret existing*
2 *standards. Advisory Opinions are issued to illustrate the applicability of appraisal standards in specific situations and*
3 *to offer advice from the ASB for the resolution of appraisal issues and problems.*

4 **SUBJECT: Scope of Work in Market Value Appraisal Assignments for Real Property**

5 **APPLICATION: Real Property**

6 **THE ISSUE:**
7 How does "market value" affect the scope of work in a real property appraisal assignment?

8 **ADVICE FROM THE ASB ON THE ISSUE:**
9 **Relevant USPAP & Advisory References**

10 • COMPETENCY RULE
11 • SCOPE OF WORK RULE
12 • DEFINITIONS section: "Appraisal," "Intended Use," "Market Value," and "Scope of Work"
13 • STANDARD 1
14 • Advisory Opinion 35 and 36

15 **Scope of Work in a Market Value Appraisal**
16 This Advisory Opinion provides guidance that appraisers, users of appraisals, and enforcement bodies can use when
17 making decisions about the scope of work in market value appraisal assignments (called a "market value assignment"
18 or a "market value appraisal" in this Advisory Opinion).

19 Competently determining the scope of work is an essential step in all assignments performed under USPAP. In a
20 real property appraisal assignment, Standards Rules 1-2(a)–(h) set forth eight identification actions or steps that an
21 appraiser must understand and complete in performing any appraisal assignment. Completing the first seven action
22 steps provides support for the eighth step, the appraiser's scope of work decision.

© The Appraisal Foundation

The Sequence and Relationship of Action Steps Required by Standards Rule 1-2 in a Real Property Appraisal – The following table illustrates the sequence and relationship of the action steps leading to the appraiser's scope of work decision and the steps taken after that decision through to completion of the appraisal process. 23 24 25

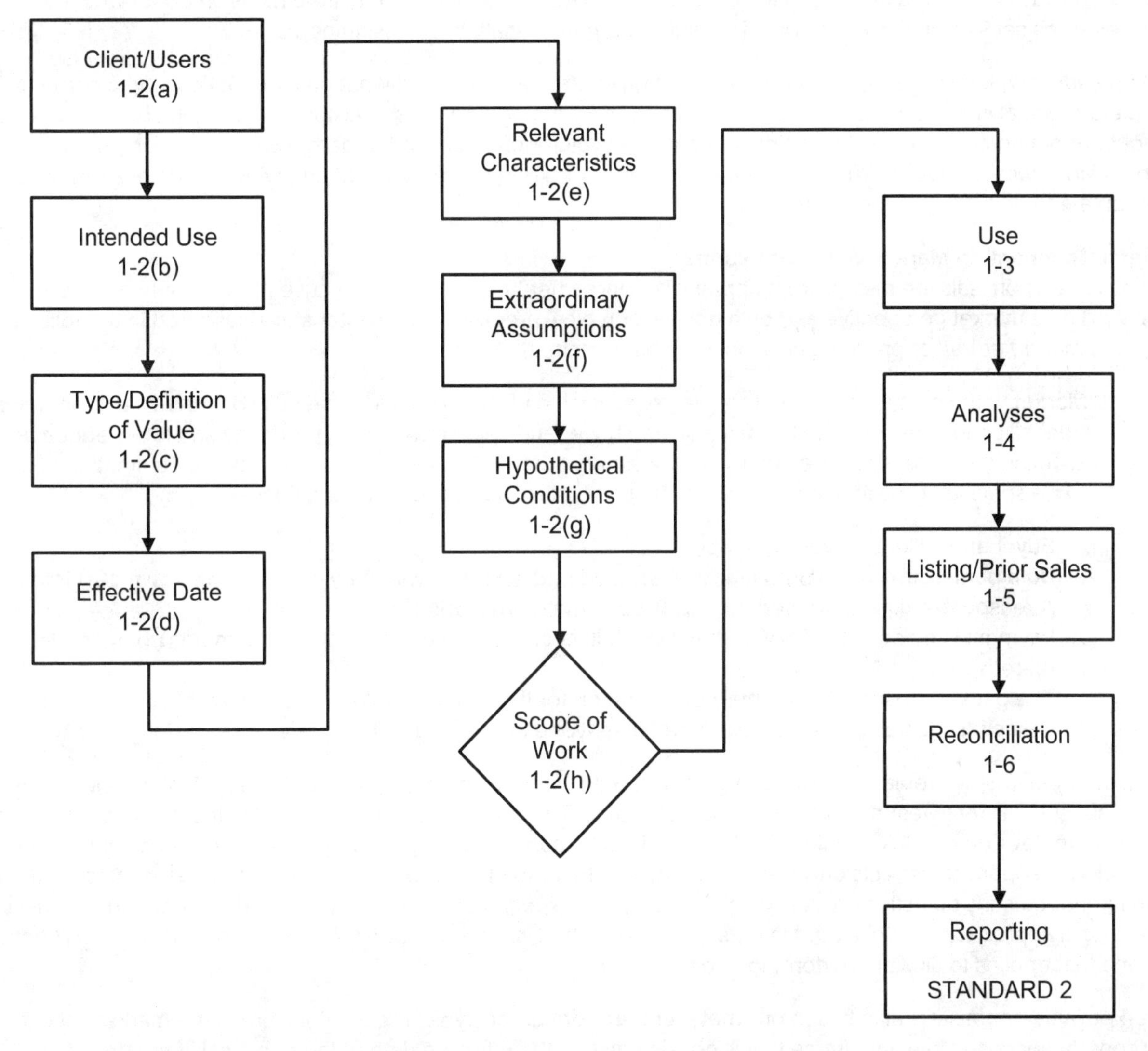

It is important to recognize that the action of identifying the client and intended users, the intended use, the type and definition of value, and the effective date (Standards Rule 1-2(a)-(d)) affects the appraiser's decisions as to the subject's relevant characteristics, the scope of work, and extraordinary assumptions or hypothetical conditions (Standards Rule 1-2(e)–(h)). The appraiser's decisions about the last four elements to be identified follow from, and must be consistent with, factual information identified in the first four elements shown in the table. 26 27 28 29 30

The sequence illustrated in the table requires the appraiser to begin the decision-making process in the early stages of an assignment. It also means the appraiser has a burden of proof for conclusions about which property characteristics are relevant and which are not. 31 32 33

<u>**Sequence and Relationship of Action Steps Required by Standards Rule 1-2 in a Real Property Appraisal**</u> 34

Competency and the Scope of Work Decision - Accomplishing the first four action steps (Standards Rule 1-2(a) through (d)) illustrated in the table provides the basis for deciding which of the property's characteristics are relevant in the assignment. This information, together with the appraiser's competency (knowledge and expertise) in appraising the specific type of property involved, permits the appraiser to determine whether any extraordinary assumptions or hypothetical conditions are necessary to complete the assignment and to make a reasonable and supportable scope of work decision. 35 36 37 38 39 40

It is important to note here that the appraiser's competency in performing similar assignments is a key factor in the scope of work decision. Without competency, the appraiser is not prepared to correctly interpret the information 41 42

© The Appraisal Foundation

43 gathered in response to Standards Rule 1-2(a)–(e) or to make well-reasoned decisions based on that information in
44 response to the requirements set forth in Standards Rule 1-2(f)–(h). Moreover, without competency, the appraiser is
45 not aware of or capable of understanding how the information gathered in compliance with Standards Rule 1-2(a)–(e)
46 and the conclusions formed in compliance with Standards Rule 1-2(f) and (g) affect the decision about which of the
47 analyses steps set forth in Standards Rules 1-3 and 1-4 are necessary in an assignment.

48 Understanding which analyses, methods and techniques are necessary and what data are necessary to correctly
49 complete the analyses is an integral part of the scope of work decision. This decision cannot be made competently
50 without understanding how the "conditions" in a market value definition work together with the other factors identified
51 in compliance with Standards Rule 1-2 to determine what kind of data are relevant and which types of analyses are
52 applicable and necessary in the assignment.

53 **General Comment on Market Value Definitions**
54 Market value appraisals are distinct from appraisals using other types of value because market value appraisals
55 are based on a market perspective and on a normal or typical premise. These criteria are illustrated in the following
56 definition of *Market Value,*[1] provided here only as an example.

57 "**Market value** means the most probable price which a property should bring in a competitive and open market
58 under all conditions requisite to a fair sale, the buyer and seller each acting prudently and knowledgeably, and
59 assuming the price is not affected by undue stimulus. Implicit in this definition are the consummation of a sale
60 as of a specified date and the passing of title from seller to buyer under conditions whereby:

61 1. Buyer and seller are typically motivated;
62 2. Both parties are well informed or well advised and acting in what they consider their own best interests;
63 3. A reasonable time is allowed for exposure in the open market;
64 4. Payment is made in terms of cash in U.S. dollars or in terms of financial arrangements comparable
65 thereto; and
66 5. The price represents the normal consideration for the property sold unaffected by special or creative
67 financing or sales concessions granted by anyone associated with the sale."

68 The market perspective replaces a user's (e.g., buyer, seller, lender, agent, etc.) perspective that might apply in other
69 appraisals, such as for investment value or insurable value. This market perspective directly affects the scope of work
70 necessary to develop credible opinions and conclusions in market value appraisals. The public's expectation that
71 a market value appraisal reflects only the perspective of the marketplace, and is not affected by such other criteria
72 as an intended user's objectives, is important. Meeting this expectation serves to foster and promote public trust in
73 professional appraisal practice, a fundamental purpose of the *Uniform Standards of Professional Appraisal Practice*
74 and one that applies to all work performed under USPAP.

75 A market value appraisal is also based on whatever the "normal" or "typical" conditions are in the marketplace for
76 the property appraised in a time frame that is consistent with the effective date of the appraisal. If the definition
77 of value used in an appraisal contains criteria that are different from those that are "normal" or "typical," the use
78 of the term "Market Value," alone, to characterize the assignment result is not appropriate. For example, a value
79 opinion developed to reflect the most probable price in a sale under forced conditions is a forced-sale value and not
80 consistent with the "normal" or "typical" premise to be reflected in a market value appraisal.

81 **Importance of Identifying the Specific Definition of Market Value**—The definition of the value to be developed in an
82 appraisal establishes specific conditions. These conditions impose parameters on the appraisal assignment that are
83 necessary to ensure that the results of the assignment are meaningful in the context of that definition of value.

84 There are many definitions of value, some of which are market value definitions. Other definitions of value appear
85 to be related to market value but are not called market value. For example, it is common practice in appraisals for
86 intended use in employee relocation assignments to use a value definition based on "anticipated sales price" rather
87 than "market value." The "anticipated sales price" definition contains very specific marketing, property condition, and
88 terms of sale requirements that replace normal or typical market conditions. Thus, while the development process

1 This example definition is from regulations published by federal regulatory agencies pursuant to Title XI of the Financial Institutions Reform, Recovery, and Enforcement Act (FIRREA) of 1989 between July 5, 1990, and August 24, 1990, by the Federal Reserve System (FRS), National Credit Union Administration (NCUA), Federal Deposit Insurance Corporation (FDIC), and the Office of Comptroller of the Currency (OCC). This definition is also referenced in regulations jointly published by the OCC, FRS, and FDIC on June 7, 1994, and in the *Interagency Appraisal and Evaluation Guidelines*, as revised and updated December 2010.

© The Appraisal Foundation

under the specific conditions may appear similar to market value assignments, the result is a value to the property user—the relocation company—under that client's specific criteria and is not market value. 89 90

Importance of Identifying the Source of a Market Value Definition—Definitions of market value from different sources contain different conditions. Those differences can directly affect the scope of work that is necessary to develop credible assignment results. Each definition is unique, with authority only in a specific jurisdiction or to a specific client group. Therefore, identification of the source for the definition of value to be applied in an assignment is essential. 91 92 93 94

The source must be consistent with the jurisdiction having authority over the transaction in which the appraisal is to be used. For example, using a definition of market value other than the definition specified in regulations published pursuant to Title XI of the Financial Institutions Reform, Recovery, and Enforcement Act of 1989 (FIRREA) may invalidate that appraisal for use in a federally related transaction. Likewise, if an appraisal is prepared for use in litigation, using a definition of value other than the definition specified by the court having jurisdiction over the matter being litigated may disqualify that appraisal for use in that court. 95 96 97 98 99 100

How the "Conditions" in a Market Value Definition Affect the Scope of Work Decision 101

In an appraisal assignment, *Market Value* is defined by a specific jurisdiction (e.g., a court, a regulatory body or public agency with legal authority), or by a client group (e.g., Fannie Mae or Freddie Mac). 102 103

In a market value appraisal, the appraiser's conclusions about how best to analyze the market and what data are necessary for the development of credible results must be consistent with the conditions set forth in the specific definition of market value applicable in the assignment. The definition of *market value* included in this Advisory Opinion as an example illustrates the type of conditions that might be part of a specific market value definition used in an assignment. 104 105 106 107 108

Market value always presumes the transfer of a property as of a certain date, under specific conditions. The "Conditions" stated in market value definitions generally fall into three categories: 109 110

1. the relationship, knowledge, and motivation of the parties (i.e., seller and buyer); 111
2. the terms of sale (e.g., cash, cash equivalent, or other terms); and 112
3. the conditions of sale (e.g., exposure in a competitive market for a reasonable time prior to sale). 113

Market value appraisals focus on understanding how buyers and sellers are most likely to respond to a subject property under the conditions stated in a specific value definition. Not all market value definitions contain the same conditions, though most contain a common subset of elements. Experienced appraisers understand the nuances in the various definitions and develop their assignments using data and analyses that match the conditions required by the specific definition used in an appraisal. 114 115 116 117 118

The "knowledge" referred to in a market value definition is knowledge about the property appraised, about the market for that property, and about alternatives available in the marketplace that the appraiser concludes are reasonable competition for the property appraised.[2] 119 120 121

An appraiser is expected to be at least as knowledgeable as the typical market participant is about the market for the type of property to be appraised. By completing research and verification steps while performing the assignment, the appraiser is expected to become as knowledgeable about the subject property and its comparables as the typical market participants. 122 123 124 125

Knowledge of the Subject Property—Of the three areas typical market participants are presumed to be knowledgeable about (subject, market, and competition), the first area that the appraiser must address is knowledge of the subject property, which is accomplished by gathering and verifying information about the subject property. This action step may or may not require a personal inspection. 126 127 128 129

In a market value assignment, the relevant characteristics are those that have a significant impact on the property's marketability (See Standard Rules 1-2(e)). These features include legal, economic and physical characteristics. The decision as to which characteristics are relevant cannot be made without knowledge of the market in which the property is sold. This is why competency in appraising a specific type of property and knowledge of the subject property's market are essential in an assignment. 130 131 132 133 134

2 See Advisory Opinion 35, *Reasonable Exposure Time in Real Property and Personal Property Opinion of Value.*

© The Appraisal Foundation

135 Knowing the property's relevant characteristics also provides the basis for deciding the applicability of an approach
136 to value.

137 **Knowledge of the Market**—The scope of work necessary to ensure an adequate knowledge of the market for
138 the subject property may range from very little (in addition to what the appraiser already knows) to extensive new
139 research. If the subject property is of a type frequently appraised and in a locality where the appraiser regularly
140 provides services, there may be little need for extensive market research beyond confirmation that the data available
141 for analysis is current, adequate, relevant, and credible.

142 However, if the property involved is not of a type regularly appraised by the appraiser or if the market area is not
143 familiar to the appraiser, the extent of research needs to be sufficient for the appraiser to acquire competency.
144 As stated in the COMPETENCY RULE, this can be achieved in several ways (self-study, association with a locally
145 knowledgeable and competent appraiser, etc.).

146 The critically important aspect of this factor in the scope of work decision is to recognize when additional research
147 is necessary. A competent, professional appraiser will not assume knowledge merely for the sake of convenience.
148 Even though the appraiser might be actively involved in appraising a particular type of property in a given locality, self-
149 imposed professional discipline will prompt that individual to ensure that the scope of work includes verification that
150 the market data used in the analyses is credible, relevant, appropriate, adequate, and as current as possible.

151 This is consistent with the requirement stated in Standards Rule 1-1(b), which is designed to ensure that the scope of
152 work completed in an appraisal is sufficient to produce credible opinions and conclusions, given the intended use of the
153 appraisal.

154 **Knowledge of Alternatives**—An understanding of market behavior requires a scope of work that includes research
155 and analyses that is sufficient to ensure competent knowledge of the supply and demand relationships that are
156 relevant to the time frame and the type of property involved in the appraisal. In a market value appraisal, this means
157 gathering, verifying, and evaluating data about sales, listings, and failed efforts to sell "competitive" property, as well
158 as more generalized market data.

159 **Conditions of Sale**—A market value appraisal requires research and analysis of market data sufficient to develop
160 a reasonable opinion of exposure time (see the Comment to Standards Rule 1-2(c) and Advisory Opinion 35) with
161 the property marketed in whatever manner is typical for that type of property in its locality. An appraiser working
162 in different market areas should guard against presuming that a marketing process common in one area is typical
163 in all areas. For example, in some markets, property is customarily sold through an auction arrangement, while in
164 others professional brokerage is the norm, and in still others so called "for sale by owner" is the typical process. Each
165 process, in a given time period and locality for the type of property involved, can be "normal." The identification of the
166 marketing process and exposure time requires an understanding of the subject's market.

167 Market value definitions imply a sale of the property wherein the buyer and seller are "typically motivated." This
168 condition requires that the level of research in a market value assignment is sufficient to understand the motivations of
169 the buyers and sellers for the sales used in the approaches to value. The motivations that lead to a sale play a critical
170 role in establishing the relevancy or irrelevancy of a sale as a comparable one in an assignment.

171 Analysis of sales data can yield numeric results, but the numbers lack real meaning without an understanding of the
172 market conditions that generated the sales involved. Without an understanding of what the market conditions were at
173 the time of a sale, as well as the conditions of a particular sale, an appraiser cannot reasonably conclude that the sale
174 price, or any element of comparison based on that price, is a reliable indicator of market value.

175 **Subject's Marketing and Sale History, and Reconciliation**
176 The appraiser's scope of work decision in a market value appraisal needs to recognize the research and analyses
177 steps that are necessary to comply with the requirements stated in Standards Rule 1-5 and Standards Rule 1-6. Those
178 requirements have two objectives, both of which are especially important in a market value appraisal.

179 The first is to ensure that the appraiser makes the effort to obtain relevant information about current and recent
180 market activity involving the subject property (Standards Rule 1-5(a) and (b)). This due diligence effort is consistent
181 with the requirement stated in Standards Rule 1-1(b). It also serves as a safeguard against confusing the price in a
182 contract (agreement of sale or option) or an offering with market value and as a safeguard against the appraiser being
183 inadvertently involved in an effort to conceal the facts in regard to one or more recent sale transactions.

© The Appraisal Foundation

The second is to ensure that the appraiser reconciles the indications of value resulting from the various approaches utilized to arrive at the value conclusion (Standards Rule 1-6). 184 185

SUMMARY: 186

The scope of work decision is a critical step in any appraisal. That decision must result in a match between the extent of the research and analyses completed in an assignment with the conditions specified in the definition of value used in that assignment. 187 188 189

In a market value appraisal, the appraiser's scope of work decision carries a burden of proof to support the appraiser's conclusion about how the appraiser addresses each "condition" in the market value definition used in the appraisal. The definition includes conditions that often require a high degree of knowledge, competency, and judgment, which are necessary to effectively develop the appraisal process. Appraisers cannot meet their obligations in a market value assignment without having competently identified and then completed a scope of work that enables development of credible opinions and conclusions. 190 191 192 193 194 195

© The Appraisal Foundation

ADVISORY OPINION 23 (AO-23)

This communication by the Appraisal Standards Board (ASB) does not establish new standards or interpret existing standards. Advisory Opinions are issued to illustrate the applicability of appraisal standards in specific situations and to offer advice from the ASB for the resolution of appraisal issues and problems.

SUBJECT: Identifying the Relevant Characteristics of the Subject Property of a Real Property Appraisal Assignment

APPLICATION: Real Property

THE ISSUE:
How does an appraiser determine which characteristics of a real property are relevant to its appraisal?

ADVICE FROM THE ASB ON THE ISSUE:
Relevant USPAP & Advisory References

- DEFINITIONS, specifically the definitions of
  - APPRAISAL: *(noun) the act or process of developing an opinion of value; an opinion of value....*

    Comment: *An appraisal is numerically expressed as a specific amount, as a range of numbers, or as a relationship (e.g., not more than, not less than) to a previous value opinion or numerical benchmark (e.g., assessed value, collateral value).*
  - ASSIGNMENT: *a valuation service that is provided by an appraiser as a consequence of an agreement with a client.*
  - REAL ESTATE: *an identified parcel or tract of land, including improvements if any.*
  - REAL PROPERTY: *the interests, benefits, and rights inherent in the ownership of real estate.*
  - VALUE: *the monetary relationship between properties and those who buy, sell, or use those properties, expressed as an opinion of the worth of a property at a given time.*

    Comment: *In appraisal practice, value will always be qualified - for example, market value, liquidation value, or investment value.*
  - Standards Rule 1-2(e): *An appraiser must identify, from sources the appraiser reasonably believes to be reliable, characteristics of the property that are relevant to the type and definition of value and intended use of the appraisal, including:*
    (i) its location and physical, legal, and economic characteristics;
    (ii) the real property interest to be valued;
    (iii) any personal property, trade fixtures, or intangible assets that are not real property but are included in the appraisal;
    (iv) any known easements, restrictions, encumbrances, leases, reservations, covenants, contracts, declarations, special assessments, ordinances, or other items of a similar nature; and
    (v) whether the subject property is a fractional interest, physical segment, or partial holding.

The Subject of a Real Property Appraisal Assignment
The subject of a real property appraisal has both physical and legal characteristics. In combination, these characteristics define the subject property and, together with the type and definition of value and intended use of the assignment results, provide the basis for deciding what data and analyses should be included in the scope of work.

Appraisers and property owners often discuss a subject property in physical terms, such as *my home, the residence, my land*, or *the building*. However, a physical object, alone, is not what is being appraised.

Taken together, the definitions of *real property* and *real estate* provided in USPAP indicate that the subject of a real property appraisal is a specific ownership of a right (or rights) in identified real estate.

The right or rights might be owned in part, as a fractional interest, or in full. Further, real estate can take many forms, such as land, land and improvements, improvements without the underlying land, or an infinite variety that involve one or more of the physical aspects of real estate. Alternatively, a type of property, such as Class A Office Space, does not signify specific ownership rights in identifiable real estate. Consequently, surveys or studies relating to a class of property do not constitute the "subject" of a real property appraisal under STANDARD 1. In such situations, the service provided by completing the survey or study is not an appraisal assignment because there is no "subject property."

Understanding these different characteristics is essential for correct identification of the subject of a real property appraisal and for determining which characteristics of the property are relevant in the assignment.

How the Characteristics of the Subject Affect the Scope of Work Decision

As discussed above, real property can have many different characteristics, each of which can significantly affect the scope of work in an assignment. Consider the following illustrations:

1. The subject is the fee simple interest owned in a single-family residence situated on an improved site. These components (the land, the improvements, and the ownership) are, together, the subject property of the appraisal assignment. In this assignment the appraiser is developing and reporting a market value opinion.

   The scope of work in this assignment should include gathering data about the characteristics of the subject that are significant in the market for this type of property under its highest and best use. Given the characteristics of the subject property, the analysis should include sales of other properties held in fee simple ownership situated in the subject's market area that are similar to the subject in as many other respects as possible.

2. If all of the same characteristics of the property in Illustration No. 1 apply, except that the land is a leased site, the subject property becomes:

   - leasehold interest, if the intended user needs to know the value of the rights in the real estate owned by the lessee in the lease, or

   - leased fee interest, if the intended user needs to know the value of the rights in the real estate owned by the lessor in the lease.

   Note that the subject real estate (physical asset) was the same, but the ownership interest of the subject changed. The impact of this change on the scope of work and on the relevant data in each assignment is significant. For example, in a market value appraisal:

   - If the subject property is the leasehold interest, the relevant analysis should include sales of leasehold interest properties that are as similar to the subject as possible, both physically and in terms of its lease (cash flow) characteristics.

   - If the subject is the leased fee interest, the relevant data should include sales of leased fee interest properties with similar physical and cash flow characteristics. The subject lease terms determine whether the improvements' characteristics are significant in this type of assignment. If the lease ends before the improvements reach the end of their economic life, the improvements' characteristics can be important to the appraisal problem. If the tenant must remove the improvements upon termination of the lease, the improvements' characteristics likely have little significance in the assignment.

3. Next, assume the same subject property characteristics as in Illustration No. 1 but change the ownership to an undivided one-third interest in the fee simple title. The scope of work in this Illustration is significantly different than that in either Illustration No. 1 or No. 2.[1]

   If available, the most relevant analysis would be of sales of similar fractional interests in similar real estate. In the absence of such sales, the research might extend to secondary sources or other less direct analyses to develop, test, and support the fractional interest value conclusion.

4. A prospective client is considering a loan secured by a portfolio of properties owned in fee simple by a loan applicant. The real property offered as loan security is an ownership, held by one party, of several nearly identical properties in different locations.

   In this situation, the appraiser must pay particular attention to the intended use of the assignment results and how that use affects the property configuration that will be relevant in the analyses. This is essential because assignment

1 See the Comment to Standards Rule 1-4(e).

© The Appraisal Foundation

results must be meaningful to the client and analyses of the market for the subject must reflect the intended use.

If the client intends to use the appraisal to secure a single loan secured with all of the properties held by the client's loan applicant, the subject property is the entire holding (i.e., the portfolio). In this situation, the appraiser must include research and analyses to address the impact of all of the subject's individual parts appearing in the market at the same time, to be sold by one owner to one buyer. The intended use drives this configuration of the subject's characteristics.

Alternatively, if the same client intended to use the appraisal to secure one loan under loan conditions that would allow each property in the holding to be released (sold) on its own, the assignment is actually for several appraisals communicated in one report or possibly in several reports. In this configuration, each individual property is a subject property to be sold by one seller in the same time frame to (potentially) different buyers. The analyses must still address the potential impact, if any, of having all of the properties in the loan applicant's portfolio on the market at one time but without the necessity of selling to one buyer in one transaction.

The intended use of the assignment results alters the characteristics of the subject that are relevant to the appraisal and clearly alters the appropriate scope of work. In the first instance, the relevant data about the subject and about its market must reflect the subject's characteristics as a property portfolio rather than as an individual property within a community. In the latter case, the relevant data must address the relevant characteristics and market conditions for each individual property. Analyzing a portfolio of properties as if each property were a separate element or increment of value when the subject of the assignment is the portfolio fails to recognize distinct differences between the markets for individual properties and portfolios. Specifically, the value of the subject, as a portfolio, is not necessarily the sum of the values for each of the properties in that portfolio; it could be less or it could be more.

5. A prospective client finances real estate development projects and requests an appraisal for use in a single-family residential tract development financing package. The client needs an opinion of value for the project and values for each of four individual floor plans as if each was a finished property on a typical or so-called "base" lot within the development. The project involves acquisition of finished sites and the construction and sale of finished homes in phases over a period of years. All of the values are to be market value and the effective value is to be a current date, all for the intended use of securing the development loan and the take-out loan commitment.

   It is important to recognize that in this illustration the assignment actually involves five properties: the entire project plus each of the four floor plans. In this case, the subject that is the project includes the land and the entitlements that allow development of the residential tract on the land. Each of the four floor plans becomes a subject under the hypothetical condition that the finished home on the typical or base lot actually exists as a finished property as of a current effective date. The appraiser must then develop and report five appraisals of five different subject properties.

   For the development loan, the subject's relevant characteristics are those of the project, not the homes, and the scope of work to analyze the market for the project must address the entire project's characteristics.

   For each take-out loan, the relevant subject property is an individual finished home, not the project, and the summation of the value for those individual homes is not meaningful in terms of the value of the project. Indeed, summation of the value of the individual homes to indicate the market value of the project is incorrect development, and reporting such a summation as market value of the project is misleading.

   The scope of work necessary to analyze the market for an individual home as a subject property is significantly different from that necessary to analyze the market for the project as a subject property.

SUMMARY:
Identifying the relevant subject property characteristics, together with the other information gathered in response to Standards Rule 1-2, enables an appraiser to make a sound scope of work decision.

Agreeing to perform a prospective assignment on the basis of incomplete information can result in a significant mismatch between the scope of work and the valuation problem to be solved in the appraisal assignment. The lack of clear communication with the client before deciding whether to perform an assignment can lead to an excessive or deficient scope of work. When the scope of work is excessive, appraisers might unnecessarily forego valuation service opportunities. When the scope of work is inadequate or the subject property

© The Appraisal Foundation

characteristics are not appropriately analyzed given the intended use of the assignment results, the results are not likely to be credible or meaningful. 137 138

An appraiser should, by communicating with a prospective client, gather information about the type and definition of value, the intended use, and the effective date of the appraisal, as well as characteristics of the subject of a real property appraisal assignment, before deciding which characteristics are relevant and the appropriate scope of work. 139 140 141

© The Appraisal Foundation

ADVISORY OPINION 24 (AO-24)

This communication by the Appraisal Standards Board (ASB) does not establish new standards or interpret existing standards. Advisory Opinions are issued to illustrate the applicability of appraisal standards in specific situations and to offer advice from the ASB for the resolution of appraisal issues and problems.

SUBJECT: Normal Course of Business

APPLICATION: Real Property, Personal Property

THE ISSUE:

Standards Rules 1-5 and 7-5 require an appraiser to analyze certain information about the subject property if the information is *available to the appraiser in the normal course of business.* How does one determine the "normal course of business" for a given assignment?

BACKGROUND:

The analysis that is required in Standards Rule 1-5 and 7-5 promotes a certain degree of due diligence on the part of the appraiser. Appropriate due diligence increases public trust in the appraisal profession. The intent is to ensure that the research of past sales and current listings, options, or agreements of sale of the subject property is sufficient to promote public trust, without creating undue hardship on the appraiser.

The availability of the data necessary to comply with the requirements in Standards Rule 1-5 and 7-5 varies greatly. In some situations, this data is available from multiple sources. In other instances, sales and listing data is not readily available.

The "normal course of business" is controlled to a large degree by the scope of work in a specific assignment. Differences in intended use, intended users, the type and definition of value, or other factors can dramatically alter the scope of work. Therefore, the "normal course of business" for one assignment might not be the "normal course of business" for a seemingly similar assignment.

ADVICE FROM THE ASB ON THE ISSUE:

Relevant USPAP & Advisory References

- The following USPAP references are applicable when ascertaining the "normal course of business" in an assignment:
  - — Standards Rules 1-2(h) and 7-2(h);
  - — Standards Rules 1-5 and 7-5.
- For additional advice, refer to Advisory Opinion 1, *Sales History.*

General Comments

The "normal course of business" is determined by the actions of an appraiser's peers and by the expectations of parties who are regularly intended users for similar assignments; it is not any one appraiser's practices or any one appraisal firm's policies.

To fully understand this concept one must examine the definitions of "Scope of Work" and "Appraiser's Peers."

"Scope of Work" is addressed in the SCOPE OF WORK RULE, Standards Rules 1-2(h) and 7-2(h), and is defined in USPAP as:

> *the type and extent of research and analyses in an appraisal or appraisal review assignment.*

Researching the subject's sales history is an aspect of the scope of work. The Comment to the Scope of Work Acceptability section in the SCOPE OF WORK RULE states:

> *The scope of work is acceptable when it meets or exceeds:*
>
> - *the expectations of parties who are regularly intended users for similar assignments; and*
> - *what an appraiser's peers' actions would be in performing the same or a similar assignment.*

© The Appraisal Foundation

Therefore, it is not the work habits of an individual appraiser that define the "normal course of business" in an assignment. Rather, it is the requirements of the Standards Rules measured against the actions of the appraiser's peers and the expectations of parties who are regularly intended users for similar assignments. 42 43 44

"Appraisers Peers" is defined as: 45

other appraisers who have expertise and competency in a similar type of assignment. 46

In addition to the concept of "normal course of business" in an assignment, an appraiser has the obligation to perform research and analysis appropriate to the intended use of the assignment. Standards Rules 1-1(b) and 7-1(b) state: 47 48

In developing a[n]...appraisal, an appraiser must: 49

not commit a substantial error of omission or commission that significantly affects an appraisal... 50

The Comments to these Standards Rules state, in part: 51

Diligence is required to identify and analyze the factors, conditions, data, and other information that would have a significant effect on the credibility of the assignment results. 52 53

Illustrations: 54

1. A reviewer noted that a real property appraisal report did not include an analysis of a sale of the subject real property that had occurred six months prior to the effective date of the appraisal. The sale was reported in the local Multiple Listing Service (MLS), which is available to appraisers in the area and to which most area appraisers subscribe. When contacted about the matter, the appraiser stated that he did not subscribe to the MLS, and checking that data source was not within his normal course of business. Is this an appropriate response? 55 56 57 58 59 60

   Answer: No. The fact that the individual appraiser does not subscribe to this data source does not excuse the lack of analysis. Since most appraisers in the market area do subscribe, and informed market participants would be aware of this and expect this level of diligence, the appraiser's lack of research and analysis did not reflect the normal course of business in *this* market. 61 62 63 64

2. A real property appraiser is engaged to appraise a property that is located in a rural area. Sales prices are a matter of public record, but the records are not computerized, and personal analysis of the public records requires a trip to the municipal building and a great deal of time searching records. Local officials will not provide this information over the telephone. Most appraisers in the area analyze sales data by using information provided by a local on-line data provider and quarterly sales reports that are mailed out by the local jurisdiction. In this situation, what action is necessary by the appraiser to comply with the requirement to analyze the subject's sales history? 65 66 67 68 69 70 71

   Answer: In this case, the normal course of business is to use the information from the local data provider and the quarterly sales reports. If a trip to the municipal building does not reflect the typical actions of most other appraisers in this market for this property type, or the expectations of clients for this specific type of assignment, then it is not required as part of the research and analysis in this assignment. 72 73 74 75

3. A personal property appraiser is engaged to appraise a painting by a well-known artist for estate tax purposes. Neither the heirs nor the executor of the estate could locate the documentation for the purchase by the decedent, even though the painting had been bought less than six months before the appraisal was ordered. However, the sale was widely reported, both in newspapers and trade publications, since the painting had been purchased at public auction and at a price that set a new high for that artist's work. The appraiser used sales of other paintings by the same artist to support the final opinion of value, but not the recent sale of the subject property, stating in the report that the documentation was not available. Does this comply with the sales history requirements of Standards Rule 7-5? 76 77 78 79 80 81 82 83

   Answer: No. This would not comply with the requirements of Standards Rule 7-5. Competent fine art appraisers would research relevant sections of newspapers and trade magazines and likely keep files or create databases of significant transactions. Therefore, this appraiser should have known at least the details of the sale that had been made public in the press. 84 85 86 87

© The Appraisal Foundation

88 4. During an appraisal assignment, the appraiser was informed by the owner that the subject property was listed
89 for sale on a prominent Internet site. The appraiser did no additional research, and in the appraisal report
90 indicated only that the property was listed for sale. Does this comply with the requirements of USPAP?

91 Answer: No. The appraiser must analyze the current listing and report the findings within the appraisal
92 report. Since the listing was placed on the Internet, where it would be available to the general public, it
93 would be available to the appraiser in the normal course of business.

© The Appraisal Foundation

ADVISORY OPINION 25 (AO-25)

This communication by the Appraisal Standards Board (ASB) does not establish new standards or interpret existing standards. Advisory Opinions are issued to illustrate the applicability of appraisal standards in specific situations and to offer advice from the ASB for the resolution of appraisal issues and problems.

SUBJECT: Clarification of the Client in a Federally Related Transaction

APPLICATION: Real Property

THE ISSUE:

The appraisal rules adopted by the Federal Financial Institutions Regulatory Agencies in August 1990 to comply with Title XI of the Financial Institutions Reform, Recovery, and Enforcement Act of 1989 (FIRREA) impose a requirement on regulated institutions that "if an appraisal is prepared by a fee appraiser, the appraiser shall be directly engaged by the regulated institution or its agent."[1]

In some cases, however, a property owner might directly engage the services of an appraiser for one intended use, but later desire to use the appraisal report in a federally related loan transaction. This and other similar scenarios lead to the question: "Do appraisers have an obligation to ensure that their services are directly engaged by a federally regulated financial institution?"

ADVICE FROM THE ASB ON THE ISSUE:

Relevant USPAP & Advisory References

- DEFINITIONS, specifically "client," "intended user," and "intended use"
- The ETHICS RULE
- SCOPE OF WORK RULE, which requires an appraiser to determine an appropriate scope of work to produce credible assignment results including all assignment conditions
- Standards Rules 1-2(a) and 1-2(b), which require an appraiser to identify the client, intended user(s), and intended use
- Standards Rule 2-1(a), which requires an appraiser to clearly and accurately set forth the appraisal in a manner that is not misleading
- Advisory Opinion 26, *Readdressing (Transferring) a Report to Another Party*
- Advisory Opinion 27, *Appraising the Same Property for a New Client*
- Advisory Opinion 30, *Appraisals for Use by a Federally Regulated Financial Institution*
- Advisory Opinion 36, *Identification and Disclosure of Client, Intended Use, and Intended Users*

Comments

USPAP requires an appraiser to identify the intended use and intended users in an appraisal assignment. USPAP also requires that appraisers not be misleading in the marketing of their services.[2] Advisory Opinion 30 provides guidance on the applicability of federal regulations and USPAP obligations when performing appraisals for use by a federally regulated financial institution.

In order to not be misleading when contacted by a prospective client, the appraiser's obligation is one of proper disclosure. If an appraiser knows that intended use of the appraisal is, or may be, for a federally related transaction by a federally regulated financial institution, it is that appraiser's responsibility to disclose to the prospective client prior to agreeing to perform the assignment that the lender or its agent is required to directly engage the appraiser. The appraiser should also disclose to the prospective client prior to agreeing to perform the assignment that it is unethical for the appraiser to later "readdress" or otherwise change the report to indicate a federally regulated financial institution was the client when the appraisal was performed for another party.[3]

1 National Credit Union Administration – 2 CFR 722.5(b)
Federal Reserve System – 12 CFR 225.65(b)
Federal Deposit Insurance Corporation – 12 CFR 323.5(b)
Office of the Comptroller of the Currency – 12 CFR 34.45(b)

2 See Management section of the ETHICS RULE

3 See Advisory Opinion-26, *Readdressing [Transferring] a Report to Another Party and* Advisory Opinion 27, *Appraising the Same Property for Another Client*

© The Appraisal Foundation

41 If the client still wishes to proceed with the appraisal after the appraiser has properly fulfilled these disclosure
42 obligations the appraiser can agree to perform the assignment. It would be prudent to recite disclosures in the
43 engagement letter and in the report.[4]

44 **Illustrations:**

45 1. Homeowner Susan Daly contacts appraiser John Hunt to perform an appraisal of her residence. She is
46 considering refinancing and wants to determine the amount of equity in the residence before completing a loan
47 application. Assuming the refinancing would be a federally related transaction at a federally regulated financial
48 institution, what is John's responsibility to this potential client?

49 Answer: Before John agrees to perform this assignment, it is his responsibility to disclose to Susan that
50 a lender or its agent is required to directly engage the services of an appraiser in a federally related
51 transaction and should not accept his appraisal report. If Susan still wants to engage John, his disclosure
52 allows him to perform the assignment.

53 2. A buyer of a commercial building contacts appraiser Jane Johnson about appraising the property for financing.
54 The buyer explains that he will likely be providing the report to an insurance company that is interested in
55 financing the property. The insurance company has no problem with the buyer being the client, as long as the
56 insurance company is identified as an intended user in this assignment. However, the buyer says that he may
57 also make application to his local bank, a federally regulated financial institution. Can Jane agree to perform
58 this assignment? If so, does she have any disclosure obligations?

59 Answer: Jane has an obligation to disclose to the buyer that the federally regulated financial institution
60 should not accept her appraisal report because a lender or its agent is required to directly engage the
61 services of an appraiser in a federally related transaction. If the buyer still wants to engage Jane, her
62 disclosure allows her to perform the assignment.

4 See Advisory Opinion 36, *Identification and Disclosure of Client, Intended Use, and Intended Users*

© The Appraisal Foundation

ADVISORY OPINION 26 (AO-26)

This communication by the Appraisal Standards Board (ASB) does not establish new standards or interpret existing standards. Advisory Opinions are issued to illustrate the applicability of appraisal standards in specific situations and to offer advice from the ASB for the resolution of appraisal issues and problems. 1 2 3

SUBJECT: Readdressing (Transferring) a Report to Another Party 4

APPLICATION: Real Property, Personal Property, and Intangible Property 5

THE ISSUE: 6

After an assignment has been completed and the report has been delivered, an appraiser may be asked to "readdress" (transfer) the report to another party. Does USPAP allow an appraiser to "readdress" (transfer) a report by altering it to indicate a new recipient as the client or additional intended user when the original report was completed for another party? 7 8 9 10

ADVICE FROM THE ASB ON THE ISSUE: 11

Relevant USPAP & Advisory References 12

- The Confidentiality and Conduct sections of the ETHICS RULE 13
- Standards Rules such as 1-2(a) and 1-2(b); 7-2(a) and 7-2(b); and 9-2(a) and 9-2(b), which require an appraiser to identify the client, intended users, and intended use 14 15
- Standards Rules such as 2-1(a), 8-1(a), 10-1(a), which require an appraiser to clearly and accurately set forth the appraisal in a manner that is not misleading 16 17
- SCOPE OF WORK RULE, which requires an appraiser to ascertain whether other laws or regulations apply to the assignment in addition to USPAP 18 19
- Advisory Opinion 25, which covers clarification of the client in a federally related transaction 20
- Advisory Opinion 27, which addresses appraising the same property for a new client 21
- Advisory Opinion 36, *Identification and Disclosure of Client, Intended Use, and Intended Users* 22

Comments 23

The answer to the question posed above is No. Once a report has been prepared for a named client(s) and any other identified intended users and for an identified intended use, the appraiser cannot "readdress" (transfer) the report to another party. 24 25 26

USPAP defines Client as: 27

> *the party or parties (i.e., individual, group, or entity) who engage an appraiser by employment or contract* ***in a specific assignment,*** *whether directly or through an agent.* (bold added for emphasis) 28 29

Assignment is defined as: 30

> *a valuation service that is provided by an appraiser as* ***a consequence of an agreement with a client.*** *(bold added for emphasis).* 31 32

Intended Use is defined as: 33

> *the use(s) of an appraiser's reported appraisal or appraisal review assignment results, as identified by the appraiser based on communication with the client* ***at the time of the assignment*** (bold added for emphasis). 34 35

Intended User is defined as: 36

> *the client and any other party as identified, by name or type, as users of the appraisal or appraisal review report by the appraiser on the based on communication with the client* ***at the time of the assignment*** (bold added for emphasis). 37 38 39

© The Appraisal Foundation

40 Identification of the client, any other intended users, and the intended use are key elements in all assignments.
41 Because these identifications drive the appraiser's scope of work decision, as well as other elements of the
42 assignment, they must be determined **at the time of the assignment**. They cannot be modified after an assignment
43 has been completed. See Advisory Opinion 36 for further clarification.

44 **Illustrations:**

45 Question #1

46 An appraiser was engaged by Client A to appraise a property. The appraiser delivered the appraisal report to
47 Client A. The client has decided not to pursue the transaction that generated the need for the appraisal report. The
48 appraiser is contacted by Client B. Client B requests that the original report be readdressed (transferred) by replacing
49 Client A's name with Client B's name in the report. Is this acceptable?

50 Answer: No. Simply changing the client name on the report cannot change or replace the original appraiser-
51 client relationship that was established with Client A. Therefore, this action is misleading.

52 Question #2

53 How can this circumstance be handled according to Standards?

54 Answer: The appraiser can consider Client B's request as a new assignment. In so doing, the appraiser
55 may establish a new appraiser-client relationship with Client B and appraise the property for this new client.
56 Important considerations, i.e., confidential information and other factors, are further addressed in AO-27,
57 *Appraising the Same Property for a New Client.*

58 Question #3

59 Why might Client B want their name on the report that was completed for Client A?

60 Answer: Client B may want to establish an appraiser-client relationship because it provides all the rights,
61 obligations and liabilities such a relationship places on the appraiser.

62 A prudent method to establish an appraiser-client relationship is to have a written engagement letter or contract
63 with any client at the time of the assignment.

© The Appraisal Foundation

ADVISORY OPINION 27 (AO-27)

This communication by the Appraisal Standards Board (ASB) does not establish new standards or interpret existing standards. Advisory Opinions are issued to illustrate the applicability of appraisal standards in specific situations and to offer advice from the ASB for the resolution of appraisal issues and problems.

SUBJECT: Appraising the Same Property for a New Client

APPLICATION: Real Property, Personal Property, and Intangible Property

THE ISSUE:

Situations often arise in which appraisers who have previously appraised a property are asked by a different party to appraise the same property. In some instances this request arises very soon after the first appraisal; in others, it may be months or years later. Under what circumstances can an appraiser agree to perform an assignment to appraise a property for a prospective client when that appraiser has previously completed an appraisal of the same property for another client?

ADVICE FROM THE ASB ON THE ISSUE:

Relevant USPAP & Advisory References:

- Conduct section of the ETHICS RULE
- Confidentiality section of the ETHICS RULE
- Advisory Opinion 25 which covers clarification of the client in a federally related transaction
- Advisory Opinion 26 which addresses reappraising/transferring a report to another party
- Advisory Opinion 36, *Identification and Disclosure of Client, Intended Use, and Intended Users*

Comments:

Agreeing to perform the assignment from the subsequent prospective client is not prohibited by USPAP, assuming appropriate disclosure is made to the client before being engaged and any existing confidential information is handled properly.

The part of the Conduct section of the ETHICS RULE that is pertinent to this matter includes the following:

If known prior to agreeing to perform an assignment, and/or if discovered at any time during the assignment, an appraiser must disclose to the client, and in the subsequent report certification:

> *any services regarding the subject property performed by the appraiser, as an appraiser or in any other capacity, within the three year period immediately preceding the agreement to perform the assignment.*
>
> *Comment: Disclosing the fact that the appraiser has previously appraised the property is permitted except in the case when an appraiser has agreed with the client to keep the mere occurrence of a prior assignment confidential. If an appraiser has agreed with a client not to disclose that he or she has appraised a property, the appraiser must decline all subsequent assignments that fall within the three year period.*

Several parts of the Confidentiality section of the ETHICS RULE are pertinent to this matter.

> *An appraiser must not disclose: (1) confidential information or (2) assignment result: to anyone other than the client;*

An appraiser cannot disclose the results of a particular assignment, performed for a particular client, to anyone other than those designated by that client. However, an understanding of the definitions of *assignment, assignment results,* and *client* are key to a complete understanding of this requirement.

> Assignment – *a valuation service that is provided by the appraiser as a consequence of an agreement with the client*
>
> Client – *the party or parties (i.e., individual, group, or entity) who engage an appraiser by employment or contract in a specific assignment, whether directly or through an agent.*
>
> Assignment Results – *An appraiser's opinions or conclusions, not limited to value, that were developed when*

© The Appraisal Foundation

43 *performing an appraisal assignment, an appraisal review assignment, or a valuation service other than an*
44 *appraisal or appraisal review.*

45 *Comment: Physical characteristics are not assignment results.*

46 As can be seen in the definitions, both the client and the assignment results are specific to an assignment. If there
47 is a new potential client, valuation services performed for that new client would constitute a new assignment and
48 the assignment results would be specific to that new assignment. Therefore, engagement for and performance of
49 the new assignment to appraise the same property would not be considered revealing the first client's assignment
50 results to the second client, even if the value conclusions were the same. It should be noted that the value conclusion
51 could easily be different if the effective date or the scope of work changed in any manner. It should also be noted that
52 USPAP requires the appraiser to provide an unbiased opinion of value to each client.

53 **Obtaining a Release:**
54 As a matter of business practice, some appraisers request a release from a prior client before agreeing to perform an
55 assignment to appraise the same property for a new client or to disclose the assignment for the second client to the
56 first client. However, USPAP does not require this. Also, appraisers should be aware that, in some cases, informing a
57 client about the existence of another client and the fact that the property was appraised for that other client may not
58 be compliant with the portion of the Confidentiality section of the ETHICS RULE, which states:

59 *An appraiser must protect the confidential nature of the appraiser-client relationship.*

60 **Confidential Information:**
61 In all assignments the appraiser must comply with the Confidentiality section of the ETHICS RULE with respect to the
62 handling of confidential information. Confidential information is defined in USPAP as:

63 *information that is either:*

64 • *identified by the client as confidential when providing it to an appraiser and that is not available from*
65 *any other source; or*
66 • *classified as confidential or private by applicable law or regulation.*

67 The Confidentiality section of the ETHICS RULE states:

68 *An appraiser must be aware of, and comply with, all confidentiality and privacy laws and regulations*
69 *applicable in an assignment.*

70 *An appraiser must not disclose: (1) confidential information; or (2) assignment results to anyone other than the*
71 *client, parties specifically authorized by the client, state appraiser regulatory agencies, third parties as may be*
72 *authorized by due process of law, and a duly authorized professional peer review committee except when such*
73 *disclosure to a committee would violate applicable law or regulation.*

74 If a prior assignment included any confidential information, its disclosure to a different client or intended user
75 would violate the ETHICS RULE if the information were still classified as confidential information. This includes the
76 requirement to comply with all confidentiality and privacy laws and regulations.

77 **Client Expectations:**
78 At times, an appraiser's client for an assignment may believe that a legitimate business interest could be harmed if
79 the appraiser provides another client with an appraisal of the same subject property. In such cases, the client and
80 the appraiser may stipulate in their service agreement the conditions under which the appraiser may or may not
81 appraise the same subject property. A client involved in litigation may stipulate that the appraiser cannot appraise a
82 subject property for the opposing party in that litigation. As another example, if an appraiser is providing the value of
83 a property to a client who is planning to sell that property in an auction, the appraiser and client may agree that the
84 appraiser will not appraise the same property for a party planning to participate in the bidding process.

85 **Illustrations:**
86 **Example A – Litigation**
87 An appraiser performs an appraisal for a client involved in litigation and then is requested to appraise the same property
88 for the opposing party. Is agreeing to perform the assignment for the second client prohibited by USPAP?

© The Appraisal Foundation

No, assuming appropriate disclosure is made to the client and confidential information is handled correctly. However, there are common business practices in such circumstances. Often, the opposing parties each hire an appraiser to appraise the subject property. If the opposing parties do not plan to hire one appraiser jointly, each party could make it a part of the agreement between the appraiser and the client (the engagement letter or contract) that the appraiser is not to appraise the property for anyone representing the opposing side of the legal action.

In the absence of such an agreement between the client and the appraiser, the appraiser should make appropriate disclosure to the client and consider the presence of confidential information. The knowledge of confidential information may prevent the appraiser from agreeing to perform the second assignment. The appraiser must decline the second assignment if:

1. the appraiser used confidential information in performing the first assignment;
2. that information would not be available from any other source; and
3. credible results cannot be derived without the use of this confidential information.

However, the appraiser may agree to perform the second assignment, making sure to not disclose any confidential information from the original assignment to the second client, if:

1. the information is available from another source (meaning it is not *confidential information*, as defined); or
2. the *confidential information* is not material to deriving credible assignment results, and
3. the client agrees to engage the appraiser after the appraiser makes the appropriate disclosure.

However, the appraiser must ensure that confidential information is not disclosed, even if it has no impact on the assignment results (such as the litigation strategy of attorneys representing the first client).

Example B – Competing Banks

If an appraiser has appraised a property for Bank A and then is approached by Bank B to appraise the same property, does USPAP prohibit agreement to perform the second assignment?

No, assuming disclosure is made to the client and confidential information is handled correctly. This constitutes a second assignment, a new client and a new agreement between a client and an appraiser.

© The Appraisal Foundation

ADVISORY OPINION 28 (AO-28)

1 *This communication by the Appraisal Standards Board (ASB) does not establish new standards or interpret existing*
2 *standards. Advisory Opinions are issued to illustrate the applicability of appraisal standards in specific situations and*
3 *to offer advice from the ASB for the resolution of appraisal issues and problems.*

4 **SUBJECT: Scope of Work Decision, Performance, and Disclosure**

5 **APPLICATION: Real Property, Personal Property, Intangible Property**

6 **THE ISSUE:**
7 The SCOPE OF WORK RULE states:

8 *For each appraisal and appraisal review assignment, an appraiser must:*

9 1. *identify the problem to be solved;*
10 2. *determine and perform the scope of work necessary to develop credible assignment results; and*
11 3. *disclose the scope of work in the report.*

12 How are the requirements in the SCOPE OF WORK RULE incorporated into the process of developing and reporting
13 assignment results?

14 **ADVICE FROM THE ASB ON THE ISSUE:**
15 **Problem Identification**
16 Problem identification is the beginning point of every assignment. The appraiser must gather and analyze the
17 information needed to properly recognize the appraisal or appraisal review problem to be solved. The information
18 necessary for problem identification is presented in each Standard that addresses the development process for an
19 appraisal or appraisal review assignment. For example, Standards Rules 1-2, 5-2, 7-2 and 9-2 provide the assignment
20 elements[1] that must be defined and analyzed in order to identify the problem to be solved in an appraisal assignment.
21 These assignment elements include the:

22 • client and any other intended users;
23 • intended use of the appraiser's opinions and conclusions;
24 • type and definition of value;
25 • effective date of the appraiser's opinions and conclusions;
26 • subject of the assignment and its relevant characteristics; and
27 • assignment conditions.

28 Identifying the problem to be solved is required in order to make critical judgments in determining the appropriate
29 scope of work. Therefore, the assignment elements necessary for problem identification in an appraisal or appraisal
30 review assignment also serve as reference points in determining whether the scope of work performed was
31 appropriate to provide credible assignment results.[2]

32 Additionally, proper identification of the problem to be solved is required for compliance with the COMPETENCY
33 RULE, which states:

34 *An appraiser must determine, prior to agreeing to perform an assignment, that he or she can perform*
35 *the assignment competently. Competency requires (1) the ability to properly identify the problem to be*
36 *addressed; (2) the knowledge and experience to complete the assignment competently; and (3) recognition*
37 *of, and compliance with, laws and regulations that apply to the appraiser or to the assignment.*

38 One of the assignment elements that affects the scope of work is assignment conditions.[3] Some assignment
39 conditions are not a matter of choice, such as an inability to inspect a property because it has been destroyed. Other
40 assignment conditions are a matter of choice, such as a client's request to perform a desktop appraisal of machinery
41 and equipment to reduce fees.

1 "See DEFINITIONS, Assignment Elements"
2 See Advisory Opinion 29, *An Acceptable Scope of Work.*
3 See DEFINITIONS, Assignment Conditions

© The Appraisal Foundation

Determining and Performing the Scope of Work

USPAP recognizes that the appropriate scope of work may differ significantly for different assignments; the SCOPE OF WORK RULE provides flexibility in determining the scope of work. The competency necessary to determine an appropriate scope of work within the allowed flexibility resides with the appraiser. Therefore, while it is common and reasonable for the client to provide input to the appraiser regarding a desired scope of work, the responsibility for determining the appropriate scope of work resides with the appraiser.

The flexibility and responsibility are linked in the SCOPE OF WORK RULE when it states:

> *Appraisers have broad flexibility and significant responsibility in determining the appropriate scope of work for an appraisal or appraisal review assignment.*

This responsibility is described when the SCOPE OF WORK RULE states:

> *The appraiser must be prepared to demonstrate that the scope of work is sufficient to produce credible assignment results.*

The client, for example, might request that the appraiser include, or exclude, specific inspections, data collection, or analysis in the scope of work. The appraiser may agree to perform an assignment with these types of assignment conditions provided that the assignment results are credible in the context of the intended use. The SCOPE OF WORK RULE addresses this issue in the Scope of Work Acceptability section:

> *An appraiser must not allow assignment conditions to limit the scope of work to such a degree that the assignment results are not credible in the context of the intended use.*
>
> *An appraiser must not allow the intended use of an assignment or a client's objectives to cause the assignment results to be biased.*

Determining the appropriate scope of work requires judgment. This judgment rests on the appraiser's identification of the assignment elements and understanding of what is required to solve the identified problem. In many assignments, experienced appraisers are able to make this judgment about the appropriate scope of work quickly because they have performed many assignments addressing a similar problem to be solved (assignment with similar assignment elements). In other assignments, the determination of the appropriate scope of work may require more analysis by the appraiser because the problem to be solved has certain unusual characteristics. In yet other assignments, the appraiser may begin with a planned scope of work but in the course of the assignment find that the planned scope of work must be modified in order to produce credible assignment results.

The SCOPE OF WORK RULE recognizes that the scope of work actually performed may differ from the scope of work initially planned, when it states:

> *Determining the scope of work is an ongoing process in an assignment. Information or conditions discovered during the course of an assignment might cause the appraiser to reconsider the scope of work.*

Disclosing the Scope of Work Performed

The SCOPE OF WORK RULE explains that proper disclosure of the scope of work:

> *...is required because clients and other intended users rely on the assignment results.*

The Rule also states that:

> *The report must contain sufficient information to allow the client and other intended users to understand the scope of work performed. The information disclosed must be appropriate for the intended use of the assignment results.*

An appraiser must disclose research and analyses not performed when such disclosure is necessary for intended users to understand the report properly and not be misled.

These disclosure requirements apply to the scope of work performed, rather than the scope of work initially planned by the appraiser. The appraiser must disclose the type and extent of research and analyses that were actually completed in the development process. Additionally, the information required to allow intended users to understand the scope of work may include disclosure of research and analyses not performed.

© The Appraisal Foundation

87 The appraiser has broad flexibility and significant responsibility in the level of detail and manner of disclosing the
88 scope of work in the appraisal report or appraisal review report. The appraiser may, but is not required to, consolidate
89 the disclosure in a specific section or sections of the report, or use a particular label, heading or subheading. An
90 appraiser may choose to disclose the scope of work as necessary throughout the report.

91 **Illustrations:**

92 1. A real property appraiser is engaged to appraise the market value of a twelve-unit apartment building. The
93 appraiser initially decided that the scope of work should include the inspection of two of each of the three unit
94 types (studio, one- and two-bedroom). In the course of conducting the inspection, the property manager had a
95 key for only one of the two-bedroom units; thus the appraiser was not able to inspect one of the two-bedroom
96 units as planned.

97 The scope of work, which includes the degree of inspection, was affected in this assignment because of lack of
98 access. If the appraiser decides that she has sufficient information to produce credible assignment results, the
99 appraiser can complete the appraisal based on the inspection completed. The report would include a description
100 of the scope of work performed, stating that five units had been inspected.

101 2. A personal property appraiser has been engaged to appraise a collection of Chinese imperial Qianlong porcelain
102 vases. The intended use of the appraisal is for litigation regarding an estate. The client has requested that all of
103 the vases be inspected, since one cause of action involves a claim that some are damaged.

104 The appraiser contacts the estate's administrator to arrange for inspection and learns that three of the vases are
105 in storage and cannot be retrieved until after the Court's deadline for the submission of expert reports. These
106 assignment conditions severely limit the appraiser's scope of work, making it impossible to obtain enough
107 information to identify the characteristics of the property in compliance with Standards Rule 7-2(e).

108 In this case, assignment conditions have changed the appraiser's scope of work. In the context of the intended
109 use of this assignment, the appraiser decides that there is no reasonable basis for making an extraordinary
110 assumption about the condition of the three vases in storage and that credible assignment results cannot be
111 produced without inspecting them. In this scenario, the appraiser informs the client that the three uninspected
112 vases cannot be appraised unless the assignment conditions can be changed. The appraiser then alters the
113 scope of work to appraise only the vases that are available for inspection.

114 3. A business appraiser is appraising a closely held business enterprise with real property and personal property
115 assets. In the course of the assignment, the appraiser's research indicates that the market for the company's
116 product is declining and management's projections are not supported. Therefore, the appraiser believes the
117 company might be worth more in liquidation than as a going concern, which would make performance of the work
118 addressed in Standards Rule 9-3 necessary for credible assignment results.

119 The scope of work must be modified because of what the appraiser learned in the course of performing research
120 and analyses.

121 4. A real property appraiser is contacted by a potential client to appraise an occupied manufacturing facility. The
122 client requests that the occupants not be disturbed by a property inspection. Additionally, the client requests
123 that the cost approach be performed in the appraisal of the building. These requests are assignment conditions
124 and will be part of the appraiser's identification of the problem to be solved and determination of the appropriate
125 scope of work.

126 To perform this assignment, the appraiser is required to:

127 • Determine that the client's assignment conditions do not limit the scope of work to such a degree that
128 assignment results are not credible in the context of the intended use;
129 • Gather information on relevant characteristics by means other than inspection and/or use extraordinary
130 assumptions;
131 • Include a cost approach in the scope of work, even if this approach is not otherwise necessary for credible
132 assignment results; and
133 • Properly reconcile the applicability or suitability of the cost approach in arriving at the value conclusion.

© The Appraisal Foundation

5. A real property appraiser agreed to perform an assignment to appraise a three-unit residential property. The intended use of the appraisal was for mortgage financing. The client requested that the appraiser not verify the legal status (e.g., compliance with zoning, building codes, use permits) of the three units with municipal officials. 134 135 136

   The appraiser withdrew from the assignment because she concluded that the client's assignment condition limited the scope of work to such a degree that assignment results would not be credible in the context of the intended use. The use of an extraordinary assumption about the legal use of the property would not produce credible assignment results in the context of the mortgage financing use. 137 138 139 140

6. A real property appraiser was engaged to appraise a one-unit residence. Based on the appraiser's identification of the appraisal problem, the appropriate scope of work was determined to include development of the sales comparison approach and cost approach. However, at the time of the inspection the appraiser discovered that the property was not a one-unit, but instead a three-unit property. 141 142 143 144

   Based on this new information, the appraiser reconsidered the appraisal problem and the appropriate scope of work. The change in relevant property characteristics for the subject property significantly changed the appropriate scope of work; the initially planned scope of work was no longer suitable and would not produce credible assignment results. The type of data to be researched and the type of analysis to be applied changed when the property type changed from a single-unit to a three-unit. 145 146 147 148 149

   A new appraisal problem requires reexamination of the scope of work. The appropriate scope of work for the new appraisal problem includes an income approach, and the cost approach is not necessary for credible assignment results. 150 151 152

   The appraiser should consult with the client since the appraisal problem has changed. 153

7. A real property appraiser is contacted by a potential client to appraise a one-unit residence. The client informs the appraiser that a property inspection completed by others will be provided to the appraiser, and that the property will not be available for inspection by the appraiser. This is an assignment condition, and the appraiser must consider this in the identification of the problem to be solved and the determination of the scope of work. 154 155 156 157

   To perform this assignment, the appraiser is required to: 158

   - Determine that the client's assignment condition does not limit the scope of work to such a degree that assignment results are not credible in the context of the intended use; and 159 160
   - Identify, from sources the appraiser reasonably believes to be reliable, relevant characteristics of the property. 161 162

   If the appraiser cannot gather sufficient information about the property's relevant characteristics from the third-party property inspection, the appraiser must seek additional information, which could include interviewing the inspector or gathering data from other sources. If uncertainties remain, but the appraiser can still develop credible assignment results, the appraiser may need to use an extraordinary assumption regarding the decision to rely on the information contained in the third-party inspection report. 163 164 165 166 167

   Otherwise, if the appraiser cannot gather sufficient information from the third-party inspection report and other sources to produce credible assignment results, the appraiser must either seek to change the scope of work or withdraw from the assignment. 168 169 170

© The Appraisal Foundation

ADVISORY OPINION 29 (AO-29)

This communication by the Appraisal Standards Board (ASB) does not establish new standards or interpret existing standards. Advisory Opinions are issued to illustrate the applicability of appraisal standards in specific situations and to offer advice from the ASB for the resolution of appraisal issues and problems.

SUBJECT: An Acceptable Scope of Work

APPLICATION: Real Property, Personal Property, Intangible Property

THE ISSUE:

The SCOPE OF WORK RULE states that an appraiser's scope of work is acceptable when it meets or exceeds:

- *the expectations of parties who are regularly intended users for similar assignments; and*
- *what an appraiser's peers' actions would be in performing the same or a similar assignment.*

What makes an assignment similar?

Who are an appraiser's peers?

Must an acceptable scope of work satisfy both benchmarks?

ADVICE FROM THE ASB ON THE ISSUE:

Similar Assignments

Assignment elements define and characterize the problem to be solved in appraisal and appraisal review assignments. The assignment elements necessary for proper identification of the appraisal problem are addressed in the applicable Standards Rules (i.e., SR 1-2, 3-2, 5-2, 7-2 and 9-2). The applicability of Standards Rules depends on the type of asset being appraised (real property, personal property, or intangible property including business interests) and the type of assignment (appraisal or appraisal review).

Assignments are similar when the assignment elements used to identify the appraisal problem are comparable. Assignment elements include such things as the intended use, intended users, type and definition of value, effective date, relevant characteristics of the subject property, and assignment conditions.

The information gathered about the assignment elements is used by the appraiser to identify the problem to be solved and determine an acceptable scope of work. The greater the commonality among assignment elements, the more similarity there is between assignments.

An Appraiser's Peers

USPAP defines Appraiser's Peers as:

> *other appraisers who have expertise and competency in a similar type of assignment.*

To be an appraiser's peer for a particular assignment, one must have the competency to address the appraisal problem presented in that assignment. This includes the knowledge and experience to:

- properly identify the appraisal or appraisal review problem to be solved;
- determine the type and extent of research and analyses to include in the development process; and
- perform the required research and analyses properly.

Because assignments can require different types of expertise and competency, it is possible to be considered an appraiser's peer for some assignments, but not for others. Identifying an appraiser's peer is always done in the context of a particular assignment.

Within appraisal practice there are three disciplines (real property, personal property, and intangible property including business interests), and within those disciplines there are many areas of specific expertise. An appraiser can have a focused area of expertise and competency or a wide variety of expertise and competency. Merely holding the same type or level of credential does not make one an appraiser's peer.

© The Appraisal Foundation

Determining if an individual is an appraiser's peer requires examining the individual's expertise regarding each of the elements that define the assignment. For example, solely having expertise in appraising the same type of property is not sufficient to make someone an appraiser's peer.

Application

The scope of work is acceptable when it leads to credible assignment results. The SCOPE OF WORK RULE establishes two benchmarks for measuring the acceptability of the scope of work, both of which need to be met. The scope of work is acceptable when it meets or exceeds **both** (1) the expectations of parties who are regularly intended users for similar assignments; and (2) what an appraiser's peers' actions would be in performing the same or a similar assignment. An acceptable scope of work must satisfy both benchmarks.

Illustrations:

1. An appraiser has been engaged to perform an "exterior only" appraisal of a single-family property for a potential home equity loan. Another appraiser has been asked to appraise a single-family property in the same development for an FHA loan. Since the subject properties are similar, would the assignments require the same scope of work?

   No. The subject of the assignment and its relevant characteristics is just one of several assignment elements that define an appraisal problem. Because of critical differences in the intended use and the appraisal problem to be solved, the scope of work that is acceptable for the first assignment would not be acceptable for the second assignment. For example, an appraisal performed for an FHA loan is subject to additional inspection requirements.

2. A state certified general appraiser is appraising a highly specialized industrial facility, and is concerned that the assignment is so complex that many appraisers who are knowledgeable about industrial property would not be qualified to judge whether or not the scope of work was appropriate. Who would be considered the appraiser's peers in this assignment?

   The appraiser's peers for this assignment would be other appraisers competent to complete a similar assignment. If special expertise is required, other state certified general appraisers without the required expertise and knowledge would not be the appraiser's peers for this assignment. Identifying appraisers with expertise and competency in appraising similar complex property types or unusual intended uses may require seeking appraisers from other geographic areas.

3. A business appraiser is engaged to value a 25% minority interest in the equity of a small privately held company for estate tax reporting purposes. The standard of value is fair market value as defined in the tax regulations. The engagement requires that a second appraiser, meeting the definition of an appraiser's peer, be retained to review the work and to opine on the value of the subject interest. Another appraiser is experienced in valuing companies in the same industry, but typically appraises them for purposes of sale, valuing 100% of the equity and has never performed appraisals of minority interests for estate tax reporting purposes. Is this other appraiser an appraiser's peer for this assignment?

   No. Part of problem identification for a business appraisal includes identification of the extent to which the subject interest contains elements of ownership control. Part of the appraisal process includes analyzing the effect on value, if any, of the extent to which the interest appraised contains elements of ownership control. Individuals who meet the definition of appraiser's peers would need to have expertise and competency in valuing minority interests. Additionally, the fact that the second appraiser has not performed appraisals for the same intended use could also render him or her to not be a peer in this assignment.

4. An appraiser has agreed to complete an assignment in the next two days. While conducting research, the appraiser discovers that the primary data source for the assignment, a regional computer database, is off-line and will not be available for three days. What is the appropriate course of action?

   If an appraiser is unable to perform research that the appraiser's peers would conduct and intended users would expect, the appraiser must modify the assignment to allow time for the research to be conducted, or withdraw from the assignment.

© The Appraisal Foundation

ADVISORY OPINION 30 (AO-30)

This communication by the Appraisal Standards Board (ASB) does not establish new standards or interpret existing standards. Advisory Opinions are issued to illustrate the applicability of appraisal standards in specific situations and to offer advice from the ASB for the resolution of appraisal issues and problems.

SUBJECT: Appraisals for Use by a Federally Regulated Financial Institution

APPLICATION: Real Property

THE ISSUE:

In order to comply with Title XI of the Financial Institutions Reform, Recovery, and Enforcement Act of 1989 (FIRREA), the federal financial institutions regulatory agencies ("agencies")[1] of the United States have adopted appraisal regulations and guidelines. These laws, regulations and guidelines are established to protect federally insured depository institutions and include the requirement that appraisals be prepared in compliance with the *Uniform Standards of Professional Appraisal Practice* (USPAP).

What are an appraiser's obligations when performing a real property appraisal for use by a federally regulated financial institution?

ADVICE FROM THE ASB ON THE ISSUE:

Recognition of Assignment Conditions

USPAP creates an obligation for appraisers to recognize and adhere to applicable assignment conditions. The appraiser's identification of the intended use and intended users drives the applicable assignment conditions. The relevant laws and agencies' appraisal regulations and guidelines are assignment conditions for real property appraisals for use by a federally regulated financial institution. These assignment conditions include, but are not limited to, the following:

- Laws, principally Title XI of the Financial Institutions Reform, Recovery, and Enforcement Act of 1989 (FIRREA);
- Regulations, primarily the following agency appraisal regulations:
  - Office of the Comptroller of the Currency (OCC) 12 CFR 34, Subpart C;
  - Federal Reserve Board (FRB) 12 CFR 225, Subpart G;
  - Federal Deposit Insurance Corporation (FDIC) 12 CFR 323;
  - National Credit Union Administration (NCUA) 12 CFR 722.
- Guidelines provided in the agencies' bulletins and issuances, including documents such as:
  - *Interagency Appraisal and Evaluation Guidelines;*
  - *Independent Appraisal And Evaluation Function;*
  - *Frequently Asked Questions on Residential Tract Development Lending;*
  - *Frequently Asked Questions on the Appraisal Regulations and the Interagency Statement on Independent Appraisal and Evaluation Functions.*

The guidelines identified in this Advisory Opinion are subject to change. Appraisers are cautioned to communicate with their client on the current guidance that is applicable in a given assignment. Reference can be made to the website of the applicable federal financial institutions regulatory agency for these documents and more information on current bulletins and applicable issuances.

USPAP Applicability

A client that is a federally regulated financial institution expects compliance with the applicable regulations and guidelines. An appraiser's obligations are established in the course of considering and agreeing to perform an assignment. Appraisers must recognize and adhere to assignment conditions that apply in an assignment to satisfy the following USPAP requirements:

1. The PREAMBLE requires that appraisers develop and communicate assignment results in a manner that is meaningful and not misleading.

[1] Office of the Comptroller of the Currency (OCC), Federal Reserve Board (FRB), Federal Deposit Insurance Corporation (FDIC), and the National Credit Union Administration (NCUA).

© The Appraisal Foundation

2. The ETHICS RULE requires that appraisers perform assignments ethically and competently. 44

3. The COMPETENCY RULE requires appraisers to provide competent service, including the specific requirement to recognize and comply with applicable laws and regulations. 45 46

4. In developing assignment results, the SCOPE OF WORK RULE requires appraisers to determine, perform, and disclose the scope of work necessary to produce credible assignment results. Determining the appropriate scope of work requires identification of the problem to be solved, which includes identification of assignment conditions. 47 48 49

   The scope of work is acceptable when it meets or exceeds the expectations of parties who are regularly intended users for similar assignments. Upon agreeing to perform an assignment, an appraiser is obligated to competently satisfy the applicable assignment conditions. 50 51 52

5. Standards Rule 1-1(a) is an extension of the COMPETENCY RULE that specifically requires that *the appraiser be aware of, understand, and correctly employ those recognized methods and techniques that are necessary to produce a credible appraisal.* 53 54 55

6. Standards Rules 2-1(a) and 2-1(b) require that each written appraisal report (a) *clearly and accurately set forth the appraisal in a manner that will not be misleading;* and (b) *contain sufficient information to enable intended users of the appraisal to understand the report properly.* 56 57 58

7. STANDARD 2 also requires that report content be appropriate for the intended use of the appraisal. 59

Use of the JURISDICTIONAL EXCEPTION RULE is not appropriate because none of the requirements in the agencies' appraisal laws and regulations preclude compliance with USPAP. 60 61

Appraisers must identify and consider the intended use and intended users in an assignment to understand their USPAP development and reporting obligations. The agencies' appraisal regulations and guidelines contain assignment conditions that are part of competent performance when they apply in an assignment. Therefore, compliance with USPAP requirements for proper development and reporting require adherence to those assignment conditions that apply in an assignment. 62 63 64 65 66

Failure to Adhere to Assignment Conditions 67

Failure to recognize and adhere to applicable assignment conditions violates one or more of the USPAP requirements previously identified. 68 69

- An appraiser who represents that an assignment is or will be completed in compliance with applicable assignment conditions and who then knowingly fails to comply with those assignment conditions violates the ETHICS RULE. 70 71 72
- An appraiser who unintentionally fails to comply with or fails to recognize those assignment conditions violates the COMPETENCY RULE. 73 74
- An appraiser who fails to develop assignment results in accordance with the assignment conditions necessary for credible assignment results violates the SCOPE OF WORK RULE and STANDARD 1. 75 76
- An appraiser who fails to report assignment results in accordance with the assignment conditions that are necessary to enable intended users to understand the report properly violates STANDARD 2. 77 78

Obligations for Appraisers Performing Appraisals for Use by a Federally Regulated Financial Institution 79

Note: All quotations in this section are from the agencies' appraisal regulations.[2] The quoted text is only a portion of the complete regulations, and the applicable regulations should be reviewed in their entirety. 80 81

Appraiser Independence[3] 82

The agencies' appraisal regulations state, in part: 83

> "If an appraisal is prepared by a staff appraiser, that appraiser must be independent of the lending, investment, and collection functions and not involved, except as an appraiser, in the federally related transaction, and have no direct or indirect interest, financial or otherwise, in the property. If the only qualified persons available to perform an appraisal are involved in the lending, investment, or collection functions of 84 85 86 87

2 Office of the Comptroller of the Currency – 12 CFR 34.45(b), Federal Reserve Board – 12 CFR225.65(b), Federal Deposit Insurance Corporation – 12 CFR 323.5(b), National Credit Union Administration - 12 CFR 722.5(b).

3 See Advisory Opinion 25, *Clarification of the Client in a Federally Related, Transaction* and Advisory Opinion 26, *Readdressing (Transferring) a Report to Another Party.*

© The Appraisal Foundation

88 the regulated institution, the regulated institution shall take appropriate steps to ensure that the appraisers
89 exercise independent judgment. Such steps include, but are not limited to, prohibiting an individual from
90 performing an appraisal in connection with federally related transactions in which the appraiser is otherwise
91 involved and prohibiting directors and officers from participating in any vote or approval involving assets on
92 which they performed an appraisal."

93 "If an appraisal is prepared by a fee appraiser, the appraiser shall be engaged directly by the regulated
94 institution or its agent, and have no direct or indirect interest, financial or otherwise, in the property or the
95 transaction."

96 "A regulated institution also may accept an appraisal that was prepared by an appraiser engaged directly by
97 another financial services institution, if:

98 (i) The appraiser has no direct or indirect interest, financial or otherwise, in the property or the transaction;
99 and
100 (ii) The regulated institution determines that the appraisal conforms to the requirements of this subpart and
101 is otherwise acceptable."

102 **Appraisal Development and Reporting**
103 The agencies' appraisal regulations state, in part:

104 "For federally related transactions, all appraisals shall, at a minimum:

105 (a) Conform to generally accepted appraisal standards as evidenced by the *Uniform Standards of Professional*
106 *Appraisal Practice* (USPAP) promulgated by the Appraisal Standards Board of the Appraisal Foundation
107 (1155 15th Street, Suite 1111, NW., Washington, DC 20005), unless principles of safe and sound banking require
108 compliance with stricter standards;
109 (b) Be written and contain sufficient information and analysis to support the institution's decision to engage in
110 the transaction;
111 (c) Analyze and report appropriate deductions and discounts for proposed construction or renovation, partially
112 leased buildings, nonmarket lease terms, and tract developments with unsold units;
113 (d) Be based upon the definition of market value as set forth in this subpart; and
114 (e) Be performed by State licensed or certified appraisers in accordance with requirements set forth in this
115 subpart."

116 **Market Value Definition**
117 The agencies' appraisal regulations state, in part:

118 "*Market value* means the most probable price which a property should bring in a competitive and open market
119 under all conditions requisite to a fair sale, the buyer and seller each acting prudently and knowledgeably, and
120 assuming the price is not affected by undue stimulus. Implicit in this definition are the consummation of a sale
121 as of a specified date and the passing of title from seller to buyer under conditions whereby:

122 (1) Buyer and seller are typically motivated;
123 (2) Both parties are well informed or well advised, and acting in what they consider their own best interests;
124 (3) A reasonable time is allowed for exposure in the open market;
125 (4) Payment is made in terms of cash in U.S. dollars or in terms of financial arrangements comparable
126 thereto; and
127 (5) The price represents the normal consideration for the property sold unaffected by special or creative
128 financing or sales concessions granted by anyone associated with the sale."

129 **Commonly Asked Questions**
130 1. How do the assignment conditions that apply to appraisals for use by a federally regulated financial institution
131 affect the appraiser's scope of work and report content?

132 An appraiser agreeing to perform an assignment under the agencies' appraisal regulations and guidelines is
133 obligated to complete that assignment in a manner that adheres to the applicable appraisal regulations and
134 guidelines.

© The Appraisal Foundation

2. What is a "real estate-related financial transaction"? 135

The term is defined in Title XI of FIRREA and the agencies' appraisal regulations as "any transaction involving — 136

(1) The sale, lease, purchase, investment in or exchange of real property, including interests in property, or the financing thereof; or 137 138
(2) The refinancing of real property or interests in real property; or 139
(3) The use of real property or interests in property as security for a loan or investment, including mortgage-backed securities." 140 141

3. What is a "federally related transaction"? 142

The term is defined in Title XI of FIRREA as "any real estate-related financial transaction which — 143

(A) a federal financial institutions regulatory agency or the Resolution Trust Corporation engages in, contracts for, or regulates; and 144 145
(B) requires the services of an appraiser." 146

The agencies' appraisal regulations define when the services of an appraiser are required. The agencies' appraisal regulations also list specific categories of transactions that do not require the services of an appraiser. 147 148 149

4. Do the agencies' appraisal regulations apply to FHA, VA, Fannie Mae, Freddie Mac, Farmer Mac, or Sallie Mae? 150

FHA, VA, Fannie Mae, Freddie Mac, Farmer Mac and Sallie Mae are not under the supervision of the federal financial institutions regulatory agencies and therefore are not subject to their appraisal regulations. 151 152

© The Appraisal Foundation

ADVISORY OPINION 31 (AO-31)

This communication by the Appraisal Standards Board (ASB) does not establish new standards or interpret existing standards. Advisory Opinions are issued to illustrate the applicability of appraisal standards in specific situations and to offer advice from the ASB for the resolution of appraisal issues and problems.

SUBJECT: Assignments Involving More than One Appraiser

APPLICATION: Real Property, Personal Property, Intangible Property

THE ISSUE:
What are the specific USPAP obligations when an appraisal or appraisal review assignment involves more than one appraiser?

BACKGROUND:
Many appraisal assignments involve participation by more than one appraiser. Typical scenarios include, but are not limited to:

- Two appraisers working together as equals on an assignment.
- A staff appraiser whose work is reviewed and/or directed by a more senior appraiser.
- A person who is being trained as an appraiser ("trainee") and requires supervision and direction by an appraiser already fully qualified to complete the assignment.
- An independent appraiser/contractor performing work for an appraisal firm.
- Two or more appraisers from different appraisal disciplines working on an assignment.

When assignments involve more than one appraiser there are often questions about the proper way to deal with USPAP requirements relating to record keeping, signatures and certifications.

It is important to realize that USPAP does not define an "appraiser" in terms of state licensing or certification requirements. USPAP defines an appraiser as one who is expected to perform valuation services competently and in a manner that is independent, impartial, and objective. Expectation is the crucial element in determining when one is acting as an appraiser. As a result, one could be a trainee by state licensing requirements and also identified as an appraiser by USPAP definition. Reference to applicable state law should be made to clarify the specific definition of appraiser and trainee in a jurisdiction.

ADVICE FROM THE ASB ON THE ISSUE:
<u>Relevant USPAP References</u>

- SCOPE OF WORK RULE, which requires that the appraiser disclose the scope of work performed
- RECORD KEEPING RULE
- Standards Rules 2-2(a)(ix), 2-2(b)(xi), 4-2(h), 6-2(h), 8-2(a)(ix), 8-2(b)(xi), 10-2(a)(x) and 10-2(b)(xii), which specify the reporting requirements when any portion of the work involves significant assistance
- Standards Rules 2-3, 4-3, 6-3, 8-3 and 10-3, which identify the requirements for an appraiser who is signing a certification and also for instances when appraisers provide significant assistance but do not sign a certification

<u>Record Keeping Requirements</u>
The RECORD KEEPING RULE requires:

> *An appraiser must prepare a workfile for each appraisal or appraisal review assignment. A workfile must be in existence prior to the issuance of any report or other communication of assignment results.*

The Rule also mandates that workfiles be retained for a specified time, and states,

> *An appraiser must have custody of the workfile, or make appropriate workfile retention, access and retrieval arrangements with the party having custody of the workfile.*

> *An appraiser having custody of a workfile must allow other appraisers with workfile obligations related to an assignment appropriate access and retrieval for the purpose of:*

© The Appraisal Foundation

- *submission to state appraiser regulatory agencies;* 44
- *compliance with due process of law;* 45
- *submission to a duly authorized professional peer review committee; or* 46
- *compliance with retrieval arrangements.* 47

When an assignment is performed by more than one appraiser, each appraiser is subject to the same obligations regarding the workfile for the assignment, whether or not the appraiser signs a certification. These obligations may be met by creating a copy of the workfile for every appraiser involved in the assignment. Alternatively, the appraisers might agree to an access arrangement whereby the workfile is stored in a single location but access is provided to all appraisers involved. In whatever manner this USPAP requirement is met, all appraisers involved with the assignment must meet it. 48 49 50 51 52 53

Certifications/Signatures 54

A signed certification is required for all appraisal and appraisal review reports. An appraiser who signs any part of a report, including a letter of transmittal, must also sign a certification. 55 56

A signed certification provides important disclosures about aspects of the assignment. It provides evidence that the appraiser is aware of the ethical obligations of acting as an appraiser. In single-discipline appraisals, a certification also attests that the analyses, opinions, and conclusions expressed are those of the signatory. A certification is also where significant appraisal assistance from others not signing a certification must be acknowledged. Any appraiser who provides significant appraisal or appraisal review assistance in the assignment must sign a certification or be identified in a certification. When more than one appraiser is involved in an assignment, USPAP allows for certification in a variety of ways, including: 57 58 59 60 61 62 63

- all appraisers could sign a certification accepting responsibility for the entirety of the analyses and the report if they are all competent to do so; or 64 65
- one appraiser could sign a certification and provide the name of each individual who provided significant appraisal or appraisal review assistance. In such a case, the exact nature of the assistance must be reported, but this need not be in a certification; or 66 67 68
- for assignments involving multiple disciplines (e.g., real property appraisal and personal property appraisal), an appraiser could sign a certification accepting responsibility only for the elements of the certification, assignment results and report contents applicable to the appraiser's discipline; or 69 70 71
- for personal property assignments involving multiple appraisers with different specialties (e.g., antiques, fine art, gems and jewelry, machinery and equipment) an appraiser could sign a certification accepting responsibility only for the elements of the certification, assignment results, and report contents specific to the appraiser's specialty. 72 73 74 75

Significant Appraisal Assistance 76

Assistance is related to the appraisal process and requires appraisal competency. Therefore, only those acting as an appraiser sign a certification, or are identified as providing significant appraisal assistance in a certification. Examples of significant appraisal assistance may include: 77 78 79

- research and selection of comparable properties and data; 80
- inspection of the subject property and comparable properties; 81
- estimating accrued depreciation; or 82
- forecasting income and expenses. 83

An appraiser often uses assistance that does not constitute significant appraisal assistance. Although it is the responsibility of the appraiser to determine the role of any individual providing assistance, tasks such as, but not limited to, writing down measurements the appraiser provides when measuring a structure, taking photographs of the subject property, and providing clerical duties are not considered significant appraisal assistance. 84 85 86 87

An appraiser providing assistance must comply with those parts of USPAP that apply to the assistance that he or she provides. So, for example, if an appraiser's assistance includes only developing a cost approach in a real property appraisal assignment, that appraiser must comply with the applicable Rules (i.e., the ETHICS RULE, etc.), Standards Rules 1-1, 1-3, 1-4(b) and any other applicable sections of Standards Rule 1-4, and Standards Rule 1-6(a). 88 89 90 91

© The Appraisal Foundation

Illustrations:

Workfile Obligations When Trainee Signs the Report

1. Jennifer is currently being trained as an appraiser (a trainee) working toward her state license as a real property appraiser. Her work includes completing and co-signing appraisal reports with her supervising appraiser. Must she keep a copy of the workfile for every assignment she works on?

   If Jennifer acted as an appraiser in the assignment, USPAP provides two options: 1) she can maintain custody of the workfile, either the original or a copy; or 2) she can make appropriate access arrangements for the retention period, for example, with her employer or supervising appraiser.

   Some common scenarios in such an assignment may include the trainee appraiser and the supervising appraiser each keeping a copy of the workfile. Or, the supervising appraiser may retain custody of the workfile and provide for access by the trainee appraiser. Both of these arrangements meet the record keeping requirements.

Certification Requirements When Trainee Does Not Sign the Report

2. Using the same scenario from Illustration 1 except only the senior appraiser signs the report and **not** the trainee appraiser, what certification requirements must each appraiser meet to comply with USPAP?

   USPAP states that when a signing appraiser relies on work done by others who do not sign a certification, the signing appraiser is responsible for the decision to rely on the trainee appraiser's work.

   The name of the trainee appraiser who provided significant assistance, but does not sign a certification, must be stated in a certification. It is not required that the description of the assistance appear in a certification, but the extent of the assistance must be set forth in the report as required in STANDARDS 2, 4, 6, 8 and 10.

Possession of Workfiles

3. An appraiser is an employee of an appraisal firm. The firm has announced that the office is moving to another city. All appraisers not moving to the new location have been asked to turn over their workfiles to the company. The appraiser believes that he is required to keep the workfiles. Who is correct?

   The RECORD KEEPING RULE does not mandate that an appraiser have possession of assignment workfiles. Employment contracts and other employment arrangements often require appraisers to leave their workfiles with an employer should the appraiser leave that firm, or in other situations. However, if an appraiser must relinquish actual possession of the workfiles, the appraiser must establish appropriate access arrangements for the length of the retention period. In the circumstances described, another solution may be for the appraiser to obtain permission from the employer to make copies of his or her workfiles.

4. Jonathan is a trainee appraiser who has been working with the same supervising appraiser for some time. Recently, his supervising appraiser told him that since he was only a trainee, he had no right to access workfiles on appraisals where he had provided significant professional assistance. Is the supervising appraiser correct? Do trainees have any rights regarding access to workfiles?

   The supervising appraiser is not correct. USPAP places workfile retention requirements on the **appraiser**. Jonathan, since he is acting as an appraiser, is an appraiser as defined in USPAP. In assignments where more than one appraiser is involved (e.g. a trainee appraiser and a supervising appraiser) each appraiser shares responsibility for complying with the RECORD KEEPING RULE.

   Supervising appraisers should be aware that all appraisers, including trainee appraisers, must maintain access to workfiles for a minimum of five years. A supervising appraiser must not impede a trainee appraiser's ability to access a workfile under the following conditions:

   - submission to state appraiser regulatory agencies;
   - compliance with due process of law;
   - submission to a duly authorized professional peer review committee; or
   - compliance with retrieval arrangements.

   Denying access to a workfile that the trainee worked on is a violation of the ETHICS RULE.

   An individual appraiser employed by a group or organization that conducts itself in a manner

© The Appraisal Foundation

that does not conform to these Standards should take steps that are appropriate under the circumstances to ensure compliance with the Standards. 139 140

Acknowledging Significant Appraisal Assistance 141

5. Matthew, an appraiser, is working with a more senior appraiser on a complex appraisal assignment. His only task has been to develop the income approach based on information provided by the senior appraiser. What is the appropriate way to acknowledge Matthew's role in the assignment? 142 143 144

   Since Matthew's work is limited to part of the assignment, signing a certification accepting responsibility for the entire assignment would not be appropriate. USPAP requires that Matthew be named in a certification, and the nature of his significant assistance summarized in the report. 145 146 147

6. Margaret is performing a specific portion of a complex appraisal assignment, but is not competent to complete the entire assignment. As part of her training, she read the report and discussed it with the senior appraiser. Having now expanded her knowledge of the assignment, she wants to sign a certification along with the senior appraiser on the project. Is this appropriate? 148 149 150 151

   No. By signing a certification, she would be accepting full responsibility for all elements of a certification, for the assignment results, and for the contents of the appraisal report. Although she was competent to perform her assigned task, reading the report and discussing it with the senior appraiser does not confer competence. Therefore, she cannot accept full responsibility for the assignment results or sign a certification. 152 153 154 155

7. I am an appraiser trainee in a large firm. We recently transmitted a report to a client for an appraisal in which I provided significant professional assistance. The report stated that I assisted in all aspects of the process and I was named in the certification. The client's reviewer sent me a request that said, "If you assisted in all aspects of the appraisal you should sign it because you are an appraiser." The principal appraiser who signed the report feels it looks better if only he signs because I am unlicensed. For this assignment, there is no law or regulation that prohibits me from signing a certification. What should I do? 156 157 158 159 160 161

   The unlicensed appraiser should discuss the situation with the principal appraiser in this instance as USPAP allows for certification in a variety of ways. The principal appraiser elected to acknowledge the significant professional assistance of the appraiser trainee in a certification rather than allowing her to sign. The exact nature of the assistance must also be reported but it does not have to be stated in a certification. The specific portions of the assignment that the appraiser trainee completed should have been summarized in the report, rather than just a statement simply indicating the appraiser trainee assisted in all aspects of the assignment. 162 163 164 165 166 167

© The Appraisal Foundation

ADVISORY OPINION 32 (AO-32)

This communication by the Appraisal Standards Board (ASB) does not establish new standards or interpret existing standards. Advisory Opinions are issued to illustrate the applicability of appraisal standards in specific situations and to offer advice from the ASB for the resolution of appraisal issues and problems.

SUBJECT: Ad Valorem Property Tax Appraisal and Mass Appraisal Assignments

APPLICATION: Real Property, Personal Property

THE ISSUE:

Ad valorem is Latin for "according to value." In ad valorem taxation assignments, the appraisal or mass appraisal is used to establish a value basis for a political subdivision's tax burden. This guidance is provided to address the application of USPAP to appraisal and mass appraisal assignments for ad valorem taxation.

As used in this Advisory Opinion, "appraisal assignments" are those covered by STANDARDS 1 and 2 or STANDARDS 7 and 8. "Mass appraisal assignments" are those covered by STANDARDS 5 and 6.

ADVICE FROM THE ASB ON THE ISSUE:

Application of Standards

Ad valorem taxation assignments include both appraisal assignments and mass appraisal assignments.

- STANDARDS 1 and 2 address the requirements for development of an appraisal and reporting of appraisal results for a particular real property interest as of a given date.
- STANDARDS 5 and 6 address the requirements for the development of a mass appraisal and reporting of mass appraisal results for real property and personal property. Mass appraisal is the valuation of a universe of properties (many properties) as of a given date using standard methodology, employing common data, and allowing for statistical testing. Mass appraisal provides for a systematic approach and uniform application of appraisal methods and techniques to obtain estimates of values that allow for statistical review and analysis of results.
- STANDARDS 7 and 8 address the requirements for development of an appraisal and reporting of appraisal results for a particular personal property interest as of a given date.

The keys to distinguishing a mass appraisal are: 1) the subject of the appraisal is a "universe" of properties, meaning more than one property; and 2) the assignment involves standard methodology employing common data that allows for statistical testing. These models may be based on the cost approach, the income approach, the sales comparison approach or any combination of these approaches to value.

Identification of Intended Users

In ad valorem taxation assignments, the client is typically the government or taxing authority that engages the appraiser. As defined in USPAP, the client is an intended user. Through communication with the client, the appraiser may identify other intended users. A party receiving a copy of a report in order to satisfy disclosure requirements does not become an intended user of the appraisal or mass appraisal unless the appraiser identifies such party as an intended user.

Scope of Work

The determination of an appropriate scope of work in all appraisal and mass appraisal assignments, including ad valorem taxation assignments, is based on problem identification. The assignment elements necessary for problem identification are identified in Standards Rule 1-2 (real property appraisal), Standards Rule 5-2 (real property and personal property mass appraisal) and Standards Rule 7-2 (personal property appraisal). This information provides the appraiser with the basis for determining the scope of work necessary to develop credible assignment results.

In ad valorem taxation assignments, applicable laws and regulations of an assessing jurisdiction may define the assignment elements needed for problem identification. For example, the type and definition of value is usually established by statute, as is the effective date of the appraiser's opinions and conclusions (tax year, levy year, valuation date, etc.). Whatever the source of the assignment elements needed for problem identification, the appraiser must identify the problem to be solved, and determine and perform the scope of work necessary to develop credible assignment results.

© The Appraisal Foundation

In the interests of equity, the scope of work in mass appraisal assignments for ad valorem taxation can include consideration of appraisal level (the overall proximity between appraised values and actual prices) and the uniformity of property values (equity within groups of like properties). Standard Rule 5-1 (a) states:

> *In developing a mass appraisal, an appraiser must: (a) be aware of, understand, and correctly employ those recognized methods and techniques necessary to produce a credible mass appraisal;*

The appraiser is responsible for recognizing when the concepts of appraisal level and appraisal uniformity are necessary for credible assignment results in a mass appraisal assignment for ad valorem taxation.

Reporting

Standards Rules 6-1 and 6-2 address the requirements for reporting mass appraisal results for real property and personal property. The Mass Appraisal Report must clearly communicate the elements, results, opinions, and value conclusions of the mass appraisal. In mass appraisals for ad valorem taxation, local statutes may prescribe additional reporting requirements and procedures for the delivery of the assignment results.

In mass appraisal, the value opinion for each property is developed using the standard methods applied in the mass appraisal model for a universe of properties. There may be many mass appraisal models used to value an entire universe of properties. An individual property record or worksheet may describe the valuation of the specific property after the application of the mass appraisal model. A written report of the mass appraisal as described in Standards Rule 6-2 is not provided for each individual property. To understand the individual property result developed in a mass appraisal requires the examination of all the information and analysis required by Standards Rule 6-2.

STANDARDS 2 and 8 address the requirements for reporting of appraisal results for real property and personal property (respectively). The written report must be presented in an Appraisal Report or Restricted Appraisal Report.

An appraiser may be asked to communicate the assignment results for a single property that was appraised as part of a mass appraisal assignment. USPAP does not address this specific circumstance. The reporting requirements of STANDARD 2 apply to appraisal assignments developed under STANDARD 1 and do not apply to mass appraisal assignments prepared under STANDARD 6. However, the second sentence of the PREAMBLE states: *It is essential that appraisers develop and communicate their analyses, opinions, and conclusions to intended users of their services in a manner that is meaningful and not misleading.* Additionally, the ETHICS RULE states: *An appraiser must not communicate assignment results with the intent to mislead or defraud.* The ETHICS RULE also states: *An appraiser must not use or communicate a report that is known by the appraiser to be misleading or fraudulent.* Therefore, if an appraiser communicates mass appraisal or assignment results for a single property, the communication must be meaningful and must not be misleading.

In assignments for ad valorem taxation, public policy may direct property owner notification of the property values rendered as a result of a mass appraisal. Notifications are commonly required within the jurisdiction to meet due process requirements. These property owner notifications are not "reports" as defined in USPAP. Further, a party receiving a notification in order to satisfy disclosure requirements does not become an intended user unless the appraiser identifies such party as an intended user as part of the assignment.

Workfile Requirements

The RECORD KEEPING RULE requirement to prepare a workfile applies to appraisals and mass appraisals performed for ad valorem taxation assignments. An appraiser's assignment workfile preserves evidence of the appraiser's compliance with USPAP and other information as may be required to support the appraiser's opinions and conclusions.

For a mass appraisal assignment, compliance with the RECORD KEEPING RULE requires a workfile for the mass appraisal assignment, not a workfile for each property in the mass appraisal. The workfile for a mass appraisal contains the information to support the valuation of all properties in the mass appraisal. This supporting material may be documented in any form of media, including electronic files, and includes such items as property records, market data, sales ratios and other statistical studies, appraisal manuals and documentation, market studies, model building documentation, regulations, statutes, property photos, sketches, aerial imagery, maps, automated mapping and geographic information systems, worksheets, spreadsheets, and analysis reports. USPAP does not dictate the form or format of workfile documentation. There is no requirement that the contents of the workfile be held in a single location.

The retention of the workfile in support of an assignment for ad valorem taxation is governed by USPAP and may also be subject to retention schedules in the jurisdictions. The record retention time frames referenced in the RECORD KEEPING

© The Appraisal Foundation

96 RULE are minimums. Retention beyond the USPAP requirements is permitted. Unless compelled by law or regulation,
97 USPAP does not permit appraisers to destroy records prior to five years after preparation **for any reason**.

98 **JURISDICTIONAL EXCEPTION RULE**

99 The JURISDICTIONAL EXCEPTION RULE exempts appraisers from the part or parts of USPAP that are precluded by
100 the law or regulation of a particular jurisdiction. If compliance with a part of USPAP is precluded by any applicable
101 federal, state, or local law or regulation, only that part shall be of no force and effect in that assignment. Appraisers
102 using the JURISDICTIONAL EXCEPTION RULE must properly disclose the legal authority justifying the exemption of
103 part or parts of USPAP that are precluded by law.

104 Use of the JURISDICTIONAL EXCEPTION RULE is triggered by a contradiction between the requirements of USPAP
105 and the law or regulations of a jurisdiction, not by client or appraiser discretion.

106 USPAP does not establish who or which assignments must comply. Therefore, the JURISDICTIONAL EXCEPTION
107 RULE cannot be applied to the decision to comply with USPAP.

108 An individual's identification as an appraiser is the basis for determining who should comply with USPAP. This is
109 because an individual's public identification as an appraiser establishes an expectation that valuation services will
110 be performed in compliance with USPAP. An individual must comply with USPAP when required by law, regulation,
111 or agreement. Even if the governing authority's policy does not require USPAP compliance, other applicable law or
112 regulation might require compliance.

113 **Illustrations:**

114 1. An appraiser is in the process of developing appraisals for the next year's tax roll. The residential properties,
115 condominiums, and general commercial and major commercial properties will be valued with a mass appraisal
116 model. Which development standards apply?

117 Because the subject of the appraisal is a universe of properties, and because they are being appraised with a
118 mass appraisal model, STANDARD 5 applies to the development portion of a mass appraisal assignment and
119 STANDARD 6 applies to the reporting portion.

120 2. An appraiser has completed a mass appraisal for ad valorem taxation using a mass appraisal model. There is
121 a special use property for which it has been determined that the mass appraisal model is not appropriate. This
122 property will be appraised as an individual property. Which development standard applies to the appraisal of the
123 special use property?

124 Even though the special use property is being appraised for ad valorem taxation, STANDARD 1 would apply
125 because the subject is an individual property, not a universe of properties.

126 3. An assessment appeal is in process, and an appraisal of an individual property is being conducted as part of that
127 appeal. Which development standards apply?

128 STANDARD 1 or STANDARD 7 would apply because an individual property is being appraised rather than a
129 universe of properties.

130 4. An appraiser is conducting a mass appraisal for ad valorem taxation. A property record card is produced for each
131 property. Is each property record card considered a report under STANDARD 6?

132 No. The property record card is not the mass appraisal report; it is only a portion of the information and
133 analysis supporting the mass appraisal.

134 5. The Comment to Standards Rule 5-5 (a)(v) requires an appraiser conducting a mass appraisal assignment to take
135 reasonable steps to ensure that the quantity and quality of the factual data that are collected are sufficient to
136 produce credible appraisals. What are some examples of these steps?

137 In real property, where applicable and feasible, systems for routinely collecting and maintaining ownership,
138 geographic, sales, income and expense, cost, and property characteristics data must be established.

139 Geographic data must be contained in as complete a set of cadastral maps as possible, compiled according
140 to current standards of detail and accuracy. Sales data must be collected, confirmed, screened, adjusted,
141 and filed according to current standards of practice. The sales file must contain, for each sale, property

© The Appraisal Foundation

characteristics data that are contemporaneous with the date of sale. Property characteristics data must be appropriate and relevant to the mass appraisal models being used. The property characteristics data file must contain data contemporaneous with the date of appraisal including historical data on sales, where appropriate and available. 142 143 144 145

The data collection program must incorporate a quality control program, including checks and audits of the data to ensure current and consistent records. 146 147

© The Appraisal Foundation

ADVISORY OPINION 33 (AO-33)

1 *This communication by the Appraisal Standards Board (ASB) does not establish new standards or interpret existing*
2 *standards. Advisory Opinions are issued to illustrate the applicability of appraisal standards in specific situations and*
3 *to offer advice from the ASB for the resolution of appraisal issues and problems.*

4 **SUBJECT: Discounted Cash Flow Analysis**

5 **APPLICATION: Real Property**

6 **THE ISSUE:**
7 Discounted cash flow (DCF) analysis is an accepted analytical tool and method of valuation within the income
8 approach to value. DCF analysis is typically utilized to identify the potential for profit or return on an investment.
9 Because it is dependent on the analysis of uncertain future events, it is vulnerable to misuse or misapplication. What
10 steps can the appraiser take to comply with USPAP in completing a DCF analysis?

11 **BACKGROUND:**
12 DCF analysis can be employed when valuing a variety of asset types. DCF techniques may be applied in the
13 valuation or analysis of proposed construction, land development, condominium development or conversion,
14 rehabilitation development, and income-producing assets of various types. DCF analysis has become a requirement
15 of many real property clients and other intended users. These users of appraisal services favor the inclusion of DCF
16 analysis as a management tool in projecting cash flow and return expectations, capital requirements, refinancing
17 opportunities, and timing of future property dispositions. DCF analysis is regarded as one of the best methods of
18 replicating steps taken to reach many investor buy/sell/hold decisions and is often a part of the exercise of due
19 diligence in the evaluation of an asset.

20 DCF methodology is based on the principle of anticipation - i.e., value is created by the anticipation of future
21 benefits. DCF analysis reflects investment criteria and requires the appraiser to make rational and supportable
22 assumptions. DCF analysis can be used for investment value and market value appraisals, as well as for other
23 purposes such as sensitivity tests.

24 DCF analysis is a tool available to the appraiser and is often applied in developing value opinions in concert with
25 one or more other approaches. However, in certain circumstances it may be the most credible method to solve the
26 valuation problem. This Advisory Opinion focuses on the criteria for proper DCF analysis and does not imply that DCF
27 analysis is or should necessarily be the only method employed.

28 The COMPETENCY RULE specifically states that competency may apply to an analytical method. Discounted
29 cash flow analysis is complex and requires specialized education and experience to achieve competency in its
30 application. In addition, due to the complexity and the potential for misuse of technology, it also requires a high
31 degree of care and diligence.

32 **ADVICE FROM THE ASB ON THE ISSUE:**
33 To avoid misuse or misunderstanding when DCF analysis is used in an appraisal assignment to develop an opinion
34 of market value, it is the responsibility of the appraiser to ensure that the controlling input is consistent with market
35 evidence and prevailing market attitudes. Market value DCF analyses should be supported by market derived data,
36 and the assumptions should be both market and property specific. Appraisal assignments that require the appraiser
37 to employ assumptions that are not based on market data, or to use assumptions provided by the client do not reflect
38 market value but rather investment value.

39 Market value DCF analyses, along with available factual data, are intended to reflect the expectations and perceptions
40 of market participants. They should be judged on the support for the forecasts that existed when made, not on whether
41 specific items in the forecasts are realized at a later date. An appraisal report that includes the results of DCF analysis
42 must clearly state and accurately disclose the assumptions on which the analysis is based (per Standards Rule 2-1) and
43 must set forth the relevant data used in the analysis.

44 Standards Rule 1-1 states that the appraiser must not commit a substantial error of omission or commission that
45 significantly affects an appraisal. Standards Rule 1-1 states that the appraiser must not render appraisal services in
46 a careless or negligent manner, such as making a series of errors that, although individually might not significantly

© The Appraisal Foundation

affect the results of an appraisal, in the aggregate would affect the credibility of those results. These Standards Rules are significant for DCF analysis because of the potential for the compounding effect of errors in the input, unrealistic assumptions, or possible programming errors.

Computer printouts showing the results of DCF analysis may be generated by readily available means such as an appraiser's own spreadsheet, a commercially available spreadsheet template, or specialized DCF software. Regardless of the method chosen the appraiser is responsible for the entire analysis including the controlling input, the calculations, and the resulting output. If using commercial DCF software the appraiser should cite the name and version of the software and provide a brief description of any assumptions and/or methodology unique to that software, if any. Standards Rule 1-4 requires that projections of anticipated future rent and/or income potential and expenses be based on reasonably clear and appropriate evidence.

DCF accounts for and reflects those items and forces that affect the revenue, expenses, and ultimate earning capacity of an asset and represents a forecast of events that would be considered likely within a specific market. For example, in the appraisal of a multi-tenant property, a lease-by-lease analysis addresses contract and market rents, specific escalations, operating expenses, pass-through provisions, market-derived or specific concessions, capital expenditures, and any other measurable specific provisions applicable. Revenue growth rate or decline rate assumptions are premised on analysis of supply/demand factors and other economic conditions and trends within the market area of the subject. Operating expense change rates should reflect both overall expense trends and the specific trend of significant expense items.

Discount rates applied to cash flows and estimates of reversion should be derived from data and information in the real estate and capital markets. Surveys of investor opinion and yield indices are also useful in the rate selection process, but only when the type of and market for the asset being appraised is consistent with the type of and market for the asset typically acquired by the investors interviewed in the survey. Primary considerations used in the selection of rates are risk, inflation, and real rates of return.

When reversion capitalization rates are used, they should reflect investor expectations considering the asset type, physical characteristics, age and condition, cash flow projections, and related factors. The projection or forecast period is a variable and should be based upon the same factors that typical market participants are using. The results of DCF analysis should be tested and checked for errors and reasonableness. Because of the compounding effects in the projection of income and expenses, even slight input errors can be magnified and can produce unreasonable results. For example, it is good practice to test whether cash flows are changing at reasonable rates and to compare the reversion capitalization rate with the inferred going-in capitalization rate to see if the relationship between these rates is reasonable.

STANDARD 2 requires the appraiser to communicate each analysis, opinion, and conclusion in a manner that is not misleading. Appraisals using the DCF method in the income capitalization approach may contain computerized projections of itemized future cash flow supported by exhaustive printouts that can be misleading. The seeming precision of computer-generated projections may give the appearance of certainty to projections and forecasts that are actually variable within a wide range. In DCF analysis, all of the assumptions (growth rates, decline rates, rental rates, discount rates, financing terms, expense trends, capitalization rates, etc.) directly affect the conclusion and must be clearly and accurately disclosed in the appraisal report.

SUMMARY:

- Use of DCF analysis requires specialized knowledge and experience. Its application requires a high degree of diligence.
- DCF analysis is a tool available to the appraiser and is often applied in developing value opinions in concert with one or more other approaches. It is the responsibility of the appraiser to ensure that the controlling input is consistent with market evidence and prevailing market attitudes. The appraiser is also responsible for the resulting output.
- Market value DCF analyses should be supported by market-derived data and the assumptions should be both market- and property-specific.
- Appraisal assignments that require the appraiser to employ assumptions that are not based on market data or assumptions provided by the client, are not market value but rather investment value.
- If using commercial DCF software the appraiser should cite the name and version of the software and provide a brief description of any assumptions and/or methodology unique to that software, if any.
- DCF accounts for and reflects those items and forces that impact the revenue, expenses, and ultimate earning capacity of an asset and represents a forecast of events that would be considered likely within a specific market.
- The results of DCF analysis should be tested and checked for errors and reasonableness.

© The Appraisal Foundation

ADVISORY OPINION 34 (AO-34)

1 *This communication by the Appraisal Standards Board (ASB) does not establish new standards or interpret existing*
2 *standards. Advisory Opinions are issued to illustrate the applicability of appraisal standards in specific situations and*
3 *to offer advice from the ASB for the resolution of appraisal issues and problems.*

4 **SUBJECT: Retrospective and Prospective Value Opinions**

5 **APPLICATION: Real Property, Personal Property**

6 **THE ISSUE:**
7 Two dates are essential to an appraisal report. Standards Rules 2-2(a)(vii) and (b)(ix), 6-2(d), 8-2(a)(vii) and (b)(ix)
8 require that each appraisal report state the effective date of the appraisal and the date of the report. The date of
9 the report indicates the perspective from which the appraiser is examining the market. The effective date of the
10 appraisal establishes the context for the value opinion. Three categories of effective dates - retrospective, current, or
11 prospective - may be used, according to the intended use of the appraisal assignment.

12 How should the appraisal be communicated when either a retrospective or prospective date is used so that the report
13 is not misleading?

14 **BACKGROUND:**
15 Current appraisals occur when the effective date of the appraisal is contemporaneous with the date of the report.
16 Because most appraisals require current value opinions, the importance of specifying both the date of the report and
17 the effective date of the analysis is sometimes lost.

18 Retrospective appraisals (effective date of the appraisal prior to the date of the report) may be required for property
19 tax matters, estate or inheritance tax matters, condemnation proceedings, suits to recover damages, and other
20 similar situations.

21 Prospective appraisals (effective date of the appraisal subsequent to the date of the report) may be required for
22 valuations of property interests related to proposed developments, as the basis for value at the end of a cash flow
23 projection, and for other reasons.

24 **ADVICE FROM THE ASB ON THE ISSUE:**
25 **<u>Relevant USPAP References</u>**

26 Standards Rules 2-1, 6-1, and 8-1 state that each written or oral appraisal report must: "clearly and accurately set forth
27 the appraisal in a manner that will not be misleading..." In order to accomplish this, appraisers must use care when
28 developing the appraisal to analyze appropriate market data when retrospective or prospective opinions of value are
29 a part of the assignment.

30 **<u>Retrospective Appraisals</u>**
31 The use of clear and concise language and appropriate terminology in appraisal reports helps to eliminate misleading
32 reports. To avoid confusion, the appraiser must clearly establish the date to which the value opinion applies. In
33 retrospective value opinions, use of a modifier for the term market value and past verb tenses increases clarity. If
34 a report written in 2017 states, "On August 19, 2009 the value was $X", the retrospective perspective is clear from
35 the context. It would also be correct to state that "the retrospective value as of August 19, 2009 is $X" because
36 on August 19, 2009, the value opinion would not have been retrospective – it is retrospective because it has been
37 developed now and looks back. The use of an appropriate qualifier is necessary for clear understanding.

38 A retrospective appraisal is complicated by the fact that the appraiser already knows what occurred in the market
39 after the effective date of the appraisal. Data subsequent to the effective date may be considered in developing a
40 retrospective value as a confirmation of trends that would reasonably be considered by a buyer or seller as of that date.
41 The appraiser should determine a logical cut-off for the data to be used in the analysis because at some point distant
42 from the effective date, the subsequent data will no longer provide an accurate representation of market conditions as of
43 the effective date. This is a difficult determination to make. Studying the market conditions as of the date of the appraisal
44 assists the appraiser in judging where to make this cut-off. With market evidence that data subsequent to the effective
45 date was consistent with market expectations as of the effective date, the subsequent data should be used. In

© The Appraisal Foundation

the absence of such evidence, the effective date should be used as the cut-off date for data considered by the appraiser. 46 47

When direct excerpts from then-current appraisal reports prepared at the time of the retrospective effective date are available and appropriate, they may help the appraiser and the intended users understand market conditions as of the retrospective effective date. 48 49 50

Prospective Appraisals 51

The use of clear and concise language and appropriate terminology in appraisal reports helps to eliminate misleading reports. To avoid confusion, the appraiser must clearly establish the date to which the value opinion applies. In prospective value opinions, use of the term "market value" without a modifier such as "forecasted" or "prospective" and without future verb tenses is improper (i.e., "...the prospective market value is expected to be..." and not "...the market value is..."). 52 53 54 55 56

Prospective value opinions, along with available factual data, are intended to reflect the current expectations and perceptions of market participants. They should be judged on the support for the forecasts that existed when made, not on whether specific items in the forecasts are realized at a later date. 57 58 59

When prospective value opinions are required with regard to proposed improvements to real property, the Comment to Standards Rule 1-2(e) regarding identification of the extent and character of the proposed improvements and Standards Rule 1-4(c)(iv) regarding the basis for anticipated future rent and expenses are relevant. Evidence that proposed improvements can be completed by the effective date of the appraisal is important. Support for projected income and expenses at the time of completion of proposed improvements and during the rent-up or sell-out period require the incorporation of sufficient market research in the appraisal and the consideration of existing and future competition. It is appropriate to study comparable projects for evidence of construction periods, development costs, income and expense levels, and absorption. Items such as rental concessions, commissions, tenant finish allowances, add-on factors, and expense pass-throughs must be studied to develop realistic income expectancy. 60 61 62 63 64 65 66 67 68

With regard to proposed developments of real property, two prospective value opinions may be required: one as of the time the development is to be completed and one as of the time the development is projected to achieve stabilized occupancy. These prospective values form a basis for investment decisions and loan underwriting. 69 70 71

In a prospective appraisal, the appraiser analyzes market trends to provide support for forecasted income and expense or sell-out opinions, absorption periods, capitalization rates, and discount rates as of the effective date of the appraisal. Economic trends such as growth in population, employment, and future competition are also analyzed. The overall economic climate and variations in the business cycle should be considered and weighed in the performance of the appraisal process. All value conclusions should include reference to the time frame when the analysis was prepared to clearly delineate the market conditions and the point of reference from which the appraiser developed the prospective value opinion. It is essential to clearly and accurately disclose any appropriate assumptions, extraordinary assumptions, and/or limiting conditions when citing the market conditions from which the prospective value opinion was made. 72 73 74 75 76 77 78 79 80

© The Appraisal Foundation

ADVISORY OPINION 35 (AO-35)

1 *This communication by the Appraisal Standards Board (ASB) does not establish new standards or interpret existing*
2 *standards. Advisory Opinions are issued to illustrate the applicability of appraisal standards in specific situations and*
3 *to offer advice from the ASB for the resolution of appraisal issues and problems.*

4 **SUBJECT: Reasonable Exposure Time in Real Property and Personal Property Opinions of Value**

5 **APPLICATION: Real Property, Personal Property**

6 **THE ISSUE:**
7 The concept of exposure time has an important role in the appraisal process. When reasonable exposure time is a
8 component of the definition of value, appraisers must develop an opinion of the reasonable exposure time linked to
9 the value opinion.

10 **BACKGROUND:**
11 Reasonable exposure time is one of a series of conditions in most market value definitions. Exposure time is always
12 presumed to precede the effective date of the appraisal.

13 **Relevant USPAP and Advisory References**
14 • DEFINITIONS, specifically the definition of EXPOSURE TIME: *an opinion, based on supporting market data, of*
15 *the length of time that the property interest being appraised would have been offered on the market prior to*
16 *the hypothetical consummation of a sale at market value on the effective date of the appraisal.*
17 • The Comments to Standards Rules 1-2(c) and 7-2(c) which states: *When reasonable exposure time is a*
18 *component of the definition for the value opinion being developed, the appraiser must also develop an*
19 *opinion of reasonable exposure time linked to that value opinion.*
20 • The Comments to Standards Rules Rules 2-2(a)(vi) and 2-2(b)(viii) which states: *When an opinion of*
21 *reasonable exposure time has been developed in compliance with Standards Rule 1-2(c), the opinion must*
22 *be stated in the report.*
23 • Similar Comments appear in Standards Rules 8-2(a)(vi) and 8-2(b)(viii).

24 How is the opinion of reasonable exposure time developed? Is it presumed to occur prior to or starting from the
25 effective date of the appraisal?

26 **ADVICE FROM THE ASB ON THE ISSUE:**
27 Exposure time is different for various types of property and under various market conditions. It is noted that the overall
28 concept of reasonable exposure encompasses not only adequate, sufficient, and reasonable time but also adequate,
29 sufficient, and reasonable effort.

30 The fact that exposure time is always presumed to occur prior to the effective date of the appraisal is substantiated
31 by related facts in the appraisal process: supply/demand conditions as of the effective date of the appraisal; the use
32 of current cost information; the analysis of historical sales information (sold after exposure and after completion of
33 negotiations between the seller and buyer); and the analysis of future income expectancy projected from the effective
34 date of the appraisal.

35 **The Importance of Exposure Time**
36 The answer to the question "what is reasonable exposure time," should always incorporate the answers to the
37 question "for what kind of property at what value range," rather than appear as a statement of an isolated time period.

38 Take for example an appraisal of a desirable mountainside second home. In this immediate resort neighborhood,
39 these homes often sell for upwards of $1,000,000 and average 120 to 180 days to sell. Research reveals that overall
40 the community generally has an average exposure time of 60 to 90 days and that home values are typically below
41 $300,000. The appraiser must be certain that research is based upon locations, price ranges and overall appeal
42 similar to the subject property. Failure to do so may impact the appraiser's ability to deliver credible results.

43 An analysis of exposure time also impacts comparable selection. If a particular property sold faster than one
44 would expect, the appraiser must investigate whether this property was underpriced or if the buyer or seller were

© The Appraisal Foundation

highly motivated. The opposite is true when it took much longer than market evidence would suggest. Apparent inconsistencies such as these may also provide vital insight into changes in the market, neighborhood, and the subject property's appeal within the market in general. 45 46 47

These sales may not reflect the conditions requisite to the requirement of the definition of market value. Failure of the appraiser to investigate these circumstances may impact the appraiser's ability to deliver credible results. It is possible these sales can still be used with the application of appropriate adjustments. Nonetheless, this determination cannot be made without market research. 48 49 50 51

Rationale and Method for Developing an Opinion of Reasonable Exposure Time 52

The opinion of the time period for reasonable exposure is not intended to be a prediction of a date of sale. Instead, it is an integral part of the analyses conducted during the appraisal assignment. Sources that may be relied upon include one or more of the following: 53 54 55

- statistical information about days on market; 56
- information gathered through sales verification; 57
- interviews of market participants; and 58
- information from data collection services 59

Related information garnered through this process may include the identification of typical buyers and sellers for the type of property involved and typical equity investment levels and/or financing terms. 60 61

The opinion of reasonable exposure time may be expressed as a range (e.g., the appraiser's opinion of reasonable exposure time for the subject property is 90 to 120 days) or a specific number (e.g., the appraiser's opinion of reasonable exposure time for the subject property is 6 months). 62 63 64

The reasonable exposure period is a function of price, time, and use, not an isolated opinion of time alone. As an example, an office building, an important work of art, a fine jewel, a process facility, or an aircraft could have been on the market for two years at a price of $2,000,000, which informed market participants considered unreasonable. Then the owner lowered the price to $1,600,000 and started to receive offers, culminating in a transaction at $1,400,000 six months later. Although the actual exposure time was 2.5 years, the reasonable exposure time at a value range of $1,400,000 to $1,600,000 would be six months. The answer to the question, "what is reasonable exposure time," should always incorporate the answers to the question, "for what kind of property at what value range," rather than appear as a statement of an isolated time period. 65 66 67 68 69 70 71 72

Applications to Client Uses of an Appraisal 73

When an appraisal is commissioned as the result of a mortgage application after a potential seller and buyer enter into a Contract for Sale, no conflict exists between the presumption in the appraisal process that exposure time occurs prior to the effective date of the appraisal and the intended use of the appraisal. 74 75 76

Appraisers need to be aware that clients and other intended users often confuse exposure time with marketing time. A key difference is that exposure time is assumed to occur before the effective date, and marketing time occurs after the effective date. The misconception is easily understood because most sources of market information report historical information about days on market as "marketing time."[1] 77 78 79 80

When the value opinion developed is not predicated on reasonable exposure time, the appraiser's opinion of reasonable exposure time is not required. For example, many appraisals commissioned for employee relocation, asset evaluation, foreclosure, or asset management purposes require a value based on a client imposed limited marketing period. In these cases, the resulting opinion of value is usually not market value. Problems may arise when clients attempt to make business decisions or account for assets without understanding the difference between reasonable exposure time and marketing time (see related Advisory Opinion 7, *Marketing Time Opinions*). 81 82 83 84 85 86

Most residential appraisal report forms have a field in which the appraiser must enter an opinion of the neighborhood marketing time. However, most residential appraisal report forms do not have a field for which the appraiser must report the reasonable exposure time. In these cases, the appraiser must supplement the form to comply with USPAP. 87 88 89

1 See Advisory Opinion 7, *Marketing Time Opinions*

© The Appraisal Foundation

90 **SUMMARY:**

91 • The reasonable exposure time inherent in the market value concept is always presumed to precede the
92 effective date of the appraisal.
93 • Exposure time is different for various types of property and under various market conditions.
94 • Exposure time may be a single period of time or a range.
95 • Exposure time is dependent on the characteristics of the subject property and the market conditions as of the
96 effective date.
97 • When the client specifies a time period upon which the appraiser is to base the opinion of value, and that
98 period differs from the appraiser's opinion of a reasonable exposure time, the final opinion of value may not
99 be market value as typically defined.

© The Appraisal Foundation

ADVISORY OPINION 36 (AO-36)

This communication by the Appraisal Standards Board (ASB) does not establish new standards or interpret existing standards. Advisory Opinions are issued to illustrate the applicability of appraisal standards in specific situations and to offer advice from the ASB for the resolution of appraisal issues and problems. 1 2 3

SUBJECT: Identification and Disclosure of Client, Intended Use, and Intended Users 4

APPLICATION: Real Property, Personal Property, Intangible Property 5

THE ISSUE: 6
An appraiser must identify and consider the client, any other intended users, and the intended use of the appraiser's reported opinions and conclusions in order to identify the problem to be solved and to understand the appraiser's development and reporting responsibilities in an appraisal or appraisal review assignment. An appraiser must state the intended use and intended users of the opinions and conclusions in a report. 7 8 9 10

What kind of information must an appraiser identify and consider regarding the intended use and intended users in the course of accepting and completing an assignment, and how much of that information must an appraiser include in the report? 11 12 13

ADVICE FROM THE ASB ON THE ISSUE: 14
<u>Relevant USPAP and Advisory References</u> 15

The term "Client" is defined in the DEFINITIONS section of USPAP as: 16

> *the party or parties (i.e., individual, group, or entity) who engage an appraiser by employment or contract in a specific assignment, whether directly or through an agent.* 17 18

The term "Intended Use" is defined as: 19

> *the use(s) of an appraiser's reported appraisal or appraisal review assignment results, as identified by the appraiser based on communication with the client at the time of the assignment.* 20 21

The term "Intended User" is defined as: 22

> *The client and any other party as identified, by name or type, as users of the appraisal or appraisal review report by the appraiser, based on communication with the client at the time of the assignment.* 23 24

<u>Issues to be Addressed in the Development of the Appraisal</u> 25
An appraiser must identify the client and other intended users in order to properly define the problem and to understand the appraiser's responsibilities in an assignment. This is accomplished by communication with the client at the time of the engagement. 26 27 28

An appraiser should use care when identifying the client to avoid violations of the <u>Confidentiality</u> section of the ETHICS RULE. In instances where the client wishes to remain anonymous, the appraiser must still document the identity of the client in the workfile but may omit the client's identity in the appraisal or appraisal review report. The client may be identified as a person or entity, or as an agent of an intended user. When the identity of the client is withheld from the report, the report must state that the client's identity has been withheld at the client's request. 29 30 31 32 33

The appraiser is obligated to identify additional intended users by name only in a Restricted Appraisal Report. If identification by name, in an Appraisal Report, is not appropriate or practical, the appraiser may identify an intended user by type. 34 35 36

An appraiser's obligations to the client are established in the course of considering and accepting an engagement. If, during the assignment, an appraiser becomes aware of a change in the intended use, the appraiser must consider whether the extent of the development process and report content initially planned are still appropriate. If they are not, the appraiser must make the necessary changes. 37 38 39 40

© The Appraisal Foundation

41 An appraiser's obligations to other intended users may impose additional development and reporting requirements
42 in the assignment. Because an appraiser's obligations to other intended users may impose additional development
43 and reporting requirements in the assignment, it is essential to establish a clear understanding of the needs of all
44 intended users.

45 A party receiving a report copy from the client does not, as a consequence, become a party to the appraiser-client
46 relationship. Parties who receive a copy of an appraisal or appraisal review report as a consequence of disclosure
47 requirements applicable to an appraiser's client do not become intended users of the report unless they were
48 specifically identified as intended users by the appraiser at the time of the assignment.

49 **Disclosure of Client and Other Intended User(s) in an Appraisal or Appraisal Review Report**
50 Except when specifically requested by the client not to do so, an appraiser must state the identity of the client in the
51 report.

52 Within an Appraisal Report an appraiser may *state the identity* of other intended users, if any, by name or by type.
53 However, in a Restricted Appraisal Report, the appraiser must *state the name(s)* of non-client intended user(s). A
54 Restricted Appraisal Report is inappropriate for users only known and identified by type because they could be misled
55 by the abbreviated reporting format which may not contain supporting rationale for the opinions and conclusions. The
56 appraiser has an obligation to ensure that the report contains sufficient information to enable the intended users of
57 the appraisal to understand the report properly. This obligation cannot be fulfilled unless the intended users are only
58 the client and those other intended users specifically named by the appraiser.

59 The purpose of this reporting requirement is to (1) ensure that the client and other intended users can recognize their
60 relationship to the assignment and report, and (2) ensure that parties other than intended users will not mistakenly
61 assume that they are the client or an intended user. For example, a statement similar to the following may be
62 appropriate in an Appraisal Report:

63 *This report is intended for use only by (identify the client) and (identify any other intended users by*
64 *name or type). Use of this report by others is not intended by the appraiser.*

65 While a statement similar to the following may be appropriate in a Restricted Appraisal Report:

66 *This report is intended for use only by (identify the client) and (identify any other intended users by*
67 *name). Use of this report by others is not intended by the appraiser.*

68 If the client's identity is omitted from a report, the appraiser must (1) identify the client in the workfile, and (2) provide a
69 notice in the report that the identity of the client has been omitted in accordance with the client's request and that the
70 report is intended for use only by the client and any other identified intended users. In such cases, a statement similar
71 to the following may be appropriate in an Appraisal Report:

72 *This report is intended for use only by the client and (identify any other intended users by name or*
73 *type). Use of this report by others is not intended by the appraiser.*

74 While a statement similar to the following may be appropriate in a Restricted Appraisal Report:

75 *This report is intended for use only by the client and (identify any other intended users by name).*
76 *Use of this report by others is not intended by the appraiser.*

77 **Identification of the Intended Use in an Appraisal or Appraisal Review Assignment**
78 Identification of the intended use is one of the assignment elements necessary to properly identify the appraisal or
79 appraisal review problem. Identification of the intended use helps the appraiser and the client make two important
80 decisions about the assignment:

81 • the appropriate scope of work for the appraisal or appraisal review development process; and
82 • the level of detail to provide in the appraisal or appraisal review report.

83 **Disclosure of the Intended Use in an Appraisal or Appraisal Review Report**
84 An appraiser can avoid misleading parties in possession of an appraisal or appraisal review report by clearly
85 identifying the intended use in the report and stating that other uses are not intended. For example, a statement
86 similar to the following may be appropriate:

© The Appraisal Foundation

This report is intended only for use in (state the use). This report is not intended for any other use. 87

The intended use description provided in the statement must be specific to the assignment. Each of the following assignments involves the same subject property and the same type and definition of value. What changes are the intended use and intended users. 88 89 90

Illustrations: 91

1. A homeowner calls an appraiser and asks for an appraisal of the owner's home. The owner wants to determine how much equity is in the property. The owner is content to know the market value of his home in the form of a range of value. He does not want to pay for a written report or the time involved in a property inspection. The owner does not intend to give the appraisal to the lender because the owner knows the lender will order a new appraisal when a loan application is submitted. 92 93 94 95 96
2. The next week a lender calls the appraiser for a "drive-by appraisal" on the same property in connection with a home equity loan. The lender is happy with the owner's credit rating and plans to keep the loan in their portfolio. The lender sees very little risk in the transaction and seeks the appraiser's opinion of the property's market value based on an exterior inspection only. 97 98 99 100
3. Several months later an attorney for the wife asks the appraiser for an appraisal on the same property because the owners are getting a divorce. The attorney needs the appraiser to conduct a thorough inspection of the home and to provide an in-depth study of the sales of comparable homes in the market area making sure to verify the sales information with the buyers, real estate agents and the county recorder's office. The attorney wants the appraiser's report to contain a complete and exhaustive description of the subject property, the comparable sales, and of the analysis leading to the appraiser's opinion. 101 102 103 104 105 106

What is the impact of the different intended users on the scope of work in the three assignments? 107

In the first assignment, the client was the only intended user. In the second assignment, the lending institution that engaged the appraiser may not be the only intended user. In the third assignment, the attorney is the intended user. In the third assignment the intended use entails scrutiny of the report by the court and/or opposing counsel. When additional intended users are identified, the scope of work may increase. This is because the assignment results typically need to satisfy more objectives as the number of intended users increase. 108 109 110 111 112

What is the impact of the different intended use on the scope of work in the three assignments? 113

The objective of the appraisal in the first assignment was to establish a range of value so the owner could resolve a question about his equity. The owner was only interested in the appraiser's opinion and had no intention of reviewing the evidence or reasoning used to support the appraiser's opinion. In this case, the appraiser could develop an opinion of value without a property inspection, relying on an interview with the owner, assessment records, or other data to identify the property's relevant characteristics. Without personal inspection by the appraiser, however, such information is assumed to be correct. Because some of these assumptions will have a significant effect on the assignment results, the assignment will involve the use of extraordinary assumptions and require proper disclosure. 114 115 116 117 118 119 120

In the second assignment, the intended use requires a property inspection by the appraiser to gather some key information, though it also permits assumptions with respect to interior components of the subject property. The development process in this assignment is likely to be expanded by the lender's appraisal guidelines as well. 121 122 123

In the third assignment, the intended use requires a higher degree of inspection of the subject property and a more thorough verification and analysis of the comparable sales. The information gathered during these investigations may affect the analysis and may extend the development process beyond what is required in the other assignments. 124 125 126

PERSONAL PROPERTY AND INTANGIBLE PROPERTY 127

Changing the above illustrations' subject property from real property to an item or group of items of personal property (works of art, machinery, jewelry, etc.) or an interest in a business would not change the assignment's results, i.e., the impact of the different intended use and different intended users on the scope of work would still be the same, with possible differences of discipline-specific terminology. Therefore, Illustration #1 would involve an owner of the property seeking a range of value for the owner's own knowledge. Illustration #2 would involve some form of loan against the property, but at an amount that did not exceed some percentage of the value. Illustration #3 would involve a lawsuit in which the value of the property, or the value of the owner's interest in the business, is an important issue. 128 129 130 131 132 133 134

© The Appraisal Foundation

135 Illustration Conclusions
136 There are two important points to be made here. First, the needs of the client and other intended users established the
137 type of information and analysis required in the development and reporting process. Second, the intended use provided
138 the context for the depth of the analysis required in development and the level of detail required in reporting.

139 **SUMMARY:**

140 • An appraiser must identify the client and other intended users as part of the process of identifying
141 the intended use of an appraisal or appraisal review report, based on communication with the client.
142 • Identification of the intended use and intended users are necessary steps in determining the
143 appropriate scope of work.
144 • Whether or not assignment results are credible is measured in the context of the intended use of the
145 opinions and conclusions.
146 • An appraiser should use care when identifying the client to avoid violations of the Confidentiality
147 section of the ETHICS RULE.
148 • The appraiser's obligations to the client are established in the course of considering and accepting
149 an engagement.
150 • The appraiser's obligation to intended users other than the client is limited to addressing their
151 requirements as identified by the appraiser at the time of the assignment.
152 • Appraisers can avoid misleading parties in possession of a report by clearly identifying the intended
153 use and any intended users in the report and stating that other uses and/or users are not intended.
154 • Except when specifically requested not to do so as part of the agreement with the client, an appraiser
155 must disclose the identity of the client in the report.
156 • If the client's identity is withheld from a report, the appraiser must (1) document the identity of the
157 client in the workfile, and (2) provide a notice in the appraisal report that the identity of the client has
158 been omitted in accordance with the client's request.
159 • The report must state the intended use of the appraisal or appraisal review.
160 • The report must state the identity of any other intended user(s) by name or type in an Appraisal
161 Report, or in a Restricted Appraisal Report only by name.

© The Appraisal Foundation

ADVISORY OPINION 37 (AO-37)

This communication by the Appraisal Standards Board (ASB) does not establish new standards or interpret existing standards. Advisory Opinions are issued to illustrate the applicability of appraisal standards in specific situations and to offer advice from the ASB for the resolution of appraisal issues and problems.

SUBJECT: Computer Assisted Valuation Tools

APPLICATION: Real Property

THE ISSUE:
Appraisers rely upon market data as the basis for their opinions and conclusions. This data is used by appraisers to analyze and report on market trend information (e.g., median sale prices, rent trends, marketing time, etc.), or the impact different features have on their subject's value (i.e., appropriate adjustments).

Appraisers have access to technology that enables them to automate some aspects of the appraisal process. Regression analysis is a common example, but there are others as well. These tools generate information that once had to be calculated by hand. The information generated by this technology can enable appraisers to produce appraisals and appraisal reviews with greater credibility, but its misuse can have the opposite effect. What steps should an appraiser take to comply with USPAP when using information generated by these types of resources?

BACKGROUND:
This Advisory Opinion addresses an appraiser's obligations when relying upon adjustments, trend analyses, or other information generated by software or various online services. Two such examples of these tools are:

- Regression Analysis Tools: A regression analysis tool is a computer software program that analyzes data using an automated process. It is a statistical process used for determining relationships among variables. For example, an appraiser may wish to determine if the market recognizes a relationship between the size of a property and its price per square foot.
- Multiple Listing Services: These services publish listings of properties for sale in a given marketplace. Typically, these services have a function that can provide subscribers with an analysis of past sale trends, such as average prices, sales volume, days on market, etc.

Automated Valuation Models (AVMs) and Discounted Cash Flow Analysis (DCF) are addressed separately in other advisory opinions, AO-18 and AO-33, respectively. The output of an AVM or DCF may become a basis for appraisal or appraisal review if the appraiser believes the output to be credible for use in a specific assignment. The output of computer assisted valuation tools are most often used as analytical tools within one or more approaches to value.

Stand-alone software or various online services can be useful tools that allow appraisers to enhance their appraisals. Some residential lenders are increasingly requiring appraisers to provide additional support for their adjustments. In the past, these forms of analysis would have been prohibitively difficult for an appraiser to provide in the normal course of business. Appraisers sometimes meet this request by providing a regression analysis, or a software generated matched-pair analysis. There are software packages available to appraisers that make this relatively simple. Some residential form software vendors include these functions as an integral part of their product. Many modern Multiple Listing Services now have integrated analytical tools to accommodate the needs of their appraiser members. Some appraisers create their own tools using commercially available spreadsheet software.

ADVICE FROM THE ASB ON THE ISSUE:
Relevant USPAP and Advisory References

- The Conduct section of the ETHICS RULE states, in part:
  - *An appraiser must not communicate assignment results with the intent to mislead or to defraud.*
  - *An appraiser must not use or communicate a report or assignment results known by the appraiser to be misleading or fraudulent.*

- The RECORD KEEPING RULE states, in part, that the workfile must include all other data, information, and documentation necessary to support the appraiser's opinions and conclusions and to show compliance with USPAP, or references to the location(s) of such other data, information, and documentation.

© The Appraisal Foundation

46 • The COMPETENCY RULE states, in part:

47 *Competency requires: (1) the ability to properly identify the problem to be addressed; (2) the knowledge and*
48 *experience to complete the assignment competently; and (3) recognition of, and compliance with, laws and*
49 *regulations that apply to the appraiser or to the assignment.*

50 • The Comment to the COMPETENCY RULE states, in part:

51 *Competency may apply to factors such as, but not limited to, an appraiser's familiarity with a specific type*
52 *of property or asset, a market, a geographic area, an intended use, specific laws and regulations, or an*
53 *analytical method.*

54 • The SCOPE OF WORK RULE includes:
55 - *The scope of work must include the research and analyses that are necessary to develop credible*
56 *assignment results.*
57 - *Appraisers have broad flexibility and significant responsibility in determining the appropriate scope of*
58 *work for an appraisal or appraisal review assignment.*
59 - *An appraiser must be prepared to demonstrate that the scope of work is sufficient to produce credible*
60 *assignment results*
61 - *An appraiser must not allow the intended use of an assignment or a client's objectives to cause the*
62 *assignment results to be biased.*

63 • Standards Rule 1-1(a):
64 *An appraiser must be aware of, understand, and correctly employ those recognized methods and*
65 *techniques that are necessary to produce a credible appraisal.*
66 • Standards Rule 1-1(b):
67 *An appraiser must not commit a substantial error of omission or commission that significantly affects an*
68 *appraisal.*
69 • Standards Rule 1-1(c):
70 *An appraiser must not render appraisal services in a careless or negligent manner, such as by making a*
71 *series of errors that, although individually might not significantly affect the results of an appraisal, in the*
72 *aggregate affect the credibility of those results.*
73 • Standards Rule 1-6(a):
74 *An appraiser must reconcile the quality and quantity of data available and analyzed within the approaches*
75 *used;*
76 • Standards Rule 1-6(b):
77 *An appraiser must reconcile the applicability and relevance of the approaches, methods and techniques*
78 *used to arrive at the value conclusion(s).*
79 • STANDARD 2:
80 *In reporting the results of a real property appraisal, an appraiser must communicate each analysis, opinion,*
81 *and conclusion in a manner that is not misleading.*
82 • STANDARDS 3 and 4:
83 *In developing an appraisal review, an appraiser must identify the problem to be solved, determine the*
84 *scope of work necessary to solve the problem, and correctly complete research and analyses necessary to*
85 *produce a credible appraisal review. In reporting the results of an appraisal review assignment, an appraiser*
86 *must communicate each analysis, opinion, and conclusion in a manner that is not misleading.*
87 • Advisory Opinion 18, *Use of an Automated Valuation Model.*
88 • Advisory Opinion 33, *Discounted Cash Flow Analysis.*

89 **Competency**
90 The COMPETENCY RULE specifically states that competency may apply to an analytical method. Technology that
91 performs statistical analyses is simple to use but still requires competence. When using computer assisted valuation
92 tools in an appraisal or appraisal review assignment, an appraiser should have a basic understanding of how it
93 analyzes data to determine whether the computer assisted valuation tool measures and reflects market activity for
94 the property that is being analyzed.

95 The appraiser does not need to know, or be able to explain, the tool's algorithm, or the intricacies of its statistical or
96 mathematical formulae. However, the appraiser should be able to describe the overall process and verify that the

© The Appraisal Foundation

computer assisted valuation tool is consistent in producing results that accurately reflect prevailing market behavior for the property that is being analyzed. 97 98

For example, a calculation of both the mean (average) and median of a given data sometimes yield different results. Either may be appropriate for use but it is the appraiser's responsibility to make that determination. Proper application of these results must also be consistent. For example, it would not be appropriate to compare the mean sale price of office space in one year to the median sale price of office space from a different year. Likewise, an appraiser should not employ terminology (e.g., standard deviation, coefficient of variation, etc.) without understanding what that terminology means. 99 100 101 102 103 104

Data 105

The credibility of any analysis that incorporates output from computer assisted valuation tools depends on the quality of its data and how well the tool is designed to analyze that data. When using one of the tools in an appraisal or appraisal review assignment, the appraiser must have reason to believe it appropriately uses data that are relevant. 106 107 108 109

The size of the database does not necessarily mean that the output is directly applicable. A sample of dozens of sales may appear to yield a well-supported correlation between size and price per acre. But if the sales would not otherwise be deemed comparable, they should not be included as part of the sample. The sales may be credible comparisons if the analysis takes into account the differences, but it is the appraiser's responsibility to determine if the source data is comparable as is, or if some adjustments are necessary prior to generating a relationship. 110 111 112 113 114

Use of Computer Assisted Valuation Tools 115

Standards Rule 1-1(b) states that the appraiser must not commit a substantial error of omission or commission that significantly affects an appraisal. Output from computer assisted valuation tools is typically used only as a portion of the analysis the appraiser relies upon to develop assignment results. A single error, which on the surface may appear minor, could have a compounding effect that could have a noteworthy impact on the results of the assignment. 116 117 118 119

When using computer assisted valuation tools, the appraiser is responsible both for selecting the appropriate input parameters and also for being proficient in the use of the technology to ensure the correct input of those parameters. The calculations performed by a computer assisted valuation tool may always be mathematically correct and easily duplicated. But if either of these criteria is not met, reliance upon the output of the computer assisted valuation tool's calculation may not provide credible results. Depending on how the appraiser relies upon this data, inappropriate information may impact the results of the assignment. 120 121 122 123 124 125

Statistical tools may be employed to support adjustments. Because of the number of independent variables required for analysis of both residential and non-residential properties, a useful statistical tool is multiple linear regression. The number of variables requires the utilization of an adequate sample size. Multiple linear regression may also be a valuable analytical tool in quantifying and supporting adjustments. 126 127 128 129

Appraisers must also have at least a basic understanding of statistics. For example, regression analysis is based upon complex calculations. Appraisers do not need to be able to duplicate those calculations, but must understand how to use the output. They must be able to recognize a graph that shows a strong relationship between the variables and one that does not. Reliance on a weak correlation of the data will directly impact the credibility of the conclusion drawn using that information. 130 131 132 133 134

The appraiser must also be aware of what information is used as the input and how to properly apply the output. The appraiser may have developed a credible adjustment for market conditions in one appraisal, but the appraiser must consider whether or not the data upon which that adjustment was supported is based upon data that is suitable for comparison to the subject of another appraisal. 135 136 137 138

A regression analysis that correlates the sale prices per acre of land sales to the size of each lot may either be based upon the unadjusted or adjusted sale prices. If unadjusted, the appraiser may need to perform additional analysis before applying the result to the subject. 139 140 141

When using any of these analytical tools, the appraiser is responsible for the accuracy of the output. Thus, the appraiser must have confidence that the technology uses data that is relevant and that the output is mathematically correct and sufficiently reliable for use in the assignment. 142 143 144

© The Appraisal Foundation

Regardless of the tool chosen, the appraiser is responsible for the entire analysis, including selection of the source data, the calculations, and the resulting output. Appraisers should use sufficient care to avoid errors that would significantly affect their opinions and conclusions. Diligence is required to identify and analyze the factors, conditions, data, and other information that would have a significant effect on the credibility of the assignment results.

When using a computer assisted valuation tool, an appraiser must not simply rely on the output of data programs which claim to give support for adjustments without an understanding that the output is credible. Reliance on this data without understanding the output could place credibility of assignment results in doubt.

Additional Considerations

Appraisers may rely upon forms of technology other than computer assisted valuation tools. The advice provided in this Advisory Opinion can, in large part, be applied to those tools as well. One such example is software that calculates the size of the subject property (CAD, or computer-aided design software). Appraisers use these programs to illustrate the floor plan of the subject and, by including dimensions, calculate building size. As with valuation tools, the appraiser is responsible for the accuracy of the measurements, correctly identifying how each area is to be classified (e.g., living area, basement, garage, etc.), and that the resulting calculation is accurate and appropriate for use in producing credible assignment results.

Reporting Requirements

Standards Rule 2-2(a)(x) states, in part:

> *The content of an Appraisal Report must be appropriate for the intended use of the appraisal and, at a minimum: provide sufficient information to indicate that the appraiser complied with the requirements of STANDARD 1 by: (1) summarizing the appraisal methods and techniques employed, and (5) stating the information analyzed and the reasoning that supports the analyses, opinions, and conclusions, including reconciliation of the data and approaches.*

This could be accomplished by summarizing the input parameters and the analysis in the report and the rationale for selecting those parameters. The summary might also be supported by graphs, tables, charts, screen captures, etc. that are generated by the tools.

This may include all of the input parameters, how the source data was obtained, the resulting output, the software used, including the version number, or the online service relied upon, and the date of the analysis. Events beyond the appraiser's control may make it impossible to reproduce the exact same output results at a later date. For example, a software vendor might refine the algorithm, or there may be a different vendor altogether. The information retained in the workfile must be sufficient to support the analyses that were the basis for the report.

Illustrations:

1. Q: A stand-alone program will calculate the replacement cost of the office building that is being appraised. The software's output is notably different from the actual costs submitted by the builder. On which cost estimate should the appraiser rely?

   A: Standard Rule 1-4(b)(ii) requires that the appraiser "analyze such comparable cost data as are available to estimate the cost new of the improvements (if any)." Therefore, the appraiser should not simply accept one cost calculation or another without careful analysis.

   The appraiser should double-check and reconsider the factual data being input. Likewise, the appraiser should review the cost contract submitted to verify that it also is based upon the same assumptions (e.g., all items included, any personal property included, arm's-length transaction, etc.) and that the calculations are correct. After doing so, the appraiser can determine whether the proposed cost or the software's output is more credible.

2. Q: An appraiser has purchased a software package that has multiple functions, such as market analysis, deriving adjustments for physical characteristics, automatically inputting information from the local MLS, and more. He uses the program to develop an adjustment for an in-ground pool. The program provides that amount and reports the standard deviation. The appraiser is not familiar with this term. He assumes that a large standard deviation is better so he decides to employ that adjustment. Is the appraiser correct in deciding that the output was credible?

© The Appraisal Foundation

A: No. The COMPETENCY RULE requires that an appraiser have the knowledge to complete the assignment competently. An appraiser must have at least a basic understanding of statistics in order to rely upon the output. By relying upon unfamiliar terminology, the appraiser is not complying with the COMPETENCY RULE. 193 194 195 196

SUMMARY: 197

- Computer assisted valuation tools that are available to the appraiser are often used in developing value opinions in concert within one or more approaches. 198 199
- The output of computer assisted valuation tools is most often used as an analytical tool within one or more approaches to value. 200 201
- The information generated by these types of valuation tools is merely a calculation that once had to be calculated by hand; it is not a substitute for an appraiser's judgment. 202 203
- Appraisers may find analytic tools useful for supporting their adjustments. 204
- Regardless of the tool chosen, the appraiser is responsible for the entire analysis including the controlling input, the calculations, and the resulting output. 205 206
- Appraisers must be proficient in the use of their chosen technology to ensure that they have correctly selected and input appropriate parameters. 207 208
- If the appropriate parameters are not correctly entered into the program, the information provided may neither meet the requirements of the assignment nor provide credible assignment results. 209 210
- Appraisers must have an understanding of statistical analysis and not employ terminology and/or methodology with which they are not familiar. 211 212
- It is the responsibility of the appraiser to ensure that the controlling input is consistent with market evidence and prevailing market attitudes. 213 214
- Output should be tested and checked for errors and reasonableness. 215
- Information retained in the workfile must be sufficient to support the analyses. 216

© The Appraisal Foundation

ADVISORY OPINION 38 (AO-38)

1 *This communication by the Appraisal Standards Board (ASB) does not establish new standards or interpret existing*
2 *standards. Advisory Opinions are issued to illustrate the applicability of appraisal standards in specific situations*
3 *and to offer advice from the ASB for the resolution of appraisal issues and problems.*

4 **SUBJECT: Content of an Appraisal Report and Restricted Appraisal Report**

5 **APPLICATION: Real Property, Personal Property, Intangible Property**

6 **THE ISSUE:**
7 Standards Rules 2-2, 8-2, and 10-2 contain the minimum content requirements for an Appraisal Report and for a
8 Restricted Appraisal Report.

9 This Advisory Opinion addresses the following questions about the required content of a report.

10 • Since USPAP allows flexibility in reporting assignment results, does this mean that for some assignments
11 an appraiser is permitted to be less thorough in developing an appraisal?
12 • If there are only two written reporting options (Appraisal Report and Restricted Appraisal Report), does this
13 mean that USPAP allows only two ways to report an appraisal?
14 • Does USPAP require appraisal reports to have a specific label?
15 • Under what conditions does USPAP permit a Restricted Appraisal Report?
16 • When may it be appropriate to issue a Restricted Appraisal Report?
17 • What are the differences between the required content of an Appraisal Report and Restricted Appraisal
18 Report?
19 • What is an example of the difference between "state" and "summarize" in the context of a real property
20 appraisal report?
21 • How must the appraiser disclose restrictions on the use of a Restricted Appraisal Report?
22 • When might an appraiser need to exceed the minimum requirements for an Appraisal Report or Restricted
23 Appraisal Report?
24 • Is it permitted to issue an Appraisal Report if an appraiser exceeds some of the minimum reporting
25 requirements for a Restricted Appraisal Report but does not meet all of the requirements for an Appraisal
26 Report?
27 • Is the appraiser required to make workfile retrieval arrangements with the client?
28 • What if the report is sufficient for the needs of the client, but a reviewer requests more information from the
29 workfile?
• For oral reports, what is meant by *substantive matters*?

30 **Relevant USPAP References**

31 According to the SCOPE OF WORK RULE Disclosure Obligations:

32 *The report must contain sufficient information to allow the client and other intended users to understand*
33 *the scope of work performed. The information disclosed must be appropriate for the intended use of the*
34 *assignment results.*

35 According to the General Reporting Requirements in Standards Rules 2-1, 8-1, and 10-1, each written or oral
36 appraisal report must:

37 *(a) clearly and accurately set forth the appraisal in a manner that will not be misleading;*

38 *(b) contain sufficient information to enable the intended user(s) of the appraisal to understand the report*
39 *properly; and*

40 *(c) clearly and accurately disclose all assumptions, extraordinary assumptions, hypothetical conditions,*
41 *and limiting conditions used in the assignment.*

© The Appraisal Foundation

ADVICE FROM THE ASB ON THE ISSUE:

Since USPAP allows flexibility in *reporting* assignment results, does this mean that for some assignments an appraiser is permitted to be less thorough in *developing* an appraisal?

STANDARDS 1, 7, and 9 set requirements for developing an appraisal. These *development* requirements apply to all appraisals along with the ETHICS RULE, the RECORD KEEPING RULE, the COMPETENCY RULE, the SCOPE OF WORK RULE, and the JURISDICTIONAL EXCEPTION RULE. Thus, regardless of whether a *report* contains only the minimum contents, the SCOPE OF WORK RULE still requires an appraiser to "determine and perform the scope of work necessary to *develop* credible assignment results."

Since the development process for an appraisal is separate from the reporting process, the choice of different reporting options does not affect the USPAP requirements for development. The appraiser must comply with STANDARDS 1, 7, or 9 to *develop* credible assignment results, regardless of the length or type of form or format used to *report* the appraisal.

If there are only two written reporting options (Appraisal Report and Restricted Appraisal Report), does this mean that USPAP allows only two ways to report an appraisal?

No. USPAP sets minimum requirements but does not limit the ways in which opinions of value may be reported. STANDARDS 2, 8 AND 10 state that "the substantive content of a report determines its compliance."

Does USPAP require appraisal reports to have a specific label?

Yes. However, Standards Rules 2-2, 8-2, and 10-2 explicitly permit an appraiser to use other labels *in addition to* "Appraisal Report" and "Restricted Appraisal Report." It is not required that either "Appraisal Report" or "Restricted Appraisal Report" be the only label.

Under what conditions does USPAP permit a Restricted Appraisal Report?

According to Standards Rules 2-2(b), 8-2(b), and 10-2(b) "A Restricted Appraisal Report may be provided when the client is the only intended user; or, when additional intended users are identified by name." For a Restricted Appraisal Report, other intended users are permitted only if they are identified by name in the report.

When may it be appropriate to issue a Restricted Appraisal Report?

According to Standards Rules 2-2(b), 8-2(b), and 10-2(b), the content of a Restricted Appraisal Report must be "appropriate for its intended use." Thus it is not appropriate to issue a Restricted Appraisal Report solely because the client is the only intended user.

Further, an appraiser should carefully consider the obligation for a report to "contain sufficient information to enable the intended user(s) of the appraisal to understand the report properly" when considering whether it is appropriate to have other intended users.

It may be appropriate to issue a Restricted Appraisal Report if:

- the client understands the limited utility of this option;
- the intended use of the appraisal is appropriate for a report which may not contain supporting rationale for all of the opinions and conclusions set forth in the report; and
- the client (and, if applicable, named other intended users) do not need the level of information required in an Appraisal Report.

Some examples of situations in which a Restricted Appraisal Report may be appropriate are:

- The intended use is consultation for acquisition or disposition by a collector who is knowledgeable about the subject property.
- A real property owner wants to know the market value of their property, but does not need to know details as to how the appraiser arrived at that conclusion.
- A business orders a yearly or quarterly appraisal of property that the appraiser has appraised many times in the past.
- The appraisal is for a preliminary hearing to dispute property taxes at the assessor's office.

© The Appraisal Foundation

85 **What are the differences between the required content of an Appraisal Report and Restricted Appraisal Report?**

86 The comparison chart below shows the required contents of an Appraisal Report and Restricted Appraisal Report
87 in Standards Rule 2-2. The requirements in Standards Rules 8-2 and 10-2 are similar. In most cases the difference
88 between an Appraisal Report and Restricted Appraisal Report is whether the information must be summarized or
89 whether it may be stated. Bold type is used to highlight some of the other differences.

Appraisal Report	Restricted Appraisal Report
(i) state the identity of the client, or if the client requested anonymity, state that the identity is withheld at the client's request;	(i) state the identity of the client, or if the client requested anonymity, state that the identity is withheld at the client's request;
(ii) state the identity of any other intended users by name **or type**;	(ii) state the identity of any other intended user(s) **by name**;
n/a	(iii) clearly and conspicuously **state a restriction** that limits use of the report to the client and the named intended user(s);
n/a	(iv) clearly and conspicuously **warn that the report may not contain supporting rationale** for the all of the opinions and conclusions set forth in the report
(iii) state the intended use of the appraisal;	(v) state the intended use of the appraisal;
(iv) **contain information, documents, and/or exhibits** sufficient to identify the real estate involved in the appraisal, including the physical, legal, and economic property characteristics relevant to the assignment	(vi) state information sufficient to identify the real estate involved in the appraisal;
(v) state the real property interest appraised;	(vii) state the real property interest appraised;
(vi) state the type **and definition** of value and cite the source of the definition;	(viii) state the type of value and cite the source of its definition;
(vii) state the effective date of the appraisal and the date of the report;	(ix) state the effective date of the appraisal and the date of the report;
(viii) **summarize** the scope of work used to develop the appraisal	(x) state the scope of work used to develop the appraisal
(ix) **summarize** the extent of any significant real property appraisal assistance;	(xi) state the extent of any significant real property appraisal assistance;
(x) provide sufficient information to indicate that the appraiser complied with the requirements of STANDARD 1 by: 1. **summarizing** the appraisal methods and techniques employed 2. stating the reasons for excluding the sales comparison, cost, or income approach(es) if any have not been developed; 3. summarizing the results of analyzing the subject sales, agreements of sale, options, and listings in accordance with Standards Rule 1-5; and 4. stating the value opinion(s) and conclusion(s); and 5. **summarizing the information analyzed and the reasoning that supports the analyses, opinions, and conclusions, including reconciliation of the data and approaches.**	(xii) provide sufficient information to indicate that the appraiser complied with the requirements of STANDARD 1 by: 1. **stating** the appraisal methods and techniques employed 2. stating the reasons for excluding the sales comparison, cost, or income approach(es) if any have not been developed; 3. summarizing the results of analyzing the subject sales, agreements of sale, options, and listings in accordance with Standards Rule 1-5; and 4. stating the value opinion(s) and conclusion(s). Comment: An appraiser must maintain a workfile that includes **sufficient information to indicate that the appraiser complied with the requirements of STANDARD 1 and for the appraiser to produce an Appraisal Report.**

© The Appraisal Foundation

(xi) state the use of the real estate existing as of the effective date and the use of the real estate reflected in the appraisal;	(xiii) state the use of the real estate existing as of the effective date and the use of the real estate reflected in the appraisal;
(xii) when an opinion of highest and best use was developed by the appraiser, state that opinion and **summarize the support and rationale for that opinion;**	(xiv) when an opinion of highest and best use was developed by the appraiser, state that opinion;
(xiii) clearly and conspicuously: • state all extraordinary assumptions and hypothetical conditions; and • state that their use might have affected the assignment results;	(xv) clearly and conspicuously: • state all extraordinary assumptions and hypothetical conditions; and • state that their use might have affected the assignment results;
(xiv) include a signed certification in accordance with Standards Rule 2-3.	(xvi) include a signed certification in accordance with Standards Rule 2-3.

What is an example of the difference between "state" and "summarize" in the context of a real property appraisal report? 90 91

The following presentations of the zoning section of a commercial appraisal report are used to exemplify the content differences in the two appraisal report options. These examples show a relative illustration of depth and detail of presentation and are not intended to characterize the format for an entire appraisal report. The examples are not intended to imply that information on zoning is necessary in all appraisal reports. Furthermore, an appraiser may need to provide additional information in the valuation of a complex property wherein the issues of what is physically possible, legally permissible, financially feasible, and maximally productive are explored in much greater detail, to enable the client and intended users to understand the report properly. 92 93 94 95 96 97 98

Example of "summarize" - zoning 99

> *The General Business B-4 zoning classification applies. Its purpose is to encourage local commercial development of banking facilities, retail stores, and service establishments along arterial streets on minimum lots of 10,000 sq. ft. with a width of 100 feet. Building coverage is limited to 50% of the lot, and building height is limited to two stories or 20 feet. John N. Forcer of the Anytown planning and zoning office indicates that the existing use and subject improvements conform.* 100 101 102 103 104

Example of "state" - zoning 105

> *General Business, B-4; existing use and subject improvements conform.* 106

The purpose of the above examples is to show one view of the differences between the application of the terms "summarize" and "state." The examples should not be extended beyond this Advisory Opinion to every section of an appraisal report. 107 108 109

How must the appraiser disclose restrictions on the use of a Restricted Appraisal Report? 110

Standards Rules 2-2(b), 8-2(b) and 10-2(b) state that restrictions on the use of a Restricted Appraisal Report must be disclosed clearly and conspicuously: 111 112

> *... clearly and conspicuously state a restriction that limits use of the report to the client and the named intended user(s);* 113 114

> *... clearly and conspicuously warn that the report may not contain supporting rationale for all of the opinions and conclusions set forth in the report.* 115 116

When might an appraiser need to exceed the minimum requirements for an Appraisal Report or Restricted Appraisal Report? 117 118

USPAP does not prescribe a one-size-fits-all level of information regardless of the required minimum contents of a report. An appraiser will need to exercise judgment and may need to exceed the minimum requirements to ensure that a report is meaningful and not misleading to the intended user(s). 119 120 121

© The Appraisal Foundation

122 The minimum content requirements do not prohibit an appraiser from providing more extensive explanation and
123 background. In some cases, for example, if a client is not a knowledgeable user of valuation services, an appraiser
124 may need to exceed the requirements in order to ensure that an Appraisal Report is meaningful and not misleading
125 to the intended user(s). In other cases, the intended use of an appraisal may require an appraiser to exceed the
126 minimum report content requirements.

127 Some examples of intended uses when the appraiser might need to summarize information even if USPAP only
128 requires a statement are:

129 • Charitable contribution for which IRS reporting requirements apply
130 • Litigation matter
131 • A financing transaction in the primary or secondary mortgage market, such as when VA, FHA, or Fannie
132 Mae report content requirements apply

133 **Is it permitted to issue an Appraisal Report if an appraiser exceeds some the minimum reporting requirements**
134 **for a Restricted Appraisal Report but does not meet all of the requirements for an Appraisal Report?**

135 No.

136 **Is the appraiser required to make workfile retrieval arrangements with the client?**

137 No. This is not required by USPAP. However, an appraiser may make these arrangements with a client.

138 **What if the report is sufficient for the needs of the client, but a reviewer requests more information from the**
139 **workfile?**

140 As long as the client gives the appraiser approval to share assignment results with the reviewer, USPAP neither
141 requires nor prohibits sharing workfile information with a reviewer.

142 **For oral reports, what is meant by *substantive matters*?**

143 Standards Rules 2-4, 8-4, and 10-4 specify that an oral appraisal report must "to the extent that it is both possible
144 and appropriate" address the *substantive matters* set forth in Standards Rules 2-2, 8-2 and 10-2.

145 The flexibility in this requirement reflects the varied circumstances in which oral appraisal reports are delivered.
146 The appraiser is expected to use judgment about which elements of Standards Rules 2-2, 8-2 and 10-2 are
147 "substantive" or, as defined in the Merriam-Webster dictionary, "matters of major or practical importance to all
148 concerned."

149 In many cases it is critically important to state (and explain) the type and definition of value, but it may not be necessary
150 in an oral report to cite the source of the definition. Similarly, it may be very important to summarize information
151 sufficient to identify the property involved in the appraisal, but it may not be necessary in every oral presentation to
152 state the property interest appraised or to state the reasons for the exclusion of some approaches to value.

© The Appraisal Foundation

2020-2021 EDITION

USPAP FREQUENTLY ASKED QUESTIONS

Authorized by Congress as the Source of Appraisal Standards and Appraiser Qualifications

APPRAISAL STANDARDS BOARD

USPAP FREQUENTLY ASKED QUESTIONS

2020-2021 EDITION

APPRAISAL STANDARDS BOARD

Published in the United States of America.

All Rights Reserved
Copyright © 2020, The Appraisal Foundation.

The Appraisal Foundation reserves all rights with respect to this material. No part of this publication may be reproduced, duplicated, altered or otherwise published in electronic or paper means or in any format or form without the express written permission of the publisher.

EFFECTIVE:

January 1, 2020 through December 31, 2021

FOREWORD

The Appraisal Standards Board (ASB) of The Appraisal Foundation develops, interprets, and amends the *Uniform Standards of Professional Appraisal Practice* (USPAP) on behalf of appraisers and users of appraisal services. **The 2020-2021 edition of USPAP is effective January 1, 2020 through December 31, 2021.** It is important that individuals understand and adhere to changes in each edition of USPAP. State and federal authorities enforce the content of the current or applicable edition of USPAP.

USPAP Frequently Asked Questions (USPAP FAQ) is a form of guidance issued by the ASB to respond to questions raised by appraisers, enforcement officials, users of appraisal services and the public to illustrate the applicability of USPAP in specific situations and to offer advice from the ASB for the resolution of appraisal issues and problems. The advice presented may not represent the only possible solution to the issues discussed and the advice provided may not be applied equally to seemingly similar situations. USPAP FAQ does not establish new standards or interpret existing standards. USPAP FAQ is not part of USPAP and is approved by the ASB without public exposure and comment.

The ASB periodically issues the USPAP Q&A, which is posted on The Appraisal Foundation website (www.appraisalfoundation.org). The USPAP Q&A is issued to inform appraisers, enforcement officials, and users of appraisal services of the ASB responses to questions received by the Board.

The ASB compiles the USPAP Q&A into the USPAP FAQ for publication with each edition of USPAP. For this 2020- 2021 edition of USPAP, Q&As through June 2018 have been included. In addition to incorporating the most recent questions and responses issued by the ASB, the USPAP FAQ is reviewed and updated to ensure that it represents the most recent guidance from the ASB.

Contacting the Appraisal Standards Board

The ASB invites questions about USPAP, commentary on USPAP, and proposed changes to USPAP from all interested parties, including appraisers, state enforcement agencies, users of appraisal services, and the public.

If you have any comments, questions, or suggestions regarding USPAP, please contact the ASB.
Appraisal Standards Board
The Appraisal Foundation
1155 15th Street, NW, Suite 1111
Washington, DC 20005
Phone: 202-347-7722
E-Mail: info@appraisalfoundation.org
www.appraisalfoundation.org

© The Appraisal Foundation

TABLE OF CONTENTS

© The Appraisal Foundation

© The Appraisal Foundation

© The Appraisal Foundation

© The Appraisal Foundation

© The Appraisal Foundation

© The Appraisal Foundation

© The Appraisal Foundation

© The Appraisal Foundation

USPAP COMPOSITION, STRUCTURE, AND COMPLIANCE

1. APPLICABLE EDITION OF USPAP

Question: **The new edition of USPAP became effective January 1, 2020. I prepared an appraisal with an effective date in December 2019; however, my date of report was in January 2020. Which edition of USPAP applies – the 2018-19 edition or the 2020-21 edition?**

Response: Appraisers must comply with the USPAP edition that is in effect as of the date of the report. The 2020-21 edition applies because the date of the report was on or after January 1, 2020. The effective date of the appraisal has no bearing on which edition of USPAP applies.

2. COMPLYING WITH USPAP BY CHOICE

Question: **I have been asked to complete an appraisal assignment for a client who has no policy regarding compliance with USPAP. As an appraiser, may I still comply with USPAP on this particular assignment?**

Response: Yes. The PREAMBLE states:

> *USPAP does not establish who or which assignments must comply... Compliance with USPAP is required when either the service or the appraiser is obligated to comply by law or regulation, or by agreement with the client or intended users.* ***When not obligated, individuals may still choose to comply.*** (Bold added for emphasis)

In addition, the ETHICS RULE states:

> *An appraiser must comply with USPAP when obligated by law or regulation, or by agreement with the client or intended users. In addition to these requirements, an individual should comply any time that individual represents that he or she is performing as an appraiser.*

So, it is clear that even in an assignment where compliance is not required of an individual who is acting as an appraiser, not only may the appraiser comply, the appraiser should comply.

Refer to Advisory Opinion 21, *USPAP Compliance,* for further guidance.

3. USPAP APPLICABILITY IN VALUATION FOR FINANCIAL REPORTING

Question: **I am an appraiser in a firm that performs valuations of business interests and assets (both tangible and intangible) for financial reporting purposes in accordance with Financial Accounting Standards Board (FASB) standards. Does USPAP apply to valuations for financial reporting purposes?**

Response: USPAP does not establish who or what assignments must comply with USPAP. Such requirements are established by law, regulation, or agreement with the client. Additionally, certain professional organizations require that their members comply with USPAP.

Therefore, regarding ***who*** must comply: Individuals providing appraisals (defined in USPAP as an opinion of value) who fall under one of the above requirements must comply with USPAP in valuations for financial reporting.

And, regarding ***what assignments*** must comply: Appraisals that are required by law to comply with USPAP must comply regardless of whether the individual performing the appraisal would otherwise be required to comply. In some states, it is mandatory for real

© The Appraisal Foundation

estate appraisals (an opinion of value of real estate) to comply with USPAP, no matter what the intended use.

Additionally, regardless of the intended use of the appraisal, individuals who hold themselves out as appraisers should comply.

It is important to note that, Fair Value assignments performed in compliance with Accounting Standards Codification (ASC) 805, *Business Combinations* issued by the Financial Accounting Standards Board, are often referred to as allocations. However, the asset values determined in these assignments are appraisals as defined in USPAP because they are opinions of value. Therefore, these allocations must comply when the appraiser, or the assignment, is required by law, regulation, agreement of the client, or when the appraiser belongs to a professional organization that requires compliance. In addition, any individuals holding themselves out to be appraisers should comply, even when not required to do so.

4. ASSIGNMENT INVOLVING ANALYSIS OF LEASES

Question: **An investment firm hired an appraiser to abstract leases, input the data into a lease-by-lease analysis software program, estimate market rents and expenses, estimate the discount rate, run ten discounted cash flows, and provide a value using the Income Capitalization Approach. The appraiser completed the assignment, including providing a conclusion of market value, and delivered the electronic lease-by-lease analysis file to the client. Does USPAP apply to this service?**

Response: Yes. This service is an appraisal. In order to be in compliance with USPAP, the appraiser must observe the development and reporting requirements applicable to a real property appraisal assignment (STANDARDS 1 and 2). It is not possible to determine from the information provided whether the appraiser properly developed the assignment results. However, it does appear that the reporting of the assignment results fails to comply with STANDARD 2. USPAP prescribes the minimum content requirements for two real property appraisal reporting options: Appraisal Report and Restricted Appraisal Report. The communication of solely a lease-by-lease analysis file does not satisfy the reporting requirements of USPAP.

5. USPAP COMPLIANCE AS AN INSTRUCTOR

Question: **In addition to my job as an appraiser, I spend a significant amount of my professional time as an instructor of appraisal courses and seminars. One of the prerequisites for my teaching position is that I must also be a practicing appraiser. Am I subject to USPAP when I am teaching appraisal courses?**

Response: Yes. Since you are acting in the role of an appraiser in these teaching assignments, you are engaged in appraisal practice, which is defined in USPAP as:

> *Valuation services performed by an individual acting as an appraiser, including,* ***but not limited to*** *appraisal and appraisal review.* (Bold added for emphasis)

While USPAP does not include Standards Rules for teaching assignments, all services performed as part of appraisal practice must comply with USPAP. The portions of USPAP that apply generally to appraisal practice include the PREAMBLE, the DEFINITIONS, the ETHICS RULE, the COMPETENCY RULE, and the JURISDICTIONAL EXCEPTION RULE.

See Advisory Opinion 21, *USPAP Compliance,* for discussion of the application of USPAP in valuation services.

© The Appraisal Foundation

6. PERSONAL PROPERTY APPRAISAL REQUIREMENTS

Question: **I'm a personal property appraiser, and I've been asked to donate my professional services to help raise funds for a charitable organization. The charity wants to hold an event where individuals can bring in their personal property items and, for a nominal fee that is paid to the charity, receive an oral report of my opinion as to the value of their item(s). This appears to be similar to television shows where people bring in their personal items to be valued. If I decide to participate, would my opinions be considered appraisals and if so, how could I comply with USPAP in performing these assignments?**

Response: USPAP defines appraisal as:

the act or process of developing an opinion of value; an opinion of value.

Therefore, the opinions you describe would be appraisals.

To comply with USPAP, a personal property appraiser would have to comply with the requirements of STANDARD 7 and STANDARD 8, in addition to the applicable rules (e.g., the ETHICS RULE, the COMPETENCY RULE, and the SCOPE OF WORK RULE). This means the appraiser would have to perform the level of research and analyses required to produce credible assignment results (given the intended use). Since the appraiser would be communicating the appraisal as an oral report, the report must address (to the extent that it is both possible and appropriate) the substantive matters of an Appraisal Report. In addition, the appraiser would have to prepare a workfile as required by the RECORD KEEPING RULE.

These television shows may make it appear that the appraisers are providing their appraisals off the cuff and not in compliance with USPAP. However, it is more likely the appraisers have been provided with the personal property item to be appraised prior to the actual taping of the show. The appraisers may also be providing the property owner with a written appraisal report, although it may not be discussed during the television show.

Therefore, it is possible the appraisers are rendering a USPAP-compliant appraisal and report, even if it does not appear that way during the airing of the show.

See Advisory Opinion 21, *USPAP Compliance,* for further guidance.

7. USPAP COMPLIANCE WITH OTHER VALUATION STANDARDS

Question: **I have been asked to perform an appraisal that complies with USPAP and with valuation standards from an international appraisal organization. If my appraisal complies with USPAP, will it automatically comply with other valuation standards as well?**

Response: No. Although there are similarities among all major appraisal standards, it is impossible to say that compliance with USPAP ensures compliance with any other standards. It would be necessary to review the actual content of the valuation standards in question to determine whether different actions would be necessary to comply with those standards.

The ASB worked with the International Valuation Standards Council (IVSC) to create a Bridge Document that provides guidance to appraisers performing USPAP-compliant appraisals on how to comply with the International Valuation Standards at the same time. This document is available free of charge at www.appraisalfoundation.org.

© The Appraisal Foundation

8. DIFFERENCES BETWEEN APPRAISAL AND APPRAISAL REPORT

Question: **I have heard some very experienced appraisers and appraisal clients use the terms appraisal and appraisal report interchangeably. I know they are each defined separately in USPAP; what is the difference between the two?**

Response: It is important to understand that USPAP distinguishes an appraisal from an appraisal report. An appraisal is an opinion of value. An appraisal report is the communication of an appraisal, which is transmitted to the client upon completion of an assignment. In other words, the appraisal is the opinion itself, while the appraisal report is the communication of that opinion to the client.

9. PUBLIC TRUST

Question: **The expression "public trust" is used in USPAP. What is public trust and who or what is the public in the USPAP context?**

Response: USPAP mentions public trust three times. The PREAMBLE states that the purpose of USPAP is to "... promote and maintain a high level of public trust in appraisal practice by establishing requirements for appraisers." The PREAMBLE also states "The appraiser's responsibility is to protect the overall public trust and it is the importance of the role of the appraiser that places ethical obligations on those who serve in this capacity." Lastly, the ETHICS RULE reinforces this concept with "An appraiser must promote and preserve the public trust inherent in appraisal practice by observing the highest standards of professional ethics."

While USPAP does not define public trust, it is clear from the context that it refers to the need for the public to be able to have confidence that services provided by an appraiser are performed competently and in a manner that is independent, impartial, and objective.

The public, whose trust the appraiser must promote and preserve, exists on several levels. The most direct is the appraiser's client. In addition to the client, any additional intended users would be part of the appraiser's public. But, even beyond the client and other intended users, there are other parties who may rely on the work an appraiser and the appraiser must be careful not to mislead such third parties. Finally, it could be said that the general public is also part of that public. If the general public cannot depend on appraisers to act as independent professionals and provide credible results, the economy could suffer.

© The Appraisal Foundation

10. DON'T AGREE TO PERFORM THE ASSIGNMENT UNLESS YOU CAN APPRAISE FOR $XXX,000

Question: **I received an appraisal request that says: "If you can't appraise the property for $XXX,000, you must not agree to perform the appraisal assignment." How should I respond to this appraisal request?**

Response: This request would be seen as an attempt to violate the appraiser's independence, and the request itself may be illegal. Agreeing to perform such an assignment would violate the Management section of the ETHICS RULE, which states, in part:

An appraiser must not agree to perform an assignment, or have a compensation arrangement for an assignment, that is contingent on any of the following:

1. ***the reporting of a predetermined result (e.g., opinion of value);***
2. *a direction in assignment results that favors the cause of the client;*
3. *the amount of a value opinion;*
4. *the attainment of a stipulated result (e.g., that the loan closes or taxes are reduced); or*
5. *the occurrence of a subsequent event directly related to the appraiser's opinions and specific to the assignment's purpose.* (Bold added for emphasis)

You could respond to this request with the following statement: "I cannot perform the assignment with this condition because it violates professional ethics. You should be aware that I must develop the appraisal before I will know the results. I can only perform the assignment if you remove the predetermined value requirement."

See Advisory Opinion 19, *Unacceptable Assignment Conditions in Real Property Appraisal Assignments,* for additional guidance on appraisal requests with conditions.

11. APPRAISER COERCION

Question: **Does USPAP require appraisers to certify in the appraisal report that they have not been coerced to provide predetermined results?**

Response: No. However, such a statement is not be inconsistent with the requirements of USPAP. Standards Rule 2-3(a) essentially requires appraisers to certify that they have not been coerced, without specifically using that term. For example, Standards Rule 2-3 requires the appraiser to certify, among other things, that:

my engagement in this assignment was not contingent upon developing or reporting predetermined results.

It would be unethical to affirm this statement in the certification if the appraiser had been coerced into providing predetermined assignment results.

12. PLAGIARISM

Question: **Is plagiarism considered unethical or improper?**

Response: Yes. Plagiarism is unethical. The Conduct section of the ETHICS RULE states that an appraiser must not use or communicate a misleading or fraudulent appraisal report. Presenting an appraisal report as yours when all or part is the work of someone else is clearly misleading.

© The Appraisal Foundation

13. USE OF QUALITATIVE TERMS

Question: **Does USPAP permit appraisers to use terms that reflect a scale, such as high, low, good, or the like?**

Response: Yes. USPAP does not prohibit the use of such qualitative terms in an appraisal report. However, the Conduct section of the ETHICS RULE states:

> *An appraiser must not use or rely on unsupported conclusions relating to characteristics such as race, color, religion, national origin, gender, marital status, familial status, age, receipt of public assistance income, handicap, or an unsupported conclusion that homogeneity of such characteristics is necessary to maximize value.*

Appraisers should exercise care to avoid comments in a report that may be perceived as biased or illegally discriminatory. Factual descriptions and qualitative terms allow the users of a report to draw their own conclusions. The use of terms that reflect a scale such as high, low, good, fair, poor, strong, weak, rapid, slow, average or the like should also provide contextual information that properly explains the frame of reference and relative position of the subject property on the scale.

For example, if absorption is stated as rapid, the context of the rating should also be cited (rapid relative to what?). Additional guidance is provided in Advisory Opinion 16, *Fair Housing Laws and Appraisal Report Content*.

14. CONFLICTS OF INTEREST

Question: **The principals of a local mortgage company propose to acquire an appraisal firm and have the appraisal firm complete assignments for the mortgage company. Is this a conflict of interest for the appraisers completing assignments for the mortgage company?**

Response: An appraiser should review the ETHICS RULE and Standards Rule 2-3 when completing appraisal assignments in situations where the appraisal company that engages (by employment or contract) the appraiser is owned by the client.

It is important to note that USPAP does not prohibit the agreement to perform an assignment in this specific situation. In an appraisal assignment developed under STANDARD 1 and reported under STANDARD 2, appraisers must specify the particulars in a situation where they have any present or prospective interest with respect to the parties involved in the property that is the subject of the report.

The engagement of an appraiser by an appraisal company that is owned by the client or by owners of the client does not, in and of itself, mean that the appraiser has an interest or bias with respect to the property or parties involved. If the appraiser has an interest but can provide the service in an ethical, unbiased manner, then the appraiser can agree to perform the assignment as long as the appraiser is competent and properly discloses the interest in accordance with Standards Rule 2-3.

If the appraiser's interest in the property or the parties involved in the assignment prevents the appraiser from providing an unbiased service, then the appraiser must not perform the assignment because it would be in violation of the ETHICS RULE and parts of the appraiser's certification in Standards Rule 2-3.

© The Appraisal Foundation

15. DISCLOSING PRIOR APPRAISAL OF A PROPERTY

Question: **I occasionally receive requests to appraise a property that I have appraised in the past. Since the ETHICS RULE requires me to disclose all prior services that I performed within the three years immediately preceding the agreement to perform the assignment, isn't disclosing that I previously performed an appraisal on the property a violation of an appraiser's responsibility under the Confidentiality section of the ETHICS RULE?**

Response: Generally, no. The Confidentiality section of the ETHICS RULE prohibits, with some exceptions, the disclosure of "confidential information or assignment results prepared for a client." The mere fact that an appraiser appraised a property is not confidential information as defined in USPAP. However, the appraiser must be careful not to disclose confidential information from a previous assignment in the new assignment.

16. APPRAISING A PROPERTY MORE THAN ONCE IN THREE YEARS

Question: **I am aware of the USPAP requirements to disclose to the client, both prior to agreeing to perform an assignment as well as in the certification of the report, services I performed on a property within the prior three years. However, I have been told that based on this requirement, USPAP prohibits me from appraising a property more than once within a three-year period. Is this true?**

Response: No. The requirements in the Conduct section of the ETHICS RULE exist to inform the client of services that the appraiser has performed within the prior three years. USPAP places no restrictions on how many times an appraiser can appraise a specific property.

It should be noted that some appraisers may contractually agree with a client not to appraise a property for another client within a specified time frame, but agreements of this type are business decisions made by appraisers and are not USPAP requirements.

17. DISCLOSURE REQUIREMENTS WHEN AN APPRAISER HAS NOT PERFORMED SERVICES REGARDING A PROPERTY IN THE PRIOR THREE YEARS

Question: **I am aware of the disclosure requirements in the Conduct section of the ETHICS RULE to disclose any services I performed regarding the subject property (or the work under review) within the prior three years. If I have not performed any such services, am I required to make that disclosure as well?**

Response: Yes. Standards Rules 2-3, 4-3, 6-3, 8-3, and 10-3 require the signed certification to include a statement with each report about whether the appraiser has performed any services regarding the property that is the subject of the report (or, for appraisal reviews, regarding the property that is the subject of the work under review).

Examples of appropriate disclosures for (1) an appraisal and (2) an appraisal review when the appraiser has performed no services within the past three years are, as follows:

(1) I have performed no services, as an appraiser or in any other capacity, regarding the property that is the subject of this report within the three-year period immediately preceding the agreement to perform this assignment.

(2) I have performed no services, as an appraiser or in any other capacity, regarding the property that is the subject of the work under review within the three-year period immediately preceding the agreement to perform this assignment.

© The Appraisal Foundation

18. DISCLOSURE OF ANY PRIOR SERVICES REGARDING THE SUBJECT PROPERTY, WHEN AN APPRAISER HAS APPRAISED THE PROPERTY MULTIPLE TIMES

Question: **If I have appraised a property multiple times within the previous three years, do I have to disclose the number of appraisal services? (e.g., "I have appraised the subject property three times during the previous three years immediately preceding the agreement to perform this assignment.")**

Response: In most cases the answer is yes. However, there are some situations, particularly for mass appraisals and appraisals of inventory or large quantities of machinery and equipment, when enumerating prior services for each item may be unreasonable.

According to the Conduct section of the ETHICS RULE any prior service regarding the subject property must be disclosed to the client. And according to Standards Rules 2-3(a), Standards Rules 4-3(a), Standards Rules 6-3(a), Standards Rules 8-3(a), and Standards Rules 10-3(a) the prior services must also be specified in the certification. Thus, in most cases the appraiser must both disclose the number of prior services and specify the nature of the service (e.g., as an appraiser, or in some other capacity such as a broker, mortgage broker, builder, etc.).

An example of a certification disclosure when there have been three prior appraisals is as follows:

I have performed three appraisal services as an appraiser, but I have provided no other services, as an appraiser or in any other capacity, regarding the property that is the subject of this report within the three-year period immediately preceding the agreement to perform this assignment.

Below is an example of an appropriate certification disclosure of all prior services when there are so many assets with prior services that it is unreasonable to enumerate them. The example shows how full disclosure of prior services can be accomplished with a description:

I have performed appraisals of most of the 200 aircraft that are the subject of this report twice per year during the three-year period immediately preceding my engagement to perform this assignment. The exceptions are approximately 85 that I have appraised more frequently than twice per year due to refinancing or those that I have never appraised because they were acquired this year. I have provided no other services as an appraiser or in any other capacity regarding these subject properties within the three-year period immediately preceding the agreement to perform this assignment.

19. DISCLOSURE OF PRIOR SERVICES

Question: **I know USPAP requires an appraiser, prior to agreeing to perform an assignment (or if discovered at any time during the assignment), to disclose any prior services performed on a property within the last three years. I have recently seen some reports where the appraiser stated, "I have performed no prior services regarding this property within three years of the effective date of this report." Is it acceptable to base the three years from the effective date of the appraisal?**

Response: No. The Conduct section of the ETHICS RULE specifies the three-year time frame to be immediately preceding the agreement to perform the assignment:

If known prior to agreeing to perform an assignment, and/or if discovered at any time during the assignment, an appraiser must disclose to the client, and in the subsequent report certification:

© The Appraisal Foundation

any services regarding the subject property performed by the appraiser, as an appraiser or in any other capacity, ***within the three-year period immediately preceding the agreement to perform the assignment***, (Bold added for emphasis)

Although the effective date of the appraisal may be relatively close to the date the appraiser agreed to perform the assignment, there may be cases when there are significant differences between the two dates, which could result in a different response from the appraiser.

20. DISCLOSURE OF ANY PRIOR SERVICES REGARDING THE SUBJECT PROPERTY BEFORE AGREEING TO PERFORM AN ASSIGNMENT, WHEN THE APPRAISER ONLY WORKS FOR ONE CLIENT

Question: **I am a staff appraiser for a company and only complete appraisals for my employer's (the company's) internal use. Am I required to inform the company that I have previously completed an appraisal within the three-year period when the company is already aware of it?**

Response: If you consistently correspond with the same person in the company when completing subsequent assignments regarding the same property, the risk of misleading that person is probably minimal. However, your prior services must still be disclosed. When you are working with the same person and they understand your professional responsibilities, it is unlikely this will be a problem.

It is also possible that the specific person you deal with from one instance to the next may change. In this case, the new contact must certainly be informed if you have performed services regarding the subject property within the last three years.

While it is not included in your question, there is also the possibility that you may have performed services regarding that property for a different client within the three-year period, or performed another type of service.

21. DISCLOSURE OF ANY PRIOR SERVICES REGARDING THE SUBJECT PROPERTY, WHEN AN APPRAISER HAS PERFORMED SERVICES OTHER THAN APPRAISAL PRACTICE

Question: **If I have performed a service other than appraisal practice, such as acting as a general contractor within the prior three years, do I have to describe the specific service or merely state a service was performed?**

Response: You must disclose to the client the type of prior service you performed regarding the property, and this must be included in the report certification. This disclosure is not limited to services provided as part of appraisal practice. Therefore, each service must be disclosed to the client and must appear in the certification.

Examples of appropriate disclosures in these cases are as follows:

I have performed a general contracting service regarding the subject property. I have provided no other services, as an appraiser or in any other capacity, regarding the property that is the subject of this report within the three-year period immediately preceding the agreement to perform this assignment.

OR

I have performed a brokerage service regarding the subject property. I have provided no other services, as an appraiser or in any other capacity, regarding the property that is the subject of this report within the three-year period immediately preceding the agreement to perform this assignment.

© The Appraisal Foundation

If you have provided both of these services, an example of the appropriate disclosure is as follows:

> *I have performed a general contracting service and a brokerage service regarding the subject property. I have provided no other services, as an appraiser or in any other capacity, regarding the property that is the subject of this report within the three-year period immediately preceding the agreement to perform this assignment.*

22. DISCLOSING PRIOR SERVICES PROVIDED BY MY COMPANY

Question: **If the firm that employs me as an appraiser has provided leasing or property management services in the past three years for the subject property, must this be disclosed?**

Response: Not necessarily. The ETHICS RULE requires disclosure of services "provided by the appraiser." However, if appraisers believe that the provision of a service by their firm or other related entity may be relevant, they *should* disclose that information to a potential client.

23. DISCLOSING PROSPECTIVE INTEREST IN A PROPERTY

Question: **If I will be conducting an auction of the subject property after the appraisal, does this have to be disclosed?**

Response: Yes. This is an example of a "current or prospective interest in the subject property." USPAP requires that such an interest be disclosed in the certification and prior to agreement to perform an assignment or upon discovery during the assignment.

24. DISCLOSING PRIOR SERVICES WHEN FORMS DO NOT INCLUDE ALL OF THE REQUIRED CERTIFICATION ELEMENTS

Question: **Most of my assignments are completed using common residential appraisal report forms. I am concerned that my clients do not allow changes to the certification on the report forms. The Conduct section of the ETHICS RULE requires that I disclose prior to agreeing to perform the assignment and in the report certification whether prior services were performed regarding the subject property. Does this mean that I will not be allowed to appraise a property for these clients if I have performed a service regarding that property in the previous three years?**

Response: USPAP compliance is the appraiser's responsibility. While deletion or modification of client-imposed certifications may not always be allowed, most clients allow *additional* certifications that do not constitute material alterations to the appraisal report. In these circumstances, it would be necessary for the appraiser to include a supplemental certification unless and until such forms are revised to comply with the requirements of Standards Rule 2-3(a).

25. DOES A REQUEST FOR A "FINAL INSPECTION" REQUIRE DISCLOSURE OF PRIOR SERVICES?

Question: **If I performed an appraisal that was "subject" to completion of repairs, and subsequently received a request to perform a "final inspection" confirming that the work had been completed, am I required to disclose that I previously appraised the property even if it is obvious to the client that I've done so?**

Response: A "final inspection" is **not** an extension of the original assignment unless it is part of the original agreement for services. A subsequent request would be a *new assignment* and as such requires disclosure in accordance with the Conduct section of the ETHICS RULE. This holds true even if it may be obvious to the client that you've already previously performed an appraisal on the property.

© The Appraisal Foundation

26. DOES USING A PROPERTY AS A COMPARABLE SALE REQUIRE DISCLOSURE OF PRIOR SERVICES?

Question: **If I perform an appraisal and use a property as one of my comparable sales, and later receive a request to appraise the property that was used as a comparable sale, must I disclose I "performed a service" on that property because I used it as a comparable sale?**

Response: No. Using a property as a comparable sale in an appraisal does not constitute "performing a service" regarding that property. Therefore, a subsequent request to appraise the comparable sale would not require disclosure under the Conduct section of the ETHICS RULE.

27. FORMAT FOR DISCLOSING PRIOR SERVICES AT THE TIME OF ASSIGNMENT

Question: **May the appraiser make an oral disclosure to the client of prior services performed on the property prior to agreeing to perform an assignment? May it be made in an email to the client?**

Response: USPAP does not specify how the disclosure must be made. It may be appropriate in some cases to provide an initial oral disclosure. If the client decides to proceed, it may be appropriate that the appraiser's disclosure be restated in writing. One way to accomplish this is by including it in a letter of engagement. In other cases an email would be appropriate.

The RECORD KEEPING RULE requires that the appraiser's workfile include "all data, information, and documentation necessary to...show compliance with USPAP." So, the disclosure prior to the agreement or upon discovery must be documented in the appraiser's workfile.

28. VALUE OPINIONS THAT EQUAL CONTRACT PRICES

Question: **I know appraisers who consistently conclude that the market value of any property they appraise is equal to the contract sale price. In doing so, they facilitate sales and financing of sales, which is apparently what keeps their clients happy. Is this a violation of USPAP?**

Response: A contract sale price can be a good indicator of a property's market value, and it may be logical and reasonable for the appraiser to conclude that they are the same. However, this is not always the case. In some situations, a contract price will exceed what is typical in a market. In other situations, a contract price will be less than what is typical. A contract sale price, while a significant piece of market data, must not become a target in an appraisal assignment. Rather, competent analysis of relevant and credible market data must be the appraiser's basis for a market value conclusion.

If an appraiser consistently concludes that the contract sale price of every appraised property equals market value, particularly when a competent analysis of credible market data indicates otherwise, the appraiser's impartiality, objectivity and independence appear to have been compromised. The ETHICS RULE clearly prohibits such a practice. The Conduct section of the ETHICS RULE includes the following statements:

An appraiser must perform assignments with impartiality, objectivity, and independence, and without accommodation of personal interests.

An appraiser must not agree to perform an assignment with bias.

An appraiser must not advocate the cause or interest of any party or issue.

An appraiser must not agree to perform an assignment that includes the reporting of predetermined opinions and conclusions.

© The Appraisal Foundation

An appraiser must not use or communicate a report or assignment results known by the appraiser to be misleading or fraudulent.

An appraiser must not knowingly permit an employee or other person to communicate a report or assignment results that are misleading or fraudulent.

The Management section of the **ETHICS RULE** also states that:

An appraiser must not agree to perform an assignment, or have a compensation arrangement for an assignment, that is contingent on any of the following:

1. ***the reporting of a predetermined result (e.g., opinion of value);***
2. ***a direction in assignment results that favors the cause of the client;***
3. *the amount of a value opinion;*
4. *the attainment of a stipulated result (e.g., that the loan closes or taxes are reduced); or*
5. *the occurrence of a subsequent event directly related to the appraiser's opinions and specific to the assignment's purpose.* (Bold added for emphasis)

An appraiser must develop an opinion of market value impartially and objectively. An appraiser who selects only data that complements a contract sale price or analyzes data in a manner to purposefully support a contract sale price violates the ETHICS RULE.

29. ARE CONDITION AND MARKETABILITY REPORTS COVERED BY USPAP?

Question: **I am a state certified appraiser and was recently asked by a client to perform a condition and marketability report. A value conclusion is not required as part of the assignment; however, I must sign the report as an appraiser. Is this assignment covered by USPAP?**

Response: Yes. Since the condition and marketability of a property directly pertain to its value, this is a valuation service. Furthermore, because you are being asked to perform the service as an appraiser, the assignment involves appraisal practice. USPAP defines appraisal practice as:

*valuation services performed by an individual acting **as an appraiser**, including but not limited to appraisal and appraisal review.*

Comment: Appraisal practice is provided only by appraisers, while valuation services are provided by a variety of professionals and others. The terms appraisal and appraisal review are intentionally generic and are not mutually exclusive. For example, an opinion of value may be required as part of an appraisal review assignment. Bold added for emphasis)

All services performed as part of appraisal practice must comply with USPAP. The portions of USPAP that apply generally to appraisal practice include the PREAMBLE, the DEFINITIONS, the COMPETENCY RULE, and the JURISDICTIONAL EXCEPTION RULE (See Advisory Opinion 21, *USPAP Compliance* for further advice.)

30. UNACCEPTABLE ASSIGNMENT CONDITIONS – NONDISCLOSURE OF FACTS

Question: **I have an assignment that involves a tract of land that is improved with two structures. However, the client has requested that I appraise the underlying land and only one of the two structures, without mentioning the other structure. Is it ethical to not disclose the presence of the second structure?**

© The Appraisal Foundation

Response: No. The Conduct section of the ETHICS RULE states:

An appraiser must not use or communicate a report or assignment results known by the appraiser to be misleading or fraudulent.

An appraiser must not knowingly permit an employee or other person to communicate a report or assignment results that are misleading or fraudulent.

In the situation described, performing an appraisal without disclosing the existence of both structures in the report would be misleading.

31. DOES DISCLOSURE OF PRIOR SERVICES APPLY TO APPRAISER OR PROPERTY?

Question: **An appraiser performed a review of an appraisal report for 123 Main Street. Seven months later, he was asked to review another appraisal report regarding the same property prepared by the same appraiser. The appraiser is unsure if he must disclose to the client that he provided a prior service regarding the subject property. He knows an appraisal review is the development and communication regarding the quality of another appraiser's work. He thinks a review assignment is not about a property, it is about an appraiser. Is the reviewer correct that the subject of an appraisal review is the appraiser and no disclosure of any prior services is necessary?**

Response: No. An appraisal review assignment is not about an appraiser, but the work of the appraiser. As such, an appraisal review is a prior service. Standards Rule 3-2 provides additional insight into developing an appraisal review. The reviewer must:

(c) *identify the purpose of the appraisal review, including whether the assignment includes the development of the reviewer's own opinion of value or review opinion related to the work under review.*

(d) *identify the work under review and the characteristics of that work which are relevant to the intended use and purpose of the appraisal review, including:*

(iv) *the physical, legal, and economic characteristics of the property, properties, property type(s), or market area in the work under review.*

Comment: *The subject of an appraisal review assignment may be all or part of a report, a workfile, or a combination of these, and may be related to an appraisal or appraisal review assignment.*

32. DISCLOSURE OF PRIOR SERVICES INVOLVING A PARTNERSHIP (NEW)

Question: **I am a business appraiser. Two years ago I appraised a 5% limited partnership interest for Estate A. Now I am appraising a 7% limited partnership interest for Giftor B. Estate A and Giftor B are brothers. Estate A and Giftor B are founding partners of the partnership and have not moved interests in the partnership amongst themselves.**

Since interest A and interest B have never been owned by the same person within the partnership, am I required to disclose any prior services since I did not previously value the Giftor B interest? Although it is the same partnership, I believe they are different interests; therefore, is there a requirement to disclose my previous appraisal as a prior service?

Response: Yes. By definition, a Limited Partnership interest is "property." A common definition of property includes "something tangible or intangible to which the owner has legal title." Therefore, if any services performed within the past three years regarding the *Partnership* (including any

© The Appraisal Foundation

interest in the Partnership) must be disclosed in accordance with the Conduct section of the ETHICS Rule and Standards Rule 10-3.

33. DISCLOSURE OF PRIOR SERVICES FOR MULTIPLE ASSIGNMENTS ON A PROPERTY (NEW)

Question: **A lender contracts with AMC A for an appraisal. The subject property is currently under contract for over $3,000,000. Given the price and the lender's high-dollar policy, the lender also orders a second appraisal from AMC B. Each AMC unknowingly engages the same appraiser on the same day. The appraiser subsequently completes and delivers two reports, one for AMC A and one for AMC B. As one might expect, the reports are identical except for the AMC name.**

The lender receives both reports and is very upset because neither report discloses any prior services had been performed. When contacted, the appraiser states that since both orders were received on the same day, his statements in each report that there had been no prior services were both correct. Is the appraiser correct?

Response: No. One assignment was performed prior to the other. Therefore, in the second assignment the appraiser would have to comply with the USPAP requirements to disclose the first assignment as a prior service.

© The Appraisal Foundation

34. FEES PAID FOR PROCUREMENT OF AN ASSIGNMENT

Question: **It has come to my attention that a local appraiser is paying a home inspection firm a $25.00 referral fee for each appraisal assignment the home inspector refers to the appraiser. Are appraisers required by USPAP to disclose the payment of cash or other things of value to clients in order to obtain assignments?**

Response: Yes. The Management section of the ETHICS RULE states that:

An appraiser must disclose that he or she paid a fee or commission, or gave a thing of value in connection with the procurement of an assignment.

Comment: The disclosure must appear in the certification and in any transmittal letter in which conclusions are stated; however, disclosure of the amount paid is not required. In groups or organizations engaged in appraisal practice, intra-company payments to employees for business development do not require disclosure.

35. COUPONS FOR PRICE DISCOUNTS

Question: **Is it a violation of USPAP for an appraiser to offer a 10% discount coupon as a marketing tool to attract potential clients?**

Response: No. The use of a coupon as a marketing tool would not be a violation of the ETHICS RULE. However, a coupon for a reduced fee would be a thing of value connected to the procurement of an assignment. Therefore, proper disclosure must be made in the certification of the report and in any transmittal letter in which value conclusions are stated.

The Management section of the ETHICS RULE states:

An appraiser must disclose that he or she paid a fee or commission, or gave a thing of value in connection with the procurement of an assignment.

Comment: The disclosure must appear in the certification and in any transmittal letter in which conclusions are stated; however, disclosure of the amount paid is not required. In groups or organizations engaged in appraisal practice, intra-company payments to employees for business development do not require disclosure.

36. PAYMENT OF FEES TO BE INCLUDED ON APPROVED APPRAISERS LIST

Question: **Is it ethical for an appraiser to pay a fee to be included on a lender's approved appraiser list?**

Response: Yes. It is ethical for appraisers to pay a fee to be included on a lender's approved appraiser list provided that the appraisers disclose payment of a fee in their appraisal reports.

The Management section of the ETHICS RULE states that:

An appraiser must disclose that he or she paid a fee commission, or gave a thing of value in connection with the procurement of an assignment.

© The Appraisal Foundation

*Comment: The **disclosure must appear in the certification and in any transmittal letter in which conclusions are stated**; however, disclosure of the amount paid is not required. In groups or organizations engaged in appraisal practice, intra-company payments to employees for business development do not require disclosure.* (Bold added for emphasis)

37. CONDUCTING DRAWINGS TO PROCURE APPRAISAL ASSIGNMENTS

Question: **Is it a violation of USPAP for an appraisal firm to conduct a random drawing with prizes and allow clients a certain number of entries in the drawing that is based on the number of appraisals ordered within a certain period of time?**

Response: This is not a violation if proper disclosure is made. The payment of **undisclosed** fees, commissions or things of value in the procurement of appraisal assignments is unethical, as stated in the Management section of the ETHICS RULE:

> *An appraiser must disclose that he or she paid a fee or commission, or gave a thing of value in connection with the procurement of an assignment.*

An entry into a drawing would be considered a thing of value. The Comment further states that:

> *The disclosure must appear in the certification and in any transmittal letter in which conclusions are stated; however, disclosure of the amount paid is not required.*

38. REDUCING APPRAISAL FEES WHEN TRANSACTIONS FAIL TO CLOSE

Question: **Is it ethical for an appraiser to offer a client a reduced fee on an appraisal if the client's loan does not close?**

Would the result be different if the client agreed to pay extra for other assignments?

Response: Neither practice would be ethical. Offering a client a reduced fee on an appraisal if the client's loan does not close is a violation of the ETHICS RULE. The Management section of the ETHICS RULE states:

> *An appraiser must not agree to perform an assignment, or have a compensation arrangement for an assignment, that is contingent on any of the following:*
>
> 1. *the reporting of a predetermined result (e.g., opinion of value);*
> 2. *a direction in assignment results that favors the cause of the client;*
> 3. *the amount of a value opinion;*
> 4. ***the attainment of a stipulated result (e.g., that the loan closes or taxes are reduced); or***
> 5. ***the occurrence of a subsequent event directly related to the appraiser's opinions and specific to the assignment's purpose.*** (Bold added for emphasis)

Standards Rule 2-3(a), 4-3(a), 6-3(a), 8-3(a), or 10-3(a), as applicable, also requires an appraiser to state that their compensation for completing the assignment is not contingent upon a subsequent event. Being paid an extra amount for other assignments does not change this result.

© The Appraisal Foundation

39. APPRAISAL FEES AS PERCENTAGES OF VALUE CONCLUSIONS

Question: **Is it acceptable for an appraisal fee to be based on a percentage of the value conclusion?**

Response: No. The Management section of the ETHICS RULE states:

An appraiser must not agree to perform an assignment, or have a compensation arrangement for an assignment, that is contingent on any of the following:

1. *the reporting of a predetermined result (e.g., opinion of value);*
2. *a direction in assignment results that favors the cause of the client;*
3. ***the amount of a value opinion;***
4. *the attainment of a stipulated result (e.g., that the loan closes or taxes are reduced); or*
5. *the occurrence of a subsequent event directly related to the appraiser's opinions and specific to the assignment's purpose.* (Bold added for emphasis.)

This is reiterated in the signed certification (Standards Rule 2-3, 4-3, 6-3, 8-3, and 10-3) that must be included in each appraisal or appraisal review report.

40. APPRAISAL FEE IS CONTINGENT ON THE APPRAISED VALUE

Question: **A potential client has asked me to complete a form indicating what my appraisal fees would be for different assignments. The form asks me to indicate my appraisal fees according to appraised value, e.g., to list the fee for assignments with appraised values between $100,000 and $299,000, $300,000 to $499,000, etc. Is it a violation of USPAP to quote fees in this manner?**

Response: Yes. This is in violation of USPAP. Completing and submitting such a form to a potential client establishes a compensation arrangement for assignments that is contingent on the amount of the value opinion. This is prohibited by the Management section of the ETHICS RULE, which states, in part:

An appraiser must not agree to perform an assignment, or have a compensation arrangement for an assignment, that is contingent on any of the following:

1. *the reporting of a predetermined result (e.g., opinion of value);*
2. *a direction in assignment results that favors the cause of the client;*
3. ***the amount of a value opinion;***
4. *the attainment of a stipulated result (e.g., that the loan closes or taxes are reduced); or*
5. *the occurrence of a subsequent event directly related to the appraiser's opinions and specific to the assignment's purpose.* (Bold added for emphasis.)

41. APPRAISAL FEE BASED ON OUTCOME OF ASSIGNMENT

Question: **I am aware of some appraisers who perform property tax assessment appeal assignments where their fee is based on a percentage of the tax savings to the property owner. Doesn't USPAP prohibit appraisers from agreeing to perform assignments where the fee is based on a specific outcome?**

Response: Yes. The Management section of the ETHICS RULE states, in part:

An appraiser must not agree to perform an assignment, or have a compensation

© The Appraisal Foundation

arrangement for an assignment, that is contingent on any of the following:

1. *the reporting of a predetermined result (e.g., opinion of value);*
2. *a direction in assignment results that favors the cause of the client;*
3. *the amount of a value opinion;*
4. ***the attainment of a stipulated result** (e.g., that the loan closes, or taxes are reduced); or*
5. *the occurrence of a subsequent event directly related to the appraiser's opinions and specific to the assignment's purpose.* (Bold added for emphasis)

42. ACTING AS AN APPRAISER

Question: **I know that appraisers are prohibited from agreeing to perform appraisal assignments in which the fee is contingent upon the attainment of a stipulated result, such as a reduction in property taxes. However, I've heard of some appraisers who believe that they are able to perform such assignments, claiming that they are not "acting as an appraiser." Are these appraisers correct?**

Response: USPAP only applies to individuals when they are performing as an appraiser. If an individual is providing this service in some other role, the individual's USPAP obligation would be to not misrepresent that role. If individuals perform a *valuation service* which is outside of *appraisal practice*, they may be able to perform such a service without complying with USPAP, subject to applicable laws and regulations. It is extremely important, however, for all state licensed or certified appraisers to fully understand the laws and regulations related to their state appraiser credentials; **most states require their credentialed appraisers to comply with USPAP when engaged in appraisal practice**, which would prohibit the appraiser from agreeing to perform assignments where the fee is contingent upon attainment of a stipulated result.

43. "USPAP CERTIFIED" ADVERTISEMENT

Question: **Recently I have seen numerous advertisements from individuals who may have completed a USPAP course and describe themselves as "USPAP Certified Appraisers," or their reports as "USPAP Certified Appraisals." Is this an actual credential, and if not, is that wording misleading?**

Response: There is no such credential. The use of the expression "USPAP Certified Appraiser" is misleading. Completing a USPAP course does not entitle one to call oneself a USPAP Certified Appraiser.

One requirement for an appraisal or appraisal review is that the report include the appraiser's certification that: "to the best of my knowledge and belief my analyses, opinions, and conclusions were developed, and this report has been prepared, in conformity with the *Uniform Standards of Professional Appraisal Practice*." The use of language such as "USPAP Certified Appraisal" could be taken by intended users to mean that there was some independent certification of compliance. If that could be inferred from the language used, this would also be misleading.

44. APPRAISER'S FEES BASED ON PENDING SALE PRICE

Question: **I'm aware that an appraiser's fee cannot be based on the amount of the appraiser's value conclusion. However, does USPAP allow an appraiser's fee to be based on the amount of the owner's estimate or a pending sale price of the subject property?**

Response: USPAP does not prohibit an appraiser's fee from being based on an owner's estimate, a pending sale price of the subject property, loan amount, or any other factor outside the appraiser's control.

© The Appraisal Foundation

This is in contrast to a fee based on the amount of the appraiser's opinion of value, which is within the appraiser's control. A fee arrangement based on the appraiser's opinion of value violates the ETHICS RULE.

45. DISCOUNTED APPRAISAL FEES

Question: **Is it a violation of USPAP to offer reduced appraisal fees for clients that send me a large volume of business? Could I also offer a discount for the method of payment, such as collecting the fee from the borrower at the time of inspection?**

Response: Appraisers may establish their fees based on a number of factors, including the amount of business received, business relationships, method of payment, and client-specific requirements. However, appraisers must ensure that they comply with the Management section of the ETHICS RULE.

46. DISCLOSURE OF REFERRAL FEE AMOUNTS

Question: **The Management section of the ETHICS RULE requires an appraiser to disclose *fees or commissions paid, or things of value given* in connection with the procurement of an assignment. If a referral fee was paid in conjunction with an assignment, must the amount of the fee be disclosed, or is it sufficient to simply disclose that a fee was paid?**

Response: Disclosing the fact that a payment was made in the appraisal certification and any transmittal letter where the conclusions are stated is sufficient to meet the requirement. However, this is a minimum requirement and does not prohibit full disclosure of the amount of the fee.

47. RECIPROCAL BUSINESS ARRANGEMENTS

Question: **A new bank client recently sent me a letter acknowledging that my firm is approved to perform appraisal assignments for their company. It goes on to state that we are now preferred providers and expresses the bank's desire to embark on a mutually beneficial long-term relationship. The letter ends with a solicitation for my firm's banking business as part of this mutually beneficial relationship. I would like to make them happy because they could provide my firm a great deal of business. If I bring my banking business to this company, while I'm engaged as an appraiser, would I be violating USPAP?**

Response: The answer to this question depends on whether the bank's approval of your firm as a preferred provider is conditional on you moving your banking business to that bank. The Management section of the ETHICS RULE states:

> *An appraiser must disclose that he or she paid a fee or commission, or gave a thing of value in connection with the procurement of an assignment.*
>
> *Comment: The disclosure must appear in the certification and in any transmittal letter in which conclusions are stated; however, disclosure of the amount paid is not required. In groups or organizations engaged in appraisal practice, intra-company payments to employees for business development do not require disclosure.*

If the lender has stated that your firm can only have their appraisal business if you bank with them, this relationship must be disclosed as described in the ETHICS RULE.

However, if the client is merely soliciting your business as it would any other potential customer, and you subsequently moved your banking business to that bank, there is no requirement in USPAP to disclose your banking relationship.

© The Appraisal Foundation

48. DOES USPAP APPLY IF THERE IS NO ASSIGNMENT FEE?

Question: **I am an appraiser who performs appraisal and appraisal review assignments, and I am required to comply with USPAP. I have been asked to perform one such assignment without charging a fee. Is my requirement to comply with USPAP impacted if I do not charge a fee?**

Response: No. The applicability of USPAP is not affected by the amount of the fee, or lack of a fee.

49. CAN APPRAISERS PERFORM COMP CHECK ASSIGNMENTS FOR FREE?

Question: **Does USPAP allow appraisers to perform comp check assignments for free?**

Response: Yes. However, the appraiser would have to ensure that receiving a full appraisal assignment is not contingent upon the result of the comp check assignment. The Management section of the ETHICS RULE states, in part:

> *An appraiser must not agree to perform an assignment, or have a compensation arrangement for an assignment, that is contingent on any of the following:*
>
> 1. *the reporting of a predetermined result (e.g., opinion of value);*
> 2. *a direction in assignment results that favors the cause of the client;*
> 3. *the amount of a value opinion;*
> 4. *the attainment of a stipulated result (e.g., that the loan closes, or taxes are reduced) ; or*
> 5. ***the occurrence of a subsequent event directly related to the appraiser's opinions and specific to the assignment's purpose***. (Bold added for emphasis.)

50. IS DISCLOSURE OF A FREE COMP CHECK ASSIGNMENT REQUIRED?

Question 1: **If I perform a free comp check assignment and my client subsequently asks me to perform a full (or traditional) assignment on the same property, do I have to disclose the free comp check assignment as having provided a thing of value to procure the new assignment?**

Response: No. The Management section of the ETHICS RULE states, in part:

> *An appraiser must disclose that he or she paid a fee or commission, or gave a thing of value in connection with the procurement of an assignment.*

Since USPAP prohibits the second assignment from being contingent upon the first, the free comp check could not be considered part of procuring the second assignment. Disclosure of the free comp check assignment would not be required as a "thing of value." However, the Conduct section of the ETHICS RULE requires disclosure of all prior services performed related to the subject property within the prior three years.

An appraiser may provide a free comp check. However, an appraiser must not provide a free comp check and the pursuant appraisal if the engagement was contingent upon developing or reporting predetermined results.

Question 2: **Must I also disclose that this comp check was a prior service in the subsequent assignment?**

Response: Yes. The comp check was a prior service and must be disclosed to the client at the time the appraiser agrees to perform the new assignment. The prior service must also be disclosed in the report certification.

© The Appraisal Foundation

51. APPRAISAL FEE PAID AT CLOSE OF FINANCING TRANSACTION

Question: **I have a potential lending client that wants to arrange for my appraisal fees to be paid at the closing of each financing transaction. Does USPAP permit this fee arrangement?**

Response: USPAP does not address the time frame for payment of fees. In the situation described there must be a clear agreement that the fee cannot depend on the closing of the financing transaction. Agreeing to perform an assignment where the appraisal fee is paid *only* upon successful closing of the transaction is a violation of the Management section of the ETHICS RULE:

> *An appraiser must not agree to perform an assignment, or have a compensation arrangement for an assignment, that is contingent on any of the following:*
>
> 1. *the reporting of a predetermined result (e.g., opinion of value);*
> 2. *a direction in assignment results that favors the cause of the client;*
> 3. *the amount of a value opinion;*
> 4. ***the attainment of a stipulated result (e.g., that the loan closes or taxes are reduced);*** *or*
> 5. ***the occurrence of a subsequent event directly related to the appraiser's opinions and specific to the assignment's purpose****.* (Bold added for emphasis.)

One way appraisers can avoid any ambiguity is by having a written agreement with the client detailing the manner in which the appraisal fee will be paid if the transaction does not close.

52. PAYMENT OF A PORTAL FEE (NEW)

Question: **Does the Management section of the ETHICS RULE in USPAP require the disclosure of a portal fee?**

Response: No. The payment of a fee to use a portal is not connected to the procurement of an assignment. Payment of a portal fee is not an inducement. The client who uses the portal typically indicates that they require delivery of the assignment via a portal when offering the assignment to the appraiser in the engagement process. This agreed-upon delivery method is similar to other conditions such as fee, due date and appraisal form type.

The obligation to use a portal is similar to requiring the appraiser to deliver the report via overnight delivery with a specified number of hard copies, or requiring that the appraiser deliver the file electronically in XML format via email. In both examples the cost of overnight shipping, printing, paper, etc. or the cost of buying a software solution that can produce a file in XML format would not require disclosure.

There are many examples of obligations or contractual terms that are part of an assignment but do not require disclosure, such as:

- Electronic delivery in a specified method or format (computer, internet, software)
- Fees associated with receiving electronic payment
- Number of hard copies of color printed photographs of the subject property (requires a camera, film, photo-processing/printing costs)
- Report delivery via an overnight courier

© The Appraisal Foundation

53. REPORTING OF ADVERSE CONDITIONS

Question: **I just inspected a property and found an adverse condition. I informed my client (a bank) and was told not to proceed because the client cannot lend on such property. Under USPAP, am I obligated to inform any other party, such as the city or county health department?**

Response: No. USPAP does not contain a specific requirement to report the existence of the adverse condition. However, there may be some state or local law or regulation that applies.

54. DUE PROCESS OF LAW

Question: **I am a personal property appraiser that specializes in the appraisal of coins and currency. I am required, by federal law, to report United States counterfeit coins and currency to the U.S. Secret Service. In reporting these counterfeit coins and currency, I am also required under federal law to provide them with the name and contact information of my client. Would disclosing my client's name under these circumstances be a jurisdictional exception under USPAP?**

Response: No, this issue does not constitute a jurisdictional exception. The Confidentiality section of the ETHICS RULE in USPAP prohibits an appraiser from disclosing *confidential information* (as defined in USPAP). However, it is not a violation of USPAP to disclose the name of the appraiser's client. Exceptions would be if the client's name qualified as *confidential information* (as defined in USPAP), or if the appraiser contractually agreed with the client not to disclose the client's name.

Even if the appraiser agreed not to disclose the name of the client, the Confidentiality section of the ETHICS RULE permits the appraiser to disclose the client's name to "such third parties as may be authorized by due process of law." If federal law mandates an appraiser to communicate confidential information, the appraiser must comply with that law.

55. DISCLOSING RESULTS OF APPRAISAL ASSIGNMENTS

Question: **I have been asked by my client's business associate for information relating to an appraisal report I prepared for my client. Can I disclose the results of an appraisal assignment to parties other than the client?**

Response: You can, but *only* if you receive authorization from the client before sharing assignment results with the client's associate. The Confidentiality section of the ETHICS RULE states, in part:

> *An appraiser must protect the confidential nature of the appraiser-client relationship.*
>
> *An appraiser must not disclose: (1) confidential information or (2) assignment results to anyone other than:*
>
> - *the client;*
> - ***parties specifically authorized by the client;***
> - *state appraiser regulatory agencies;*
> - *third parties as may be authorized by due process of law; or*
> - *a duly authorized professional peer review committee except when such disclosure to a committee would violate applicable law or regulation.* (Bold added for emphasis.)

© The Appraisal Foundation

56. "VERIFYING" COMPLETION OF AN APPRAISAL

Question: **I have received inquiries from various companies regarding appraisals I have completed for others. Typically, I receive a letter that includes the address of a property I previously appraised, along with the effective date of my appraisal, and my appraised value. The letter asks me to confirm that the information agrees with my records, and also asks me to confirm that my appraisal was performed without violating any appraiser independence requirements. Since the company requesting the information was not my client, does USPAP allow me to comply with such requests for information?**

Response: No. Unless you have received permission from your client, you may not communicate assignment results or confidential information (both, as defined in USPAP) to this third party (or any other entity that your client did not authorize).

Acknowledging the fact that you performed an appraisal on a property is not prohibited by USPAP. However, in this instance, acknowledging assignment results or confidential information without permission from the client is prohibited.

There are also instances where appraisers contractually agree with some clients to not disclose the fact that an appraisal was performed; in such cases the appraiser's contractual obligation would preclude the appraiser from disclosing even the fact that an appraisal was performed.

57. APPRAISAL REPORT RECEIVED BY OTHERS

Question: **I was recently contacted by a lender regarding an appraisal I had performed for another client. The lender had somehow obtained a copy of my appraisal report and wanted me to answer some questions. However, this lender was not my original client and was not named as an intended user. Are there any USPAP prohibitions against discussing my appraisal with this lender?**

Response: Yes. USPAP prohibits the appraiser from communicating *assignment results or confidential information* (as defined in USPAP) to anyone other than the client and parties specifically authorized by the client (with the exception of those authorized by due process of law, state appraiser regulatory agencies, and a duly authorized professional peer review committee under certain conditions). Even if the lender who had contacted the appraiser was identified as an intended user in the original appraisal report, that lender is not part of the appraiser-client relationship. Therefore, authorization from the client would be needed if that lender wanted to discuss *assignment results or confidential information*.

Barring an agreement between the appraiser and the original client prohibiting disclosure of any information pertaining to the assignment, appraisers may confirm that they performed an appraisal on the subject property, and may communicate anything other than *assignment results* (which include the appraiser's opinions and conclusions, in addition to the value conclusion) or *confidential information* (as defined in USPAP).

58. DISCLOSURE OF A PRIOR ASSIGNMENT

Question: **As a condition of engagement, a financial institution requires that I disclose any prior appraisals I have completed on the subject property. If I disclose that I have previously appraised the subject property, am I violating USPAP?**

Response: Disclosing the fact that you have previously appraised the property is permitted, **and required by USPAP as explained in the following paragraph**, except in the case when an appraiser has agreed to keep the mere occurrence of a prior assignment confidential.

The Conduct section of the ETHICS RULE states, in part:

© The Appraisal Foundation

If known prior to agreeing to perform an assignment, and/or if discovered at any time during the assignment, an appraiser must disclose to the client, and in the subsequent report certification:

any current or prospective interest in the subject property or parties involved; and
any services regarding the subject property performed by the appraiser within the ***three year period immediately the agreement to perform the assignment,*** *as an appraiser or in any other capacity (Bold added for emphasis)*

There are some cases in which appraisers are asked by the client not to reveal that they have appraised that particular property. In such cases, the fact that the appraiser previously appraised the property is confidential information.

If the occurrence of a prior appraisal is confidential, and disclosure of prior appraisals is a condition of a potential new assignment or a requirement of USPAP, the appraiser must decline the new assignment because the appraiser could not make the requested disclosure.

59. SAMPLE APPRAISAL REPORTS AND THE ETHICS RULE

Question: **I am a fee appraiser currently seeking to get on the approved list for a prospective client. In order to be considered for approval, this lender requires appraisers to provide sample appraisal reports performed within the past year. Is there a way that I can accomplish this without violating USPAP?**

Response: In order to provide this information an appraiser must satisfy the Confidentiality section of the ETHICS RULE. This section states:

An appraiser must protect the confidential nature of the appraiser-client relationship.

An appraiser must act in good faith with regard to the legitimate interests of the client in the use of confidential information and in the communication of assignment results.

An appraiser must be aware of, and comply with, all confidentiality and privacy laws and regulations applicable in an assignment.

An appraiser must not disclose: (1) confidential information or (2) assignment results to anyone other than:

- *the client;*
- *parties specifically authorized by the client;*
- *state appraiser regulatory agencies;*
- *third parties as may be authorized by due process of law; or*
- *a duly authorized professional peer review committee except when such disclosure to a committee would violate applicable law or regulation.*

The Comment further explains that if all essential elements of confidential information are removed through redaction or the process of aggregation, client authorization is not required for the disclosure of the remaining information, as modified.

The appraiser in this case has three options:

1. Decline the request to provide the information, or
2. Obtain authorization from the client of each sample appraisal report, or
3. Provide sample reports, but redact all information that should not be provided to anyone other than the client, such as confidential information or assignment results.

© The Appraisal Foundation

60. PROVIDING SAMPLE APPRAISAL REPORTS

Question: **Recently I've heard that some appraisers are using a questionable technique to provide sample appraisal reports for prospective clients. These appraisers will redact all confidential information from the report (as required to comply with the Confidentiality section of the ETHICS RULE in USPAP) and send the redacted sample report to a prospective client, but then will follow-up with an additional e-mail that provides the client with all of the information that had been redacted from the sample report. Is this practice acceptable?**

Response: No. Although the confidential information and assignment results are not being communicated simultaneously with the initial submission of the sample report, they are nonetheless being communicated in the subsequent e-mail transmission.

The Confidentiality section of the ETHICS RULE does not permit communicating confidential information and assignment results without the client's consent, even if that information is provided in a separate communication.

61. CONFIDENTIALITY AND SAMPLE APPRAISAL REPORTS

Question: **I have found that many prospective clients request samples of my appraisal reports. I'm concerned that I would be in violation of appraiser-client confidentiality by providing them. To alleviate this problem, I'm considering including the following disclaimer in the fine print of my reports:**

"The appraiser reserves the right to use this report in its entirety as sample work for the purpose of soliciting prospective clients unless written refusal is received from the client."

Does USPAP allow me to do this?

Response: No. The client, not the appraiser, determines who may receive the appraisal report. The Confidentiality section of the ETHICS RULE states, in part:

An appraiser must protect the confidential nature of the appraiser-client relationship.

An appraiser must act in good faith with regard to the legitimate interests of the client in the use of confidential information and in the communication of assignment results.

An appraiser must be aware of, and comply with, all confidentiality and privacy laws and regulations applicable in an assignment.

An appraiser must not disclose: (1) confidential information or (2) assignment results to anyone other than:

- *the client;*
- *parties specifically authorized by the client;*
- *state appraiser regulatory agencies;*
- *third parties as may be authorized by due process of law; or*
- *a duly authorized professional peer review committee except when such disclosure to a committee would violate applicable law or regulation.*

Including a statement indicating that the report may be used as a sample does not constitute client authorization to distribute copies of the report.

One solution is to obtain client authorization to use each report as a work sample. An alternative solution may be to redact all confidential information from the report before providing it as a sample. The Comment to the Rule states:

© The Appraisal Foundation

When all confidential elements of confidential information, and assignments results are removed through redaction or the process of aggregation, client authorization is not required for the disclosure of the remaining information, as modified.

62. DELIVERING A REPORT BY EMAIL TO A CLIENT

Question: **I have been told that since email is not secure, delivering reports to my clients by email violates the confidentiality requirements of USPAP. Does emailing a report violate USPAP?**

Response: No. It is the opinion of the Appraisal Standards Board that sending reports via email does not violate the confidentiality requirements in USPAP.

In all assignments the appraiser and the client should agree to a delivery method, and should understand any security risks associated with the delivery method. Whether a report is sent by government mail service, private mail service, email, courier or some other mechanism, there is always some risk that the security of the original document may be compromised.

63. CONFIDENTIALITY AND INTENDED USERS

Question: **I recently performed an appraisal. Yesterday, an intended user who is not the client contacted me to discuss the appraisal. Do I need the client's authorization to discuss the appraisal with this intended user?**

Response: Yes. Although intended users have an important role in the appraiser's decisions about the appropriate scope of work and the content of the report, the appraiser cannot discuss the appraisal with an intended user without the client's authorization. The Confidentiality section of the ETHICS RULE states:

An appraiser must not disclose: (1) confidential information; or (2) assignment results to anyone other than:

- ***the client;***
- ***parties specifically authorized by the client***... (Bold added for emphasis)

The appraiser-client relationship is distinct from the appraiser's relationship to intended users.

64. CONFIDENTIALITY AND REVIEW APPRAISERS

Question: **A few weeks ago I performed an appraisal for a lender client. I was recently contacted by an individual who claimed to be a review appraiser hired by the lender. She wanted to ask me some questions about my appraisal. Can I discuss my appraisal with her?**

Response: Yes; but *only* if you receive authorization from the client. The Confidentiality section of the ETHICS RULE states, in part:

An appraiser must protect the confidential nature of the appraiser-client relationship.

An appraiser must not disclose: (1) confidential information; or (2) assignment results to anyone other than:

- *the client;*
- *parties specifically authorized by the client;*
- *state appraiser regulatory agencies;*
- *third parties as may be authorized by due process of law; or*
- *a duly authorized professional peer review committee except when such disclosure to a committee would violate applicable law or regulation.*

© The Appraisal Foundation

65. DISCLOSURE OF ASSIGNMENT RESULTS TO STATE APPRAISER REGULATORY AGENCY

Question: **A new state law requires all real estate appraisers in my area to regularly submit a log to the State Appraiser Board reporting the address of properties appraised along with the value opinion. Does this violate the confidentiality requirements in USPAP?**

Response: No. This does not violate USPAP.

The Confidentiality section of the ETHICS RULE states, in part:

An appraiser must not disclose: (1) confidential information or (2) assignment results to anyone other than:

- *the client;*
- *persons specifically authorized by the client;*
- ***state appraiser regulatory agencies;***
- *third parties as may be authorized by due process of law; and*
- *a duly authorized professional peer review committee except when such disclosure to a committee would violate applicable law or regulation.* (Bold added for emphasis.)

Disclosure of assignment results to the state board, or to any other entity required by law, is specifically permitted.

66. DUE PROCESS UNDER CONFIDENTIALITY

Question: **I received a request from my state attorney general's office to turn over some appraisal reports I had prepared. Can I comply with this simple request or must it be in the form of a subpoena?**

Response: The Confidentiality section of the ETHICS RULE states, in part:

An appraiser must not disclose: (1) confidential information or (2) assignment results to anyone other than:

- *the client;*
- *parties specifically authorized by the client;*
- ***state appraiser regulatory agencies;***
- *third parties as may be authorized by due process of law; or*
- *a duly authorized professional peer review committee except when such disclosure to a committee would violate applicable law or regulation.* (Bold added for emphasis.)

USPAP does not identify what constitutes due process of law. While a subpoena or court order might clearly constitute due process, a simple verbal or written request might not. Therefore, for requests of this type, it may be necessary to seek legal counsel to determine what constitutes due process.

67. COMMUNICATING CONFIDENTIAL INFORMATION TO A SWORN PEACE OFFICER

Question: **I was contacted by a sworn peace officer who simply requested the workfile of an assignment I had previously completed. The officer made this request without a subpoena or any form of court order. If the workfile contains confidential information, does USPAP allow me to comply with the officer's request?**

Response: The answer to the question depends on whether or not the officer's request qualifies as due process of law.

© The Appraisal Foundation

The Confidentiality section of the ETHICS RULE states, in part:

An appraiser must not disclose: (1) confidential information or (2) assignment results to anyone other than:

- *the client;*
- *parties specifically authorized by the client;*
- *state appraiser regulatory agencies;*
- *third parties as may be authorized by due process of law; or*
- *a duly authorized professional peer review committee except when such disclosure to a committee would violate applicable law or regulation.*

It is likely that this determination would need to be made by a court or other legal body, since USPAP does not define what due process of law constitutes. You may want to seek legal advice to determine an appropriate response.

It is also important to note that if the officer made the request on behalf of a state enforcement agency, the portion of the Confidentiality section of the ETHICS RULE quoted above allows the appraiser to communicate confidential information.

68. CONFIDENTIALITY AND PEER REVIEW COMMITTEES

Question: **Is it ethical to disclose confidential information to a duly authorized professional peer review committee?**

Response: Yes. However, the appraiser must be aware of and comply with applicable laws or regulations that would pertain to such disclosure. The Confidentiality section of the ETHICS RULE states, in part:

An appraiser must protect the confidential nature of the appraiser-client relationship.

An appraiser must act in good faith with regard to the legitimate interests of the client in the use of confidential information and in the communication of assignment results.

An appraiser must be aware of, and comply with, all confidentiality and privacy laws and regulations applicable in an assignment.

An appraiser must not disclose: (1) confidential information or (2) assignment results to anyone other than:

- *the client;*
- *parties specifically authorized by the client;*
- *state appraiser regulatory agencies;*
- *third parties as may be authorized by due process of law; or*
- ***a duly authorized professional peer review committee except when such disclosure to a committee would violate applicable law or regulation.*** (Bold added for emphasis.)

A member of a duly authorized professional peer review committee must not disclose confidential information presented to the committee.

Comment: *When all confidential elements of confidential information, and assignment results are removed through redaction or the process of aggregation, client authorization is not required for the disclosure of the remaining information, as modified.*

© The Appraisal Foundation

69. CONFIDENTIALITY AND PRIVACY REGULATIONS

Question: **Does USPAP address the federal privacy laws? And, if it does, where does it address them?**

Response: Yes. USPAP takes into account 16 CFR Part 313 both in the definition of confidential information and in the Confidentiality section of the ETHICS RULE, which states that "an appraiser must be aware of, and comply with, all confidentiality and privacy laws and regulations applicable in an assignment."

USPAP defines confidential information as:

information that is either:

- *identified by the client as confidential when providing it to an appraiser and that is not available from any other source; or*
- *classified as confidential or private by applicable law or regulation.*

A footnote regarding the federal privacy regulations is also included in this definition.

70. WHEN DOES APPRAISER-CLIENT CONFIDENTIALITY END?

Question: **I performed an appraisal assignment for a lender client who has subsequently gone out of business. Now the borrower is requesting a copy of the appraisal report from me since the company is defunct, and there is no way to contact them. Does my obligation for appraiser-client confidentiality end since the client no longer exists?**

Response: No. USPAP has no provision for terminating appraiser-client confidentiality. An appraiser is required to comply with the requirements of the Confidentiality section of the ETHICS RULE, regardless of the status of the client.

71. COPYRIGHTING AN APPRAISAL REPORT

Question: **Does registration of a copyright on an appraisal report with the U.S. Copyright Office violate the confidentiality provisions of USPAP?**

Response: The ASB is taking no position as to whether an appraisal report is copyrightable, and this response does not constitute a legal opinion of the ASB.

If an appraisal report is copyrightable, and if the process of registration with the U.S. Copyright Office includes public disclosure of the appraisal report, such registration would disclose assignment results. Such disclosure would, therefore, result in a breach of the Confidentiality section of the ETHICS RULE of USPAP, unless the appraiser/registrant had the prior approval of the client for such registration.

72. SELLING AN APPRAISAL FIRM AND ETHICAL OBLIGATIONS

Question: **I am considering the sale of my appraisal practice. What are my USPAP obligations regarding confidentiality and record keeping?**

© The Appraisal Foundation

Response: In the sale of an appraisal practice, the selling appraiser must comply with the Confidentiality section of the ETHICS RULE and the RECORD KEEPING RULE.

The Confidentiality section of the ETHICS RULE states, in part:

An appraiser must protect the confidential nature of the appraiser-client relationship.

An appraiser must act in good faith with regard to the legitimate interests of the client in the use of confidential information and in the communication of assignment results.

An appraiser must be aware of, and comply with, all confidentiality and privacy laws and regulations applicable in an assignment.

The RECORD KEEPING RULE states, in part:

An appraiser must have custody of the workfile, or make appropriate workfile retention, access, and retrieval arrangements with the party having custody of the workfile.

The selling appraiser can retain possession of the workfiles to satisfy confidentiality and record keeping obligations. This would also satisfy any client confidentiality agreements and applicable privacy laws and regulations.

The selling appraiser must adhere to the requirement to (1) protect the appraiser-client relationship and (2) not disclose assignment results and confidential information to anyone other than the client and persons specifically authorized by the client. This can be accomplished by seeking client authorization to disclose assignment results and confidential information that would be part of the workfile. Providing the acquiring appraiser with access to the selling appraiser's workfiles without client authorization is a violation of the Confidentiality section of the ETHICS RULE.

With client authorization, the selling appraiser can provide the acquiring appraiser with access to the selling appraiser's workfiles. However, the selling appraiser should also consider the impact of applicable privacy laws and regulations.

To comply with the RECORD KEEPING RULE, the selling appraiser should make appropriate workfile retention, access, and retrieval arrangements as part of the sale terms.

73. PURCHASING AN APPRAISAL FIRM AND ETHICAL OBLIGATIONS

Question: **I am considering the purchase of another appraiser's appraisal practice. What are my USPAP obligations regarding record keeping and confidentiality?**

Response: The acquiring appraiser has general USPAP obligations to protect public trust in appraisal practice. The PREAMBLE, in part:

The appraiser's responsibility is to protect the overall public trust and it is the importance of the role of the appraiser that places ethical obligations on those who serve in this capacity.

The ETHICS RULE states, in part:

An appraiser must promote and preserve the public trust inherent in professional appraisal practice, observing the highest standards of professional ethics.

In the sale of an appraisal practice, the acquiring appraiser should respect the selling appraiser's obligations under the Confidentiality section of the ETHICS RULE and the

© The Appraisal Foundation

RECORD KEEPING RULE.

The acquiring appraiser does not have an appraiser-client relationship with the clients of the selling appraiser, but the acquiring appraiser's obligation to protect public trust creates a responsibility when access is provided to another appraiser's workfile. The acquiring appraiser should treat the acquired assignment results and confidential information in the workfiles in compliance with USPAP.

The acquiring appraiser should honor the workfile retention, access, and retrieval arrangements made by the selling appraiser in compliance with the following RECORD KEEPING RULE.

An appraiser having custody of a workfile must allow other appraisers with workfile obligations related to an assignment appropriate access and retrieval for the purpose of:

- *submission to state appraiser regulatory agencies;*
- *compliance with due process of law;*
- *submission to a duly authorized professional peer review committee; or*
- *compliance with retrieval arrangements.*

74. PROVIDING A COPY OF A WORKFILE

Question: **I recently received a notice from an Appraisal Management Company (AMC) asking that I provide a copy of my complete workfile upon their request. What steps should I take to comply with this request without violating USPAP?**

Response: Providing the AMC with a copy of the workfile is not prohibited by USPAP. However, the appraiser must comply with the Confidentiality section of the ETHICS RULE. The workfile might contain assignment results from another assignment, or confidential information obtained from another client. If so, the appraiser must have authorization from that other client to disclose assignment results or any confidential information related to that assignment.

In addition, the appraiser must be aware of any other laws or regulations applicable to those past assignments, including privacy requirements such as those contained in the Gramm-Leach-Bliley Bank Modernization Act.

75. ARE PHYSICAL CHARACTERISTICS CONFIDENTIAL?

Question: **I am aware that the definition of *assignment results* specifies that physical characteristics are not assignment results. Does this mean that physical characteristics are not confidential?**

Response: Yes. Because physical characteristics are not assignment results, they are not confidential unless identified as such by the client and unless they are not available from any other source. USPAP defines physical characteristics as:

attributes of a property that are observable or measurable as a matter of fact, as distinguished from opinions and conclusions, which are the result of some level of analysis or judgment.

76. PHYSICAL CHARACTERISTICS OR ASSIGNMENT RESULTS?

Question: **I read an appraisal report that included the paragraph below regarding the subject property's Improvements. The paragraph appears to include both a description of the physical characteristics, as well as the appraiser's opinions (i.e., assignment results). I would like clarification on which items are physical characteristics and which are assignment results.**

© The Appraisal Foundation

The subject property is located at 245 Broad Street. The improvements were constructed in 1985 and were renovated in 2010 with all new appliances, bathroom fixtures, and heat/AC. The house, however, has functional problems. There are two bedrooms on the second floor with no bathroom on that floor. The interior decor is dated, and some of the walls are pink, yellow, and purple.

Response: Items that fall under the category of physical characteristics include: the address (245 Broad Street); the age of the improvements (constructed in 1985); the appliances, bathroom fixtures, and heat/AC; the number of bedrooms and baths on the second floor; and the color of the walls (pink, yellow, and purple).

Assignment results (the appraiser's analyses, opinions, and conclusions) include: identifying "functional problems"; and the "interior décor is dated."

77. PHYSICAL CHARACTERISTICS OR ASSIGNMENT RESULTS – RESIDENTIAL REAL PROPERTY EXAMPLE

Question: **I am trying to distinguish between physical characteristics and assignment results in a residential appraisal assignment. Which of the following ten terms are physical characteristics and which are assignment results?**

1. ***Living area is 2,000 SF***
2. ***Property is in good condition***
3. ***The property has functional problems***
4. ***The improvements were constructed in 2005***
5. ***The carpet is new***
6. ***2nd floor has 2 bedrooms, no baths***
7. ***Well landscaped***
8. ***Poor floor plan***
9. ***Carpet needs replacing***
10. ***Walls are painted pink, yellow, and purple***

Response: Physical characteristics do not include an appraiser's opinions. The items listed above shown as #1, 4, 5, 6 & 10 are examples of physical characteristics.

Assignment results include an appraiser's opinions. The items listed above shown as #2, 3, 7, 8 & 9 are examples of an appraiser's opinions, and therefore, are assignment results.

78. PHYSICAL CHARACTERISTICS OR ASSIGNMENT RESULTS – NON-RESIDENTIAL REAL PROPERTY EXAMPLE

Question: **I am trying to distinguish between physical characteristics and assignment results in a non-residential appraisal assignment. Which of the following ten terms are physical characteristics and which are assignment results?**

1. ***Building contains 10,316 SF***
2. ***There is a low land to building ratio***
3. ***The mechanicals are in fair condition***
4. ***The heat/AC equipment is 20 years old***
5. ***Parking access is poor***
6. ***There is 2,000 SF of mezzanine office space***
7. ***There are 4 parking spaces per 1,000 SF of office area***
8. ***The warehouse ceiling height is 14 feet***
9. ***The building has functional problems***
10. ***The building is Class A construction according to Marshall & Swift description***

© The Appraisal Foundation

Response: Physical characteristics do not include an appraiser's opinions. The items listed above shown as #1, 4, 6, 7, 8 & 10 are examples of physical characteristics.

Assignment results include an appraiser's opinions. The items listed above shown as #2, 3, 5 & 9 are examples of an appraiser's opinions, and therefore, are assignment results.

79. PHYSICAL CHARACTERISTICS OR ASSIGNMENT RESULTS – MACHINERY AND EQUIPMENT EXAMPLE

Question: **I recently completed a personal property appraisal of a group of machinery and equipment. My client was the business owner and the intended use was to appeal the tax value established by the local assessor. My client provided a copy of the appraisal to the assessor. I was authorized by my client to share information with the assessor about his machinery and equipment but I was not authorized to share any assignment results.**

The assessor sent me a list of questions via email. Which questions can I answer without violating the Confidentiality section of the ETHICS RULE by disclosing assignment results or confidential information?

Response: Without client authorization, you may not share any assignment results (i.e., opinions or conclusions that you formed as part of the assignment). You may disclose physical characteristics.

Following are examples of questions that you could answer (assuming you know the answer), as they address physical characteristics or other factual information. The answers to the questions would not include opinions or conclusions formed during the assignment.

- *What is the age of Machine A?*
- *Machine A is noted as being rebuilt; when was it rebuilt?*
- *What, specifically, was replaced when Machine A was rebuilt?*
- *The photograph for Machine B shows a larger collection of fluid next to the machine; is that coming from the machine?*
- *If so, what would the cost to repair the leak be?*
- *According to the description for Machine C, it is stored outside. How long has it been outside?*

Conversely, the answers to the following questions would be your opinions, and therefore could not be answered.

- *Immediately after Machine A was rebuilt, on a percentage basis, how would it compare in value to a brand new machine of the same make and model?*
- *What would the value of Machine B be if it was repaired and no longer leaking fluid?*
- *What is the condition of Machine C?*

80. PHYSICAL CHARACTERISTICS OR ASSIGNMENT RESULTS – FINE ART EXAMPLE

Question: **Last year I appraised a painting that was subsequently sold by an auction house. My client was the owner of the painting. A fellow appraiser, who is now appraising a similar painting by the same artist, recently contacted me. This other appraiser is using the painting I appraised as a comparable example and has asked me several questions about its physical condition.**

I would like to help this colleague but want to be sure that I am not violating the Confidentiality section of the ETHICS RULE. My client did not request that I keep the condition report prepared by the auction house confidential, and I still have it in my workfile.

May I share the auction house condition report?

© The Appraisal Foundation

Response: Yes. Even though the condition report includes opinions about the subject painting's condition, they are the opinions of the auction house, not of the appraiser. Therefore, they are not assignment results as defined in USPAP.

To meet the USPAP definition of confidential information, the information must be both identified by the client as confidential, and not available from another source. The auction house condition report was not identified by the client as confidential, and it also may still be available from another source (directly from the auction house). So sharing the auction house's condition report is not a violation.

It should be noted that an appraiser's own opinion as to the condition of the painting would qualify as assignment results under USPAP and, therefore, could not be disclosed without permission from the appraiser's client.

81. WHAT ARE "REASONABLE STEPS"?

Question: **USPAP requires that an appraiser "take reasonable steps to safeguard access to confidential information." What are reasonable steps?**

Response: The Confidentiality section of the ETHICS RULE stipulates that except in certain circumstances, the appraiser must not disclose confidential information or assignment results (both as defined in USPAP). Safeguarding confidential information and assignment results requires the appraiser to make a decision as to what is reasonable.

One dictionary defines reasonable as being based in sound judgment. Sound judgment is not a one-size-fits-all proposition. For example, what are reasonable steps for an appraiser who is working in a public space where others might be able to see the work papers or computer screen? The reasonable steps necessary to safeguard private documents from public view could vary.

The same judgment extends to the appraiser's office. It is up to the appraiser to determine when confidential information and assignment results should be kept under lock and key or in a closed folder. The answer could vary depending on the office environment; reasonable steps for an appraiser working from a home office might be different from those required in a large firm with appraisers and others having access to the workspace. USPAP requires an appraiser to exercise good judgment; it does not list steps the appraiser should take to comply.

Confidential information and assignment results can also be stored electronically. This information kept in desktop computers can be safeguarded in the same manner as physical files. The information can also be kept on an array of portable devices (e.g., laptops, external disk drives, small flash drives, smart phones, etc.). These devices may be easily misplaced, lost or stolen. The loss of one of these devices carries the same risk as orally disclosing confidential information or misplacing printed copies of reports.

USPAP cannot specify the steps an appraiser should take to prevent losing these devices or documents, nor can it specify what to do if that happens. Over time, new data storage and security technologies will evolve. USPAP does not specify whether these devices must be encrypted or password protected, nor the level of protection. USPAP cannot specify whether the appraiser must have the ability to remotely erase confidential information.

USPAP can only require the appraiser to exercise sound judgment. Therefore, relying on best professional practices, individual appraisers must seek "reasonable" and practical solutions to maintaining client confidentiality.

© The Appraisal Foundation

82. CONTENTS OF A WORKFILE

Question: **What information must be retained in an appraiser's workfile?**

Response: An appraiser must prepare a workfile for each appraisal or appraisal review assignment. The RECORD KEEPING RULE states:

The workfile must include:

- *the name of the client and the identity, by name or type, of any other intended users;*
- *true copies of all written reports, documented on any type of media (A true copy is a replica of the report transmitted to the client. A photocopy or an electronic copy of the entire report transmitted to the client satisfies the requirement of a true copy.);*
- *summaries of all oral reports or testimony, or a transcript of testimony, including the appraiser's signed and dated certification; and*
- *all other data, information, and documentation necessary to support the appraiser's opinions and conclusions and to show compliance with USPAP, or references to the location(s) of such other data, information, and documentation.*

A workfile in support of a Restricted Appraisal Report or an oral appraisal report must be sufficient for the appraiser to produce an Appraisal Report. A workfile in support of an oral appraisal review report must be sufficient for the appraiser to produce an Appraisal Review Report.

The appraiser's assignment workfile serves several purposes. As in many other professions, the discipline of enforcement by public agencies and peer review, together with one's self-discipline and dedication of effort, serves to ensure performance of assignments in compliance with professional standards. In addition to facilitating enforcement, a workfile aids the appraiser in handling questions from the client or an intended user subsequent to the date of the report.

An appraiser's assignment workfile preserves evidence of the appraiser's compliance with USPAP and other information as may be required to support the appraiser's opinions and conclusions.

83. DISPOSAL OF WORKFILES

Question: **I am aware of and comply with the workfile retention requirements in the RECORD KEEPING RULE in USPAP. However, once the required retention period has passed, does USPAP dictate a method I must employ to dispose of the workfiles?**

Response: No, USPAP does not dictate a particular method for disposal of workfiles. However, because there are no provisions in USPAP for termination of the appraiser-client relationship and the appraiser's respective confidentiality obligations, appraisers must ensure that they do not violate the Confidentiality section of the ETHICS RULE even when disposing of workfiles.

This means that appraisers must ensure that whatever method they employ to dispose of workfiles does not allow for the communication of *assignment results* or *confidential information* (both, as defined in USPAP) in the disposal process.

© The Appraisal Foundation

84. PHOTOCOPIES OF APPRAISAL REPORTS IN WORKFILES

Question: **In order to satisfy the RECORD KEEPING RULE, must an appraiser retain a complete photocopy of the finished appraisal report that was sent to the client?**

Response: The workfile must contain a true copy of all reports. A photocopy or an electronic copy of the entire appraisal report transmitted to the client satisfies the USPAP requirement of a true copy.

85. WORKFILES FOR APPRAISAL REVIEW ASSIGNMENTS

Question: **I am a manager for an Appraisal Management Company that performs commercial and residential appraisals in various parts of the country. Our company acts as the agent for our clients who consist of numerous regional and national lenders. In that capacity, we take in appraisal orders from our clients and order those appraisals from fee appraisers on our approved list of appraisers. We also perform USPAP compliant reviews on those appraisals. We forward the appraisal and appraisal review reports to our client. Are we required to keep a file of the appraisal reviews?**

Response: Yes. The RECORD KEEPING RULE requires, in part:

*An appraiser must prepare a workfile for each appraisal or **appraisal review** assignment.*

The workfile must include:

- *the name of the client and the identity, by name or type, of any other intended users;*
- ***true copies of all written reports** documented on any type of media (A true copy is a replica of the report transmitted to the client. A photocopy or an electronic copy of the entire report transmitted to the client satisfies the requirement of a true copy.);*
- *summaries of all oral reports or testimony or a transcript of testimony, including the appraiser's signed and dated certification; and*
- *all other data, information, and documentation necessary to support the appraiser's opinions and conclusions and to show compliance with USPAP, or references to the location(s) of such other data, information, and documentation.*

A workfile in support of a Restricted Appraisal Report or an oral appraisal report must be sufficient for the appraiser to produce an Appraisal Report. A workfile in support of an oral appraisal review report must be sufficient for the appraiser to produce an Appraisal Review Report.

Further, it is important to note that USPAP requires the **appraiser** to retain a copy of:

the workfile for a period of at least five (5) years after preparation or at least two (2) years after final disposition of any judicial proceeding in which the appraiser provided testimony related to the assignment, whichever period expires last.

Therefore, it is incumbent upon the appraisers, not their employer, to ensure that a copy of the workfile is available for the time periods stipulated.

86. PURGING WORKFILES AT A CLIENT'S REQUEST

Question: **If requested by a client, can I purge my appraisal files and records of an appraisal that was not used in loan underwriting or in any other manner by the client?**

Response: No. USPAP does not permit appraisers to destroy records prior to five years after preparation **for any reason**, including a client's request to do so or the fact that an appraisal was not used by the client. The RECORD KEEPING RULE states, in part:

An appraiser must prepare a workfile for each appraisal or appraisal review assignment.

© The Appraisal Foundation

An appraiser must retain the workfile for a period of at least five (5) years after preparation or at least two (2) years after final disposition of any judicial proceeding in which the appraiser provided testimony related to the assignment, whichever period expires last.

In addition, the Conduct section of the ETHICS RULE states, in part, that an appraiser:

must not willfully or knowingly violate the requirements of the RECORD KEEPING RULE.

87. WORKFILE RETENTION WITH MORE THAN ONE APPRAISER

Question: **If two appraisers sign an appraisal report, what are the obligations related to record keeping? Specifically, must both appraisers keep a copy of the workfile?**

Response: No. It is not necessary for both appraisers to have a copy of the workfile.

The RECORD KEEPING RULE states, in part:

An appraiser must have custody of the workfile, or make appropriate workfile retention, access, and retrieval arrangements with the party having custody of the workfile.

Neither appraiser is required to have custody of the workfile. However, an appraiser who does not have custody must make appropriate arrangements for retention, access, and retrieval.

See Advisory Opinion 31, *Assignments Involving More than One Appraiser,* for further guidance.

88. RESPONSIBILITY FOR WORKFILE RETENTION

Question: (1.) **Jim, an independent contractor, works for my appraisal company on a regular basis. I have always kept all appraisal file documentation (including hard copies of appraisal reports, field notes, drawings, photographs, and data) at my office. Now Jim wants to keep the files relating to his work in his own possession. Under USPAP, which appraiser should keep the workfile?**

Question: (2.) **Is the RECORD KEEPING RULE upheld if institutionally-employed appraisers ensure that the institution retains copies of their appraisal work for five years? Or, must the appraiser also maintain a personal file of all work performed?**

Question: (3.) **A client's attorney requested that I supply all of my files/records regarding an assignment. Can I do this and still be in compliance with the record keeping requirements for USPAP? Also, what must I retain in my files as proof that the files are now the responsibility of the attorney? Will a simple letter from the client be sufficient?**

Response: In responding to each of the three preceding questions, what should be considered is that, according to USPAP, **the appraiser**, not the appraiser's employer or client, is ultimately responsible for the retention of the workfile for the prescribed period. (Bold added for emphasis) (See RECORD KEEPING RULE)

When workfiles will be retained by an employer, client, co-appraiser or any other party, the appraiser must make arrangements with that party to protect and preserve the workfile, and to allow the appraiser to make the workfile available to other parties such as state appraiser regulatory agencies, professional peer review committees, or when required by due process of law.

© The Appraisal Foundation

There are a number of ways an appraiser who works for or with another party can ensure that files are retained so that the appraiser can have access to the files to meet the requirements of the RECORD KEEPING RULE. For example, an appraiser and the employer or colleague may agree that the files will remain in the employer's or colleague's custody for the duration of the requisite retention period and that the appraiser will have access to those files, if needed.

USPAP does not dictate the form or format of workfile documentation. It is not necessary to include original documents in the file; photocopies and electronic copies are acceptable as true copies. Because there have been cases where employers and others have denied appraisers access to workfiles, an appraiser may wish to make and retain copies of workfiles. However, USPAP does not address any specific manner by which an employer or contractor and appraiser should handle record retention. This is a business matter which should be arranged in the context of the employer- or contractor-appraiser relationship.

By the same token, providing the workfile to a duly authorized party, such as a client's attorney, is permitted by USPAP. However, this does not relieve the appraiser of the responsibility for that workfile. At no time may an appraiser abdicate responsibility for maintaining a workfile. Therefore, when an appraiser relinquishes possession of a file to a client or the client's representative, the appraiser should retain either a copy of the workfile or a written reference to an agreement with the client that the appraiser will have access to the workfile, if the need arises.

89. TRAINEE ACCESS TO WORKFILES

Question: **I am a trainee appraiser and have been working with the same supervising appraiser for some time. Recently, my supervising appraiser told me that since I was only a trainee, I had no right to access workfiles on appraisals where I provided significant professional assistance. Is my supervising appraiser correct? Do trainees have no rights regarding access to workfiles?**

Response: As background, USPAP places workfile retention requirements on the appraiser. In assignments where more than one appraiser is involved (e.g., a trainee appraiser and a supervising appraiser) each appraiser shares responsibility for complying with the RECORD KEEPING RULE.

Supervising appraisers should be aware that all appraisers, including trainee appraisers, must maintain access to workfiles for a minimum of five years. A supervising appraiser must not impede a trainee appraiser's ability to access workfiles. Denying access to workfiles is a violation of the RECORD KEEPING RULE.

An appraiser having custody of a workfile must allow other appraisers with workfile obligations related to an assignment appropriate access and retrieval for the purpose of:

- *submission to state appraiser regulatory agencies;*
- *compliance with due process of law;*
- *submission to a duly authorized professional peer review committee; or*
- *compliance with retrieval arrangements.*

An appraiser who willfully or knowingly fails to comply with the obligations of this RECORD KEEPING RULE is in violation of the ETHICS RULE.

See Advisory Opinion 31, *Assignments Involving More than One Appraiser*, for further guidance.

© The Appraisal Foundation

90. APPROPRIATE WORKFILE RETENTION AND ACCESS ARRANGEMENTS

Question: **USPAP requires appraisers who do not have custody of their workfile to make appropriate retention and access arrangements. What does this mean?**

Response: The RECORD KEEPING RULE states, in part:

> *An appraiser must have custody of the workfile, or* ***make appropriate workfile retention, access, and retrieval arrangements with the party having custody of the workfile****.* (Bold added for emphasis)

There are a number of ways an appraiser who works for or with another party can ensure that the assignment workfile is retained so that the appraiser may access the workfile. The following is a common example: an appraiser and his employer or colleague agree that the workfile will remain in the employer's or colleague's custody for the duration of the requisite retention period and that the appraiser will have access to the workfile. In practice, having such an agreement in writing could prove beneficial to all parties if access and retrieval arrangements are subsequently called into question.

91. MAY ACCESS TO A WORKFILE BE DENIED?

Question: **Two appraisers perform an appraisal assignment together. Appraiser A retains the workfile, and Appraiser B has made access and retrieval arrangements. Are there any conditions under which USPAP allows Appraiser A to deny Appraiser B access to the workfile?**

Response: Yes. USPAP does not set conditions for workfile access and retrieval. However, the RECORD KEEPING RULE states:

> *An appraiser having custody of a workfile* ***must allow other appraisers with workfile obligations*** *related to an assignment appropriate access and retrieval for the purpose of:*
>
> - *submission to state appraiser regulatory agencies;*
> - *compliance with due process of law;*
> - *submission to a duly authorized professional peer review committee; or*
> - *compliance with retrieval arrangements.* (Bold added for emphasis.)

In this scenario, if Appraiser B is seeking access for purposes outside those specified, access may be denied.

92. ACCESS AND RETRIEVAL OF WORKFILES

Question: **I am an appraiser in a large firm and assist several of the senior appraisers in appraisal research, analysis and report preparation. In a recent USPAP class, the instructor said that associates must have either copies of their workfiles, or an agreement with their employer regarding access to the workfiles, for appraisals on which they provided significant assistance. Does that agreement have to be in writing?**

Response: No. USPAP does not specify whether the access and retrieval arrangements you make must be in writing. The RECORD KEEPING RULE states:

> *An appraiser must have custody of the workfile, or make appropriate workfile retention, access, and retrieval arrangements with the party having custody of the workfile.*

This agreement can be either written or oral. However, there is less chance for a misunderstanding about the agreement if it is in writing.

© The Appraisal Foundation

93. SIGNED CERTIFICATION IN TRUE COPIES

Question: **The RECORD KEEPING RULE states, in part:**

The workfile must include...true copies of all written reports...

Does a true copy have to include a signature on the certification?

Response: Yes. A true copy is a replica of the report sent to the client. Any signatures that were affixed to the original report must also exist on the copy for the workfile.

94. CREATING A WORKFILE AFTER REPORT DELIVERY

Question: **I was recently told that USPAP allows appraisers to wait and create a workfile after the report has been delivered to the client for an appraisal or appraisal review assignment. Is this true?**

Response: No. The RECORD KEEPING RULE states:

A workfile must be in existence ***prior to*** *the issuance of any report or other communication of assignment results. A written summary of an oral report must be added to the workfile within a reasonable time after the issuance of the oral report.* (Bold added for emphasis)

It is advisable to create a workfile as soon as an agreement between an appraiser and a client results in an assignment.

95. IS A TRANSCRIPT REQUIRED FOR ORAL REPORT AND TESTIMONY?

Question: **Is a transcript of an oral report or testimony required for the workfile when an appraiser testifies about an appraisal assignment?**

Response: No. There is no absolute requirement to have a transcript of the appraisal oral report testimony. The RECORD KEEPING RULE requirement is for the workfile to contain summaries (which are typically prepared by the appraiser) or a transcript. In cases where summaries are retained, a transcript is not required.

96. IS A TRANSCRIPT REQUIRED IF A WRITTEN APPRAISAL REPORT WAS PREPARED?

Question: **Does the requirement to have a transcript or summary of testimony apply if the appraiser has a written appraisal report and testifies only to the information contained in that report?**

Response: Yes. A transcript or summary of the testimony must be included in the workfile when the appraiser testifies about a written report. While the report that is the subject of the appraiser's testimony must also be included in the assignment workfile, it does not replace a summary of the testimony.

97. RECORD KEEPING REQUIREMENTS FOR ORAL REPORTS AND TESTIMONY

Question: **Does the requirement to have a transcript or a summary of the appraiser's testimony apply only in assignments when an appraiser provides an oral report?**

Response: No. The requirements identified in the RECORD KEEPING RULE apply to both oral reports and testimony in an appraisal or appraisal review assignment.

© The Appraisal Foundation

98. IS A SEPARATE CERTIFICATION REQUIRED IF A WRITTEN APPRAISAL REPORT WAS PREPARED?

Question: **If an appraiser prepares a written appraisal report, is the workfile required to contain a separate signed certification for any testimony the appraiser provided in support of that report?**

Response: In cases where testimony is provided about information contained in a written appraisal report or appraisal review report, a signed certification is required to be included in the written report. The requirement to include a signed certification is satisfied by including a true copy of the report in the workfile, consistent with the RECORD KEEPING RULE.

99. IS A TRANSCRIPT OF THE ENTIRE PROCEEDING REQUIRED?

Question: **Must the workfile contain a transcript or summary of an appraiser's testimony for the entire proceeding, or only for that portion that contains the appraiser's testimony?**

Response: The appraiser's workfile must contain a summary or a transcript of the appraiser's testimony in an appraisal or appraisal review assignment. The appraiser is not obligated to retain summaries or transcripts for other segments of the proceedings in which testimony was provided by individuals other than the appraiser.

100. ELECTRONIC WORKFILE STORAGE

Question: **Recently I have considered maintaining only electronic workfiles (i.e., saving only electronic versions of my reports and supporting data, and scanning any paper documents used so that copies may be stored on electronic media). Is this prohibited by USPAP?**

Response: No. There is nothing in USPAP that would prohibit an appraiser from maintaining only electronic versions of workfiles.

The RECORD KEEPING RULE states, in part:

An appraiser must prepare a workfile for each appraisal or appraisal review assignment.

The workfile must include:

- *the name of the client and the identity, by name or type, of any other intended users;*
- *true copies of all written reports documented on any type of media (A true copy is a replica of the report transmitted to the client. A photocopy or* ***an electronic copy of the entire report transmitted to the client satisfies the requirement of a true copy.****);*
- *summaries of all oral reports or testimony, or a transcript of testimony, including the appraiser's signed and dated certification; and*
- *all other data, information, and documentation necessary to support the appraiser's opinions and conclusions and to show compliance with USPAP, or references to the location(s) of such other data, information, and documentation. (Bold added for emphasis)*

A workfile in support of a Restricted Appraisal Report or an oral appraisal report must be sufficient for the appraiser to produce an Appraisal Report. A workfile in support of an oral appraisal review report must be sufficient for the appraiser to produce an Appraisal Review Report.

As long as an electronic workfile contained these items, it would be sufficient.

© The Appraisal Foundation

Care should be exercised in the selection of the form, style, and type of medium for records to ensure that they are retrievable by the appraiser throughout the prescribed record retention period. The appraiser must ensure that the proper software is maintained to allow access to the electronic files.

101. ADEQUACY OF WORKFILE DOCUMENTATION

Question: **In the course of preparing my appraisals, I often research Multiple Listing Service (MLS) and other data sources. I use this information to develop conclusions regarding neighborhood value ranges and market trends. Is it necessary for me to include copies of this information in my workfile? Alternatively, can I simply reference the data sources in my workfile?**

Response: References in the workfile to the location of documentation used to support an appraiser's analyses, opinions, and conclusions can be adequate. It is not always necessary for the appraisal workfile to include all the documentation provided the referenced material is retrievable by the appraiser throughout the workfile retention period. Care should be exercised in the selection of the format and location of documentation.

The RECORD KEEPING RULE states that the workfile must include:

> *all other data, information, and documentation necessary to support the appraiser's opinions and conclusions and to show compliance with USPAP,* ***or references to the location(s) of such other data, information, and documentation.*** (Bold added for emphasis)

102. JURISDICTIONAL EXCEPTION AND WORKFILE RETENTION

Question: **My state law requires an appraiser to retain workfiles for three years after the valuation date. Is this an example of a jurisdictional exception?**

Response: No. The JURISDICTIONAL EXCEPTION RULE states:

> *If any applicable law or regulation precludes compliance with any part of USPAP, only that part of USPAP becomes void for that assignment.*

In the scenario described in this question, complying with the RECORD KEEPING RULE would exceed the requirements of the law, but it would not be precluded by the law.

By retaining access to workfiles for the longer period required by USPAP, the appraiser would also be in compliance with the law. Therefore, this would not be a jurisdictional exception.

103. MINIMUM WORKFILE RETENTION

Question: **My state appraisal board is asking me to send a copy of the workfile for an appraisal I performed eight years ago. Since I provided no testimony in the assignment, I was only required to maintain access to the workfile for five years. Given that this time period has expired, can the state board still take action in this case?**

Response: Yes. The time frames referenced in the RECORD KEEPING RULE are only minimums. Enforcement proceedings by individual State Boards are independent of the USPAP RECORD KEEPING RULE. Nothing in USPAP would prevent an enforcement proceeding from taking place after the applicable time period had expired. An appraiser should always be aware of state laws which may exceed the minimum USPAP requirements.

© The Appraisal Foundation

104. WORKFILE REQUIREMENTS WHEN COMMUNICATING ASSIGNMENT RESULTS (NEW)

Question: **I was engaged to perform an appraisal of a single-unit residential property for a mortgage lending transaction. After inspecting the property and collecting the necessary data, I concluded that the highest and best use was as a two-unit dwelling. I informed the client of this conclusion prior to completing the appraisal, and the client then canceled the assignment. Since there was no appraisal performed and no appraisal report transmitted, must a workfile be kept for the prescribed timeframes?**

Response: Yes. The RECORD KEEPING RULE states, "An appraiser must prepare a workfile for each appraisal or appraisal review assignment." The Rule is not limited to completed assignments or to assignments in which a report was transmitted. In fact, it specifies that the workfile "must be in existence prior to the issuance of any report or other communication of assignment results."

105. WORKFILES AFFECTED BY A NATURAL DISASTER (NEW)

Question: **My appraisal workfiles were recently damaged due to a natural disaster. I am salvaging what I can but will likely have to discard many. What does USPAP require in this situation?**

Response: USPAP requires that workfiles be retained "for a period of at least five years after preparation or at least two years after final disposition of any judicial proceeding in which the appraiser provided testimony related to the assignment, whichever period expires last." If the workfiles are older than the prescribed period, then there is no USPAP violation in discarding them.

However, if the natural disaster has destroyed workfiles that must be retained, a real property appraiser is advised to contact the applicable state appraiser regulatory agency to see if they have any guidance on what steps to take to document the loss.

Storing workfiles and electronic copies off site, and implementing a system of regular backups may serve to minimize future risk.

106. APPRAISING AFTER A NATURAL DISASTER (NEW)

Question: **A client has asked me to complete an appraisal of a property that was damaged in a recent natural disaster, but I have no experience with appraisals of this type. What are my USPAP obligations in this situation?**

Response: USPAP requires appraisers to perform competently when completing assignments. However, USPAP allows appraisers to acquire the necessary competency during the assignment. The COMPETENCY RULE states, in part:

If an appraiser determines he or she is not competent prior to accepting an assignment, the appraiser must:

1. *disclose the lack of knowledge and/or experience to the client before*
2. *take all steps necessary or appropriate to complete the assignment competently; and*
3. *describe, in the report, the lack of knowledge and/or experience and the steps taken to complete the assignment competently*

In addition, being competent includes the requirement to recognize and comply with laws and regulations applicable to the appraiser and the assignment. In the aftermath of a natural disaster some clients, particularly lenders, may include additional assignment conditions for developing and reporting an appraisal, and may waive others. In order to perform competently, appraisers involved in such assignments must remain current on these topics.

© The Appraisal Foundation

107. MAINTAINING RECORDS FOR A DECEASED APPRAISER (NEW)

Question: **I have worked with another appraiser for many years, starting with simply sharing office space and most recently as members of a limited liability company (LLC). Unfortunately, this appraiser recently passed away unexpectedly. All of our appraisal assignments were performed independently, so I never signed certifications for any of his appraisal reports.**

Am I required to maintain his records in accordance with the record keeping requirements in USPAP?

Response: No. USPAP places the record keeping obligations on the appraiser, not the appraiser's firm, family, or other party. Therefore, the obligation to comply with the RECORD KEEPING RULE in USPAP ceases to apply if an appraiser is no longer living. Some business associates or family members may be required to maintain a deceased appraiser's workfiles for other reasons, but there is no such requirement in USPAP.

108. GOVERNMENT AGENCY WORKFILE RETENTION (NEW)

Question: **I am a review appraiser employed by a federal government agency. The agency's record retention policies for appraisal and appraisal review reports meet or exceed the requirements of the RECORD KEEPING RULE in USPAP. My workfile is considered a government record, which I have access to throughout the USPAP retention period. Am I required to keep a separate workfile in my personal custody?**

Response: No. The RECORD KEEPING RULE states that an "appraiser must have custody of the workfile, or make appropriate workfile retention, access, and retrieval arrangements with the party having custody of the workfile." Since your employer's record retention policies meet or exceed the requirements of USPAP and you have access to the workfile during that retention period, you are not required to maintain a separate copy of your workfile.

109. TESTIMONY AND DEPOSITION (NEW)

Question: **I completed an appraisal report that was used by my client in litigation. My report was entered into evidence, but I did not provide a deposition and did not testify at the trial. How long must I retain my workfile since there was a judicial proceeding?**

Response: The RECORD KEEPING RULE states:

> *"An appraiser must retain the workfile for a period of at least five years after preparation or at least two years after final disposition of any judicial proceeding* ***in which the appraiser provided testimony*** *related to the assignment, whichever period expires last." (Bold added for emphasis)*

In this scenario, the appraiser did not provide testimony, therefore the workfile must be retained for a minimum of five years after preparation.

110. RETENTION REQUIREMENTS FOR PRELIMINARY COMMUNICATIONS AFTER COMPLETION OF THE ASSIGNMENT (NEW)

Question: **During the course of the assignment, my client has asked me to provide the sale comparables I plan to use, as well as information on my rent and expense conclusions, prior to the completion of my Appraisal Report. If I subsequently provide an Appraisal Report, does my workfile need to contain a written copy or summary of the communication previously transmitted to the client?**

© The Appraisal Foundation

Response: No. Upon completion of the assignment, the assignment results are communicated to the client within the Appraisal Report. The RECORD KEEPING RULE requires the workfile to contain a true copy of the report as well as all data, other information and documentation necessary to support the appraiser's opinions and conclusions. State requirements may add to USPAP obligations therefore appraisers should check with their state to see if additional requirements apply

© The Appraisal Foundation

111. ACQUIRING KNOWLEDGE AND EXPERIENCE TO COMPLY WITH THE COMPETENCY RULE

Question: **How does an appraiser gain the knowledge and experience required by the COMPETENCY RULE if the appraiser lacks the knowledge and experience to complete an assignment competently?**

Response: The COMPETENCY RULE requires an appraiser who lacks the knowledge and experience to complete an assignment competently to (1) disclose the lack of knowledge and/or experience to the client before agreeing to perform the assignment, or (2) disclose the lack of knowledge and/or experience to the client during the assignment if discovered by the appraiser during the assignment. In either instance, the appraiser must then take all steps necessary to appropriately complete the assignment competently and document the steps in the appraisal report. An appraiser may gain the knowledge and experience required through any or all of the following: personal study by the appraiser; association with an appraiser reasonably believed to have the necessary knowledge or experience; or, retention of others who possess the required knowledge or experience.

In addition, the COMPETENCY RULE requires an appraiser to withdraw from the assignment if competency cannot be achieved prior to completion of the assignment.

Refer to the COMPETENCY RULE for further guidance.

112. ASSIGNMENT CONDITIONS, SCOPE OF WORK ACCEPTABILITY, AND GEOGRAPHIC COMPETENCY

Question: **I am a residential appraiser performing work for several Appraisal Management Companies. Often, I am asked to perform an appraisal assignment outside the areas I am most familiar with. The assignments come with a requirement that a completed report be submitted within 48 hours or less. This time frame does not permit me to adequately research the subject property market. Is it permissible for me to agree to perform an assignment under these conditions?**

Response: The COMPETENCY RULE in USPAP requires appraisers to notify the client if they do not have the necessary competency to complete an assignment prior to agreeing to perform an assignment. Because your question states that the "time frame does not permit me to adequately research the subject property market," you have already made the determination that becoming geographically competent for this assignment is a concern. The client must be notified, appropriate steps must be taken to become competent, and the lack of competency, plus the steps taken to become competent, must be disclosed in the appraisal report. If an appraiser is not in a position to spend the necessary time in a market area to attain geographic competency, affiliation with a qualified local appraiser may be an appropriate response to ensure development of credible assignment results. Alternatively, the appraiser must decline the assignment.

This situation is also addressed by the SCOPE OF WORK RULE in USPAP:

For each appraisal and appraisal review assignment, an appraiser must:

1. *identify the problem to be solved;*
2. ***determine and perform the scope of work necessary to develop credible assignment results; and***
3. *disclose the scope of work in the report.* (Bold added for emphasis)

© The Appraisal Foundation

Scope of work is defined as *the type and extent of research and analyses in an assignment.* If you know that the required time frame does not permit you to adequately research the subject property market in order to complete the scope of work necessary to develop credible assignment results, you should decline the assignment.

In some situations, you may initially believe that you can complete the scope of work necessary to develop credible assignment results, but subsequently determine you are unable to do so and still comply with the specific time frame. This circumstance is specifically covered in the Scope of Work Acceptability section of the SCOPE OF WORK RULE.

An appraiser must not allow assignment conditions to limit the scope of work to such a degree that the assignment results are not credible in the context of the intended use.

Comment: If relevant information is not available because of assignment conditions that limit research opportunities (such as conditions that place limitations on inspection or information gathering), an appraiser must withdraw from the assignment unless the appraiser can:

- *modify the assignment conditions to expand the scope of work to include gathering the information; or*
- *use an extraordinary assumption about such information, if credible assignment results can still be developed.*

113. CONTINUING EDUCATION COURSES

Question: **Does USPAP require appraisers to take continuing education courses?**

Response: Not directly; however, it is implied in the development Standards. For example, Standards Rule 1-1(a), states the following:

In developing a real property appraisal, an appraiser must:

(a) be aware of, understand, and correctly employ those recognized methods and techniques that are necessary to produce a credible appraisal;

Comment: This Standards Rule recognizes that the principle of change continues to affect the manner in which appraisers perform appraisal services. Changes and developments in the real estate field have a substantial impact on the appraisal profession. Important changes in the cost and manner of constructing and marketing commercial, industrial, and residential real estate as well as changes in the legal framework in which real property rights and interests are created, conveyed, and mortgaged have resulted in corresponding changes in appraisal theory and practice. Social change has also had an effect on appraisal theory and practice. To keep abreast of these changes and developments, the appraisal profession is constantly reviewing and revising appraisal methods and techniques and devising new methods and techniques to meet new circumstances. ***For this reason, it is not sufficient for appraisers to simply maintain the skills and the knowledge they possess when they become appraisers. Each appraiser must continuously improve his or her skills to remain proficient in real property appraisal.*** *(Bold added for emphasis)*

The last sentence of the Comment to Standards Rules 1-1(a) clearly indicates that appraisers must continuously improve their knowledge and skills. Therefore, some form of continuing education is required, although not explicitly stated in the USPAP document.

© The Appraisal Foundation

114. COMPETENCY STATEMENT IN THE REPORT

Question: **Does USPAP require an appraiser to include a competency statement in all reports?**

Response: No. USPAP does not require that an appraiser provide a statement of competency in all reports. Only when the appraiser agrees to perform an assignment with a lack of knowledge and/or experience does the COMPETENCY RULE require the report to contain a description of the appraiser's lack of knowledge and/or experience and the steps taken to complete the assignment competently.

115. ERRORS AND OMISSIONS INSURANCE

Question: **Does USPAP require appraisers to be covered by errors and omissions (E&O) insurance?**

Response: USPAP does not address E&O insurance. However, if appraisers are required to have E&O insurance as a matter of law or regulation, they must comply with that requirement under the COMPETENCY RULE which requires recognition of, and compliance with, laws and regulations that apply to the appraiser or the assignment.

© The Appraisal Foundation

116. APPLICATION OF THE JURISDICTIONAL EXCEPTION RULE

Question: **When does the JURISDICTIONAL EXCEPTION RULE apply in an assignment?**

Response: The JURISDICTIONAL EXCEPTION RULE exempts appraisers from the part or parts of USPAP for which compliance is precluded by law or regulation. The Rule applies anytime there is a conflict between the requirements of USPAP and the applicable law or regulation of a jurisdiction.

An appraiser using the JURISDICTIONAL EXCEPTION RULE must properly identify and comply with the law or regulation that precludes compliance with USPAP. In addition, the appraiser must disclose in the report the part of USPAP that is voided by that law or regulation, and also cite in the report the specific law or regulation that precludes compliance with USPAP.

The Comment to the JURISDICTIONAL EXCEPTION RULE includes language that helps appraisers recognize laws and regulations. However, in every case, it is ultimately the responsibility of the appraiser, and not the client or other intended users, to determine whether the use of the JURISDICTIONAL EXCEPTION RULE is appropriate.

117. USPAP COMPLIANCE AND JURISDICTIONAL EXCEPTION

Question: **I am a real property appraiser and a government employee. The agency I work for wants me to provide a preliminary estimate of value. The agency policy states that this work is not an appraisal and is not covered by USPAP because of a jurisdictional exception. Should I comply with USPAP when I prepare a preliminary estimate of value?**

Response: This question raises a number of issues related to USPAP compliance and the application of the JURISDICTIONAL EXCEPTION RULE.

Based on your identification as an appraiser, you should comply with USPAP. This is because an individual's public identification as an appraiser establishes an expectation that valuation services will be performed in compliance with USPAP. You must comply with USPAP when required by law, regulation, or agreement. Even if the agency policy does not require USPAP compliance, other applicable law or regulation might require compliance.

The JURISDICTIONAL EXCEPTION RULE cannot be used to resolve this type of USPAP compliance question unless the agency policy is determined to be law or regulation. USPAP does not establish who or which assignments must comply; thus, the JURISDICTIONAL EXCEPTION RULE cannot be applied to a decision to comply with USPAP. To the contrary, a jurisdictional exception occurs when an applicable law or regulation precludes compliance with USPAP; therefore, no decision is necessary.

Another issue raised by this question relates to the USPAP requirements that apply to a preliminary estimate of value. USPAP does not define preliminary estimate of value. However, it is the nature of the service, not the label applied, that defines the service. An appraisal is defined as *the act or process of developing an opinion of value; an opinion of value*. If the service is an *appraisal* as defined in USPAP, then STANDARDS 1 and 2 apply to the preliminary estimate of value.

© The Appraisal Foundation

118. WHEN COMPLIANCE WITH USPAP IS PRECLUDED BY LAW OR REGULATION

Question: **Can a jurisdictional exception take away from the requirements of USPAP?**

Response: Yes. The JURISDICTIONAL EXCEPTION RULE provides for the situation in which compliance with parts of USPAP may be precluded by law or regulation in certain jurisdictions. It states:

If any applicable law or regulation precludes compliance with any part of USPAP, only that part of USPAP becomes void for that assignment.

As stated in the Comment to the JURISDICTIONAL EXCEPTION RULE:

The JURISDICTIONAL EXCEPTION RULE provides a saving or severability clause intended to preserve the balance of USPAP if compliance with one or more of its parts is precluded by the law or regulation of a jurisdiction. When an appraiser properly follows this Rule in disregarding a part of USPAP, there is no violation of USPAP.

The Comment to the JURISDICTIONAL EXCEPTION RULE also includes language that helps appraisers recognize laws and regulations.

119. PROBATE COURT STATUTE BASING THE APPRAISAL FEE ON THE APPRAISED VALUE

Question: **A property is being appraised for a probate court in a state which has a statute stipulating that appraisal fees for these assignments shall be based on the appraised value of the property. Does USPAP allow me to appraise the property under this compensation arrangement?**

Response: Yes. This is an example where the JURISDICTIONAL EXCEPTION RULE applies. In order to comply with the requirements of the JURISDICTIONAL EXCEPTION RULE, the appraiser must disclose in the appraisal report the reason(s) that prohibit compliance with USPAP, and cite the basis for the jurisdictional exception.

120. APPROPRIATE SOURCES FOR JURISDICTIONAL EXCEPTION

Question: **My client's attorney has told me to invoke the JURISDICTIONAL EXCEPTION RULE to avoid mentioning in my appraisal report an underground storage tank that I know exists in the property. The attorney did not provide any reference or citation of law or regulation justifying this action. Can I follow the instruction from this attorney, who is representing my client?**

Response: No. Use of the JURISDICTIONAL EXCEPTION RULE is triggered by a conflict between the requirements of USPAP and the law or regulation of a jurisdiction, not by client discretion.

The JURISDICTIONAL EXCEPTION RULE states:

If any applicable law or regulation precludes compliance with any part of USPAP, only that part of USPAP becomes void for that assignment.

This Rule provides a saving or severability clause when compliance with a part or parts of USPAP is precluded by law or regulation. The first sentence of the Comment to the Rule states:

The JURISDICTIONAL EXCEPTION RULE provides a saving or severability clause intended to preserve the balance of USPAP if compliance with one or more of its parts is precluded by the law or regulation of a jurisdiction. When an appraiser properly follows this Rule in disregarding a part of USPAP, there is no violation of USPAP.

© The Appraisal Foundation

The second paragraph in the Comment also provides explicit descriptions of laws and regulations that appraisers can use to determine when use of the JURISDICTIONAL EXCEPTION RULE is acceptable. It is important to note that the parameters described in the Comment apply regardless of the intended use of the assignment, whether it is an appraisal or appraisal review, or whether the type and definition of value is market value or if it is some other type of value.

An attorney's instruction, without specific citation of law or regulation, is not the equivalent of law or regulation. Attorneys may offer legal opinions, but legislative bodies and courts make laws, and administrative agencies establish regulations. While an attorney is an expert in the practice of law, it is the court that decides if the facts in a matter support an attorney's representation of how established law applies to a specific set of facts.

Absent the citation of law or regulation, which should be cited in the report together with the part or parts of USPAP from which compliance is precluded in the assignment, the attorney's instruction is not acceptable as a basis to disregard a part or parts of USPAP applicable in the assignment.

121. VALUATION METHODS AND JURISDICTIONAL EXCEPTION RULE

Question: **I am doing an appraisal assignment for a government agency that is subject to the provisions of *The Uniform Relocation Assistance and Real Property Acquisitions Act of 1970*, as Amended (commonly known as, the Uniform Act), and its implementing regulation, 49 CFR Part 24. The agency has provided me with a reference to a State Court of Appeals ruling which indicates that standing timber and landscaping impacted by a public project must be appraised based on the value it contributes to the subject property as a whole, and not as individual items. They have informed me that this appeals case is frequently cited in condemnation cases and almost always upheld by trial courts in this state. Based on this court decision, the agency has adopted a policy that all standing timber and landscaping be valued in this manner.**

On this issue of landscaping, does using contributory value versus replacement value constitute a jurisdictional exception?

Response: No. The JURISDICTIONAL EXCEPTION RULE does not apply in this circumstance since there are no requirements in USPAP addressing the proper valuation techniques for standing timber and landscaping. The Rule only applies when there is a conflict between the requirements of USPAP and the applicable law or regulation of a jurisdiction.

USPAP requires that in the development of an appraisal, an appraiser must be aware of, understand, and correctly employ those recognized methods and techniques that are necessary to produce a credible appraisal. Further, the COMPETENCY RULE requires recognition of, and compliance with, laws and regulations that apply to the appraiser or to the assignment.

The agency policy on the valuation of standing timber and landscaping is an assignment condition and must be considered in the scope of work decision. However, an appraiser cannot perform an assignment with a condition that would produce assignment results which are not credible in the context of the intended use.

© The Appraisal Foundation

122. CLIENT REQUIREMENT TO DISREGARD MARKET VALUE CHANGES PRIOR TO EFFECTIVE DATE

Question: **I have a question related to the implementing regulation, 49 CFR Part 24, for *The Uniform Relocation Assistance and Real Property Acquisitions Act of 1970*, as Amended (the Uniform Act). The issue is the relationship of Standard Rule 1-4(f) and "Before Acquisition Value." The ASB has pointed out that such a situation does not create a jurisdictional exception under USPAP but is rather an assignment condition.**

My state has a similar law that requires the appraiser to disregard any decrease or increase in market value of the property prior to the effective date caused by the public improvement for which the property is being acquired. Does this state law cause a jurisdictional exception under USPAP?

Response: No. The state law does not cause a jurisdictional exception in this case. USPAP Standards Rule 1-4(f) becomes applicable in an assignment only *if* the scope of work includes the analysis of anticipated improvements:

> ***When** analyzing anticipated public or private improvements, located on or off the site, an appraiser must analyze the effect on value, if any, of such anticipated improvements to the extent they are reflected in market actions.* (Bold added for emphasis)

The key word in Standards Rule 1-4(f) is "***When***." Your state law does not conflict with USPAP because the word ***When*** indicates that Standards Rule 1-4(f) is only applicable in the circumstance that public or private improvements must be analyzed in order to develop credible assignment results.

The JURISDICTIONAL EXCEPTION RULE states, in part:

> *In an assignment involving a jurisdictional exception, an appraiser must:*
>
> 1. *identify the law or regulation that precludes compliance with USPAP;*
> 2. *comply with that law or regulation;*
> 3. *clearly and conspicuously disclose in the report the part of USPAP that is voided by that law or regulation; and*
> 4. *cite in the report the law or regulation requiring this exception to USPAP compliance.*

123. CLIENT REQUIREMENT TO DISREGARD LINKING OPINION OF VALUE TO A SPECIFIC EXPOSURE TIME

Question: **I am aware that in the development of an opinion of value in which reasonable exposure time is a component of the definition, I am required by USPAP to develop of an opinion of reasonable exposure time linked to that value opinion. The assignment I am working on must, by regulation, comply with the *Uniform Appraisal Standards for Federal Land Acquisitions* (the Yellow Book). Those standards require that the market value opinion be based on a reasonable exposure time, but also prohibit the appraiser from linking the value to a specific exposure time. Does this prohibition represent a jurisdictional exception since compliance with the Yellow Book is required by regulation?**

Response: Yes. In this case, the Yellow Book requirement imposed by the implementing regulation applicable to your assignment ***precludes*** you from complying with USPAP. As stated in the Comment to Standards Rule 1-2(c), USPAP requires an appraiser to develop an opinion of reasonable exposure time linked to the value opinion being developed, when reasonable exposure time is a component of its definition. In contrast, the Yellow Book provides that "the appraiser shall not link an estimate of market value for federal land acquisitions to a specific exposure time."

© The Appraisal Foundation

In accordance with the JURISDICTIONAL EXCEPTION RULE the appraisal report must clearly and conspicuously disclose the part or parts of USPAP that are voided by law or regulation and cite the law or regulation which requires compliance with the *Uniform Appraisal Standards for Federal Land Acquisitions.*

124. IS A "WAIVER VALUATION" A JURISDICTIONAL EXCEPTION?

Question: **The Federal Highway Administration (FHWA) permits a "waiver valuation." To quote, 49 CFR § 24.2 (33) "The term waiver valuation means the valuation process used and the product produced when the Agency determines that an appraisal is not required, pursuant to § 24.102(c)(2) appraisal waiver provisions." Is this an application of the JURISDICTIONAL EXCEPTION RULE?**

Response: No. There is no jurisdictional exception in the situation described. USPAP does not establish who or which assignments must comply. An agency may determine that an appraisal is not required for a specific situation, and may elect to rely on a waiver valuation.

Nothing in the definition of waiver valuation *precludes the appraiser from complying with USPAP*. Compliance with USPAP sometimes requires an appraiser to develop an expanded level of analyses, or to communicate results with a different minimum set of requirements, distinct from what might be desired by a particular intended use or user. These additional obligations may impact the decision on whether the appraiser *chooses* to perform the assignment.

It is important that an appraiser take the time and effort to clearly understand all the assignment elements, and make an appropriate scope of work decision that complies with the appraiser's obligation to be able to demonstrate that the scope of work is sufficient to produce credible assignment results.

125. CLIENT REQUIREMENT TO ASSUME NO CONTAMINATION EXISTS

Question: **The Federal Highway Administration (FHWA) publishes a "Guide for Preparing an Appraisal Scope of Work." One of the items listed is that the property being acquired should be "appraised as if free and clear of contamination," unless otherwise specified. Is this a jurisdictional exception, extraordinary assumption, or hypothetical condition?**

Response: This situation is not an application of the JURISDICTIONAL EXCEPTION RULE. Rather, if contamination is an aspect of the valuation, the situation calls for either an extraordinary assumption or a hypothetical condition. In the DEFINITIONS section, an extraordinary assumption is defined as:

> *An assignment-specific assumption as of the effective date regarding uncertain information used in an analysis which, if found to be false, could alter the appraiser's opinions or conclusions.*

A hypothetical condition is defined as:

> *a condition, directly related to a specific assignment which is contrary to what is known by the appraiser to exist on the effective date, but is used for the purpose of analysis.*

If the contamination status of the property is uncertain and cannot be determined, an extraordinary assumption is appropriate. If the property is known to be contaminated, a hypothetical condition to the contrary would be required.

© The Appraisal Foundation

126. JURISDICTIONAL EXCEPTION AND CONFIDENTIALITY

Question: **I was recently hired to perform an appraisal assignment for a government agency. The agency has a regulation that requires me to provide the appraisal report to other government agencies if requested. Does this regulation create a jurisdictional exception to the Confidentiality section of the ETHICS RULE?**

Response: No. The Confidentiality section of the ETHICS RULE reads, in part:

An appraiser must not disclose: (1) confidential information or (2) assignment results to anyone other than:

- *the client;*
- ***parties specifically authorized by the client**;*
- *state appraiser regulatory agencies;*
- ***third parties as may be authorized by due process of law**; or*
- *a duly authorized professional peer review committee except when such disclosure to a committee would violate applicable law or regulation.* (Bold added for emphasis)

Since the Confidentiality section of the ETHICS RULE allows for the disclosure of confidential information to *persons specifically authorized by the client* and *third parties as may be authorized by due process of law*, the JURISDICTIONAL EXCEPTION RULE would not apply.

© The Appraisal Foundation

127. PAYMENT BY A PARTY OTHER THAN THE CLIENT

Question: **Some clients to require me to pick up the check for the appraisal fee from the property owner. Since I am being paid directly by the property owner, does the property owner become the client?**

Response: No. USPAP defines the client as:

> *the party or parties (i.e., individual, group, or entity) who engage an appraiser by employment or contract in a specific assignment, whether directly or through an agent.*

The act of the property owner or any other entity paying the appraiser does not make them the client under USPAP. However, state law could take precedence over USPAP in this situation. Therefore, you should contact the pertinent jurisdictions to ensure that there is not a conflict between applicable law and USPAP.

Situations may arise, especially in certain mortgage lending related assignments, in which this payment arrangement is not permitted.

128. DIFFERENCE BETWEEN CLIENTS AND INTENDED USERS

Question: **What is the difference between a client and an intended user?**

Response: The client is *the party or parties (i.e., individual, group, or entity) who engage an appraiser by employment or contract in a specific assignment, whether directly or through an agent.* There are special obligations and responsibilities (e.g., confidentiality, required disclosures by the appraiser, etc.) as a result of an appraiser-client relationship.

An intended user is a party identified by the appraiser, based on communication with the client at the time of the assignment, as a user of the appraisal or appraisal review. The appraiser is obligated to ensure the appraisal report is appropriate for the intended use, and can be properly understood by the intended user(s).

A party receiving a copy of an appraisal or appraisal review report is not "automatically" an intended user. To be an intended user the recipient must have been identified as such in the appraisal report by the appraiser.

129. APPRAISAL MANAGEMENT COMPANY AS AUTHORIZED AGENT FOR A CLIENT

Question: **I perform assignments from an Appraisal Management Company (AMC) that has informed me they are an authorized agent for the lenders they represent. As the AMC is not my client, they have requested that I only identify the lender they are representing as the client. USPAP says the appraiser's client is the party who engages the appraiser. Is it ethical to omit the AMC's name as the client on my reports?**

Response: Yes. If the AMC is acting as a duly authorized agent for a lender, identifying only the lender as your client is acceptable. The USPAP definition of client is: *the party or parties (i.e., individual, group, or entity) who engage an appraiser by employment or contract in a specific assignment, whether directly* ***or through an agent****.* (Bold added for emphasis.) However, the appraiser must be aware of situations where disclosure of the AMC might be required by law, regulation, or the secondary market.

© The Appraisal Foundation

130. CAN AN APPRAISAL MANAGEMENT COMPANY BE THE CLIENT?

Question: **I received an appraisal order from an Appraisal Management Company (AMC) that has requested to be identified as the client in the appraisal report. The AMC will not provide its client's name. Does USPAP allow me to identify the AMC as the client if the AMC will not disclose the name of its client?**

Response: There is nothing in USPAP that precludes an AMC from being a client; however, appraisers must comply with all applicable assignment conditions. Assignment conditions required by some users of appraisal services, including those prepared for federally-regulated financial institutions, specify who the client must be.

Therefore, the AMC may be the client under USPAP, but there could be additional applicable assignment conditions depending on the intended use and intended users.

Having an AMC as the client can be similar to the situation in which an appraiser is engaged by an attorney. The identity of the party that engaged the attorney might not be made available to the appraiser, but USPAP does not preclude the appraiser from naming the attorney as the client.

131. CLIENT CANNOT BE IDENTIFIED

Question: **I was recently asked to perform a real property appraisal assignment, but the individual that contacted my firm was not the client and indicated that the client could not be identified. Can I agree to perform this assignment and comply with USPAP?**

Response: No. Standards Rule 1-2 states, in part:

> *In developing a real property appraisal, an appraiser must:*
>
> *(a) identify the client and other intended users;*

This does not preclude a third party, acting as an agent for the client, from ordering the appraisal. In all assignments, the appraiser must know the identity of the client in order to proceed; however, the appraiser is not required to disclose the identity of the client in the appraisal report. See Advisory Opinion 36, *Identification and Disclosure of Client, Intended Use and Intended Users*, for further clarification.

132. SUBSEQUENT USER REQUESTS A RELIANCE LETTER

Question: **I delivered an appraisal report to my client. A week later, an entity other than one of the identified intended users contacted me and asked that I provide a reliance letter, enabling them to rely on the appraisal report for their own investment use. My client says they have no problem with me doing that. Can I provide this entity with such a letter, even though I had not originally identified them as an intended user?**

Response: No. You cannot add what is in effect a new intended user after the completion of an assignment, no matter what terminology you use.

USPAP defines Intended User as:

> *The client and any other party as identified, by name or type, as users of the appraisal or appraisal review report by the appraiser based on communication with the client* ***at the time of the assignment****.* (Bold added for emphasis)

© The Appraisal Foundation

The proper way to handle this is to initiate a new assignment with this entity as the client and provide them an appraisal, being careful to develop an appropriate scope of work consistent with the intended use of the new intended user(s).

This new assignment could be based on virtually the same data and analysis, and the value conclusion might be the same. However, in the new assignment you must consider the assignment elements most appropriate to the scope of work for the new client, intended users, and intended use for the assignment results, which could well be different from those of your original client.

133. READDRESS OR TRANSFER

Question: **Is it acceptable to readdress or transfer a completed appraisal report?**

Response: No. Once a report has been prepared for a named client or clients, the appraiser cannot readdress or transfer the report to another party. Simply changing the client name on the report cannot change or replace the original appraiser-client relationship. Therefore, this action is misleading.

However, you can consider the request as a new assignment. In so doing, you may establish a new appraiser-client relationship and appraise the property for this new client.

Additional information can be found in Advisory Opinion 26, *Readdressing (Transferring) a Report to Another Party*. Important considerations, such as the handling of confidential information and other factors, are addressed in Advisory Opinion 27, *Appraising the Same Property for a New Client.*

134. READDRESSING WITH LENDER RELEASE

Question: **I am aware of two advisory opinions, AO-26, *Readdressing (Transferring) a Report to Another Party,* and AO-27, *Appraising the Same Property for a New Client*. Does that guidance still apply if Lender A releases me to perform another assignment, or can I just readdress the report to Lender B since I have obtained a release?**

Response: Yes; the guidance still applies. It is never permissible to readdress a report by simply changing the client's name on a completed report, regardless of whether the first client gave a release. The request from Lender B must be treated as a new assignment.

Further guidance can be found in the Obtaining a Release section of AO-27, *Appraising the Same Property for a New Client.*

135. IDENTIFICATION OF INTENDED USERS

I know that it is my responsibility to identify the intended users when I perform an assignment, and that USPAP defines intended user as the client and any other party as identified, by name or type, as users of the appraisal or appraisal review report by the appraiser based on communication with the client.

However, I need clarification regarding whether certain parties should automatically be considered intended users in certain circumstances described below.

Question: **(1.)** **If I perform an appraisal for estate tax purposes and the client will provide my report to the IRS with her tax return, must the IRS be identified as an intended user in this situation?**

© The Appraisal Foundation

Question: (2.) I have been hired by an attorney representing a husband in a divorce to appraise certain assets held in the marital estate and to appear as an expert witness. I know my report will go to the court as well as to the parties on the other side of the litigation. Must the court and/or the parties on the other side of the litigation be identified as intended users?

Question: (3.) I frequently perform appraisals for purposes of purchase price allocation. The corporation that is my client will use the values for financial reporting purposes. My reports are provided to the auditors of the corporations for their review as part of the audit process. In such cases, must the auditors be identified as intended users?

Question: (4.) I am appraising a property for a regulated lender. I know that my appraisal will be reviewed by the bank's outside auditors and the OCC reviewers. Must the auditors and OCC reviewers be identified as intended users?

Response: The answer for each of the four questions is no. Intended users are identified by the appraiser through communication with client and are not established based on who might receive or use the report.

The definition of intended user has a specific meaning in USPAP. In the context of the USPAP definition of intended user, the fact that the IRS, the court, an independent auditor, or the OCC in the above cases will use your report for review, audit, or other purposes does not automatically make them intended users. These parties receive the report through established processes of disclosure or regulation.

One way to understand the concept is to think about what the *intended use* is for each party. The appraiser must identify both the intended users and the intended use of the appraisal, because these two factors affect many aspects of the appraisal assignment, such as the appropriate scope of work and the appropriate type of report.

In each case, the use of the report by these other parties is different from the intended use the appraiser identified, which was related to the client's use. Such other parties may be evaluating the decision made by the appraiser's client to obtain an appraisal, as well as the appraisal results, and other matters of which the appraiser may not be aware. As an example, the client filing the estate tax return is using the appraisal as an indication of the amount to state on the tax form. However, the IRS may use the appraisal report to determine whether the value reported on the tax return is adequately supported, whether the IRS agrees with the value, and/or whether the IRS should challenge the taxpayer because they disagree with the value.

See Advisory Opinion 36, *Identification and Disclosure of Client, Intended Use and Intended User.*

136. ADDRESSEES, CLIENTS, AND INTENDED USERS

Question **If the party to whom an appraisal report is addressed is the client and is also the only intended user, does USPAP require the report to state the intended user by name or type?**

Response: Yes, but the specific requirements differ depending upon whether it is an Appraisal Report or Restricted Appraisal Report. According to Standards Rule 2-2(a)(ii) an Appraisal Report must, at a minimum:

state the identity of any other intended user(s) by name or type.

According to Standards Rule 2-2(b)(ii) a Restricted Appraisal Report must, at a minimum,

state the identity of any other intended user(s) ***by name***. (Bold added for emphasis).

© The Appraisal Foundation

The Comment to Standards Rules 2-2(a)(1) and 2-2(b)(i) clarifies that *Because the client is an intended user they must be identified in the report as such.* However, if the client has requested anonymity the appraiser must use care when identifying the client to avoid violations of the Confidentiality section of the ETHICS RULE.

Advisory Opinion 36, *Identification and Disclosure of Intended Use and Intended Users*, provides extensive guidance on this topic in addition to several examples of statements that may be appropriate for inclusion in a report.

137. APPRAISING WITHOUT KNOWING THE INTENDED USE OR INTENDED USER

Question: **Does USPAP allow me to appraise a property without knowing the intended use or user(s) if there is an agreed upon scope of work?**

Response: No. The SCOPE OF WORK RULE requires an appraiser to *gather and analyze information about those assignment elements that are necessary to properly identify the appraisal or appraisal review problem to be solved.* Two of the assignment elements that an appraiser is required to identify in an appraisal assignment are: "the client and other intended users" and "the intended use of the appraiser's opinions and conclusions." (See Standards Rule 1-2, Standards Rule 5-2, Standards Rule 7-2, and Standards Rule 9-2.)

138. ARE BORROWERS INTENDED USERS?

Question: **Frequently, the borrower in a mortgage finance transaction is provided with a copy of the appraisal report; and in most cases, the appraiser knows that the borrower will be receiving a copy of the appraisal report. When the appraiser is aware that the borrower or any other third party will receive a copy of the appraisal, does this make that third party an intended user?**

Response: No. The fact that a borrower or anyone else receives a copy of the appraisal report does not make them an intended user. The concept of an intended user in USPAP is framed within the context of the appraiser-client relationship. An intended user is defined in USPAP as:

> *the client and any other party as identified, by name or type, as users of the appraisal or appraisal review report by the appraiser, based on communication with the client at the time of the assignment.*

There are several things to note in this definition. First, intended users of the appraisal report must be identified by the appraiser. Secondly, this identification is made at the time of the assignment so the appraiser can make a prudent judgment about the scope of work to apply in the assignment and the level of detail to include in the report.

It is also worth noting that the concepts of intended use and intended users are related to the type and definition of value in an assignment. Appraisal reports for loan transactions are typically used to substantiate the real property's market value as underlying collateral for a particular loan. The fact that the lending institution is required by law or regulation to make certain disclosures to the borrower about the loan and the basis for the loan decision does not alter the intended use, intended users, or type and definition of value in the appraisal assignment.

The Comments to Standards Rule 2-2(a)(ii) and 2-2(b)(ii) further clarify this issue by stating:

> *A party receiving a copy of an Appraisal Report [or, in Standards Rule 2-2(b)(ii), a Restricted Appraisal Report] in order to satisfy disclosure requirements does not become an intended user of the appraisal unless the appraiser identifies such party as an intended user as part of the assignment.*

© The Appraisal Foundation

139. IDENTIFYING INTENDED USERS BY TYPE

Question: **I recently received a request to perform an appraisal assignment. The potential client has indicated that there will be other intended users, but has not identified the intended users specifically. Is it acceptable to identify the intended users by type?**

Response: Yes, but only if the appraisal is communicated as an Appraisal Report. Standards Rules 2-2(a), 8-2(a), and 10-2(a) allow for the identification of intended users by name or type. However, for a Restricted Appraisal Report the appraiser must identify any other specific intended users by name. A Restricted Appraisal Report is inappropriate for users only known and identified by type because they could be misled by the abbreviated reporting format which may not contain supporting rationale for the opinions and conclusions.

See Advisory Opinion 36, *Identification and Disclosure of Client, Intended Use and Intended Users* for more information.

140. ENGAGED DIRECTLY BY THE HOMEOWNER

Question: **I was contacted by homeowners who want me to perform an appraisal of their home to be used for a loan at a federally regulated financial institution. What are my responsibilities in this potential assignment?**

Response: It is an appraiser's responsibility to disclose to the homeowners that a lender or its agent is required by Title XI of FIRREA to directly engage the services of an appraiser in a federally related transaction. If the homeowners still want to engage you, your disclosure allows you to perform the assignment.

Additional information can be found in Advisory Opinion 25, *Clarification of the Client in a Federally Related Transaction*.

141. CLIENT APPROVAL FOR FUTURE ASSIGNMENTS

Question: **Some of my clients include a condition in engagement correspondence that addresses future assignments for the same subject property. Specifically, my agreement to perform an assignment requires that I obtain client approval before I perform future assignments related to the subject from another party. Advisory Opinion 27, *Appraising the Same Property for a New Client*, states that USPAP does not require a release to perform the new assignment. Can I agree to perform assignments where the client requires a release for future assignments related to the subject?**

Response: Yes. Appraisers are often subject to agreements that exceed the requirements of USPAP. These additional client requirements are permissible so long as they do not conflict with the requirements of USPAP. Although USPAP does not require obtaining approval from a prior client before agreeing to perform an assignment to appraise the same property for a new client, a client can establish such a requirement.

142. REQUEST TO MODIFY A COMPLETED APPRAISAL REPORT

Question: **I have completed an appraisal assignment for a client. The report was completed using the 2005 version of the Uniform Residential Appraisal Report (URAR). The client has requested that I remove one of the comparable properties from the report because, in the underwriter's opinion, it is not sufficiently similar to the subject property. If I do this, will my action comply with USPAP?**

Response: Such an action has the potential to be misleading. Certification item #15 of the 2005 URAR states the following:

© The Appraisal Foundation

*"**I have not knowingly withheld any significant information from this appraisal report** and, to the best of my knowledge, all statements and information in this appraisal report are true and correct."* (Bold added for emphasis)

You initially concluded that the comparable you are being asked to remove was relevant in developing and communicating the assignment results. If this opinion has not changed, and you subsequently remove a comparable listing or sale from the appraisal report and sign the certification for this specific report format, it would likely be misleading because information you consider to be significant is being knowingly withheld.

In addition, Standards Rule 2-2(a)(x)(5) requires that at a minimum an Appraisal Report provide sufficient information to indicate that the appraiser complied with the requirements of STANDARD 1 by:

> ***summarizing the information analyzed and the reasoning that supports the analyses, opinions, and conclusions, including reconciliation of the data and approaches***
> (Bold added for emphasis)

If the comparable is removed as requested by the client, information that was analyzed would no longer be summarized in the report as required by this Standards Rule.

143. SHELF LIFE OF AN APPRAISAL OR APPRAISAL REPORT

Question: **I've received inquiries from some of my clients asking me how long my appraisal reports are valid. Is this addressed in USPAP?**

Response: USPAP does not determine the length of time for which an appraisal or appraisal report is valid. Various users of appraisal services may establish their own requirements or guidelines for the validity period of an appraisal or appraisal report.

It is also important to note that USPAP distinguishes an appraisal from an appraisal report. An appraisal is an opinion of value while an appraisal report is any communication, written or oral, of an appraisal that is transmitted to the client upon completion of an assignment.

Two dates are essential to an appraisal report: the effective date of the appraisal and the date of the report. The effective date of the appraisal establishes the context for the value opinion, while the date of the report indicates whether the perspective of the appraiser on the market and property as of the effective date of the appraisal was prospective, current, or retrospective.

As such, the effective date of the appraisal, the date of report, or both may be important reference points when determining when a new appraisal or appraisal report is required.

144. USE OF DISTRESS SALES IN REAL PROPERTY MARKET VALUE APPRAISALS

Question: **A client has asked me to disregard any foreclosure, real estate owned (REO), or short sales when performing market value appraisal assignments. Is this an acceptable assignment condition?**

Response: No. USPAP does not specifically address which sales should or should not be considered in an appraisal assignment. However, in real property appraisal assignments, Standards Rule 1-4(a) requires:

> *When a sales comparison approach is necessary for credible results, an appraiser must analyze such comparable sales data as are available to indicate a value conclusion.*

© The Appraisal Foundation

So, the appraiser must determine what data is relevant.

There are many appraisal assignments where, in order to achieve credible results, it is necessary to use "distress" (e.g., REO or Short Sales) properties as comparable sales. However, foreclosure sales, defined by *Black's Law Dictionary* as "the sale of mortgaged property, authorized by a court decree or a power-of-sale clause, to satisfy the debt" are seldom based on market expectations. When there is a glut of distress sales in the marketplace, and those properties are truly comparable to the subject, it would be misleading not to use them as part (or in some cases all) of the basis for a value conclusion.

A client-imposed requirement to disregard data that may be relevant and necessary for credible assignment results would be an unacceptable assignment condition.

145. ADDING AN INTENDED USER (NEW)

I am performing an appraisal of a small retail property for the property owner. The intended use of the appraisal is for estate planning. Before I could complete the Appraisal Report, the client informed me that he has hired a new financial planner, and we have agreed that the financial planner should be identified as an additional intended user. Now I have some questions regarding the assignment.

Question (1.) Does adding an intended user change the scope of work?

Response (1.) Not if the appraiser can confirm that the use of the financial planner does not trigger any additional appraisal development-related requirements. However, if the financial planner is not as familiar with the subject property as the owner, the content necessary for the intended users to understand the report may differ. This could affect the amount of information and level of detail necessary in the report.

Question (2.) Does adding an intended user require the request to be treated as a new assignment?

Response (2.) No. As long as the change is *during* the assignment, USPAP does not require it to be treated as a new assignment. On the other hand, there is nothing in USPAP that would prohibit the appraiser from calling it a new assignment.

Question (3.) What if I had been asked to make the change *after* the report was issued?

Response (3.) If the change occurs *after* the appraiser performed the scope of work and issued the report, the new intended user could not have been identified "...based upon communication with the client at the time of the assignment." (See DEFINITION of intended user.) Therefore, the only way to accommodate adding an intended user after issuing a report is in a new assignment.

146. ASSIGNMENT CONDITIONS VERSUS CLIENT CONDITIONS (NEW)

Question: **I agreed to perform a market value appraisal of a property with proposed improvements under the following client-imposed conditions:**

a. **The appraiser must develop at least two approaches to value;**
b. **The property must be appraised as if it had been completed per plans and specifications as of the date of inspection;**
c. **The report must include photographs of abutting properties;**
d. **The report must include an as-is market value for the subject property; and**
e. **The report must be transmitted to the client within 30 days of the agreement to perform the appraisal.**

© The Appraisal Foundation

I am unsure whether all of these are actual assignment conditions as defined in USPAP, and which may be client conditions only. Which, if any, of these conditions are assignment conditions?

Response: The DEFINITION of assignment conditions includes "... other conditions that affect the scope of work." So the question is which of these conditions affects the appraiser's scope of work? Only items a, b, and d are assignment conditions under USPAP.

© The Appraisal Foundation

147. EFFECTIVE DATE OF THE APPRAISAL

Question: **The Standards Rules require all appraisal reports to disclose the effective date of the appraisal. Must the date be reported as a specific day, month, and year, or is it sufficient to simply provide the month and year?**

Response: The effective date of an appraisal is determined by the intended use and the intended user. In most cases the intended use and/or the intended user dictates that the date provided is a specific day, month, and year. However, in some circumstances it may be acceptable to be less specific, (e.g., in a prospective appraisal assignment when an exact date cannot be accurately determined at the time the assignment is completed).

148. APPRAISAL DATES

Question: **I hear various terms used with respect to appraisal dates. In addition to the effective date and date of report, I've heard terms such as "date of appraisal" and "signature date." Do these terms have different meanings?**

Response: USPAP defines effective date as *the date to which an appraiser's analyses, opinions, and conclusions apply; also referred to as date of value*. This term is preferable to date of appraisal, which is ambiguous. Signature date is sometimes used to signify when the report was transmitted to the client, but the appropriate terminology is the date of the report or report date.

149. CITATION OF EFFECTIVE DATE

Question: **I've been engaged to perform a real property appraisal review assignment and have a question about the appraisal report under review. Does USPAP require the effective date to be cited each time the opinion of value is stated in the appraisal report?**

Response: No. USPAP does not require the appraiser to state the effective date of the appraisal with each statement of the value opinion. In a real property appraisal report, the requirements that apply to reporting the effective date can be found in Standards Rules Rule 2-2(a)(vii) for an Appraisal Report and Standards Rule 2-2(b)(ix) for a Restricted Appraisal Report. This rule simply requires the appraisal report to "state the effective date of the appraisal and the date of the report."

However, you should take care to ensure that intended users are not misled, and should state the effective date in a manner which clearly establishes the context for the value opinion. In most instances, it will assist intended users to understand the context if the appraiser reports the value opinion with the effective date of the appraisal, especially when the effective date is significantly different (retrospective or prospective) from the date of the report.

150. CHANGING THE EFFECTIVE DATE

Question: **I recently had a client ask me to change the effective date of my appraisal, to make it one week after the effective date shown in my report. Does USPAP permit me to simply change the effective date without taking additional steps?**

Response: No. As indicated in the SCOPE OF WORK RULE, the effective date of the appraiser's opinions and conclusions is an assignment element.

© The Appraisal Foundation

If the client is asking for an appraisal with a different effective date, the appraiser needs to determine the appropriate scope of work to produce credible assignment results for this request. Such a request would need to be considered a new assignment, but that does not necessarily require starting from scratch. As with all new assignments, the appraiser must decide the appropriate scope of work to produce credible assignment results. This would include a decision as to whether it is necessary to perform another inspection, as well as the extent of any additional research and analyses that might be required. The scope of work for the new assignment can be different from the scope of work completed in the earlier assignment. As with any assignment, the appraiser might be able to use information and analyses developed for a previous assignment.

151. DATE OF REPORT

Question: **I was recently asked by a client to change the date of an appraisal report that I had submitted. I have always used the date that I began writing the report as my report date. My client wants me to use the date the report was submitted. Is my client correct in asking me to change the date?**

Response: Yes. The date of the report is the date that it is completed and transmitted to the client. According to USPAP, a report is a communication "transmitted to the client upon completion of the assignment." Given that language, the appraiser's document is not a "report" until it is transmitted to the client.

In addition, if the certification is dated, that date should also be based on the date the report is completed and transmitted, not when it is begun. Logically, one cannot certify regarding what has been done before it has been done.

152. DATE OF REVISED REPORT

Question: **In response to a client request, I recently made some minor edits to a report. The assignment results were unchanged, but I corrected a few minor typographical errors and entered the census tract number which had been omitted from the original report. Because the results did not change, this was essentially the same report, so I did not change either the effective date or the date of the report. My client now wants me to resubmit the report with the current report and certification date. Should the new report be dated as of the date revised?**

Response: Yes. The date of the revised report should be the date that it is completed and transmitted to the client. According to USPAP, a report is a communication "transmitted to the client upon completion of an assignment." Since, in this case, a new report is being completed and transmitted, it should be dated accordingly. This is true even when the only changes are minor corrections and the assignment results are unchanged.

In addition, if the certification is dated, that date should also be based on the date the report is resubmitted. In the resubmission, the appraiser is certifying the content of the revised report, so any certification date cannot precede the completion of the revisions.

153. REVISION TO THE CONTRACT PRICE

Question: **I recently completed an appraisal for mortgage financing purposes in a purchase transaction and delivered the report to my client. My opinion of value was less than the pending sale price. One week later, the buyer and seller renegotiated the contract agreeing to a price equal to my appraised value. My client asked if I can provide a revised report wherein I replace the prior sale price with the newly agreed-upon sale price. How can I do this and comply with the requirements of USPAP?**

© The Appraisal Foundation

Response: The appraiser may not simply replace the pending sale price information in the appraisal report and resubmit the report to the client, as this would be misleading.

Under Standards Rule 1-5(a) the appraiser is required (when the value opinion to be developed is market value, and if such information is available to the appraiser in the normal course of business) to *"analyze all agreements of sale, options, and listings of the subject property current as of the effective date of the appraisal."*

If the new contract information is stated in a revised report, the appraiser should note that the second contract was provided after the effective date, and the information regarding the contract that was in place as of the effective date must remain in the report. Further, the revised report must have a new report date, as of the date the revised report is transmitted to the client.

If the client does require a more current effective date, the request must be treated as a new assignment.

Additional related guidance may be found in Advisory Opinion 1, *Sales History,* and Advisory Opinion 3, *Update of a Prior Appraisal.*

154. PROPOSED IMPROVEMENTS – CURRENT AND PROSPECTIVE VALUE OPINIONS

The real property that I am appraising involves proposed improvements, and the client needs to know my opinion of market value as if the proposed improvements were complete, both as of the current date and as of a future date. I have two questions.

Question: (1.) When the effective date is a current date, is my opinion developed on the basis of a hypothetical condition or an extraordinary assumption?

Response: When the effective date is a current date, and the appraisal is of a property with proposed improvements as if those improvements were complete on a current the effective date, the value opinion is developed on the basis of a hypothetical condition.

This is because the appraiser knows the proposed improvements do not, in fact, exist on that current effective date. Completing an analysis on the condition that something the appraiser knows to be contrary to what exists, but is supposed for purposes of reasonable analysis, is using a hypothetical condition in that analysis. (See Standards Rule 1-2[g]).)

Question: (2.) When the effective date is a future date, when the proposed improvements will be complete, is my opinion developed on the basis of a hypothetical condition or an extraordinary assumption?

Response: When the effective date is a future date and the appraisal is of a property with proposed improvements that are expected to be complete on or before that future date, the value opinion is developed on the basis of an extraordinary assumption.

This is because the appraiser presumes the proposed improvements will, in fact, exist as of that future effective date. Completing the analysis on the condition that something the appraiser reasonably believes will exist as of a future date is using an extraordinary assumption in that analysis. (See Standards Rule 1-2[f]).

© The Appraisal Foundation

155. EFFECTIVE DATE AND DATE OF THE REPORT

Question: **I have been engaged to perform a valuation assignment. The assignment is to develop an opinion of the market value of the subject property in its current "as-is" condition. In this context, what does "current" mean?**

Response: In USPAP, there are three different types of appraisals: retrospective, current, and prospective. As explained in Advisory Opinion 34, *Retrospective and Prospective Value Opinions*:

> *Current appraisals occur when the effective date of the appraisal is contemporaneous with the date of the report. Because most appraisals require current value opinions, the importance of specifying both the date of the report and the effective date of the analysis is sometimes lost.*

"Current" appraisal assignments are based on the effective date of the appraisal being contemporaneous with the date of the report. Contemporaneous means arising, existing or occurring during the same time period. In this context contemporaneous is not intended to mean simultaneous. Because the time period may very well differ from assignment to assignment, one single specific time period cannot be provided that can be used for all assignments. However, for an assignment to include a current appraisal opinion there must not have been a significant change in the property characteristics or market conditions between the effective date of the appraisal and the date of the report.

156. COMPETENCY AS OF EFFECTIVE DATE OF THE APPRAISAL

Question: **Can an appraiser prepare a retrospective appraisal, with an effective date of appraisal as of five years ago, if that appraiser wasn't even an appraiser five years ago?**

Response: Yes. The appraiser must comply with the COMPETENCY RULE at the time the appraiser develops the appraisal, regardless of the effective date of the appraisal. If appraisers are to develop a value opinion, be it retrospective, prospective, or current, the appraisers must be able to deal with the nuances of such an assignment at the time they are performing the assignment (e.g., to research data associated with the retrospective, prospective, or current effective date of the appraisal and to analyze the data in light of market conditions as of that date). It is not necessary for appraisers to be, or to have been, competent appraisers as of the effective date of the appraisal.

Appraisers could develop a retrospective appraisal with an effective date of the appraisal that is prior to the their own date of birth. Likewise, an appraiser could develop a prospective appraisal with an effective date of the appraisal that occurs after the date of the appraiser's own death. These would be legitimate assignments that could be completed according to USPAP. In such cases the appraisers could not be considered to be competent appraisers as of the effective dates of those appraisals.

157. CURRENT AND RETROSPECTIVE VALUE OPINIONS WITHIN ONE REPORT

Question: **I have been asked to perform an appraisal assignment that includes providing a retrospective opinion of value as well as a current one. Can I report both value opinions within one appraisal report?**

Response: Yes; you can communicate both opinions of value within one appraisal report. Since two opinions of value (appraisals) are included in the report, both opinions must be developed in conformance with the appropriate STANDARD (1, 5, 7, or 9).

© The Appraisal Foundation

158. POST-VALUE DATE INFORMATION IN RETROSPECTIVE APPRAISALS

Question: **The real property that I am appraising is in a market that was impacted by the the closing of a major regional employer's facility three years ago. My client needs an opinion of value as of a date that preceded any knowledge of the facility being closed. Is it appropriate to include the fact that the facility closed in my retrospective appraisal?**

Response: A thorough review of Advisory Opinion 34, *Retrospective and Prospective Value Opinions* is necessary to properly deal with the problem the appraiser faces in this question.

> *A retrospective appraisal is complicated by the fact that the appraiser already knows what occurred in the market after the effective date of the appraisal. Data subsequent to the effective date may be considered in developing a retrospective value as a confirmation of trends that would reasonably be considered by a buyer or seller as of that date. The appraiser should determine a logical cut-off for the data to be used in the analysis because at some point distant from the effective date, the subsequent data will no longer provide an accurate representation of market conditions as of the effective date. This is a difficult determination to make. Studying the market conditions as of the date of the appraisal assists the appraiser in judging where to make this cut-off. With market evidence that data subsequent to the effective date was consistent with market expectations as of the effective date, the subsequent data should be used. In the absence of such evidence, the effective date should be used as the cut-off date for data considered by the appraiser.*

The appraiser cannot include in the analyses the fact that an event subsequent to the effective date in a retrospective appraisal changed the market conditions that existed as of the effective date. Using such information is not consistent with the intended use of the appraisal because buyers and sellers had no knowledge or expectation of that subsequent event as of the effective date.

However, an appraiser may disclose facts in an appraisal report about events that occurred subsequent to the effective date of an appraisal. Such a disclosure is particularly appropriate when the appraiser has reason to believe that the intended users of the report could be misled by not knowing those facts.

159. APPRAISAL BASED ON CURRENT AND PROSPECTIVE DATES OF VALUE

Question: **My client, a federally regulated lender, has requested a market value appraisal for use in financing a commercial property development project. The client's stated loan conditions include a requirement that the property be leased before the onset of its development. The client stated they need (1) an opinion of market value for the property that actually exists as of a current date, which is the site with its entitlements and under the zoning in effect as of the current date, and (2) an opinion of market value as of the future date (a prospective value opinion) when the property will be physically completed and occupied under the pre-leasing terms and conditions. Must I develop both of these opinions of value and, if so, why?**

Response: Yes; the client needs both opinions to aid in identifying its project development loan risk and respond to regulatory requirements and guidelines.

The client's project development loan decision would typically be based, in part, on your analysis of highest and best use and the feasibility of the development project. (See Standards Rules 1-2[e], Comment on [i]-[v]).

The value of the site, with its entitlements and under the zoning in effect as of a current date (i.e., without use of a hypothetical condition), is an important component in your analysis; and it provides the client with information necessary to identify development risk and determine appropriate loan terms and conditions. Absent other factors, this value opinion could be

© The Appraisal Foundation

developed without use of either an extraordinary assumption or a hypothetical condition. The subject in the current appraisal is the site that actually exists with the zoning (including any entitlements) in effect as of that date.

The value of the property as of the prospective date, when it has been physically completed and leased under the pre-leasing terms and conditions, is also significant information the client would typically use in making its project development loan decision. Developing this value opinion typically requires the use of an extraordinary assumption because the subject in the prospective appraisal is the property as it is expected to exist as of that future date when physical development is complete and the property is leased in accordance with the lease terms and conditions.

160. USPAP COMPLIANCE IN RETROSPECTIVE APPRAISALS

Question: **When preparing an assignment with a retrospective effective date, should the appraiser comply with the USPAP in effect as of the effective date of the appraisal or as of the date of report?**

Response: Appraisers must comply with the USPAP edition in effect as of the date of the report.

161. RETROSPECTIVE APPRAISAL ASSIGNMENTS

Question: **I was recently asked to complete a retrospective market value appraisal for which the effective date of the appraisal is two years prior to the date of the report. In researching this assignment I discovered several comparable sales that were listed and placed under contract prior to the effective date of the appraisal, but actually sold well after the effective date. Would it be appropriate to use only these sales in my sales comparison approach to value?**

Response: In a retrospective appraisal the analysis should reflect the market conditions that existed on the effective date of the appraisal. Using only comparable sales information that was **not** available to the market place, or did not exist as of the effective date of the appraisal could be misleading because it would not reflect information available to the marketplace during that time period.

Retrospective appraisals and the use of data from the time period after the effective date are addressed in Advisory Opinion 34, *Retrospective and Prospective Value Opinions*. AO-34 states, in part:

> *A retrospective appraisal is complicated by the fact that the appraiser already knows what occurred in the market after the effective date of the appraisal. Data subsequent to the effective date may be considered in developing a retrospective value as a confirmation of trends that would reasonably be considered by a buyer or seller as of that date. The appraiser should determine a logical cut-off for the data to be used in the analysis because at some point distant from the effective date, the subsequent data will no longer provide an accurate representation of market conditions as of the effective date. This is a difficult determination to make. Studying the market conditions as of the date of the appraisal assists the appraiser in judging where to make this cut-off. With market evidence that data subsequent to the effective date was consistent with market expectations as of the effective date, the subsequent data should be used. In the absence of such evidence, the effective date should be used as the cut-off date for data considered by the appraiser.*

While the effective date is not an absolute cut-off point for market data, the appraiser must use particular caution in applying it in these assignments.

Refer to AO-34 for additional information.

© The Appraisal Foundation

162. CITING THE SOURCE OF THE VALUE DEFINITION AND FANNIE MAE FORM 1004/FREDDIE MAC FORM 70

Question: **USPAP requires an appraisal report to include a citation of the source of the value definition used for the appraisal. Is this information adequately addressed on Fannie Mae Form 1004/ Freddie Mac Form 70?**

Response: Yes. The value definition is on the Fannie Mae Form 1004/Freddie Mac Form 70, and there are several references indicating that Fannie Mae and Freddie Mac are the sources for the form. No additional citation is required for USPAP compliance.

© The Appraisal Foundation

163. WHAT IS SCOPE OF WORK?

Question: **What is scope of work?**

Response: In basic terms, the scope of work is the work an appraiser performs to develop assignment results. USPAP defines scope of work as *the type and extent of research and analyses in an appraisal or appraisal review assignment*. Note that this definition does not include reporting.

164. APPLICABILITY OF SCOPE OF WORK RULE

Question: **In my role as an appraiser, I perform many assignments that are not appraisal or appraisal review. Does the SCOPE OF WORK RULE apply to these assignments?**

Response: No. The SCOPE OF WORK RULE applies only to appraisal and appraisal review assignments.

Assignments other than appraisal and appraisal review (for example, teaching appraisal courses, providing sales data, collecting market data, analyzing reproduction costs, developing educational texts) still require an appraiser to comply with those portions of USPAP that apply to appraisal practice. The portions of USPAP that apply generally to appraisal practice include the PREAMBLE, the DEFINITIONS, the ETHICS RULE, the COMPETENCY RULE, and the JURISDICTIONAL EXCEPTION RULE.

165. RESPONSIBILITY FOR THE SCOPE OF WORK DECISION

Question: **Who determines the scope of work?**

Response: It is the appraiser's responsibility to determine and perform the appropriate scope of work.

166. CLIENT SPECIFIES SCOPE OF WORK

Question: **Is a scope of work specified by the client acceptable?**

Response: The scope of work specified by the client is acceptable only if it allows the appraiser to develop credible assignment results. If the scope of work specified by the client does not permit development of credible assignment results, the appraiser must either change the scope of work to what the appraiser determines is necessary to develop credible assignment results or withdraw from the assignment.

167. ALTERNATIVE VALUATION PRODUCTS

Question: **I am a state certified appraiser and as such, perform real property appraisals in compliance with USPAP. However, I have recently been asked by a client to provide them with an "alternative valuation product" that they have designed. This product, as designed, does not appear to comply with USPAP. Am I allowed to perform such an assignment as an appraiser?**

Response: First, it is important to understand that appraisers, not report forms, must comply with USPAP.

If you are able to perform an acceptable scope of work and make modifications and/or additions to the report that would result in USPAP compliance, then you may perform such an assignment as an appraiser.

Otherwise, you must decline or withdraw from the assignment.

© The Appraisal Foundation

168. CLIENT REQUEST TO LIMIT SCOPE OF WORK TO NEW CLIENT NAME

Question: **An appraiser completed an appraisal for Client A. Client B received a copy of the appraisal from Client A and finds it acceptable for their purposes, but wants to be identified as the client in the appraisal report. Client B is aware that appraisers are prohibited from readdressing (or transferring) a completed report to a different client's name. As a result, Client B would like to engage the appraiser in a new assignment, limiting the appraiser's scope of work to only identifying them as the new client. Can the appraiser complete the assignment from Client B under these terms?**

Response: No. USPAP requires the scope of work performed to produce credible assignment results. USPAP clearly establishes that the scope of work is determined by the appraiser. If a client's instructions (i.e., assignment conditions) limit the appraiser's scope of work in a new assignment to simply identifying a new client, then it would be the client, not the appraiser, who has made the scope of work decision.

In addition, even if the appraiser accepted the client's proposed scope of work as the appraiser's own, that scope of work may not be adequate to produce credible assignment results as required by USPAP.

As is the case with all assignments, when a client's assignment conditions are too restrictive to produce credible assignment results, an appraiser must decline or withdraw from an assignment, unless the appraiser can modify those assignment conditions to allow for credible assignment results.

169. THE IMPACT OF DIFFERENT CLIENTS ON ASSIGNMENT RESULTS WITH OTHERWISE IDENTICAL ASSIGNMENT ELEMENTS AND SCOPE OF WORK

Question: **Assuming otherwise identical assignment elements and scope of work, will an appraiser's value opinion for an assignment be the same regardless of the appraiser's client?**

Examples: **Assuming otherwise identical assignment elements and scope of work, will an appraiser's value opinion for an eminent domain assignment be the same regardless of whether the assignment is for the condemnee or the condemnor?**

In a litigation assignment with otherwise identical assignment elements and scope of work, will the appraiser's value opinion be the same regardless of whether the appraiser was hired by the defendant or the plaintiff or a third-party?

In an appraisal prepared for a tax assessment appeal with otherwise identical assignment elements and scope of work, will the appraiser's value opinion be the same regardless of whether the appraiser was hired by the government or the taxpayer?

In an appraisal prepared for a gift donation for tax filing purposes with otherwise identical assignment elements and scope of work, will the appraiser's value opinion be the same regardless of whether the appraiser was hired by the IRS or the taxpayer?

Assuming otherwise identical assignment elements and scope of work, will an appraiser's value opinion be the same independent of the client and other intended user(s)?

Response: Before answering these questions, it is important to review portions of the SCOPE OF WORK RULE.

In any appraisal or appraisal review assignment, the appraiser must identify the problem to be solved, then determine and perform the scope of work necessary to develop credible assignment results in the context of the intended use. Appraisers have broad flexibility and significant responsibility in determining the appropriate scope of work for an assignment. It is

© The Appraisal Foundation

the appraiser's responsibility, with input from the client, to identify the assignment elements. Assignment elements are the:

- *client and any other intended users;*
- *intended use of the appraiser's opinions and conclusions;*
- *type and definition of value;*
- *effective date of the appraiser's opinions and conclusions;*
- *subject of the assignment and its relevant characteristics; and*
- *assignment conditions.*

Assignment conditions include assumptions, extraordinary assumptions, hypothetical conditions, laws and regulations, jurisdictional exceptions and other conditions that affect scope of work.

The answer to each of the above questions is yes. If the other assignment elements (except the client) and the scope of work are the same, then the appraiser's value opinion will be the same.

As an example, suppose an appraiser is requested to provide an opinion of the market value of a property for a specific intended use, such as for a potential sale or acquisition. Unless other assignment elements are different, and the appraiser establishes and follows a different scope of work as a result of differing assignment elements, there will be no difference in the value opinion regardless of whether the intended user is the buyer, seller, or a third party.

In all assignments, the appraiser must comply with the Management section of the ETHICS RULE, which prohibits compensation that is based on *a direction in assignment results that favors the cause of the client.* In all assignments, the appraiser must comply with the Conduct section of the ETHICS RULE which states, *an appraiser must perform assignments with impartiality, objectivity, and independence, and without accommodation of personal interests*. In addition, *an appraiser must not advocate the cause or interest of any party or issue.* If an appraiser's results vary solely depending on whether the client is a buyer or seller, then the appraiser would be acting as an advocate for the cause of the client.

There are times, however, when assignments involving the same property will have different assignment elements. These could include different effective dates, different types and definitions of value (market value, as opposed to insurable value, for example) or different assignment conditions. As a result of a change in assignment elements, the value conclusion may be different; but the value conclusion will not differ simply because the client changed. The value conclusion may differ because one or more of the other assignment elements changed; and, as a result of this change, the appraiser established and followed a different scope of work.

170. HOW CREDIBLE ASSIGNMENT RESULTS ARE MEASURED

Question: **Is there an absolute measure of credible assignment results?**

Response: No. Measuring the credibility of assignment results is always in the context of the intended use of the assignment. This means that credibility is relative, not absolute. Assignment results that are credible for one intended use may not be credible for another intended use.

© The Appraisal Foundation

171. ERRORS OF COMMISSION AND OMISSION

Question: **A reviewer recently told me that my appraisal did not comply with USPAP because of errors of omission and commission. The reviewer cited Standards Rule 1-1(b). What is the difference between these two errors?**

Response: An error of *commission* is doing something incorrectly. For example, incorrectly identifying the subject property's relevant characteristics is an error of commission. In a residential appraisal assignment, this could be inaccurately measuring the property.

An error of *omission* is neglecting to do something that is necessary. For example, failing to identify the subject property's relevant characteristic is an error of omission. In a residential appraisal assignment, this could be neglecting to measure the second level of a two-story house.

172. MAKING A SERIES OF ERRORS

Question: **A reviewer told me that my appraisal did not comply with USPAP because I made several minor calculation and analytical errors. Does USPAP address this issue?**

Response: Yes. Standards Rules 1-1(c), 7-1(c), and 9-1(c) require that the appraiser not render appraisal services in a careless or negligent manner such as by making a series of errors that in aggregate affects the credibility of the assignment results. This means, for example, that the following series of errors in a residential appraisal could affect the credibility of the assignment results: making small errors in determining the property size, not recognizing minor deferred maintenance items, and making a small negative adjustment when it should have been a positive adjustment.

173. CHANGING THE SCOPE OF WORK AFTER THE REPORT HAS BEEN SUBMITTED

Question: **Sometimes after submitting my appraisal report, my client will ask me to perform additional work. This can mean looking at more or different comparables or developing another approach. Do these requests for additional work create a new assignment?**

Response: No. Requests to perform additional research or analysis change the scope of work, but do not create a new assignment. The additional work can be performed as part of the original assignment. The appraiser may decide, as a business decision, to treat the request for additional research and analysis as a new assignment, but it is not required.

174. DIFFERING SCOPES OF WORK

Question: **I recently completed an appraisal that complied with FHA guidelines, including a more detailed physical inspection of the subject property than is normally performed for conventional loans. The borrowers changed their minds and are now opting for a conventional loan. Can I simply remove any references to FHA guidelines and resubmit the appraisal for conventional loan purposes? What if I had named FHA/HUD as an intended user in my original appraisal report, can I remove them as an intended user as well?**

Response: USPAP would not preclude you from preparing a new report that removed references to any FHA guidelines. However, if you obtained any information as a result of your inspection of the subject property for FHA purposes, you would have to disclose the results of that inspection, even if it were a more thorough inspection than required for conventional financing. For example, if you noted roof problems because you entered the attic when performing your inspection for FHA, you would be obligated to disclose those same results, even if you wouldn't typically access an attic when inspecting the subject property for conventional financing.

© The Appraisal Foundation

Because FHA/HUD was named as an intended user in your original report, USPAP requires you to treat the request as a *new assignment,* since the intended user(s) are an assignment element, and as such, cannot be changed once the assignment is complete.

See Advisory Opinion 26, *Readdressing (Transferring) a Report to Another Party*, and Advisory Opinion 27, *Appraising the Same Property for a New Client*, for additional guidance.

175. JUDGING THE ACTIONS OF AN APPRAISER'S PEERS

Question: **In the SCOPE OF WORK RULE, one of the two tests regarding the acceptability of an appraiser's scope of work is what the appraiser's peers would do. There are many appraisers that do things differently, so how would I know what they would do in an assignment?**

Response: The SCOPE OF WORK RULE states that the acceptability of an appraiser's work is judged based on two tests:

- *the expectations of parties who are regularly intended users for similar assignments; and*
- *what an appraiser's peers' actions would be in performing the same or a similar assignment.*

The first step in knowing what your peers would do is to identify your peers. In USPAP, the term appraiser's peers has a specific meaning. It is defined as:

other appraisers who have expertise and competency in a similar type of assignment.

This definition illustrates that an appraiser's peers are assignment specific and may change from assignment to assignment. This is because appraisers have varying levels of expertise and competency in specific property types, geographic locations, or other important areas of appraisal. For more information on appraiser's peers, please see Advisory Opinion 29, *An Acceptable Scope of Work.*

Knowledge about what an appraiser's peers would do in a similar assignment comes through being a participant in the profession. Typical forums that allow appraisal professionals to share information about practice include appraisal journals and publications, professional meetings and conferences, education though courses and seminars, and appraisal discussion groups.

176. TYPE AND DEFINITION OF VALUE, AND CITATION OF SOURCE

Question: **USPAP requires Appraisal Reports to state the type and definition of value and cite the source of the definition. What is a type of value? What sources can be used to comply with the requirement to cite the source of the definition of value?**

Response: STANDARDS 2, 6, 8 and 10 require that Appraisal Reports state the type and definition of value and cite the source of the definition. The exact wording varies slightly for STANDARD 10.

The type of value is the general class or category of value. Examples include market value or fair value.

The definition of value provides a specific description of the characteristics and conditions of the type of value. Examples include definitions provided on a form report, in FIRREA, in U.S. accounting regulations, U.S. tax regulations, and various court rulings.

USPAP does not provide any specific definition of value or endorse any particular source. Sources of value definitions could include, for example, a regulatory agency, a legal jurisdiction, an engagement letter, or a textbook.

© The Appraisal Foundation

177. MARKET RENT OPINION

Question: **A client asked me to provide an opinion of the market rent for a commercial property. Is such an assignment considered an appraisal?**

Response: Yes. USPAP defines an appraisal as an opinion of value, and market rent is an expression of value for the right to use a property. Therefore, to comply with USPAP in this assignment, an appraiser would have to follow STANDARD 1 to develop the opinion of the market rent, and STANDARD 2 to report the assignment results.

178. USING THE DEFINITION OF VALUE PROVIDED

Question: **A client has asked me to use a definition of value included in an engagement letter for the assignment. Is this permitted?**

Response: Yes. As part of identifying the problem to be solved, the appraiser must identify the type and definition of value, but USPAP does not require the use of any specific type or definition of value.

179. SALES OR FINANCING CONCESSIONS

Question: **The real estate market I appraise in has slowed down over the last 12 to 18 months, and it is now extremely common to see seller concessions as part of a purchase transaction. What are the USPAP requirements regarding proper treatment of sales/financing concessions?**

Response: Sales or financing concessions may have an effect on the price paid for a property. As such, it is important for the appraiser to recognize this and analyze their impact. Sales or financing concessions should be considered in light of the type and definition of value used in an assignment. If the opinion of value is to be based on non-market financing or financing with unusual conditions or incentives, Standards Rule 1-2(c) requires that the appraiser identify the terms of such financing and any influences on value.

It should be noted that some assignment conditions, such as Fannie Mae appraisal guidelines, specify how sales or financing concessions are to be addressed in assignments that are subject to their guidelines. Appraisers performing assignments of this type should become familiar with all applicable guidelines in order to satisfy the requirements of the COMPETENCY RULE.

180. INTENTIONALLY DEFLATING OPINIONS OF VALUE

Question: **Most appraisers know that inflating values is unethical, but some appraisers think that deflating values is acceptable, particularly in light of difficult market conditions. I think that both actions are unethical. Am I correct?**

Response: Yes. The ETHICS RULE requires an appraiser to be independent, impartial, and objective, and to perform assignments without bias. An appraiser who intentionally inflates or deflates an opinion of value would be in violation of the Conduct section of that Rule.

© The Appraisal Foundation

181. MEASURING SINGLE FAMILY RESIDENCES USING THE ANSI STANDARD

Question: **Are appraisers bound by USPAP required to comply with ANSI Z765-2013, the Standards Method for Measuring Square Footage in Detached and Attached Single Family Houses?**

Response: No. Appraisers are not required by USPAP to comply with ANSI Z765-2013, which is a voluntary Standard. However, use of the ANSI Standards may be an assignment condition in some assignments.

Although appraisers are not required by USPAP to adhere to a specific standard of square footage measurement, appraisers are required by Standards Rule 1-1(b) to *not commit a substantial error of omission or commission that significantly affects an appraisal*. This rule requires the appraiser to gather factual information in a manner that is sufficiently diligent. Standards Rule 1-1(c) requires appraisers to *not render appraisal services in a careless or negligent manner*. Appraisers must use due diligence and due care in performing appraisal services, including gathering factual data such as square footage.

182. EXPOSURE TIME AND MARKETING TIME

Question: **What is the difference between exposure time and marketing time?**

Response: Both the DEFINITIONS and Advisory Opinion 35, *Reasonable Exposure Time in Real and Personal Property Market Value Opinions of Value*, define exposure time as:

> *an opinion, based on supporting market data, of the length of time that the property interest being appraised would have been offered on the market prior to the hypothetical consummation of a sale at market value on the effective date of the appraisal.*

In contrast, Advisory Opinion 7, *Marketing Time Opinions*, defines reasonable marketing time as:

> *an opinion of the amount of time it would likely take to sell a real or personal property interest at the concluded market value or at a benchmark price during the period immediately after the effective date of an appraisal.*

In other words, exposure time occurs **before** the effective date of the appraisal, whereas marketing time occurs **after** the effective date. An estimate of reasonable exposure time is required by USPAP when reasonable exposure time is a component of the definition for the value opinion being developed. (See the Comment to Standards Rules 1-2(c)[iv] and 7-2(c)[iv]). An estimate of marketing time is not mandated by USPAP but may be required by the client). For additional guidance, see AO-35 and AO-7.

183. MARKETING TIME ON APPRAISAL FORMS

Question: **I am completing a market value appraisal. I use standard residential report forms that ask for a neighborhood marketing time. Does *marketing time* on these forms mean the same thing as *exposure time* as it is used in USPAP?**

Response: No. Although the two may be the same length of time, the meanings are different. The exposure time opinion required by USPAP is *specific to the subject property* and represents the length of time the subject would likely have been listed for sale prior to a hypothetical sale of the subject property on the effective date of the appraisal. Marketing time, in this context, is the typical length of time the *properties in that neighborhood* would be expected to be on the market prior to a sales agreement.

© The Appraisal Foundation

As explained in Advisory Opinion 35, *Reasonable Exposure Time in Real and Personal Property Opinions of Value*, exposure time is dependent on the characteristics of the subject property and the market conditions as of the effective date.

Most residential appraisal report forms have a field in which the appraiser must enter an opinion of the neighborhood *marketing time*. However, most residential appraisal report forms do not have a field for which the appraiser must report the reasonable *exposure time*.

The Comment to Standards Rule 1-2(c)(iv) requires the appraiser to *develop* an opinion of reasonable exposure time whenever developing an opinion of value where exposure time is a component of the definition for the value opinion being developed. The Comments to Standards Rules 2-2(a)(vi) and (b)(viii) require the appraiser to *communicate* the opinion of reasonable exposure time in the appraisal report.

184. EXPOSURE TIME VALUE RANGE

Question: **I understand that reasonable exposure time needs to be developed and reported in cases when it is a component of the definition of the value opinion being developed. However, Advisory Opinion 35, *Reasonable Exposure Time in Real and Personal Property Opinions of Value* seems to suggest that a *range of values* is required when reporting exposure time. Does this mean I must reference a range of values when I report my opinion of reasonable exposure time?**

Response: No, a *range of values* is not required when reporting an opinion of reasonable exposure time. However, the appraiser's opinion of reasonable exposure time must be linked to *an* opinion of value, whether it is a specific value or a range of values.

As stated in AO-35:

> *"The reasonable exposure period is a function of price, time, and use, not an isolated opinion of time alone."*

185. CHECKING "STABLE" VS. "DECLINING" PROPERTY VALUES

Question: **When performing residential appraisal assignments I use standard appraisal software forms. The forms ask me to identify whether neighborhood property values are increasing, stable, or declining. I have been told that lenders won't accept appraisal reports where declining is checked (even when this is an accurate analysis), so I usually check stable to accommodate the underwriting process. Is this a violation of USPAP?**

Response: Yes. If the appraiser is aware that a market is declining and either intentionally or due to gross negligence, reports it as being otherwise, the appraiser is in violation of the ETHICS RULE.

If an appraisal report indicates that property values are stable when they are actually declining and the appraiser's data supports the conclusion of declining values, the report is misleading and in violation of Standards Rule 2-1(a).

In addition, if the appraiser does not properly recognize that a market is declining, the appraiser may also be in violation of other requirements in STANDARD 1, as well as the COMPETENCY RULE.

© The Appraisal Foundation

186. RANGE OF VALUE

Question: **Is a range of value considered an appraisal?**

Response: Yes. The Comment to the definition of appraisal states, in part:

An appraisal is numerically expressed as a specific amount, as a range of numbers, or as a relationship (e.g., not more than, not less than)...

187. MORE THAN ONE INTENDED USE

Question: **Can an appraisal or appraisal review assignment include more than one intended use?**

Response: Yes. USPAP requires appraisers to *identify the intended use of the appraiser's opinions and conclusions*. There is no prohibition against having more than one intended use. However, when performing an appraisal or appraisal review assignment with multiple intended uses, the appraiser must be very careful to clearly identify each of the intended uses in the report to limit the possibility of confusion.

Additionally, the appraiser must comply with all assignment conditions that are applicable to the intended uses. The appraiser must also recognize that the scope of work may need to be expanded in order to provide credible results for all of the intended uses.

188. VALUE IN USE REQUEST FROM FEDERALLY REGULATED LENDER

Question: **My client, a federally insured financial institution, has asked me to provide a value in use appraisal instead of a market value appraisal. May I do this?**

Response: USPAP does not dictate the use of any specific type or definition of value. The type and definition of value must be appropriate for the intended use and intended users.

For federally related transactions, federally insured financial institutions require an opinion of market value, as defined by regulations. Therefore, if you provide a value in use, you may also have to provide a market value, depending on the intended use.

189. DRIVE-BY AND DESKTOP APPRAISALS

Question: **Does USPAP permit real property appraisers to perform drive-by or desktop appraisal assignments?**

Response: Yes. The Comment to Standards Rule 1-2(e) states, in part:

An appraiser may use any combination of a property inspection, documents, such as a legal description, address, map reference, copy of a survey or map, property sketch, photographs, or other information to identify the relevant characteristics of the subject property.

This is also discussed in Advisory Opinion 2, *Inspection of Subject Property.* It states:

An inspection is not required by USPAP, but one is often conducted.

The extent of the inspection process is an aspect of the scope of work, and may vary based on assignment conditions and the intended use of the assignment results. It is the appraiser's responsibility to determine the appropriate scope of work, including the degree of inspection necessary to produce credible assignment results given the intended use.

© The Appraisal Foundation

For further clarification, see AO-2.

190. INSPECTION OF SUBJECT PROPERTY

Question: **Have I violated USPAP if I don't inspect the interior of the subject property?**

Response: USPAP has no requirement to inspect a subject property's interior. Standards Rule 1-1(b) requires that an appraiser *not commit a substantial error of omission or commission that significantly affects an appraisal*. The Comment to that Standards Rule states, in part:

> *Diligence is required to identify and analyze the factors, conditions, data, and other information that would have a significant effect on the credibility of the assignment results.*

Standards Rule 1-2(e)(i) requires that an appraiser identify a subject property's physical, legal, and economic characteristics. But, note that the required identification must be *relevant to the type and definition of value and intended use of the appraisal*. If an interior inspection is not relevant, it is not required. Determining whether an interior inspection is relevant is a scope of work decision. The SCOPE OF WORK RULE states:

> *An appraiser must not allow assignment conditions to limit the scope of work to such a degree that the assignment results are not credible in the context of the intended use.*

Advisory Opinion 2, *Inspection of the Subject Property* advises that if adequate information about the relevant characteristics of the subject property, such as information that could only be obtained as a result of an interior inspection, is not possible by personal inspection or from sources the appraiser reasonably believes are reliable, an appraiser must withdraw from the assignment unless the appraiser can:

- *modify the assignment conditions to expand the scope of work to include gathering the necessary information; or*
- *use an extraordinary assumption about such information, if credible assignment results can still be developed*

Additional guidance about inspecting properties can be found in Advisory Opinion 23, *Identifying the Relevant Characteristics of the Subject Property of a Real Property Appraisal Assignment*, and Advisory Opinion 28, *Scope of Work Decision, Performance, and Disclosure*.

191. DOES INSPECTING PHOTOGRAPHS CONSTITUTE A PERSONAL INSPECTION OF A SUBJECT PROPERTY?

Question: **I am a licensed trainee with approximately six months of experience. My supervisory appraiser recently determined that I am competent to perform inspections on my own; however, many of our clients require the supervisory appraiser to personally inspect the property as well. If I do the inspection by myself, but take numerous representative photos of the interior of the subject property, may my supervisory appraiser indicate in the report that he also personally inspected the property?**

Response: No. A personal inspection of the interior of the property is not the same as the inspection of photographs of the interior of the property. It would be misleading for any appraiser, including supervisory appraisers, to indicate that a personal inspection was performed when, in fact, the appraiser viewed photographs of the property. Appraisers who only inspect photographs of a property, but sign a certification indicating that they personally inspected the subject property, are in violation of the USPAP prohibition against communicating assignment results with the intent to mislead or to defraud, communicating a report that is known by the appraiser to be misleading or fraudulent, and, possibly, knowingly permitting an employee or other person to communicate a misleading or fraudulent report. (See Conduct section of the ETHICS RULE.)

© The Appraisal Foundation

192. IS IT PERMISSIBLE TO USE MLS PHOTOS FOR COMPARABLE SALES?

Question: **I use standard appraisal report forms that contain a statement saying I personally inspected the exterior of the comparable sales. The assignment conditions require me to comply with this statement and do not permit any alterations. One of my clients now requires two additional sales of comparable properties to be included with every appraisal report. However, the client told me not to inspect the exterior of these additional sale comparables and just to use the MLS photos. May I comply with the client's request?**

Response: No; you are being asked to not inspect the comparable sales when the form states that you have. You must either inspect the sales or change your report to indicate you did not inspect the sales.

193. IS IT PERMISSIBLE TO USE MLS PHOTOS FOR ACTIVE LISTINGS?

Question: **I use an appraisal report form that contains a statement saying I personally inspected the exterior of the comparable sales, but it does not address active listings. One of my clients now requires two additional active listing comparable properties to be included with every appraisal report. However, the client told me not to inspect the exterior of these active listings and just to use the MLS photos. Am I compliant with USPAP if I do not physically inspect the exterior of these properties and only use the MLS photos?**

Response: Yes; USPAP does not require inspections or photographs. However, both are often required by clients. If an inspection of the active listing comparables is not required for credible assignment results, and if it is not contrary to assignment conditions or specific statements in the report, then using an MLS photo and not performing an exterior inspection would be acceptable.

194. IS THE COST APPROACH NECESSARY FOR APPRAISAL OF VACANT LAND?

Question: **The property I am appraising is land without improvements, to be valued as is without foreseeable change in zoning or use. Does Standards Rule 1-4(b)(i) mean that for my market value opinion to be credible I must complete a cost approach?**

Response: No. Standards Rule 1-4(b) is prefaced by the phrase "When a cost approach is necessary for credible assignment results." This means that USPAP does not specify when an appraiser must develop a cost approach.

USPAP does not prescribe methods and techniques for any assignment, however Standards Rule 1-1(a) does require the appraiser to be aware of, understand, and correctly employ those recognized methods and techniques that are necessary to produce a credible appraisal. Thus it is up to the appraiser to know whether the cost approach is necessary for an appraisal to be credible.

195. IMPROVEMENT ONLY APPRAISAL

Question: **In a real estate appraisal is it permissible to appraise only the improvements?**

Response: Yes. Standards Rule 1-2(e)(v) states that the subject of an assignment may be a physical segment of a property.

The subject of a real property appraisal does not have to include all of the physical parts of an identified parcel or tract of real estate. The subject of a real property appraisal can be all or any part of an improved or unimproved parcel or tract of identified real estate. For example, the subject of a real property appraisal could be a part of the land, the improvements on or to the land, or some other configuration within a parcel or tract of identified real estate.

© The Appraisal Foundation

Use of a hypothetical condition or extraordinary assumption is not necessary in the specific case of appraising the building component of an improved property, although one or both may be necessary in other specific cases. However, to avoid communicating a misleading appraisal, the report would have to disclose the *existence* of the land as part of the property, but the land does not have to be included in the valuation.

196. APPRAISING ONLY THE UNDERLYING LAND OF AN IMPROVED PROPERTY

Question: **I have been asked by my client to appraise the underlying land of an existing shopping center. Can I perform such an assignment under USPAP and if so, would this require the use of a hypothetical condition?**

Response: Yes, you can perform this type of assignment in compliance with USPAP. Standards Rule 1-2(e) states, in part, the appraiser must:

> *identify, from sources the appraiser reasonably believes to be reliable, the characteristics of the property that are relevant to the type and definition of value and intended use of the appraisal, including:*
>
> *(i) its location and physical, legal, and economic characteristics;*
> *(ii) the real property interest to be valued;*
> *(v) whether the subject property is a fractional interest, physical segment, or partial holding.*

In addition, the Comment to this Rule states, in part:

> *An appraiser is not required to value the whole when the subject of the appraisal is a fractional interest, a physical segment, or a partial holding.*

The subject of a real property appraisal does not have to include all of the physical parts of an identified parcel or tract of real estate. The subject of a real property appraisal can be a full or fractional ownership interest in all or any part of an improved or unimproved parcel or tract of identified real estate. For example, the subject of a real property appraisal could be a partial-interest in the land, all or part of the land, the improvements only, the fee simple interest of a fully leased or otherwise encumbered property or some other configuration within a parcel or tract of identified real estate.

Use of a hypothetical condition or extraordinary assumption is not necessary in the specific case of appraising the land component of an improved property, although one or both may be necessary in other specific cases. The same is true whenever appraising any other portion of the subject. To avoid communicating a misleading appraisal, the report should disclose the *existence* of the improvements as part of the property, but the improvements do not have to be included in the valuation.

197. APPRAISING PHYSICAL SEGMENTS (5-ACRE PORTION)

Question: **A local lender has asked me to appraise only a 5-acre portion of a 62-acre parcel. Am I permitted to comply with this request?**

Response: Standards Rule 1-2(e)(v) states that the subject of an assignment may be a physical segment of a property. However, appraisers must also comply with any laws, regulations, guidelines or other assignment conditions that might apply.

If the assignment requires compliance with published assignment conditions, the appraiser must be aware of the current guidelines (or regulations, if applicable).

© The Appraisal Foundation

Failure to recognize applicable assignment conditions would be a violation of the ETHICS RULE or COMPETENCY RULE.

198. PROPOSED IMPROVEMENTS – PLANS AND SPECIFICATIONS REQUIRED

Question: **I have been asked to perform an appraisal involving proposed improvements. The client has indicated that plans and specs have not been finalized. Does USPAP require me to review the plans and specifications prior to completing this assignment?**

Response: No. The Comment to the Standards Rule 1-2(e)(i)-(v) states, in part:

> *When appraising proposed improvements, an appraiser must examine and have available for future examination, plans, specifications,* ***or other documentation sufficient to identify the extent and character of the proposed improvements.*** (Bold added for emphasis)

Hence, the appraisal can be based on other documentation if that documentation provides sufficient information to properly identify the relevant characteristics of the subject property.

Additional guidance on appraising proposed improvements can be found in Advisory Opinion 17, *Appraisals of Real Property with Proposed Improvements*.

199. IS AN AVM AN APPRAISAL?

Question: **Are the results from an Automated Valuation Model (AVM) an appraisal?**

Response: No. Advisory Opinion 18, *Use of an Automated Valuation Model (AVM)*, states:

> *An AVM's output is not, by itself, an appraisal, and communication of an AVM's output is not, in itself, an appraisal report.*

An AVM is a tool that delivers an estimation or calculation, whereas appraisers arrive at a value opinion by applying their judgment and experience. An appraisal is defined as an opinion of value, which is distinctly different from an estimate or calculation of value. An AVM uses automated processes and cannot produce an opinion of value because only individuals can exercise judgment and form opinions. An AVM is just one tool among many that an appraiser might use to arrive at an opinion of value.

Appraisers are cautioned that this response is based on the USPAP definition of appraisal. Jurisdictions that use a different definition of appraisal may reach a different conclusion.

200. APPRAISER'S USPAP OBLIGATIONS WHEN USING AN AVM

Question: **What are an appraiser's USPAP obligations when using an Automated Valuation Model (AVM)?**

Response: Many appraisers use calculators, spreadsheets, analytic software, and similar tools to analyze market data and calculate assignment results. The nature of the appraiser's service and how these tools are used are important factors in recognizing USPAP obligations. When appraisers use an AVM, it can be as part of an appraisal assignment that provides value opinions to the client, or it may be for an assignment to run the AVM and provide the output to the client.

Advisory Opinion 18, *Use of an Automated Valuation Model (AVM)*, provides advice to help appraisers properly distinguish among the uses of an AVM. Additional guidance can be found in Advisory Opinion 37, *Computer Assisted Valuation Tools*.

© The Appraisal Foundation

An appraiser who uses an AVM for any purpose must comply with USPAP. The portions of USPAP that apply generally to appraisal practice include the PREAMBLE, the DEFINITIONS, the ETHICS RULE, the COMPETENCY RULE, and the JURISDICTIONAL EXCEPTION RULE.

When the assignment includes providing an opinion of value for real property, the assignment is an appraisal and the RECORD KEEPING RULE, the SCOPE OF WORK RULE, and STANDARDS 1 and 2 also apply.

201. UNIFORM ACT AND SCOPE OF WORK

I'm doing an appraisal assignment for a government agency that is subject to the jurisdiction of The Uniform Relocation Assistance and Real Property Acquisitions Act of 1970, as Amended (commonly known as, the Uniform Act), and its implementing regulation, 49 CFR Part 24. The regulation requires the acquiring agency to develop the scope of work and define the appraisal problem cooperatively with the appraiser. This is somewhat different from USPAP's SCOPE OF WORK RULE which places that responsibility primarily on the appraiser. The agency is providing a draft scope of work and asking me to comply with that as a minimum assignment condition. This raises two possible scenarios.

Question: **(1.) If the agency scope of work seems appropriate, do I need to state somewhere in my report that the scope of work was developed by the agency with my concurrence?**

Question: **(2.) Assume that I believe the agency scope of work is inappropriate or inadequate. I discuss this with the agency and they insist that the scope of work they have developed is appropriate for their program needs. Can I complete the assignment and be in USPAP compliance?**

Response: The answer to both questions is the same. It is the appraiser's responsibility to determine and perform the appropriate scope of work.

The scope of work performed in the assignment must be disclosed in the report. However, USPAP does not address disclosure of the client's role in determining the scope of work.

Direction from the client on the scope of work is acceptable only if the appraiser is able to develop credible assignment results. If the scope of work specified by the client does not allow the development of credible assignment results, the appraiser must either (a) obtain the client's agreement for an appropriate scope of work, or (b) withdraw from the assignment.

202. APPRAISING LARGE GROUPS OF SIMILAR OR LIKE ITEMS

Question: **When an appraiser is asked to value a significantly large group of similar or like items does USPAP require that the appraiser follow STANDARD 5 for mass appraisals?**

Response: No. USPAP does not require that STANDARD 5 be followed in such cases. Mass appraisal, for which performance standards are addressed in STANDARD 5, is an appraisal method. USPAP does not dictate the use of any particular method or technique in any particular assignment or under any particular set of circumstances. While mass appraisal methods may be helpful in the appraisal of large numbers of similar assets, whether its use is appropriate in a particular assignment would depend on such things as assignment conditions, the intended use of the appraisal results, and, at times, agreement with the client.

© The Appraisal Foundation

203. BLOCKAGE DISCOUNT AND STANDARD 5

Question: **Is there any connection between the application of STANDARD 5 for mass appraisals and the application of a blockage discount?**

Response: No. There is no connection between the application of mass appraisal methods, as addressed in STANDARD 5, and the application of a blockage discount. A blockage discount may be applicable when the appraisal problem being addressed indicates an assumption that a large number of similar assets would be offered for sale on the market at once. Under some circumstances, this would create an oversupply, which would depress the value of the assets.

Whether the application of a blockage discount is appropriate depends on many factors, including the intended use of the appraisal, the type and definition of value, the conditions of the assignment, and the relevant characteristics of the assets. Relevant characteristics include the nature of the assets, their market and other factors.

204. CALCULATING BLOCKAGE DISCOUNT

Question: **Does USPAP offer guidance in how to calculate an appropriate blockage discount?**

Response: No. USPAP focuses on appraisal standards, not appraisal methodology or how to perform calculations. USPAP does require that an appraiser be competent (see the COMPETENCY RULE) and states, in Standards Rule 1-1(a) and the other development Standards, that an appraiser must:

> *be aware of, understand, and correctly employ those recognized methods and techniques that are necessary to produce a credible appraisal.*

205 BUSINESS VALUATION USING ASSET-BASED (COST) APPROACH

Question: **I am valuing a controlling interest in a business enterprise by use of an asset-based (cost) approach, and that business owns real property. Am I required to have an appraisal of the real property or may I use other indications of the real property value?**

Response: This decision is part of the scope of work determination the business appraiser must make. The appraiser's judgment of whether an appraisal is necessary depends upon whether credible assignment results can be developed for the business interest without such an appraisal.

For some intended uses, a business appraiser may determine that it is necessary to have a real property appraisal, performed by an appraiser competent to perform the appraisal in compliance with USPAP. For other intended uses, the business appraiser may determine that an indication of the real property value other than a real property appraisal may be appropriate. Such indications could be a management estimate, a recent transaction of the property, or tax assessment values.

206. ALLOCATION OF VALUE OPINIONS

I often perform real property appraisal assignments that include not only real property but also personal property and/or intangible assets (examples include property types such as hotels and restaurants).

Often times, my clients will request that I separate or allocate a portion of the defined value opinion to these non-real property components. These requests raise the following four questions.

© The Appraisal Foundation

Question: (1.) What exactly are the appraiser's USPAP obligations in performing this separation of value?

Question: (2.) May this allocation be accomplished without the appraiser developing an opinion of value in compliance with STANDARD 7 or 9?

Question: (3.) Is an allocation considered to be synonymous with an opinion of value or is it the result of a mathematical calculation?

Question: (4.) There are also occasions when the client does not specifically request separate valuations of non-real property assets, even though they may be present. Is the appraiser still required to value those assets separately?

Response: Standards Rule 1-2(e) requires an appraiser to:

> *Identify the characteristics of the property that are relevant to the type and definition of value and intended use of the appraisal, including:*
>
> > *(iii) any personal property, trade fixtures, or intangible assets that are not real property but are included in the appraisal;...*

Standards Rule 1-4(g) states:

> *When personal property, trade fixtures, or intangible assets are included in the appraisal, the appraiser must analyze the effect on value of such non-real property assets.*

And the Comment to Standards Rule 1-4(g) further states:

> *When the scope of work includes an appraisal of personal property, trade fixtures or intangible assets, competency in personal property appraisal (see STANDARD 7) or business appraisal (see STANDARD 9) is required.*

Given this background, each of the questions can be answered as follows.

Question: (1.) What exactly are the appraiser's USPAP obligations in performing this separation of value?

Response: Whether this is labeled a separation or an allocation, it is an appraisal as defined in USPAP.

Question: (2.) May this allocation be accomplished without the appraiser developing an opinion of value in compliance with STANDARD 7 or 9?

Response: No. Once it is understood that performing this separation of value is synonymous with performing an appraisal, compliance with the applicable Standards Rules is required, as is appropriate competency.

Question: (3.) Is an allocation considered to be synonymous with an opinion of value or is it the result of a mathematical calculation?

Response: As stated in the response to Question #1, an allocation is synonymous with an appraisal.

Question: (4.) There are also occasions when the client does not specifically request separate valuations of non-real property assets, even though they may be present. Is the appraiser still required to value those assets separately?

Response: No. This is a scope of work decision to be made by the appraiser; Standards Rule 1-4(g) does not require separate appraisals of these different types of assets. Standards Rule 1-4 (g) states:

© The Appraisal Foundation

When personal property, trade fixtures, or intangible assets are included in the appraisal, the appraiser must analyze the effect on value of such non-real property assets.

Comment: When the scope of work includes an appraisal of personal property, trade fixtures or intangible assets, competency in personal property appraisal (see STANDARD 7) or business appraisal (see STANDARD 9) is required.

Some appraisers and users of appraisals believe the requirement that *the appraiser must analyze the effect on value of such non-real property items* in Standards Rule 1-4(g) is a requirement for the separate appraisal of those items in all assignments. That is incorrect. Analyzing the effect on value might be appropriately made through the selection of comparable properties used in the sales comparison approach or the deduction of certain line items of expense for management fees, maintenance or replacements in the income approach, for example.

207. LEASED FEE INTEREST WHEN INTANGIBLE ASSETS EXIST

Question: **I am appraising a single tenant retail property that is being sold with financing by my client, which is a bank. The property was developed by XYZ Company and just completed last month for a total development cost (land and improvements) of $1,500,000. The developer is part of a large retail chain that will occupy the building at an above-market lease rate. The property is being sold to an investor on a sale-leaseback basis for over $2,000,000. This sale price is supported by several other sales that also have above-market leases that were also created by the same type of sale-leaseback arrangements.**

When I questioned the seller/tenant's representative, they said that *both parties recognized the lease rate was above-market* and that the price was well above replacement cost. They noted that the lease supported the sale price and that the credit strength of the XYZ Company warranted using the above-market lease rate for the valuation. Should I allocate the portion of above-market rent to the real estate or treat it as an intangible? My client insists that I attribute the entire rent to real property value. What does USPAP require in this situation?

Response: The subject of this appraisal is real property, not intangibles, specifically the leased fee estate; therefore, Standards Rule 1-2(e) applies. The characteristics of the lease must be identified in accordance with Standards Rule 1-2(e)(iv). In developing a real property appraisal, Standards Rule 1-2(e) states an appraiser must:

identify, from sources the appraiser reasonably believes to be reliable, the characteristics of the property that are relevant to the type and definition of value and intended use of the appraisal, including:

(i) its location and physical, legal, and economic characteristics;
(ii) the real property interest to be valued;
(iii) any personal property, trade fixtures, or intangible assets that are not real property but are included in the appraisal;
(iv) ***any known*** *easements, restrictions, encumbrances,* ***leases****, reservations, covenants,* ***contracts****, declarations, special assessments, ordinances, or other items of a similar nature; and*
(v) whether the subject property is a fractional interest, physical segment, or partial holding. (Bold added for emphasis)

Further, the valuation in this assignment must address the effect of the lease on value in accordance with Standards Rule 1-4(d) that states:

When developing an opinion of the value of a leased fee estate or a leasehold estate, an appraiser must analyze the effect on value, if any, of the terms and conditions of the lease(s).

© The Appraisal Foundation

In this situation you are required to analyze the effect on value of the above-market lease. The result of the analyses must be reported in accordance with Standards Rule 2-2, for example 2-2(a)(x)(5) which states, in part:

summarizing the information analyzed, and the reasoning that supports the analyses, opinions, and conclusions;...

208. PURCHASE CONTRACT IS NOT PROVIDED TO THE APPRAISER

Question: **I was recently engaged to conduct a market value appraisal of a one-to-four unit residential property. The intended use of this appraisal is to assist the client in analyzing the loan collateral associated with the property's purchase. I requested a copy of the purchase contract from the client, but they refused to provide it although they acknowledged that a contract for purchase of the property in fee simple exists. They did, however, provide a sale price orally. Can I continue this assignment, without the purchase contract, and comply with USPAP?**

Response: Yes. You can complete the assignment in compliance with USPAP; however, you will need to ensure compliance with Standards Rule 1-5(a) in developing the appraisal, and with the relevant reporting requirement in Standard 2.

Standards Rule 1-5(a) states:

When the value opinion to be developed is market value, an appraiser must, ***if such information is available to the appraiser in the normal course of business:*** *(Bold added for emphasis)*

(a) analyze all agreements of sale, options, or listings of the subject property current as of the effective date of the appraisal;

The Comment to the corresponding reporting requirements in Standards Rules 2-2(a)(x)(3) and 2-2(b)(xii)(3) states in part:

If such information is unobtainable, a statement on the efforts undertaken by the appraiser to obtain the information is required.

The appraiser has an obligation to make an effort to obtain a copy of the purchase contract, and the report must state what efforts were made. In addition, if a copy of the contract cannot be obtained, the appraiser must perform the analysis and report the results of the analysis based on the information provided. In order to avoid being misleading, the report must disclose the source of the contract information.

Complying with these Standards Rules ensures that the existence and unavailability of the purchase contract is appropriately disclosed so that intended users will not be misled.

209. AVAILABILITY OF CURRENT AGREEMENT OF SALE

Question: **When developing a real property appraisal, what is an appraiser's responsibility under USPAP if a lender refuses to provide a copy of the current agreement of sale of the subject property?**

Response: Standards Rule 1-5(a) requires an appraiser developing a market value real property appraisal, if such information is available to the appraiser in the normal course of business, to:

analyze all agreements of sale, options, or listings of the subject property current as of the effective date of the appraisal.

© The Appraisal Foundation

The normal course of business for an appraiser when the property is known to be the subject of a pending transaction is to ask the client for the terms of the agreement. If this request is denied, then the appraiser should make reasonable attempts to obtain this information from other sources through legal means commonly available to and practiced by the appraiser's peers. The Comment to Standards Rules 2-2(a)(x)(3) and (b)(xii)(3) also includes the requirement that:

If such information is unobtainable, a statement on the efforts undertaken by the appraiser to obtain the information is required. If such information is irrelevant, a statement acknowledging the existence of the information and citing its lack of relevance is required.

Refer to Advisory Opinion 1, *Sales History* for additional information.

210. RECONCILIATION OF THE APPROACHES TO VALUE

Question: **For a real property appraisal, I know that USPAP requires an appraiser to develop a reconciliation of the approaches to value that are used in an assignment. Does USPAP require the appraiser to reconcile the data utilized within each approach to value?**

Response: Yes. Standards Rule 1-6 states:

In developing a real property appraisal, an appraiser must:

*(a) reconcile the quality and quantity of the data available **and analyzed within the approaches used**; and*

(b) reconcile the applicability and relevance of the approaches, methods and techniques used to arrive at the value conclusion(s). (Bold added for emphasis)

211. ADJUSTMENTS IN SALES COMPARISON APPROACH

Question: **Does USPAP place any limitation on the size of adjustments made to comparable sales in the sales comparison approach to value?**

Response: No. USPAP places no limitations on the size of adjustments made in the sales comparison approach. However, it should be noted that certain clients and other intended users may have assignment conditions addressing this topic.

212. UPDATING A PRIOR ASSIGNMENT WITH A DIFFERENT SCOPE OF WORK

Question: **Several months ago I appraised a property using only a sales comparison approach. My client is now asking that I perform an update of my prior appraisal, but they now want me to include a cost approach. Does USPAP allow me to do this?**

Response: Yes. Update is a business term; under USPAP, the second assignment from the same client is a new assignment with its own scope of work and the requirement to produce credible assignment results. Advisory Opinion 3, *Update of a Prior Appraisal,* states, in part:

*When developing an opinion regarding a property that was the subject of a previous assignment, the scope of work in the **new assignment** may be different from the scope of work in the prior one.* (Bold added for emphasis)

Therefore, the new assignment can be performed with a scope of work greater than that performed in the original assignment.

© The Appraisal Foundation

213. APPRAISAL UPDATE WITH NO CHANGE IN VALUE

Question: **I was recently contacted by a client for whom I had previously completed an appraisal. The client asked if I could simply tell them whether there have been changes in the market since the time of my appraisal, and whether the value of the property remains the same. Am I permitted to do this under USPAP?**

Response: Yes. However, it must also be understood that an appraiser making a determination that the value of a property has not changed is performing an appraisal as defined in USPAP. The USPAP definition of appraisal states, in part:

> *An appraisal is numerically expressed as a specific amount, as a range of numbers, **or as a relationship (e.g., not more than, not less than)...*** (Bold added for emphasis)

In addition, the appraiser is obligated to comply with the reporting requirements of USPAP. The request from the client should be treated as a new assignment, which could be completed in accordance with Advisory Opinion 3, *Update of a Prior Appraisal.*

214. UPDATE OF AN APPRAISAL COMPLETED BY ANOTHER APPRAISER

Question: **I was recently asked to update an appraisal performed by another appraiser who works for a different appraisal company. Can I prepare an update if the original appraisal was performed by another appraiser?**

Response: Yes. Advisory Opinion 3, *Update to a Prior Appraisal,* provides advice on how such an assignment can be performed in conformance with USPAP.

215. DOES A NEW ASSIGNMENT REQUIRE STARTING OVER?

Question: **Advisory Opinion 26, *Readdressing (Transferring) a Report to Another Party*, and Advisory Opinion 27, *Appraising the Same Property for a New Client,* clarify that I cannot readdress an appraisal, and I must treat a subsequent request as a new assignment. Does that mean I must start from scratch since I would be performing a new assignment for a different client? Must I re-inspect the property?**

Response: A new assignment does not mean that you must start from scratch. You must decide the appropriate scope of work for the new assignment. This would include a decision as to whether it is necessary to perform another inspection. The scope of work for the new assignment can be different from the scope of work completed in the earlier assignment.

As with any assignment, you might be able to use information and analyses developed for a previous assignment. Appraisers are often selected for subsequent assignments specifically because of experience and demonstrated competency in a prior assignment.

One must be mindful of obligations relating to the use of confidential information. The Confidentiality section of the ETHICS RULE states, in part:

> *An appraiser must not disclose (1) confidential information; or (2) assignment results prepared for a client to anyone other than:*
>
> - *the client;*
> - *parties specifically authorized by the client;*
> - *state appraiser regulatory agencies;*
> - *third parties as authorized by due process of law; or*
> - *a duly authorized professional peer review committee except when such disclosure to a committee would violate applicable law or regulation.*

© The Appraisal Foundation

216. RECERTIFICATION OF VALUE

Question: **I heard that a recertification of value is no longer permitted. Is this true?**

Response: No. This is not true; however, there is confusion surrounding this question because the term recertification of value is often mistakenly used by some clients in place of the term update.

Appraisers may perform a recertification of value to confirm whether or not the conditions of a prior appraisal have been met. However, if a client wants to know whether the value of a property has changed (or remained the same) since a prior appraisal, this is an update.

Regardless of the label used, an appraisal of a property that was the subject of a prior assignment is not an extension of the prior assignment – it is a new appraisal assignment. Information about an appraiser's obligations in this situation can be found in Advisory Opinion 3, *Update of a Prior Appraisal.*

217. RECERTIFICATION OF VALUE AND APPRAISAL UPDATE

Question: **The terms recertification of value and appraisal update are often used interchangeably. Do they have the same meaning?**

Response: No, these terms do not have the same meaning. The terms update and recertification of value are discussed in Advisory Opinion 3, *Update of a Prior Appraisal.*

An update is a new appraisal assignment involving a property that was previously appraised. An update is subject to the same USPAP requirements as any other appraisal assignment.

A recertification of value is performed to confirm whether or not the conditions of a prior assignment have been met. One example of a recertification of value is a final inspection. When an appraiser is asked to complete a final inspection, the appraiser is confirming that conditions established in an assignment have, or have not, been met.

Final inspections are commonly used in the case of proposed construction where an appraisal is completed subject to completion per plans and specifications.

See AO-3 for additional information.

218. APPRAISERS PROVIDING COMPS

Question: **I have a client that just wants me to provide comps from a neighborhood. Are there any USPAP requirements I must comply with to perform this task?**

Response: To answer this question, it is important to identify exactly what the appraiser is being asked to do. If the appraiser is asked to provide comps that would typically mean the appraiser would be exercising judgment to determine which sales are most comparable to the subject property. The appraiser may choose to include only those sales the appraiser thinks are most similar to the subject in size, location, quality, or other relevant characteristics, which could mean that certain sales may be omitted. In this case, the resulting data would have been filtered by the appraiser's judgment, which would have the net effect of providing a range of value to the client. This range of value is defined as an appraisal under USPAP; therefore, the appraiser would be obligated to comply with STANDARDS 1 and 2.

This should be contrasted to a request for an appraiser to simply provide data. For example, an appraiser asked by a client to provide sales data of all homes located within a one-

© The Appraisal Foundation

mile radius of a specific address could comply with the client's request without complying with STANDARDS 1 and 2, as the appraiser would just be providing sales data pursuant to the client's defined parameters. In this example, the appraiser must be careful not to communicate any opinions or conclusions regarding the data provided.

For related guidance on this topic, please see Advisory Opinion 19, *Unacceptable Assignment Conditions in Real Property Appraisal Assignments*.

219. CAN APPRAISERS PERFORM COMP CHECK ASSIGNMENTS?

Question: **I'm a residential appraiser and have been asked to perform a comp check (or pre-comp) assignment, where a client wants to get an idea of the value of a home prior to proceeding with a mortgage financing transaction. Does USPAP allow me to perform this type of assignment?**

Response: Yes. These types of assignments are allowed under USPAP. To understand the USPAP requirements, it is important to identify exactly what the appraiser is being asked to do. If the appraiser is asked to provide comps, that would typically mean the appraiser would be exercising judgment to determine which sales are most comparable to the subject property. The appraiser may choose to include only those sales that the appraiser considers most similar to the subject in size, location, quality, or other characteristics, which could mean that certain sales may be omitted. In this case, the resulting data would have been filtered by the appraiser's judgment, which would have the net effect of providing a range of value to the client. This range of value is defined as an appraisal under USPAP; therefore, the appraiser would be obligated to comply with STANDARDS 1 and 2.

But, comp check assignments should be contrasted to requests for an appraiser to simply provide data. For example, an appraiser asked by a client to provide sales data of all homes located within a one mile radius of a specific address could comply with the client's request without complying with STANDARDS 1 and 2, because the appraiser would just be providing sales data pursuant to the client's defined parameters. In this example, the appraiser must be careful not to communicate any opinions or conclusions regarding the data provided.

For additional related guidance on this topic, please refer to Advisory Opinion 19, *Unacceptable Assignment Conditions in Real Property Appraisal Assignments*.

220. SUDDEN MARKET CHANGES RELATED TO CATASTROPHIC EVENTS

Question: **I live and work just outside an area that was devastated by a catastrophic weather event. My market area experienced sudden changes in supply and demand, and real estate sales prices climbed rapidly for a period of time following the disaster. Does USPAP provide advice to real estate appraisers on how to handle sudden market changes brought about by such catastrophic events?**

Response: Although USPAP does not directly address the appraisal issues associated with catastrophic events, the following passages may be especially important in appraisals involving properties in markets that are changing rapidly, for any reason.

Standards Rule 1-2(e) requires an appraiser to identify economic characteristics relevant to the subject property, and Standards Rule 1-3(a)(iii) specifically requires analysis of supply and demand.

For Appraisal Reports, Standards Rule 2-2(a)(iv) requires an Appraisal Report to *contain information, documents, and/or exhibits sufficient to identify the real estate involved in the appraisal, including the physical, legal,* ***and economic property characteristics*** *relevant to the assignment.* (Bold added for emphasis) Market conditions (including sudden market

© The Appraisal Foundation

changes related to catastrophic events) are economic property characteristics, and, as such, should be identified in the development of an appraisal and disclosed in the appraisal report.

221. RESTRICTIONS OR ENCUMBRANCES ON PERSONAL PROPERTY

Question: **What are some examples of a restriction or encumbrance that could have an effect on the value of personal property?**

Response: A restriction or encumbrance exists when the owner of a property is prohibited from exercising one of the traditional rights of ownership (i.e., when one of the "sticks" in the bundle of rights is removed). Examples include: constraints on the exhibition of a work of art; a prohibition or limit on the breeding of an animal; a prohibition on the use of a machine in a particular location; or the prohibition or limit on the sale of the item produced by a particular machine.

Each of these examples shows a restriction or encumbrance that prohibits a particular action, and in each case, that prohibition may have an effect on value.

222. LIENS ON PERSONAL PROPERTY

Question: **I am appraising an asset that is encumbered by a lien. Does the term encumbrances in Standards Rule 7-4(d) mean that when providing an opinion of the value of an asset that is being used as collateral, an appraiser would conclude a value based on the portion of the asset that is not encumbered by the lien (i.e., taking into consideration the remaining balance outstanding on a loan secured by the asset)? Also, must it then be stated in the report which particular asset(s) being appraised is encumbered by this lien?**

Response: Standards Rule 7-4 states, in part:

> *In developing a personal property appraisal, an appraiser must collect, verify, and analyze all information necessary for credible assignment results.*

Standards Rule 7-4 (d) further states:

> *When developing an opinion of value of a lease, leased, or encumbered property, an appraiser must analyze the effect on value, **if any**, of the terms and conditions of the lease or encumbrances.* (Bold added for emphasis)

The mere existence of a lien or other encumbrance does not necessarily affect value, even though the owner's equity in the property may be greatly impacted. The USPAP requirement is to analyze the effect on value; if there is no effect on value then no further analysis is required.

223. APPRAISING TWO LOTS AS ONE

Question: **I have a lender client that wants a market value appraisal completed. The property consists of two separate legal lots. The highest and best use for each of these lots is as a separate one-unit residential site. However, the client wants them appraised as though they were one legal lot. The intended use is for mortgage lending.**

May this assignment be completed treating these two lots as if they were one legal lot with the highest and best use as one legal lot?

Response: Yes. However, complying with the lender's request will require use of a hypothetical condition. If the client is a federally regulated financial institution, the client may also need an "as-is" appraisal.

© The Appraisal Foundation

If the appraisal were based on a hypothetical condition (i.e., market value of the subject as if it were a single lot), and if necessary for credible results, the appraiser would have to develop an opinion of highest and best use of the hypothetical parcel. If this leads to the conclusion that the highest and best use would be subdivision into two or more lots, the appraiser must perform the appraisal recognizing that potential use and may need to perform a subdivision analysis to reach a credible opinion of the highest and best use of the hypothetical parcel.

224. IMPACT ON VALUES OF SURROUNDING PROPERTIES

Question: **My state requires that when property owners seek an exception to a zoning requirement they demonstrate that the exception will not diminish the value of surrounding properties. I am occasionally engaged to render an opinion in these matters. Is the service that I am providing an appraisal?**

Response: Yes. USPAP defines *appraisal*, in part, as *the act or process of developing an opinion of value.* The Comment to the definition states that an appraisal *is numerically expressed as a specific amount, as a range of numbers, or as a relationship (e.g., not more than, not less than) to a previous value opinion or numerical benchmark (e.g., assessed value, collateral value).* In this example, the question could be restated as: Will the market value of the surrounding properties be less than their current market value if the exception is granted? Therefore, the resulting response is an appraisal.

225. IS TURNAROUND TIME AN ASSIGNMENT CONDITION

Question: **My state's appraiser regulatory agency sent out a newsletter that says a due date is an *assignment condition*, and that failing to adhere is a violation of USPAP. Is this true?**

Response: Assignment due dates are contractual obligations, but are not assignment conditions under USPAP. Turnaround times and similar items are business practice issues, and are outside the scope of USPAP.

Assignment conditions are defined in USPAP as:

> *Assumptions, extraordinary assumptions, hypothetical conditions, laws and regulations, jurisdictional exceptions, and other conditions that affect the scope of work.*

However, an appraiser failing to comply with contractual obligations could potentially be subject to civil penalties.

226. INSPECTION USING A DRONE

Question: **I specialize in eminent domain and right-of-way appraisal assignments. My subject properties are typically very large, wooded, and sometimes have rugged topography. I have begun to use a camera mounted on a drone to view more of the subject property than is practical on foot. Drones even help me view the comparable sales. The certification required by Standards Rule 2-3 requires me to disclose whether or not I personally inspected the subject property. Do aerial viewings using a drone constitute a "personal inspection"?**

Response: No. The use of unmanned aerial vehicles, or drones, now allows appraisers to view much more of the subject or comparables and with greater detail. Drones are tools that can be used to amplify vision like binoculars or a jeweler's loupe.

© The Appraisal Foundation

The use of a drone may be a critical tool in the assignment, however, just as viewing photographs of a house does not constitute a personal inspection by the appraiser, neither does viewing recordings of aerial photography. In order for a real property appraiser to include the statement, "I have made a personal inspection of the subject property" in the certification, the appraiser must have physically visited the subject property.

USPAP does not require that you inspect the property being appraised. The SCOPE OF WORK RULE requires that you disclose the extent to which you inspected the property. Therefore, just as you would disclose whether or not you entered the property, or that you relied upon surveys and topographical maps, you would disclose that a drone allowed you to view additional areas of the subject property. Conversely, if somebody provided you with footage filmed by a drone or a manned aircraft, it would be misleading to represent this as a personal inspection.

Because this is a rapidly evolving technology, regulations by government agencies, such as the Federal Aviation Administration, are also rapidly evolving. Make sure you are familiar with all relevant federal, state, and local laws, requirements and restrictions. This may be of particular importance if you use aerial technology to view comparable properties or those with access restrictions.

See Advisory Opinion 2, *Inspection of Subject Property*, for more information.

227. CAN I PERFORM AN APPRAISAL IF THE PROPERTY INSPECTION WAS DONE BY SOMEONE ELSE? (NEW)

Question: **A client has asked me to perform an appraisal, but instead of requiring me to physically inspect the subject, they will provide me with the results of an inspection of the property done by someone else. Does USPAP allow this?**

Response: Yes. USPAP does not require an appraiser to inspect the subject property. However, while an inspection is not required, appraisal reports for real and personal property must contain a signed certification that clearly states whether or not the appraiser personally inspected the property that is the subject of the report.

Standards Rule 1-2(e) requires an appraiser to identify, from sources the appraiser reasonably believes to be reliable, the characteristics of the property that are relevant to the type and definition of value and the intended use of the appraisal, including its location and physical, legal and economic characteristics.

The Comment indicates that an appraiser may use "... any combination of a property inspection, documents, such as a legal description, address, map reference, copy of a survey or map, property sketch, photographs, or other information to identify the relevant characteristics of the subject property."

Standards Rule 1-1(b) requires that an appraiser "...not commit a substantial error of omission or commission that significantly affects an appraisal." Therefore, the appraiser has to have a reasonable basis to believe the information is reliable. Furthermore, an appraiser must not allow assignment conditions to limit the scope of work to such a degree that the assignment results are not credible in the context of the intended use. If appraisers determine that the only way to meet these criteria is by inspecting the property themselves, they must either discuss changing the scope of work with the client, or withdraw from the assignment.

Additional guidance about inspecting properties can be found in Advisory Opinion 2, *Inspection of Subject Property*, Advisory Opinion 23, *Identifying the Relevant Characteristics of the Subject Property of a Real Property Appraisal Assignment*, and Advisory Opinion 28, *Scope of Work Decision, Performance, and Disclosure*.

© The Appraisal Foundation

228. ANALYZING THE SUBJECT'S OPERATING HISTORY (NEW)

Question: **I am appraising the market value of the leased fee interest in an existing, income-producing shopping center property that was built 5 years ago. I have determined that the income approach is necessary for credible assignment results. Standards Rule 1-4(d) requires me to "analyze the effect on value, if any of the terms and conditions of the lease(s)," and Standards Rule 1-4(c)(ii) requires me to "analyze such comparable expense data as are available to estimate the operating expenses of the property." Am I also required to analyze the subject property's operating expense history in such cases?**

Response: If the client or similar clients would expect you to analyze the subject's historical expense data (if available), and if an appraiser's peers (as defined in USPAP) would analyze it; then, yes, you should analyze the data as a part of your development of the income approach. Standards Rule 1-1(a) requires the appraiser to "be aware of, understand, and correctly employ those recognized methods and techniques that are necessary to produce a credible appraisal." Furthermore, the Comment to the Scope of Work Acceptability section of the SCOPE OF WORK RULE indicates that "The scope of work is acceptable when it meets or exceeds the expectations of parties who are regular intended users for similar assignments; and what an appraiser's peers' actions would be in performing the same or a similar assignment."

229. PERSONAL INSPECTION TIMING (NEW)

Question: **Both the DEFINITION of Personal Inspection and the SCOPE OF WORK RULE refer to *identifying* relevant characteristics. If I personally inspect a property to *collect* data about those relevant characteristics, am I "locked in" to only collect information about those relevant characteristics I previously identified, or may I identify additional relevant characteristics based on what I've learned from my personal inspection?**

Response: First, it is important to remember that USPAP does not require a personal inspection at all. Furthermore, if you do perform a personal inspection, USPAP does not dictate when in the process it must occur. An appraiser typically identifies the assignment elements (including the subject of the assignment and its relevant characteristics) at the beginning of an assignment in order to develop an initial Scope of Work and to establish the business terms of the engagement. However, an appraiser's Scope of Work can and often does evolve during the appraisal process based upon information gathered as a result of research and analysis. Thus, an appraiser may identify relevant property characteristics at various stages of an assignment, which could occur prior or subsequent to a personal inspection, if one is performed. For further information see Advisory Opinion 36, *Identification and Disclosure of Client, Intended Use, and Intended Users*, which offers guidance about altering the Scope of Work if the appraiser becomes aware of a change in an assignment element.

230. INTANGIBLE PERSONAL PROPERTY (NEW)

Question: **Why was the DEFINITION of "Personal Property" expanded to include intangible articles? Are these different from "intangible assets," and how can a personal property appraiser know whether to follow STANDARDS 7 and 8 or STANDARDS 9 and 10 when valuing intangible personal property?**

Response: The reason for the updated DEFINITION of Personal Property is that the world of fine art and archives is changing. Some articles that have traditionally been appraised as personal property are not tangible objects. While they could be described as "intangible assets," another term was used in the USPAP definition to help distinguish them from the traditional "franchises, trademarks, patents, copyrights, goodwill, equities, securities and contracts" that are the domain of business appraisers. The simplest way to explain the new developments is with examples.

© The Appraisal Foundation

The first example is conceptual art. Consider a "paint installation" by Sol LeWitt. This artist created "wall drawings" that consist only of instructions and diagrams that authorize others to paint the work of art. The catalogue of London's Tate museum, which owns a Sol LeWitt paint installation, explains that "... Wall Drawing #1136 can be installed, removed, and then reinstalled in another location, as many times as required for exhibition purposes. As such, there can also be periods of time in which the work **does not exist in physical form**." (bold added for emphasis)

A second example is library and museum archives. Today many of these holdings were created and are archived in digital form. In some cases the images, writings, or music, etc. were created digitally and may never have existed as tangible objects.

The COMPETENCY RULE in USPAP applies to appraisals of all types of property. Depending upon the relevant characteristics of a subject property, some conceptual art can be appraised by a personal property appraiser with a specialization in fine art. In other cases, particularly if the rights to a subject property have significant income-producing potential, a business appraiser with expertise in intangible assets may be better qualified. It is also possible for appraisers from both disciplines to collaborate on an assignment. For the types of examples described above, USPAP does not prescribe which STANDARDS are applicable.

231. APPRAISING LARGE QUANTITIES – NOT NECESSARILY A MASS APPRAISAL (NEW)

Question: **I am a personal property appraiser specializing in fine art. When I value the estate of an artist, I sometimes appraise hundreds of very similar prints or an archive of thousands of items that may include letters, photographs, sketches, memorabilia, and business documents. Due to the large quantity of items, I am wondering if these are mass appraisals and whether they should be performed in compliance with STANDARD 5 and reported in compliance with STANDARD 6.**

Response: Large quantities of personal property can be appraised according to STANDARD 5: MASS APPRAISAL, DEVELOPMENT or STANDARD 7: PERSONAL PROPERTY APPRAISAL, DEVELOPMENT. The difference depends on the methodology, not the number of items. Collections of fine art or archives are commonly appraised under STANDARD 7 in ranked groups of items. This is not the same as the development and calibration of a model structure that is required in STANDARD 5.

A mass appraisal must be based upon standard mass appraisal methods of developing, calibrating, and testing a model structure based on the cost, sales comparison and/or income approaches to value. Developing a model involves specifying a mathematical model where the relationship between property characteristics and market value is either linear or nonlinear. The model is generally applied either in tabular or equation form. Calibrating a model requires market analysis to ascertain the appropriate coefficient for each variable. A common statistical process used for calibration is regression analysis. Testing and validating the reliability of the model is often accomplished using ratio studies.

A written report of a mass appraisal must include, among other STANDARD 6 requirements, sufficient information for the intended users to have confidence in the process and procedures. The report must include a summary of the rationale for each model, the calibration techniques used, and the performance measures used. Further, the report must identify the appraisal performance tests used and the performance measures attained.

The Competency Rule specifies that an appraiser's required competence may include analytical methods. Therefore, if the fine arts appraiser is unfamiliar with mass appraisal statistical methods, then the appraiser lacks the competency to complete a mass appraisal assignment in compliance with STANDARD 5 and STANDARD 6.

© The Appraisal Foundation

232. EXTRAORDINARY ASSUMPTIONS COMPARED TO HYPOTHETICAL CONDITIONS

Question: **How does an extraordinary assumption differ from a hypothetical condition? Can you give some examples of extraordinary assumptions that might apply in a real property appraisal?**

Response: An extraordinary assumption is defined as:

> *an assignment-specific assumption as of the effective date regarding uncertain information used in an analysis which, if found to be false, could alter the appraiser's opinions or conclusions.*

A hypothetical condition is defined as:

> *a condition, directly related to a specific assignment, which is contrary to what is known by the appraiser to exist on the effective date of the assignment results, but is used for the purpose of analysis.*

Appraisers may need to use extraordinary assumptions or hypothetical conditions in performing an assignment. When used in an assignment they become part of the givens in that assignment and have a significant effect on the appraiser's opinions and conclusions.

The difference between the two terms depends upon what the appraiser knows. If an appraiser is uncertain and cannot verify a certain condition that is critical to the valuation but nevertheless has a reasonable basis to accept it as true, then the appraiser will make an extraordinary assumption.

If, on the other hand, an appraiser is basing the analysis upon a condition known to be false, the appraiser will use a hypothetical condition.

The following assumptions would be extraordinary if their use had a significant effect on the appraiser's opinions and conclusions:

1. Appraising proposed improvements, such as new construction or additions, as of the date of completion (a prospective effective date).
2. Appraising a property as if it were free of environmental contamination when it is not known to be contaminated.
3. Appraising a site as if sewer were available when the fact is unknown and there is no apparent evidence that the sewer is not available.
4. Appraising a site under an assumed zoning when the zoning is not known and there is no evidence that the assumed zoning is not possible.
5. Appraising irrigated farmland on the premise that the water supply is adequate for irrigated crop production, absent any evidence that the supply is not adequate.

233. HYPOTHETICAL CONDITIONS DESCRIBED

Question: **What is a hypothetical condition? Can you give me some examples that might apply?**

Response: A hypothetical condition is defined as:

> *a condition, directly related to a specific assignment, which is contrary to what is known by the appraiser to exist on the effective date of the assignment results, but is used for the purpose of analysis.*

© The Appraisal Foundation

Examples of hypothetical conditions that might be necessary in an appraisal assignment include:

1. Appraising proposed improvements such as new construction or additions, as if they existed as of a current date, when they do not.
2. Appraising a property as if it were free of any contamination when it is known to be contaminated.
3. Appraising a site as if the zoning were different.
4. Appraising a business as if key personnel (for example the business founder/owner) were gone, when they are in fact still actively working.
5. Appraising a glass chandelier as if it were properly conserved when it is currently non-functional and broken into many pieces.
6. Appraising an item of equipment as if it were recently rebuilt when the rebuild is either pending or in process.
7. Appraising machinery for manufacturing diesel engines as if stringent new regulations for reducing exhaust emissions had already been enacted, when in fact the regulations are not yet final.

234. WHEN A HYPOTHETICAL CONDITION MAY BE USED

Question: **May an appraiser use any type of hypothetical condition in developing an appraisal?**

Response: No. Standards Rule 1-2(g) states, in part:

*A hypothetical condition may be used in an assignment **only if**:*

(i) use of the hypothetical condition is clearly required for legal purposes, for purposes of reasonable analysis, or for purposes of comparison; and
(ii) use of the hypothetical condition results in a credible analysis.

(Bold added for emphasis)

Standards Rules 3-2(f), 5-2(j), 7-2(g) and 9-2(g) contain similar wording.

235. BEFORE ACQUISITION VALUE AND STANDARDS RULE 1-4(f)

Question: **I'm doing an appraisal assignment for a government agency that is subject to the provisions of The Uniform Relocation Assistance and Real Property Acquisitions Act of 1970, as Amended (commonly known as, the Uniform Act), and its implementing regulation, 49 CFR Part 24. In the before acquisition value appraisal, the regulation requires appraisers to disregard any decrease or increase in the market value of the property that has been caused directly by the project. This regulation appears to conflict with USPAP, Standards Rule 1-4(f), which addresses the analysis of the effect on value of anticipated public or private improvements.**

Obviously, I must comply with the Federal law and regulations, but I am unsure how to reconcile this with the requirements of USPAP, Standards Rule 1-4(f). Does this situation create a USPAP jurisdictional exception or is this simply an assignment condition?

Response: When it applies, 49 CFR Part 24 is an assignment condition. The 49 CFR Part 24 regulation that requires appraisers to disregard any decrease or increase in the market value of the property that has been caused directly by the project in the before acquisition value appraisal is not a jurisdictional exception because the regulation does not conflict with the requirements of USPAP. A jurisdictional exception is only created where USPAP compliance is precluded by a requirement of law or regulation. Standards Rule 1-4(f) becomes applicable in an assignment only when the scope of work includes the analysis of anticipated improvements.

© The Appraisal Foundation

When analyzing anticipated public or private improvements, located on or off the site, an appraiser must analyze the effect on value, if any, of such anticipated improvements to the extent they are reflected in market actions.

The intended use of the assignment drives the appraiser's decisions in identifying relevant property characteristics and assignment conditions. The decision to analyze the effect on value of an anticipated off-site improvement is part of the scope of work decision. The scope of work in before acquisition value assignments prepared under the Uniform Act is based on a condition that anticipated project improvement will not be recognized; therefore Standards Rule 1-4(f) does not apply.

In an appraisal with an assumed condition that is contrary to known fact, the assumed condition is a hypothetical condition. A before acquisition value appraisal assignment that does not include recognition of the project would require the use of a hypothetical condition because this is contrary to a known fact. Standards Rule 1-2(g) states, in part:

A hypothetical condition may be used in an assignment ***only if****: (i) use of the hypothetical condition is clearly required for legal purposes, for purposes of reasonable analysis, or for purposes of comparison; and (ii) use of the hypothetical condition results in a credible analysis.* (Bold added for emphasis)

In the reporting of a real property appraisal report, USPAP Standards Rule 2-1(c) states that the real property appraisal report must:

clearly and accurately disclose all assumptions, extraordinary assumptions, ***hypothetical conditions****, and limiting conditions used in the assignment.* (Bold added for emphasis)

This requirement creates an obligation to disclose all hypothetical conditions used in the assignment. USPAP real property appraisal report requirements state that the report must, at a minimum:

clearly and conspicuously:

- *state all extraordinary assumptions and* ***hypothetical conditions****; and*
- *state that their use might have affected the assignment results; (Bold added for emphasis)*

This requirement directs the appraiser to provide a clear and conspicuous statement of the hypothetical conditions. The form and location of the statement is left to the discretion of the appraiser, but it must be clear and conspicuous to intended users.

236. REPORTING USE OF EXTRAORDINARY ASSUMPTIONS AND HYPOTHETICAL CONDITIONS

Question: **What are the USPAP reporting requirements relating to the use of extraordinary assumptions and hypothetical conditions in an appraisal assignment?**

Response: The report must clearly disclose the use of extraordinary assumptions and hypothetical conditions and notify intended users that the extraordinary assumptions and hypothetical conditions might have affected the assignment results.

For example, Standards Rule 2-1(c) states that each written or oral real property appraisal report must, at a minimum:

clearly and accurately disclose all assumptions, extraordinary assumptions, hypothetical conditions, and limiting conditions ***used*** *in the assignment.* (Bold added for emphasis)

© The Appraisal Foundation

This requirement creates an obligation to disclose all extraordinary assumptions and hypothetical conditions used in the assignment.

For example, Standards 2-2(a)(xiii) states that an Appraisal Report must, at a minimum:

clearly and conspicuously:

- ***state** all extraordinary assumptions and hypothetical conditions; and*
- ***state** that their use might have affected the assignment results;* (Bold added for emphasis)

This requirement directs the appraiser to provide a clear and conspicuous statement of the extraordinary assumptions and hypothetical conditions. The form and location of the statement is left to the discretion of the appraiser, but it must be clear and conspicuous to intended users.

The requirement further directs the appraiser to provide notice to intended users that the use of the extraordinary assumptions and hypothetical conditions might have affected the assignment results. The appraiser is not required to report on the impact of the extraordinary assumptions and hypothetical conditions on assignment results.

Note: The requirements for other report types are similar.

237. MUST A HYPOTHETICAL CONDITION OR EXTRAORDINARY ASSUMPTION BE LABELED?

Question: **If I employ a hypothetical condition or an extraordinary assumption in an assignment, does USPAP require me to label it as such?**

Response: No. USPAP does not require use of the specific terms *hypothetical condition* or *extraordinary assumption*. USPAP requires that all hypothetical conditions and extraordinary assumptions be disclosed clearly and conspicuously, and it must be disclosed that their use might affect the assignment results.

238. VALUE AS IF COMPLETED

Question: **My client, a federally regulated lender, has requested a market value appraisal as of the current date of a site that has all necessary approvals for development of a multi-family project with 30 units. My client intends to use the appraisal in underwriting the credit in a land acquisition loan. Must I develop an opinion of value for the completed project?**

Response: No. As long as the intended use is as you described, the appraisal assignment does not require a current value of the project with the hypothetical condition of it being completed. This is because the subject of your assignment is the site with the existing entitlement to develop the multi-family project, and presumes those entitlements are consistent with the highest and best use of the site.

Since your appraisal is as of a current date, and the property that is the subject of your appraisal is a property that actually exists under the zoning and entitlements in place as of that date, there is no need to use a hypothetical condition, nor to develop an opinion of value of the property after, or as though, it has been developed.

239. APPRAISING A PROPERTY NOT IN AS-IS CONDITION

Question: **Our local community public works department has declared a parcel of land surplus and asked me to appraise the real property at market value with an effective date of the appraisal prior to its advertisement for sale. However, the public works director said there will be a covenant placed on the land immediately prior to the sale that will restrict its use to open space or**

© The Appraisal Foundation

recreation, and the value in my appraisal is to reflect that title condition. Currently, the property is in use by the public works department and does not have such a use limitation.

Since I know the as-is condition of the property title is not as the director described it, can I do the appraisal as if the covenant was in place?

If so, would this covenant be an extraordinary assumption or a hypothetical condition in the appraisal?

Response:

(a) Given the type and definition of value (market value with the title conditioned as the director described), and intended use of the assignment results (to provide the client with information for use in deciding an asking price), the appraisal must reflect an analysis as if the covenant were in place.

(b) The appraisal of the property as though it had the covenant in place requires a hypothetical condition in the appraisal, because, as of the effective date of the appraisal, the property did not have the covenant in place (i.e., the covenant is *that which is contrary to what exists, but is used for purpose of analysis as stated in the USPAP definition of hypothetical condition*).

If instead you did not know whether the covenant was or was not in place as of the effective date of the appraisal, but you based the appraisal on the covenant being in place, the appraisal would be based on an extraordinary assumption. This is because you would be presuming as fact otherwise uncertain information about the condition of title which, if found to be false, could alter your opinions or conclusions.

If, instead of saying there would be a covenant recorded after the effective date of the appraisal, the director provided a title document that said the covenant was already in place, the appraisal would not require either a hypothetical condition or an extraordinary assumption about that land use limitation. This is because the title condition used in the appraisal would have been the actual condition in place on the effective date of the appraisal.

240. ANALYZING THE LEASE WHEN APPRAISING FEE SIMPLE INTEREST

Question: **I am performing an appraisal of a single-family dwelling that is in use as a rental property. The type of value to be developed is market value for the fee simple interest. The current lease on the property is significantly below market and runs for another 24 months past the effective date in my appraisal. Furthermore, the lease would survive a transfer of ownership.**

Does USPAP require that I analyze and reflect the presence of the lease in the valuation?

Response: No; the subject of your assignment is the fee simple interest, not the leased fee interest. The appraisal report must provide adequate disclosures to intended users of the appraisal that there is a lease in effect, and that the value of the leased fee interest in the property has not been reflected in the appraisal.

241. DEFINITION OF EXTRAORDINARY ASSUMPTION

Question: **I recently agreed to perform an appraisal assignment for a property that had an affirmative surface easement granted in perpetuity. The client was also the property owner. She did not have a copy of the easement and stated that it had never been recorded. What are my development and reporting obligations under USPAP?**

Response: You should do whatever research is possible to see if the easement was recorded and consider the facts you discover in your analysis. If you cannot confirm the facts, you may use an extraordinary assumption in your analysis. The particulars of the use of the extraordinary assumption must be clearly and accurately disclosed.

The definition of an extraordinary assumption is:

an assignment-specific assumption as of the effective date regarding uncertain information used in an analysis which, if found to be false, could alter the appraiser's opinions or conclusions.

*Comment: Uncertain information might include physical, **legal**, or economic characteristics of the subject property; or conditions external to the property, such as market conditions or trends; or the integrity of data used in an analysis.* (Bold added for emphasis)

Standards Rule 2-1(c) states, in part:

Each written or oral real property appraisal report must:

(c) clearly and accurately disclose all assumptions, extraordinary assumptions, hypothetical conditions, and limiting conditions used in the assignment.

242. PROPOSED CONSTRUCTION EMPLOYING AN EXTRAORDINARY ASSUMPTION (NEW)

Question: **I have agreed to perform a market value appraisal of a property with proposed improvements. The assignment calls for a prospective appraisal with an effective date that is 120 days after the date the appraisal report is submitted.**

The client and I believe that the construction will have been completed and a certificate of occupancy issued prior to the effective date. What assumptions, extraordinary assumptions, or hypothetical conditions might apply to this assignment?

Response: In this case, there are extraordinary assumptions, but no hypothetical conditions. The extraordinary assumptions include the assumption that the construction will be complete and the certificate of occupancy issued on or before the effective date and the assumption that the construction will be completed in accordance with the plans and specifications that were provided to the appraiser.

243. EMPLOYING AN EXTRAORDINARY ASSUMPTION WHEN A CLIENT PROVIDES INSPECTION DATA (NEW)

Question: **A client has asked me to perform an appraisal, but instead of requiring me to personally inspect the subject property, they will provide me with the results of an inspection done by someone else. If I rely upon that inspection, should I employ an extraordinary assumption?**

Response: The answer to this question is dependent upon the appraiser's judgment about the reliability and completeness of the information contained in the client-provided inspection report. Standards Rule 1-2(e) requires the appraiser to:

...identify, from sources the appraiser reasonably believes to be reliable, the characteristics of the property that are relevant to the type and definition of value and intended use of the appraisal...

If the appraiser determines that the information contained in the inspection report is reliable and allows the appraiser to identify the relevant property characteristics and develop credible assignment results, then an extraordinary assumption would not be necessary.

© The Appraisal Foundation

However, Advisory Opinion 2, *Inspection of Subject Property*, contains the following advice:

> *...an appraiser must ensure that the degree of inspection is sufficient for the appraiser to understand the subject property's relevant characteristics, so the appraiser can develop a credible appraisal. Therefore, in cases when the appraiser relies upon a third-party inspector's report, it may be necessary to obtain additional information and/or examine other documents or information in order to understand the relevant characteristics of the property.*
>
> *In all cases, when adequate information about relevant characteristics is not available through a personal inspection or from sources the appraiser reasonably believes are reliable, the appraiser must:*
>
> - *modify the assignment conditions to expand the scope of work to include gathering the necessary information;*
> - *use an extraordinary assumption about such uncertain information, if credible assignment results can still be developed or*
> - *withdraw from the assignment.*

An extraordinary assumption is an **assignment-specific assumption** that is made when an appraiser must rely upon uncertain information. The Comment to the USPAP definition of extraordinary assumption explains that:

> *Uncertain information might include physical, legal, or economic characteristics of the subject property; or conditions external to the property, such as market conditions or trends; or the integrity of data used in an analysis.*

If the appraiser determines that the client-provided inspection data is not adequate to identify the relevant property characteristics, or if the appraiser believes that the data source is not reliable, the appraiser has three choices:

> *(1) expand the scope of work to include gathering the necessary information, a process that might include, for example, discussion with the property inspector, personal inspection by the appraiser, or research from other data sources;*
> *(2) use an extraordinary assumption about such information if credible assignment results can still be developed; or*
> *(3) withdraw from the assignment.*

244. CAN AN EXTRAORDINARY ASSUMPTION BE USED WITHOUT A REASONABLE BASIS? (NEW)

Question: **A client has asked me to appraise a property subject to the extraordinary assumption that it would be possible to obtain a lot split of the existing property. I have researched the marketplace and have been unable to find any properties where a lot split was granted. I have confirmed the property's zoning, and it appears that a lot split would not be possible due to the minimum lot size required for a new lot. May I use an extraordinary assumption in this case?**

Response: No. Standards Rule 1-2(f)(ii) states that an extraordinary assumption may be used in an assignment "...only if the appraiser has a reasonable basis for the extraordinary assumption." In this case, the appraiser has no reasonable basis.

© The Appraisal Foundation

APPRAISAL DEVELOPMENT – SUBJECT PROPERTY SALES HISTORY

245. MULTIPLE SALES OR TRANSFERS OF THE SUBJECT PROPERTY

Question: **If the subject property, such as a single-family dwelling, has sold more than once in the three (3) years prior to the effective date of the appraisal, am I required to analyze all of the sales, or just the most recent sale? Also, what am I required to do if a transfer of ownership is due to a foreclosure sale, or is a sale between family members or other related parties?**

Response: Standards Rule 1-5 states:

When the value opinion to be developed is market value, an appraiser must, if such information is available to the appraiser in the normal course of business;

(a) analyze all agreements of sale, options, or listings of the subject property current as of the effective date of the appraisal; and

(b) analyze all sales of the subject property that occurred within three (3) years prior to the effective date of the appraisal.

Standards Rule 2-2(a)(x)(3) requires that an Appraisal Report provide

sufficient information to indicate that the appraiser complied with the requirements of STANDARD 1 by:

(3) summarizing the results of analyzing the subject sales, agreements of sale, options, and listings in accordance with Standards Rule 1-5;

The Comment to Standards Rule 2-2(a)(x)(3) states:

if such information is unobtainable, a statement on the efforts undertaken by the appraiser to obtain the information is required. If such information is irrelevant, a statement acknowledging the existence of the information and citing its lack of relevance is required.

Therefore, you must report and analyze **all** of the sales, not just the most recent one. This would also include **any** type of sale, whether it was arm's length or not. If a transfer of ownership was the result of a sale between family members or otherwise related parties, or involved a foreclosure sale, or transfer of the deed in lieu of foreclosure, the appraiser is still obligated to analyze and report it.

In addition, if sales beyond the minimum three-year period, or options and listings that may not be current are identified and relevant to the appraisal of the subject property, they should also be analyzed and reported.

It is important to understand that assignment conditions for some appraisal assignments, particularly those in which the current version of Fannie Mae Form 1004/Freddie Mac Form 70 is used for the report, require that the appraiser also report and analyze transfers of ownership that did not necessarily result from a sale transaction.

Refer to Advisory Opinion 1, *Sales History,* for further guidance.

© The Appraisal Foundation

246. OFFERS TO PURCHASE SUBJECT PROPERTY

Question: **Are offers to purchase the subject property, prior to the effective date of the appraisal, pertinent information required to be considered under Standards Rule 1-5?**

Response: Standards Rule 1-5(a) states:

When the value opinion to be developed is market value, an appraiser must, if such information is available to the appraiser in the normal course of business:

analyze all agreements of sale, options, or listings of the subject property current as of the effective date of the appraisal;...

Standards Rule 1-5(a) does not require that an offer to purchase the subject property, that is prior to the effective date of the appraisal be considered and analyzed. Agreements of sale and options are generally significant to solving an appraisal problem because they involve a meeting of the minds about the property's value between the potential buyer and seller. A listing of the subject property is likewise significant in that it indicates the property's availability in the market. A mere offer to purchase by a potential buyer, however, does not necessarily correlate to the property's value or even to the owner's desire to sell. Furthermore, information about a purchase offer is often confidential and sometimes may not be available to the appraiser in the normal course of business.

Nevertheless, the appraiser is required by Standards Rule 1-1(b) to *not commit a substantial error of omission or commission that significantly affects an appraisal*. If information about a purchase offer is available to the appraiser, even if the offer is not current, and that information is relevant to solving the appraisal problem, it must be considered. In some cases, an offer would be relevant to the appraisal problem only because it points to other information concerning the property or the market about which the appraiser should know. For example, if the appraiser learns of an offer that seems out of character with market trends, additional research might lead the appraiser to discover property or market characteristics that support that offering price.

247. CURRENT SALES CONTRACT IS NOT PROVIDED

Question: **I am an appraiser with several clients that do not provide a copy of the current sales contract as a part of their standard appraisal ordering procedures. In addition, the parties to the transaction have been requested by the client not to provide either the contract or information contained in the sales contract to the appraiser. If the client withholds the current pending sale contract, can I still perform the assignment in compliance with USPAP?**

Response: Yes. Under certain conditions Standards Rules 1-5 and 7-5 require real and personal property appraisers to analyze all agreements of sale that are current at the effective date of the appraisal *if such information is available to the appraiser in the normal course of business*. Since these contracts are not available to you, you can complete the assignment and still be in compliance with USPAP.

However, the Comment to Standards Rules 2-2(a)(x)(3), 2-2(b)(xii)(3), 8-2(a)(x)(3) and 8-2(b)(xii)(3) require the appraiser to include a statement on the efforts of the appraiser to obtain the information in the report. Therefore, if you have attempted to obtain the current contract and could not, you must disclose how you attempted to obtain the contract.

For more information regarding the meaning of normal course of business, see Advisory Opinion 24, *Normal Course of Business*, which is applicable to both real and personal property.

© The Appraisal Foundation

248. PENDING SALES AS COMPARABLES

Question: **Can a pending sale be used as a comparable if the fact that the sale is pending is disclosed in the appraisal report?**

Response: Yes. USPAP does not require the use of a pending sale as a comparable, nor does USPAP prohibit such use.

In addition, Standards Rule 1-1(b) requires that an appraiser:

> *not commit a substantial error of omission or commission that significantly affects an appraisal;*

Not considering a pending sale of a property highly similar to the subject property could constitute an omission that would significantly affect the appraisal. USPAP requires appraisers to be complete in their analysis and convey that analysis in a way that is not misleading. Pending sale details, by their very nature, are often confidential. Appraisers must take care not to disclose information that they know is confidential.

249. SUBJECT PROPERTY AS A COMPARABLE SALE

Question: **Is it a violation of USPAP to use a recent sale of the subject property as a comparable in the sales comparison approach to value?**

Response: No. Standards Rule 1-4, states:

> *In developing a real property appraisal, an appraiser must collect, verify, and analyze all information necessary for credible assignment results.*
>
> *(a) When a sales comparison approach is necessary for credible assignment results, an appraiser must analyze such comparable sales data as are available to indicate a value conclusion.*

Additionally, Standards Rule 1-5(b), states:

> *When the value opinion to be developed is market value, an appraiser must, if such information is available to the appraiser in the normal course of business:*
>
> *(b) analyze all sales of the subject property that occurred within the three (3) years prior to the effective date of the appraisal.*

Therefore, not only could the subject property potentially be used as a comparable sale, but an analysis of the prior sale must be made in accordance with Standards Rule 1-5 if it occurred within the prior three years. However, appraisers are cautioned to be aware of possible assignment conditions that require minimum numbers of comparable sales to be reported in addition to the sale of the subject property.

250. FIVE-YEAR SALES HISTORY AS AN ASSIGNMENT CONDITION

Question: **My state appraisal board has adopted a regulation requiring appraisers to provide a five-year sales history for the subject property in all assignments. Is this situation addressed in USPAP?**

Response: Yes. In the scenario described, an administrative agency (the state appraisal board) has a regulation that adds to the requirements in USPAP. Therefore, failure to comply with the

© The Appraisal Foundation

regulation would be a violation of the Being Competent section of the COMPETENCY RULE which states in part:

Competency requires: ...

3. *recognition of, and compliance with, laws and regulations that apply to the appraiser or the assignment.*

251. SALES HISTORY FOR NEW CONSTRUCTION

Question: **I have received an assignment to appraise a property with newly constructed improvements. Because the property includes new construction, there is no prior sales history of the property as it now exists. However, I do have information pertaining to a prior sale of the site (without the improvements). Does Standards Rule 1-5(b) require me to analyze this prior sale of the site?**

Response: Yes. The goal of USPAP is to promote public trust in the appraisal profession. Standards Rule 1-5 provides a research and analysis requirement for information that is judged to be important to the credibility of the appraisal process. To be consistent with the purpose of USPAP as well as with the intent of Standards Rule 1-5, an appraiser is required to analyze *all* prior sales that include the subject property. This includes: 1) prior sales of a property that includes the subject property; and 2) prior sales of a portion of the subject property.

In this case, the analysis of the prior sale of the unimproved site would be necessary to comply with Standards Rule 1-5(b). The site in this instance is a component of the subject property.

Another example might be the appraisal of a leased fee interest in a property. The appraiser must research and analyze prior sales of the subject, even if these sales include a fee simple interest in the property.

An additional example might be the appraisal of 20 acres subdivided from a 200-acre parcel. The appraiser must research and analyze prior sales of the subject, even if these sales include the 200-acre site in its entirety.

252. APPRAISAL WITHOUT KNOWING SALE PRICE

Question: **I have been asked to perform an appraisal of a residential dwelling that I know is under contract. No lender is involved and the buyer and seller do not want the appraiser to know the amount of the sales contract. Can I perform this assignment and still comply with USPAP?**

Response: Yes. USPAP does not contain a requirement for the appraiser to know the pending sale price of a subject property. Standards Rule 1-5(a) does require the appraiser to analyze all current agreements of sale and options to purchase or listings of the subject property, when available during the normal course of business.

When the value opinion to be developed is market value, an appraiser must, if such information is available to the appraiser ***in the normal course of business****, analyze all agreements of sale, options, and listings of the subject property current as of the effective date of the appraisal.* (Bold added for emphasis)

However, if the appraiser's scope of work and the normal course of business render the subject property's pending transaction details unavailable, the appraiser may be able to comply with USPAP without obtaining the information. For more information on the normal course of business, please see Advisory Opinion 24, *Normal Course of Business.*

© The Appraisal Foundation

It should be noted that when the amount of the sale contract is unknown, this does not eliminate the appraiser's responsibility to analyze other information that is available related to the pending sale. This can include information such as marketing history and other details of the pending sale that may be available.

253. ANALYSIS OF SALES HISTORY FOR COMPARABLE SALES

Question: **I was told that USPAP now requires real property and personal property appraisers to analyze previous sales of comparable properties used in the sales comparison approach to value. Is this true?**

Response: No. However, there may be applicable laws, regulations or other assignment conditions in certain appraisal assignments that require the appraiser to provide a more detailed analysis than otherwise required by USPAP.

254. SALES HISTORY ANALYSIS FOR DEED IN LIEU OF FORECLOSURE

Question: **I am currently appraising an office building that was transferred 18 months ago via a deed in lieu of foreclosure. Am I required to analyze this transaction?**

Response: Yes. A transfer of the deed in lieu of foreclosure is a de facto sale of the property to a lienholder in lieu of the payment of the outstanding balance (or some portion thereof) of the lien.

Standards Rule 1-5(b) requires the appraiser to analyze all sales of the subject property that occurred with the three (3) years prior to the effective date of the appraisal.

255. OBLIGATION TO ANALYZE PRIOR LISTINGS OF SUBJECT PROPERTY

Question: **I know that Standards Rule 1-5(a) requires an appraiser to analyze all current listings of the subject property. Does it also require analysis of *prior* listings of the subject property?**

Response: No. However, in the development of an appraisal, an appraiser is required under Standards Rule 1-1(b), to *not commit a substantial error of omission or commission that significantly affects an appraisal*. If information about a prior listing is known by the appraiser, and that information is relevant to solving the appraisal problem, it must be considered.

Appraisers are cautioned to be aware that an analysis of the subject's prior listing history may be required by assignment conditions that apply to some assignments.

256. PROPER ANALYSIS OF AGREEMENT OF SALE

Question: **I understand that Standards Rule 1-5(a) requires the appraiser to analyze an agreement of sale (if available in the normal course of business). What constitutes proper analysis?**

Response: The term analyze is not defined in USPAP because it does not have a special meaning within the document or in Standards Rule 1-5. The term is used based on its English language meaning as found in common dictionaries.

The extent of the analysis performed to comply with the requirements of Standards Rule 1-5(a) is part of the scope of work decision. The acceptability of the appraiser's analysis is judged in the same way that any other scope of work decision is judged. For more information, see the SCOPE OF WORK RULE, Advisory Opinion 28, *Scope of Work Decision, Performance, and Disclosure*, and Advisory Opinion 29, *An Acceptable Scope of Work*.

© The Appraisal Foundation

257. VALUE CONCLUSION BELOW CONTRACT PRICE

Question: **I recently submitted an appraisal report to an Appraisal Management Company (AMC). The value conclusion in the report was below the contract sale price. The AMC, acting on behalf of the client, sent me the following request:**

"Discuss the lack of support for the contract price, considering the subject's features, any changes in market conditions between the contract and effective dates, the details of the contract, etc., which you believe may have contributed to the issue. If there is no apparent reason for the lack of support of the contract price, state that within your report."

Do I have to respond to this request to comply with USPAP?

Response: USPAP compliance does not specifically require the appraiser to respond to this particular request, but it does require that the appraiser analyze the pending sale and summarize the results of that analysis in the appraisal report.

An appraiser is not engaged for the purpose of supporting a contract price, but rather to form an opinion of, in this instance, the market value of the subject property. The appraiser must comply with the Conduct section of the ETHICS RULE, which states, in part:

> *An appraiser must perform assignments with impartiality, objectivity, and independence, and without accommodation of personal interests.*

Standards Rule 1-5(a) requires the appraiser to analyze all agreements of sale (if available in the normal course of business). Both Standards Rule 2-2(a)(x)(3) and Standards Rule 2-2(b)(xii)(3) state that a report must

> *provide sufficient information to indicate that the appraiser complied with the requirements of STANDARD 1 by summarizing the results of analyzing the subject sales, agreements of sale, options, and listings in accordance with Standards Rule 1-5;*

258. OBLIGATION TO ANALYZE WITHDRAWN OR EXPIRED LISTINGS

Question: **I was asked to appraise a single-family residence for refinancing. I am aware that the property had been previously listed but did not sell. During my data investigation and analysis, I noted that the owner's estimate of value was $375,000. When I looked up the listing history, I found it had been withdrawn from the market at the asking price of $325,000. What are my obligations under USPAP regarding a withdrawn or expired listing of the subject property?**

Response: Standards Rule 1-5(a) states:

> *When the value opinion to be developed is market value, an appraiser must, if such information is available to the appraiser in the normal course of business:*
>
> *(a) analyze all agreements of sale, options, or listings of the subject property current as of the effective date of the appraisal.*

Therefore, there is not a specific requirement in Standards Rule 1-5(a) to consider and analyze a withdrawn or expired listing of the subject property, prior to the date of the appraisal.

However, any listing of the subject property prior to the effective date of the appraisal might be significant in that it indicates the property's previous availability in the market and the market's reaction to that availability. Likewise, agreements of sale and options are generally significant

© The Appraisal Foundation

to the appraisal problem in that they involve a meeting of the minds relating to the property's value between a potential buyer and the seller.

In the development of an appraisal, an appraiser is required under Standards Rule 1-1(b), to *not commit a substantial error of omission or commission that significantly affects an appraisal.* If information about a withdrawn or expired listing is known by the appraiser, and that information is relevant to the appraisal problem, it must be considered.

259. SALES HISTORY ANALYSIS IN A RETROSPECTIVE APPRAISAL

Question: **I have been asked to perform a retrospective appraisal on the fee simple interest in a real property. The effective date of the appraisal is September 1, 1995. Must I analyze listings of the subject that were current at that time and/or the sales history of the subject?**

Response: Yes. Standards Rule 1-5 states:

When the value opinion to be developed is market value, an appraiser must, if such information is available to the appraiser in the normal course of business:

(a) analyze all agreements of sale, options, or listings of the subject property current as of the effective date of the appraisal; and
(b) analyze all sales of the subject property that occurred within the three (3) years prior to the effective date of the appraisal.

If this information is available in the normal course of business, it must be analyzed and reported in conformance with Standards Rules 2-2(a)(x)(3) and 2-2(b)(xii)(3).

260. SALES HISTORY ANALYSIS FOR CONDITION AND MARKETABILITY REPORTS

Question: **I have been asked to provide a client with a condition and marketability report on a residential property. I am to complete a form used by some lenders and secondary market participants. Since this assignment is part of appraisal practice (because I am providing this service as an appraiser), must I conform with the requirements in Standards Rule 1-5(a), to *analyze all agreements of sale, options, or listings of the subject current as of the effective date of the appraisal; and (b) analyze all sales of the subject property that occurred within the three (3) years prior to the effective date of the appraisal*?**

Response: No. Standards Rule 1-5 only applies to the development of a real property appraisal. The assignment described in this question is not an appraisal since developing an opinion of value is not part of the assignment. While the requirements of STANDARD 1 are not applicable, all services performed as part of appraisal practice must comply with USPAP. The portions of USPAP that apply generally to appraisal practice include the PREAMBLE, the DEFINITIONS, the ETHICS RULE, the COMPETENCY RULE, and the JURISDICTIONAL EXCEPTION RULE.

261. SUBJECT PROPERTY SALES HISTORY AND STANDARDS RULE 1-5(B)

We often receive appraisal reports where a prior sale of the subject property is addressed. However, the reports do not include an affirmative statement that there have been no other sales within the three years prior to the effective date of the assignment. The appraisers believe they are in compliance with USPAP as they have appropriately addressed a prior sale. As the client, I do not agree.

Question: **(1.) If, in fact, there was only one sale within the 3-year period, must the appraisal report state that there were no additional sales?**

© The Appraisal Foundation

Response: No, USPAP does not require an appraiser to state in the report that there were no additional sales.

Question: (2.) Must the appraisal report include a statement that there were no sales of the subject within the 3-year period if, in fact, there were none?

Response: No. USPAP does not require an appraiser to state in the report that there have been no sales within the 3-year period.

As the client you may, of course, require that the appraiser exceed USPAP requirements by including an affirmative statement about the absence of other sales.

262. SALES HISTORY IN MACHINERY AND EQUIPMENT APPRAISAL ASSIGNMENT (NEW)

Question: **A personal property appraiser has been engaged to perform an orderly liquidation value appraisal of the inventory of a used farm equipment dealership that owns 50 vehicles. There are no agreements of sale, validated offers or third-party offers to sell, or options related to any of the subject properties current as of the effective date of the appraisal. The appraiser determines it is not necessary for credible assignment results to research and analyze the prior sales of each of the properties. What are the appraiser's obligations under USPAP regarding the prior sales?**

Response: Standards Rule 7-5(a) requires the appraiser to consider whether the analysis of information about prior sales is necessary for credible assignment results. Because the analyses of the prior sales are not necessary for credible assignment results, analyses are not required to be performed or reported.

263. SALES HISTORY IN FINE AND DECORATIVE ARTS APPRAISAL ASSIGNMENT (NEW)

Question: **The executor of an estate has hired an appraiser to provide an opinion of value of the fine and decorative arts in the estate. No records of prior sales have been provided to the appraiser. What are the appraiser's obligations under USPAP regarding the prior sales?**

Response: Standards Rule 7-5(a) requires the appraiser to consider whether the analysis of information about prior sales is necessary for credible assignment results. If not, then such analysis is not required to be performed or reported.

If the analysis of prior sales is necessary for credible assignment results and if such information is available to the appraiser in the normal course of business (e.g., if the property was sold at a public auction), the appraiser is required to analyze all prior sales of the subject property that occurred within a reasonable and applicable time period.

For example, if the appraiser researches public sales and discovers that some of the paintings were purchased within the past few years, the summary to be included in the appraisal report for each of the paintings would likely consider whether the sales were arm's-length transactions and might also discuss the level of trade of the sale venues.

264. CHANGES IN COMPOSITION OF PARTNERSHIPS OR CORPORATIONS (NEW)

Question: **USPAP requires appraisers to analyze prior sales of the subject property. Are appraisers required to analyze and report changes related to ownership interests (e.g., partnerships, corporations, LLCs, etc.) of a property, as well as actual property transfers?**

Response: For real property appraisal assignments, appraisers are required to analyze and report prior sales of the property being appraised, not changes related to a partnership or corporation that owns a property.

© The Appraisal Foundation

If the subject of an appraisal assignment is a partnership or corporation (as opposed to real property owned by a partnership or corporation), then the analysis of prior sales of ownership interests would be required when necessary for credible assignment results. Standards Rule 9-4(b)(vi) states, in part:

> *An appraiser must, when necessary for credible assignment results, analyze the effect upon value, if any, of...*
>
> *(vi) prices, terms, and conditions affecting past sales of similar* ***ownership interests in the asset being appraised*** *or a similar asset; (Bold added for emphasis.)*

© The Appraisal Foundation

APPRAISAL REPORTING – CERTIFICATION AND SIGNATURES

265. REASON FOR SIGNED CERTIFICATION

Question: **Why does USPAP require an appraiser to include a signed certification in the workfile for oral reports and in all written reports?**

Response: A signed certification is evidence that appraisers recognize their ethical obligations.

266. USE OF CERTIFICATION WITH FORM 1004D/442

Question: **My client has asked me to re-inspect the property and provide them with a certification of completion for an appraisal that I completed for them eight months ago and submit the report on the Fannie Mae Form 1004D/Freddie Mac Form 442. The assignment does not include an updated value opinion. Does this assignment require a certification regarding the prior service?**

Response: No. Because this is neither an appraisal nor appraisal review assignment, USPAP does not require a certification. Although a disclosure of the prior service is required at the time of agreeing to perform this assignment, no certification is required. The Conduct section of the ETHICS RULE states in part:

> *In assignments in which there is no appraisal or appraisal review report, only the initial disclosure to the client is required.*

267. CHANGING THE CERTIFICATION

Question: **Must the certification be exactly the same as that presented in USPAP? May an appraiser add items to the certification?**

Response: USPAP states that the report must contain a signed certification. The wording of a certification does not have to match the content verbatim, but each of the elements must be addressed. An appraiser may modify or add to the certification as necessary. For example, the names of appraisers providing significant appraisal assistance who do not sign the certification must be stated in the certification. There are also certification requirements in some jurisdictions for real property appraisal certifications and licenses as well as requirements related to membership in a professional association. Clients, intended users, and the intended use may also require additional certification items.

Appraisers using preprinted appraisal forms should be aware that clients and client groups may prohibit altering the preprinted certification used in assignments performed for them, but any such prohibition is not contained in USPAP.

268. REVISING APPRAISAL FORM CERTIFICATION TO DISCLOSE PRIOR SERVICES

Question: **I perform residential real estate appraisals using "standard" appraisal forms, such as those developed by Fannie Mae. I've heard that Fannie Mae does not allow any changes to their certifications, so how can I comply with the USPAP requirement to disclose, in the certification, any prior services I have or have not performed on the property within the prior three years?**

© The Appraisal Foundation

Response: Fannie Mae does **not** prohibit additional certifications to their appraisal forms, as long as those additional certifications do not conflict with or diminish the "standard" certification items appearing on their forms. Therefore, appraisers may create a supplemental certification to comply with the obligations of the Conduct section of the ETHICS RULE as well as the requirements of Standards Rules 2-3(d) and 4-3(d).

269. REQUIREMENT FOR SIGNING REPORTS

Question: **What is the USPAP requirement regarding signing a report?**

Response: USPAP requires that each written report include a signed certification. Although many written reports include the appraiser's signature on the report or a letter of transmittal, this is not required by USPAP. However, an appraiser who signs any part of the report must also sign the certification. For an oral report, USPAP requires that a signed and dated certification be part of the workfile.

270. SIGNATURE ON LETTER OF TRANSMITTAL

Question: **Does USPAP require an appraiser to sign the letter of transmittal?**

Response: No. USPAP does not require that any report include a letter of transmittal. However, USPAP does require that an appraiser who signs a letter of transmittal must also sign the certification required in Standards Rules 2-3, 4-3, 6-3, 8-3, and 10-3.

For example, Standards Rule 2-3(b) states:

> ***An appraiser who signs any part of the appraisal report, including a letter of transmittal, must also sign a certification.*** (Bold added for emphasis)

271. MULTIPLE SIGNATURES ON APPRAISAL REPORTS

Question: **I am a review appraiser for a national mortgage company. I recently received a residential appraisal reported on a commonly used form that has two signatures on the appraiser line (left hand side of the form). Both appraisers also signed the certification. Does this violate *Uniform Standards of Professional Appraisal Practice* (USPAP)?**

Response: This does not violate USPAP. Standards Rule 2-3 states, in part:

> *An appraiser who signs any part of the appraisal report, including a letter of transmittal, must also sign a certification.*

Therefore, if both real property appraisers signed the appraisal report, then both must sign the certification. The Comment to Standards Rule 2-3(b) goes on to say:

> *any appraiser who signs a certification accepts full responsibility for all elements of the certification, for the assignment results, and for the contents of the appraisal report.*

In this scenario, both real property appraisers will have complete responsibility for the appraisal in its entirety.

272. SIGNATURE AUTHORIZATION

Question: **Can I authorize someone else to sign an appraisal report for me, using my signature? If so, could you identify what steps I must take to do this correctly?**

© The Appraisal Foundation

Response: USPAP does not specifically state that the appraiser can only personally sign a report. It does state, in the definition of signature, that the signature be *personalized evidence indicating authentication*. The ETHICS RULE of USPAP also states, in part:

> *An appraiser may authorize the use of his or her signature only on an assignment-by-assignment basis.*
>
> *An appraiser must not affix the signature of another appraiser without his or her consent.*

The USPAP reporting standards (for example, Standard Rules 2-2(a)(xiv) and 2-2(b)(xvi)) specify that a report must: include a signed certification ...

In the DEFINITIONS section, a signature is defined as:

> *personalized evidence indicating authentication of the work performed by the appraiser and the acceptance of the responsibility for content, analyses, and the conclusions in the report.*

Unless specifically contrary to the law of a particular jurisdiction, USPAP allows another person to sign for an appraiser, as long as it is with the appraiser's specific authorization and is clear and does not result in a misleading report. One solution would be for that other person to sign the appraiser's name and then write their own initials by the signature, preceded by the word by (for example, "by sbk").

273. PROVIDING SIGNATURE TO CREATE A SIGNATURE FILE

Question: **I am a residential appraiser and I use software to generate my appraisal reports. The software company requires me to provide a copy of my signature to create an electronic signature file for use with the software. Does this action violate USPAP?**

Response: No. This situation is similar to providing a copy of your signature to a rubber stamp company for purposes of creating a signature stamp. Common business agreements in these situations limit use of the signature to creating the signature image. In providing a signature to a software company or rubber stamp company, the appraiser is not authorizing use of the signature.

274. LOSING CONTROL OF A DIGITAL SIGNATURE

Question: **If my digital signature is stolen and applied to reports without my knowledge or consent, am I in violation of USPAP?**

Response: No. Unauthorized use of the appraiser's signature is not a violation of USPAP. If the appraiser's digital signature is stolen, the appraiser is the victim of a crime. Any such use of the appraiser's signature is not authorized, and that use is beyond the appraiser's control. However, an appraiser must use due care to prevent unauthorized use of his/her signature. The Management section of the ETHICS RULE states, in part:

> *An appraiser may authorize the use of his or her signature only on an assignment-by-assignment basis.*
>
> *An appraiser must not affix the signature of another appraiser without his or her consent.*
>
> Comment: *An appraiser must exercise due care to prevent unauthorized use of his or her signature. An appraiser exercising such care is not responsible for unauthorized use of his or her signature.*

© The Appraisal Foundation

This is similar to a party who uses an appraiser's rubber signature stamp without permission from the appraiser, or a party who simply puts pen and ink to paper and forges an appraiser's signature. In these cases, the appraiser did not give permissionfor the signature's use.

275. RESPONSIBILITY OF AN APPRAISER SIGNING AS A SUPERVISOR

Question: **I have been told that a supervisor or employer who signs a report is not as responsible as the individual preparing the appraisal and that using a conditional label next to the signature of the supervisor or employer exempts that individual from adherence to USPAP. Is this true?**

Response: No, it is not true if the supervisor or employer is an appraiser. Standards Rule 2-3(b) (as well as similar language in Standards Rules 4-3(b), 6-3(b), 8-3(b) and 10-3(b)) specifically states:

An appraiser who signs any part of the appraisal report, including a letter of transmittal, must also sign this certification.

In an assignment that includes only assignment results developed by the real property appraiser, any appraiser who signs a certification accepts full responsibility for all elements of the certification, for the assignment results, and for the contents of the appraisal report.

276. SIGNING DIGITAL (ELECTRONIC) REPORTS

Question: **What is the USPAP requirement for signing a digitally created (electronic) report?**

Response: The requirement for paper (hard copy) and digital (electronic) reports is the same. The appraiser must include a signed certification with each report.

277. BUSINESS ENTITY SIGNING AN APPRAISAL REPORT

Question: **Can a business entity, such as a corporation, sign an appraisal report?**

Response: Yes. There is no prohibition against an entity signing a transmittal letter or the page stating the value conclusion of a report. However, USPAP does require that an individual appraiser(s) sign a certification. Standards Rules 2-3(b) and (c), 4-3(b) and (c), 6-3(b) and (c), 8-3(b) and (c), and 10-3(b) and (c) all refer to an appraiser or a signing appraiser. Clearly, this language refers to an individual or individuals, not a corporate or business entity.

278. SIGNIFICANT APPRAISAL ASSISTANCE

Question: **In preparing an appraisal assignment, I talk with many different people. I know the report certification must identify individuals who provide significant real property appraisal assistance. What is significant appraisal assistance?**

Response: USPAP does not include a definition of significant appraisal assistance. However, aspects of this phrase can be explored to clarify its meaning.

First, the adjective significant means that the contribution must be of substance to the development of the assignment results. In other words, the individual must contribute to the valuation analysis in a noteworthy way. An individual who merely collects or provides data for use in the analysis does not provide significant appraisal assistance.

Second, the reference to the term appraisal assistance means that the contribution is related to the appraisal process or requires appraiser competency. One misconception is that non-appraisers who provide assistance should be identified in the certification. This is incorrect

© The Appraisal Foundation

because the certification requirements in USPAP apply only to appraisers. Thus, only appraisers sign the certification or are identified as providing significant appraisal assistance. For example, the use of an environmental expert to determine wetland boundaries would not be considered significant real property appraisal assistance.

Examples of contributions made by appraisers that constitute significant real property appraisal assistance include the identification of comparable properties and data, inspection of the subject property and comparables, estimating accrued depreciation, or forecasting income and expenses.

279. USING A DATA ENTRY SERVICE

Question: **I primarily perform residential appraisal assignments for mortgage finance purposes. I recently received a solicitation from a company that is offering to enter all the data into my appraisal software program for me at a very low cost. Is this something that is allowed under USPAP?**

Response: There are two primary concerns. The first concern is whether the service provider is performing significant real property appraisal assistance. If the service provider simply performs clerical tasks, such as entering information provided by the appraiser, USPAP does not require disclosure; this would be a clerical service, not significant real property appraisal assistance. However, if the service includes performing tasks that require appraisal competency, the name of each individual performing that service must be stated in the certification as having provided significant real property appraisal assistance, and the extent of the assistance must be addressed within the appraisal report. Tasks that require appraisal competency include, but are not limited to, rating a property's quality or condition, estimating remaining economic life, and selecting comparable data.

The second concern deals with the issue of appraiser-client confidentiality. The Confidentiality section of the ETHICS RULE states, in part:

> *An appraiser must not disclose: (1) confidential information; or (2) assignment results to anyone other than:*
>
> - *the client;*
> - *parties specifically authorized by the client*
> - *state appraiser regulatory agencies;*
> - *third parties as may be authorized by due process of law; or*
> - *a duly authorized professional peer review committee except when such disclosure to a committee would violate applicable law or regulation.*
>
> *An appraiser must take reasonable steps to safeguard access to confidential information and assignment results by unauthorized individuals, whether such information or results are in physical or electronic form.*
>
> *An appraiser must ensure that employees, co-workers, sub-contractors, or others who may have access to confidential information or assignment results, are aware of the prohibitions on disclosure of such information or results.*

Therefore, the appraiser is prohibited from disclosing *confidential information* or *assignment results* (both, as defined in USPAP) to anyone other than the parties identified in the ETHICS RULE without the client's permission.

© The Appraisal Foundation

280. HAVE I PROVIDED SIGNIFICANT APPRAISAL ASSISTANCE?

Question: **I am a research assistant with an appraisal firm that has three state certified or licensed real property appraisers. My responsibilities include preparing an appraisal file on each new assignment, researching past sales of the subject, obtaining zoning information, tax data, market information and sales research (including confirming the sales) for the three associates. The licensed or certified appraisers usually inspect the property and prepare the appraisal themselves. Currently, they do not recognize me in these reports, and I am not permitted to sign them.**

I also sometimes go with them on inspections and write portions of the reports. In these cases they do recognize me, as required by USPAP. I am concerned about receiving experience credit for all my appraisal assistance from my state's appraiser licensing board or a professional association if I apply for a designation. Should my participation be referenced in all the reports when I provide assistance, or only when I inspect the property and write portions of the report?

Response: USPAP does not address the specific experience requirements of state appraiser licensing agencies or professional appraisal organizations. You will have to contact those entities directly to obtain that information.

USPAP *does* specifically address what to do when an individual provides significant appraisal assistance in the development of appraisal and appraisal review assignments. For example, in real property appraising, Standards Rule 2-2(a) (ix) states:

> ***summarize the extent of any significant real property appraisal assistance;***

Clerical responsibilities such as file preparation, typing reports, and similar activities are not considered significant appraisal assistance. However, the participation you described could go beyond clerical duties. If, as part of the work you perform, you decide what, where, or how to research, you have applied judgment. Applying judgment or performing analysis for an assignment would likely be considered significant appraisal or appraisal review assistance. You can, obtain more guidance on how to make a decision on whether your contributions to an assignment should be considered significant within USPAP by reviewing Advisory Opinion 31, *Assignments Involving More than One Appraiser.*

281. REPORTING SIGNIFICANT APPRAISAL ASSISTANCE IN AN ORAL REPORT

Question: **How must recognition of my significant appraisal assistance be included when there is no written report, but significant assistance was provided and documentation of my work is in the workfile?**

Response: The RECORD KEEPING RULE states that the workfile must include:

> *summaries of all oral reports or testimony, or a transcript of testimony, including the appraiser's signed and dated certification*

Standards Rule 2-4 states:

> *To the extent that it is both possible and appropriate, an oral real property appraisal report must address the substantive matters set forth in Standards Rule 2-2(a).*

© The Appraisal Foundation

Therefore, based on the requirements in USPAP, the workfile of an oral report must include a **signed certification stating the name of the person or persons providing significant appraisal assistance.** The oral report must also include a summary of the extent of that assistance because Standards Rule 2-4 requires that oral reports address the substantive matters set forth in Standards Rule 2-2(a), which are the requirements for an Appraisal Report. (Bold added for emphasis)

NOTE: This FAQ focuses on significant real property appraisal assistance. The same type of disclosure is also required in Standards 4, 6, 8, and 10 as they relate to the appraisal of other types of property, appraisal review, and mass appraisal.

282. DOES USPAP DEFINE SUPERVISORY APPRAISER?

Question: **The term supervisory appraiser is used in many appraisal reports, particularly residential appraisal reports. Does USPAP define supervisory appraiser?**

Response: No. USPAP does not define or otherwise address this term. The term supervisory appraiser was introduced by the authors of several widely used residential appraisal report forms.

However, it should be noted that an appraiser who signs any part of the appraisal report, including a letter of transmittal, must also sign the certification.

283. REPORTING SIGNIFICANT REAL PROPERTY APPRAISAL ASSISTANCE

Question: **I am currently working in an appraisal firm as a trainee. As part of my training I contribute significant real property appraisal assistance in appraisal assignments performed by other appraisers in the firm, but I do not sign the appraisal report or the certification. I understand that my name must be stated in the certification. Must the certification include a description of my assistance?**

Response: No. A description of your assistance or contribution to the assignment is not required in the certification. However, in accordance with Standards Rule 2-2(a)(ix) the extent of the assistance must be summarized (or stated, in accordance with Standards Rule 2-2(b)(xi)) within the report. This required disclosure could be included within the certification, but it could also be included in some other section of the report.

See Advisory Opinion 31, *Assignments Involving More than One Appraiser,* for further guidance.

284. RELYING ON THE REPORTS OF OTHERS

Question: **I am a business appraiser and do not perform real property appraisal assignments. As a result, I sometimes rely on the results of a real property appraisal to determine the value of business equity. The real property appraisal report is not contained in my business valuation report; however, the real property value conclusion (the dollar amount) is indicated in my report. An example of this would be a real property holding company in which the value of the equity may be significantly dependent on the value of the owned real property. What is the appropriate way to address such reliance on the real property appraisal within my business appraisal report?**

Response: Standards Rule 10-3(c) states:

> *When a signing appraiser has relied on work done by appraisers and others who do not sign the certification, the signing appraiser is responsible for the decision to rely on their work.*

© The Appraisal Foundation

(i) The signing appraiser is required to have a reasonable basis for believing that those individuals performing the work are competent.

(ii) The signing appraiser also must have no reason to doubt that the work of those individuals is credible.

Additionally, the Conduct section of the ETHICS RULE states, in part:

An appraiser must not use or communicate a misleading or fraudulent report...

The business valuation report should specifically reference the source of the real property value and may incorporate that value conclusion by use of an extraordinary assumption. Disclosure of the extraordinary assumption could be similar to the following:

"The fair market value of the subject interest in XYZ Company is dependent on the market value of the real property owned by the Company, as provided to us. We have not verified the validity of this asset value, which we assume to be reliable. The use of this assumption might have affected our assignment results."

The business appraisal report must contain a certification by the business appraiser(s). A signed certification related to the real property appraisal will be in the report provided by the real property appraiser (or in the workfile in the case of an oral report.)

The business appraiser must rely on a real property appraiser because the business appraiser in this scenario is not competent to perform a real property appraisal or to review the real property appraisal.

In deciding that the individual providing the real property appraisal is competent, the business appraiser might note such things as the real property appraiser's:

- declaration in a signed certification that the analyses, opinions and conclusions were developed, and the report was prepared, in conformance with USPAP;
- relevant experience, education, or references; or
- evidence of professional status, such as license, professional designation, or other recognition of professional or academic achievement.

It is important to note that the determination of another appraiser's competency may not be established by a single factor, but instead may require a combination of factors. Ultimately, it would be the business appraiser's decision as to whether the real property appraiser is competent, and that decision must be based on reasonable criteria. In addition, it is of paramount importance that the business appraiser has no reason to doubt that the work of the real property appraiser is credible.

© The Appraisal Foundation

285. DISAGREE WITH SUPERVISOR ON VALUE CONCLUSION

Question: **I am employed at a firm where my reports are reviewed by a supervisory appraiser. The supervisory appraiser recently asked me to make changes to a report that resulted in a value opinion with which I do not agree. I am not comfortable signing the amended report. What are my obligations under USPAP?**

Response: If the report does not represent your own opinions and conclusions, then you must not sign the report or the certification.

Standards Rule 2-3(b) states: *An appraiser who signs any part of an appraisal report, including a letter of transmittal, must also sign a certification.*

One of the required elements of the certification is:

> *I certify that, to the best of my knowledge and belief, the reported analyses, opinions, and conclusions are limited only by the reported assumptions and limiting conditions and are* ***my personal****, impartial, and unbiased professional analyses, opinions, and conclusions.* (Bold added for emphasis)

If appraisers are required to make changes with which they do not agree, they cannot truthfully certify that they are reporting their own personal analyses, opinions, or conclusions.

286. DOES THE CERTIFICATION ON THE UNIFORM RESIDENTIAL APPRAISAL REPORT (URAR) FORM ALSO EXTEND TO THE MARKET CONDITIONS ADDENDUM?

Question: **When I complete the Market Conditions form (i.e., Fannie Mae 1004MC/Freddie Mac 71) and include it within my report, does the certification contained in the URAR form apply to the Market Conditions form as well?**

Response: Yes. The name of the form in question is the *Market Conditions Addendum to the Appraisal Report*. Any addendum is part of a larger report (in this case, a URAR form). In addition, the Market Conditions form is clearly identified as an addendum, as evidenced by the following language at the top of the form:

> *The purpose of this addendum is to provide the lender/client with a clear and accurate understanding of the market trends and conditions prevalent in the subject neighborhood. This is a required addendum for all appraisal reports with an effective date on or after April 1, 2009.*

The Comment to Standards Rule 2-3(b) states:

> *In an assignment that includes only assignment results developed by the real property appraiser(s), any appraiser who signs a certification accepts full responsibility for all elements of the certification, for the assignment results, and for the contents of the appraisal report.*

Thus, the certification applies to the entire appraisal and report, including any addenda.

© The Appraisal Foundation

287. MULTI-DISCIPLINE CERTIFICATION – REAL PROPERTY APPRAISER

Question: **I am a real property appraiser who sometimes participates in assignments that include the appraisal of real property, personal property (machinery and equipment), and intangible assets. The value conclusions for each asset type are separately prepared by an appraiser with competency in the asset type. A single report is jointly issued that communicates the assignment results for all of the assets. What is the appropriate wording for the certification in these situations?**

Response: Standards Rule 2-3(a) states, in part:

> *The wording of a certification does not have to match the following verbatim, but each of the elements must be addressed:*
>
> *I certify that, to the best of my knowledge and belief:*
>
> - *the reported analyses, opinions, and conclusions ... are my personal, impartial, and unbiased professional analyses, opinions, and conclusions...*
> - *my analyses, opinions, and conclusions were developed, and this report has been prepared, in conformity with the Uniform Standards of Professional Appraisal Practice...*

The Comment to Standards Rule 2-3(b) states, in part:

> *In an assignment that includes only assignment results developed by the real property appraiser(s), any appraiser who signs a certification accepts full responsibility for all elements of the certification, for the assignment results, and for the contents of the appraisal report.* ***In an assignment that includes personal property, business or intangible asset assignment results not developed by the real property appraiser(s), any real property appraiser who signs a certification accepts full responsibility for the real property elements of the certification, for the real property assignment results, and for the real property contents of the appraisal report.*** (Bold added for emphasis)

When reporting assignment results that are separately prepared by appraisers from different disciplines, the certification must clearly define responsibility for all assignment results and report content. The certification language may be altered to indicate which reported conclusions each appraiser is certifying to. The certification language is not required to be exactly as presented in USPAP.

One solution would be for each appraiser to sign a separate certification that identifies the assignment results and report content for which they take responsibility. Another solution to this circumstance would be to include a single certification altered to indicate the assignment results and report content certified to by each appraiser.

Whatever solution is adopted, the certification language must identify the assignment results and report content for which the real property appraiser takes responsibility. One example of such language would be:

- the reported **real property** analyses, opinions, and conclusions ... are my personal, impartial, and unbiased professional analyses, opinions, and conclusions...
- my **real property** analyses, opinions, and conclusions were developed, and the **real property content** of this report has been prepared, in conformity with the *Uniform Standards of Professional Appraisal Practice.* (Bold added for emphasis)

Each personal property appraiser must take responsibility for the personal property assignment results and report content. Each business and/or intangible asset appraiser must take responsibility for the business and/or intangible asset assignment results and report content.

© The Appraisal Foundation

288. SIGNIFICANT APPRAISAL ASSISTANCE – PERSONAL PROPERTY APPRAISER

Question: **I am a personal property appraiser specializing in machinery and equipment. My value opinions are sometimes influenced by analysis performed by a business appraiser, such as in determining whether the earnings of the business are sufficient to justify the otherwise-determined value of the machinery and equipment. What are the certification requirements in this scenario?**

Response: The key to the disclosure requirement is the significance of the assistance that is provided by the business appraiser. In cases where the earnings of the business support a value that greatly exceeds the value that you have otherwise determined, the information from the business appraiser does not appear to be significant.

In a case where your otherwise determined value is impacted or influenced by the information that you receive from the business appraiser, this appears to be assistance that is significant and disclosure of that assistance is required.

Standards Rule 8-2(a)(viii) requires that an Appraisal Report must, at a minimum:

> *summarize the scope of work used to develop the appraisal;*
>
> *Comment: Summarizing the scope of work includes disclosure of research and analyses performed and might also include disclosure of research and analyses not performed.*

(NOTE: If reporting assignment results in a Restricted Appraisal Report format, the appraiser must state the scope of work used to develop the appraisal, per Standards Rule 8-2(b)(x).)

When any portion of the work involves significant personal property appraisal assistance, the appraiser must summarize (or state) the extent of that assistance. The name(s) of those providing the significant personal property appraisal assistance must be stated in the certification, in accordance with Standards Rule 8-3.

Therefore, if the assistance provided by the business appraiser is significant, the extent of the assistance must be summarized in an Appraisal Report or stated in a Restricted Appraisal Report, and the business appraiser must be named in the certification.

For additional guidance, refer to Advisory Opinion 28, *Scope of Work Decision, Performance, and Disclosure,* and Advisory Opinion 29, *An Acceptable Scope of Work.*

289. USE OF CERTIFICATION WITH FORM 1004D/442 – APPRAISAL UPDATE

Question: **My client has asked me to update an appraisal that I completed for them eight months ago and submit the report on the Fannie Mae Form 1004D/Freddie Mac Form 442. Does this assignment require a certification regarding the prior service?**

Response: Yes. Because an appraisal update is a new appraisal assignment, regardless of the form used to report the results, the report must include a certification disclosing whether you have provided a service regarding the subject property in the three years prior to agreeing to perform the new assignment.

Each real property appraisal report, including those for update assignments, must include a signed certification that, at a minimum, addresses the items specified in Standards Rule 2-3(a). The certification in the prior report cannot be incorporated by reference, since it would not be possible to have certified in the past that the work done in the present meets all of the requirements to which the appraiser must certify.

© The Appraisal Foundation

290. USE OF CERTIFICATION WITH FORM 1004D/442 – SATISFACTORY COMPLETION

Question: **My client has asked me to re-inspect the property and provide them with a certification of completion for an appraisal that I completed for them eight months ago and submit the report on the Fannie Mae Form 1004D/Freddie Mac Form 442. The assignment does not include an updated value opinion. Does this assignment require a certification regarding the prior service?**

Response: No. Because this is neither an appraisal nor appraisal review assignment, USPAP does not require a certification. Although a disclosure of the prior service is required at the time of agreeing to perform this assignment, no certification is required. The Conduct section of the ETHICS RULE states in part:

> *In assignments in which there is no appraisal or appraisal review report, only the initial disclosure to the client is required.*

291. CERTIFICATION WITH MULTIPLE APPRAISERS

Question: **When the certification for a commercial appraisal report is signed by two certified general appraisers, does USPAP require each appraiser to specify which part of the appraisal the appraiser performed?**

Response: No. If both appraisers sign the certification, they both accept full responsibility for all elements of the certification, for the assignment results, and for the contents of the appraisal report. When more than one person signs the certification, USPAP requires only that that they disclose which individuals did and which individuals did not inspect the subject property.

According to Standards Rule 2-3(a):

> *If more than one person signs this certification, the certification must clearly specify which individuals did and which individuals did not make a personal inspection of the appraised property.*

For additional guidance, see Advisory Opinion 31: *Assignments Involving More than One Appraiser.*

292. PERSONAL PROPERTY APPRAISAL ASSIGNMENT INVOLVING MULTIPLE APPRAISERS (NEW)

Question: **I have been hired to coordinate the appraisal of personal property for a large estate. The project will involve four different appraisers. I will appraise the furniture, decorative arts, and residential contents but will subcontract with three other specialty appraisers to appraise the gems and jewelry, fine arts, and automobiles. What is the correct way to prepare the signed certification?**

Response: The Comment to Standards Rule 8-3(b) states that appraisers with different specialties may accept responsibility for the parts of the appraisal that are specific to their specialty. USPAP does not prescribe a single correct way to prepare the certification. If the terms of the certification are identical (i.e., if all appraisers have inspected and if none have performed any services within the prior three years), one way to accomplish this would be to state a limitation by each appraiser's signature (e.g., John Doe for furniture, David Jones for automobiles). Another way to address this would be to include separate certifications from each of the appraisers beginning with language such as, "For the furniture in this appraisal, I certify that, to the best of my knowledge and belief..." Another option is for all appraisers to sign the certification and state in the report who worked on what.

© The Appraisal Foundation

Appraisers must remember that in addition to the certification requirement, the Comment to Standards Rule 8-3(b) states, "the role of each appraiser signing the certification must be disclosed in the report." Clear disclosure of each appraiser's role helps to ensure that the report is not misleading.

293. DOES USPAP REQUIRE DISCLOSURE OF ASSISTANCE BY A NON-APPRAISER? (NEW)

Question: **A client has asked me to perform an appraisal, but instead of requiring me to personally inspect the subject, they will provide me with the results of an inspection of the property done by someone else. Does USPAP require me to disclose this person's name as having provided significant appraisal assistance and describe the assistance they provided?**

Response: Generally, no. If the information provided in the inspection only includes *factual data* regarding the subject, then significant appraisal assistance has not been provided. However, if the appraiser relies upon opinions and conclusions of the inspector regarding quality, condition and/or functional utility, then this qualifies as significant appraisal assistance. In this case, if the individual performing the assistance is an appraiser, then yes, you must disclose the inspector's identity and also describe the assistance. It is a misconception that non-appraisers who provide assistance must be identified in the certification. The certification requirements in USPAP apply only to appraisers.

Even if disclosure is not required because an individual providing information is not an appraiser, the appraiser relying on such information still has obligations pertaining to the information used.

First, it's important to remember that the appraiser signing the certification is taking full responsibility for the appraisal. The Comment to Standards Rule 2-3(b) states, in part:

> *In an assignment that includes only assignment results developed by the real property appraiser(s), any appraiser who signs a certification accepts full responsibility for all elements of the certification, for the assignment results, and for the contents of the appraisal report...*

Second, Standards Rule 2-3(c) states:

> *(c) When a signing appraiser has relied on work done by appraisers and others who do not sign the certification, the signing appraiser is responsible for the decision to rely on their work.*
>
> *(i) The signing appraiser is required to have a reasonable basis for believing that those individuals performing the work are competent; and*
>
> *(ii) The signing appraiser must have no reason to doubt that the work of those individuals is credible.*
>
> Comment: *Although a certification must contain the names of individuals providing significant real property appraisal assistance, it is not required that a summary of the extent of their assistance be located in a certification. This disclosure may be in any part(s) of the report.*

Standard Rule 1-2(e), one of the first steps in the development of an appraisal, requires the appraiser to identify the relevant characteristics of the property. If the scope of work requires that the appraiser consider physical aspects that they would not already know without inspecting the property, the source and accuracy of this information becomes critically important.

© The Appraisal Foundation

USPAP neither requires nor prohibits the disclosure of the name of a non-appraiser inspector or the source of the inspection data.

294. SIGNING AND LABELING OF SUPPLEMENTAL CERTIFICATIONS (NEW)

Question: **I use appraisal reporting software that includes a fixed certification which cannot be altered. The certification does not include USPAP's required disclosure certifying whether I performed any services on the property in the three years prior to agreeing to perform the assignment. May I add this or other certification elements required by USPAP elsewhere in the report, outside of the provided certification?**

Response: Yes. Standards Rule 2-3(d) states:

> *When an assignment requires the use of a certification that does not include all of the certification elements in this Standards Rule, the appraisal report must contain a supplemental certification, which includes the remaining required certification elements.*

295. LABELING SUPPLEMENTAL CERTIFICATIONS (NEW)

Question: **I use appraisal reporting software that includes a fixed certification which cannot be altered. Therefore I need to add a supplemental certification to include all of the disclosures required by USPAP. Must I label these certification elements as a "Supplemental Certification," and am I required to sign a supplemental certification?**

Response: While it is not a requirement to use the exact words "Supplemental Certification," it is a good idea. Standards Rule 2-3(d) states that under these circumstances "...the appraisal report must contain a supplemental certification." A clear and simple way to meet this requirement is to group the missing required certification elements in a single location under this heading.

USPAP does not require that a supplemental certification be signed. However, nothing would prohibit an appraiser from signing a supplemental certification.

296. PRIOR SERVICE AND PROFESSIONAL ASSISTANCE DISCLOSURES – PART 1 (NEW)

Question: **I work for "Large National Appraisal Firm," which has multiple offices. In situations where appraisers on staff have valued properties within the prior three years, the firm's management recommends its appraisers utilize the following language in the certification to disclose prior services: "Large National Appraisal Firm has provided a prior service, as appraisers, but has provided no other services, as appraisers or in any other capacity." Is this a proper disclosure under USPAP?**

Response: No. Firms do not sign certifications. Appraisers sign certifications. The disclosure in the certification must clarify whether the individual appraiser who signs the certification has provided prior services. The same requirements apply if the certification is signed by appraisers who have different records of prior services. The certification must indicate which appraisers provided prior services (and what services) and which appraisers have not provided any services, as an appraiser or in any other capacity, during the three-year period immediately preceding engagement to complete the assignment.

© The Appraisal Foundation

297. PRIOR SERVICE AND PROFESSIONAL ASSISTANCE DISCLOSURES – PART 2 (NEW)

Question: **I work for the multi-office "Large National Appraisal Firm." The firm's management recommends staff appraisers include the following generic disclosure language in the certification to identify instances where staff members have provided significant real property appraisal assistance: "Staff members of Large National Appraisal Firm have provided significant professional appraisal assistance to the persons signing this certification." Is this a proper disclosure under USPAP?**

Response: No, this is not a proper disclosure. The names of individuals providing significant appraisal assistance must be stated in the certification. It is not required that the description of their assistance be contained in the certification, but the extent of their assistance must be stated or summarized within the appraisal report in accordance with Standards Rule 2-2(a)(ix) or 2-2(b)(xi) as applicable.

© The Appraisal Foundation

APPRAISAL REPORTING – USE AND FORMAT ISSUES

298. OWNERSHIP OF APPRAISAL REPORTS

Question: **A property owner has requested a copy of an appraisal report I prepared for a lender. Who owns an appraisal report, its associated research and supporting documentation?**

Response: USPAP does not specifically address who owns an appraisal report, the research necessary to produce that report and the report's supporting documentation.

An appraiser who receives a request from any party for a copy of an appraisal report must comply with the Confidentiality section of the ETHICS RULE which states, in part:

An appraiser must protect the confidential nature of the appraiser-client relationship.

An appraiser must act in good faith with regard to the legitimate interests of the client in the use of confidential information and in the communication of assignment results.

The Confidentiality section of the ETHICS RULE further states:

An appraiser must not disclose: (1) confidential information or (2) assignment results to anyone other than:

- *the client;*
- *parties specifically authorized by the client;*
- *state appraiser regulatory agencies;*
- *third parties as may be authorized by due process of law; or*
- *a duly authorized professional peer review committee except when such disclosure to a committee would violate applicable law or regulation.*

299. ELECTRONIC REPORT DELIVERY

Question: **I am an appraiser who has been asked by my client to submit my appraisal reports to them electronically. Assuming that I have satisfied the reporting obligations in the creation of the report, what are my obligations in the use of electronic delivery systems?**

Response: USPAP does not specifically address this issue, but there are general ethical obligations that are relevant. The Conduct section of the ETHICS RULE states, in part,

An appraiser:

- *must not communicate assignment results with the intent to mislead or to defraud;*
- *must not use or communicate a report or assignment results known* ***by the appraiser*** *to be misleading or fraudulent;*
- *must not knowingly permit an employee or other person to communicate a report or assignment results that are misleading or fraudulent;* (Bold added for emphasis)

Communication in this instance means transmission of the report or assignment results, which can occur through such mechanisms as U.S. mail, private courier service, fax, e-mail, or web portal. The appraiser's obligation is to not transmit a misleading or fraudulent report.

© The Appraisal Foundation

In the transmission of electronic reports, the appraiser's obligation is to ensure that the report that is transmitted is not misleading or fraudulent. Therefore, the appraiser needs to be familiar with the electronic report created by the software used in the assignment. The appraiser must have a sufficient understanding of the report generating software used in an assignment to avoid the communication of misleading reports. In order to comply with USPAP, the electronic report that will be sent to the client must be examined by the appraiser prior to transmission to ensure that it is not misleading or fraudulent.

An appraiser cannot control what a client or intended user does with the appraisal report. USPAP establishes requirements only for appraisers, not clients, intended users, or others. Once an appraisal report has been transmitted to the client, USPAP places no further responsibility on the appraiser for the client's use of that report.

300. LABEL DIFFERENT FROM REPORTING OPTIONS

Question: **May I label an appraisal report using another term in place of Appraisal Report or Restricted Appraisal Report?**

Response: No. Standards Rules 2-2, 8-2, and 10-2 state, in part:

> *An appraiser may use any other label in addition to, but not in place of, the label set forth in this Standard for the type of report provided.*

301. FANNIE MAE FORM 1004

Question: **I appraise residential properties and use the Fannie Mae 1004 (URAR) appraisal report form. I'm aware USPAP requires me to label my reports as an "Appraisal Report" or "Restricted Appraisal Report". But my appraisal software program won't let me change the report type from the old "Summary Appraisal Report" to the now required "Appraisal Report". Does that mean my reports do not comply with USPAP?**

Response: No. Standards Rule 2-2 states, in part:

> *An appraiser may use any other label* ***in addition to****, but not in place of, the label set forth in this Standard for the type of report provided.* (Bold added for emphasis.)

Therefore, use of the label "Summary Appraisal Report" does not violate USPAP, unless use of that label in a specific report results in that report being misleading.

302. IS A LETTER OF TRANSMITTAL PART OF AN APPRAISAL REPORT?

Question: **I recently completed an appraisal report that included a letter of transmittal as part of my report. Some of the items required to comply with the reporting requirements of USPAP appear only in the letter of transmittal. My client states that a letter of transmittal is not part of the appraisal report, and these items must appear within the body of the report to comply with USPAP. Is my client correct?**

Response: No; the client is not correct. Although a letter of transmittal is not required by USPAP, there is nothing in USPAP that prohibits making a letter of transmittal part of the appraisal report. It should be noted that USPAP does require an appraiser signing any part of an appraisal report, including a letter of transmittal, to also sign the certification.

© The Appraisal Foundation

303. COPY OF LICENSE IN APPRAISAL REPORT

Question: **I have several clients that request I include a copy of my state appraisal license in each appraisal report I perform. Does USPAP permit me to do this?**

Response: USPAP does not directly address issues of appraiser licensing or credentials. However, some licensing jurisdictions have laws that govern the circumstances under which licensees may provide a copy of their license. If so, appraisers are required to comply with such laws in order to comply with USPAP.

304. DOES USPAP REQUIRE IDENTIFYING APPRAISAL CREDENTIALS?

Question: **I am a state certified real estate appraiser and typically list my state license number directly below my signature on appraisal reports. I spoke with an appraiser in another state who said USPAP has certain requirements pertaining to identification of credentials in an appraisal report. Is this correct, does USPAP address how appraiser credentials must appear in an appraisal report?**

Response: No. There are no requirements in USPAP specifying how appraisers must identify their credentials in an appraisal report. That is a matter of individual state laws for state licensed or certified appraisers. There may also be specific requirements from professional appraiser organizations for appraisers who possess designations from those organizations.

305. RESTRICTED APPRAISAL REPORT AND THIRD PARTIES

Question: **I have been asked to prepare a Restricted Appraisal Report that the client plans to provide to another intended user. Does USPAP allow me to use this report option in such a circumstance?**

Response: Yes. Additional intended users besides the client are permitted for a Restricted Appraisal Report, as long as the other intended users are named in the report (i.e., not merely identified "by type.") The Comment to Standards Rule 2-2(b)(ii) states:

> *A Restricted Appraisal Report may be provided when the client is the only intended user; or, when additional intended users are identified by name;*

306. ARE INSTANT MESSAGES OR TEXT MESSAGES APPRAISAL REPORTS?

Question: **I perform appraisal assignments for a client who asks to be notified of my final value conclusion via instant message or text message. Is this communication to the client an appraisal report that must comply with USPAP?**

Response: Yes; this communication of assignment results is considered an appraisal report. Instant messages or text messages are written communications and, for assignments involving real property, are subject to the requirements of Standards Rules 2-2.

Oral appraisal reports of real property (where assignment results are communicated by the spoken word) are subject to the requirements of Standards Rule 2-4.

307. REPORTING APPRAISAL UPDATES

Question: **I recently received an assignment for an update of an appraisal. The original appraisal was reported on a commonly used single-family residential report form. Must I use this same form to report the results of the update assignment?**

© The Appraisal Foundation

Response: No. Using the same form as the original report is not required for an update appraisal report. The update is a new appraisal assignment, and it may be reported in any format that is acceptable for the intended use and complies with the applicable reporting Standard (STANDARD 2 for a real property assignment). The report must contain sufficient information to be meaningful and not misleading to the intended users, but it is not required to have the same level of detail as the original report.

For additional information, refer to Advisory Opinion 3, *Update of a Prior Appraisal*.

308. FANNIE MAE UPDATE REPORT FORM 1004D/FREDDIE MAC FORM 442

I have been asked to provide an update of a previous appraisal assignment and to report the results on Fannie Mae Form 1004D/Freddie Mac Form 442. The form asks me to check yes or no in response to the question "Has the subject's market value declined since the original appraisal date?" I have the following two questions.

Question: (1.) Does this constitute a new appraisal of the property?

Response: Yes; this is a new appraisal with a new effective date. Additional guidance can be found in Advisory Opinion 3, *Update of a Prior Appraisal*.

Question: (2.) How much of my analysis must I include in the report?

Response: The analysis will vary from assignment to assignment, so the information required in the report will also vary. In some cases, it might be possible to summarize the analysis using the three lines provided on the form itself. If the space provided is insufficient, then the appraiser must supplement the form.

As with any written appraisal report, the appraiser is also required to include a signed certification. For Fannie Mae Form 1004D, which would be used for a real property appraisal assignment, the signed certification must be similar in content to that required in Standards Rule 2-3(a). If the certification included on the form does not cover all of the elements required in Standards Rule 2-3(a), then in accordance with Standards Rule 2-3(d), the appraisal report must contain a supplemental certification, which includes the remaining required certification elements.

309. LEGAL DESCRIPTION

Question: I've been told that I have to report a complete legal description for the subject property in every appraisal I perform. Is this required by USPAP?

Response: No. USPAP does not require a complete legal description for the subject property to be included in every report, since it is recognized that it is not always possible to do so. However, the reporting standards for real property, personal property, and business appraisals do have similar minimum identification requirements.

In the reporting standards for real property, Standards Rule 2-2(a), for example, the content of an Appraisal Report must be appropriate for the intended use of the appraisal and, at a minimum:

> *Contain information, documents, and/or exhibits sufficient to identify the real estate involved in the appraisal, including the physical, legal, and economic property characteristics relevant to the assignment;*

© The Appraisal Foundation

For personal property and business or intangible asset appraisals, the requirements include similar language to present information sufficient to identify the property or assets (refer to Standards Rule 8-2(a)(iv) for personal property appraisals and to Standards Rule 10-2(a)(iv) for business appraisals).

310. PROPERTY ADDRESS

Question: **Does USPAP require that an address for the subject property be reported in every real property Appraisal Report?**

Response: No. Standards Rule 1-2(e) states, in part:

> *In developing a real property appraisal, an appraiser must:*
>
> *(e) identify, from sources the appraiser reasonably believes to be reliable, the characteristics of the property that are relevant to the type and definition of value and intended use of the appraisal, including:*
>
> *(i) its location and physical, legal, and economic characteristics; ...*

Additionally, Standards Rule 2-2(a) states, in part:

> *The content of an Appraisal Report must be appropriate for the intended use of the appraisal and, at a minimum:*
>
> *(iv) contain information, documents, and/or exhibits sufficient to identify the real estate involved in the appraisal, including the physical, legal, and economic property characteristics relevant to the assignment;*

The appraiser must provide information sufficient to *identify the real estate involved in the appraisal.* In some cases an address, particularly a post office box or other rural address may be misleading if no other identifying information such as a legal description is provided. In other cases, an address is sufficient to meet USPAP requirements.

311. WHY REPORT SCOPE OF WORK?

Question: **Why are appraisers required to report the scope of work in an appraisal and/or appraisal review report?**

Response: Documenting the scope of work provides the intended users with a clear understanding of the extent of the research and analyses performed. It also serves as protection for both the client and the appraiser by detailing things that were, and were not, done in the assignment.

In the SCOPE OF WORK RULE, a Comment states:

> *Proper disclosure is required because clients and other intended users rely on the assignment results. Sufficient information includes disclosure of research and analyses performed and might also include disclosure of research and analyses not performed.*

(Note: other professions, such as engineering, have a long history of requiring the development and reporting of the scope of work in their assignments.)

© The Appraisal Foundation

312. REPORTING WORK NOT DONE IN AN ASSIGNMENT

Question: **Does the report need to explain what wasn't done in an assignment?**

Response: Possibly; in addition to the disclosure of research and analyses performed, disclosure of research and analyses not performed might be needed to allow intended users of the report to understand your scope of work. The report must explain why the cost approach, sales comparison approach or income approach was not developed. It may also be necessary to disclose other research and analysis not performed.

313. EXPLAINING THE EXCLUSION OF APPROACHES

Question: **Standards Rules 2-2(a)(x)(2) and 2-2(b)(xii)(2) and other reporting standards require that I state the reasons for excluding the sales comparison, cost, or income approach(es) if any have not been developed. In this context, what does "state the reasons" mean?**

If, for example, the cost approach is not developed:

- **Is it sufficient to state that the cost approach was considered, but not developed?**
- **Is it sufficient to state that the appraiser does not consider the cost approach necessary for credible results, thus it has not been developed? If not, what should the appraiser do to comply with USPAP?**

Response: Simply stating that an approach was not developed does not meet the USPAP requirement to state the reasons why it was not developed.

Stating that an approach was not necessary, without providing some basis for that opinion, also fails to meet the requirement. The report must give some explanation of why an excluded approach is not necessary for credible results.

The USPAP requirement to state the reasons for the exclusion of an approach to value from the analysis is necessary to provide the client and other intended users with insight into why the analysis was not performed.

314. SEPARATE SCOPE OF WORK SECTION IN THE REPORT

Question: **Am I required to have a separate section in my reports describing my scope of work?**

Response: No. USPAP does not dictate where information must be included in reports, and the description of the scope of work performed is no exception.

The SCOPE OF WORK RULE states, in part:

> *The report must contain sufficient information to allow the client and other intended users to understand the scope of work performed. The information disclosed must be appropriate for the intended use of the assignment results.*
>
> *Comment: The appraiser has broad flexibility and significant responsibility in the level of detail and manner of disclosing the scope of work in the appraisal report or appraisal review report. The appraiser may, but is not required to, consolidate the disclosure in a specific section or sections of the report, or use a particular label, heading, or subheading. An appraiser may choose to disclose the scope of work as necessary throughout the report.*

The scope of work performed may be described in one section, or throughout the report.

© The Appraisal Foundation

315. IDENTIFICATION OF INTENDED USERS IN APPRAISAL REPORTS

Question: **When reporting assignment results, must an appraiser state the identity of the client and other intended users by name?**

Response: Unless the client has requested anonymity, the name of the client must be stated in the report. The rules for stating the identity of other intended users depend upon whether the assignment results are in an Appraisal Report or in a Restricted Appraisal Report.

In an Appraisal Report, the identity of the other intended users may be stated either by name or by type. However, in a Restricted Appraisal Report, the appraiser must state the identity of any other intended user(s) by name.

Refer to Advisory Opinion 36, *Identification and Disclosure of Client, Intended Use and Intended Users,* for additional information.

316. IDENTIFICATION OF THE CLIENT IN APPRAISAL REPORTS

Question: **Is an appraiser required to disclose the identity of the client in an appraisal report?**

Response: Yes. Unless the client has requested anonymity, the client must be identified as required by Standards Rules 2-2(a) and (b), 4-2(a), 6-2(a), 8-2(a) and (b), and 10-2(a) and (b) (as applicable). Standards Rule 2-2(a)(i) states, in part:

> *State the identity of the client, or if the client requested anonymity, state that the identity is withheld at the client's request but is retained in the appraiser's workfile;*
>
> *Comment: Because the client is an intended user, they must be identified in the report as such. However, if the client has requested anonymity the appraiser must use care when identifying the client to avoid violations of the Confidentiality section of the ETHICS RULE.*

Refer to Advisory Opinion 36, *Identification and Disclosure of Client, Intended Use, and Intended Users,* for additional guidance.

317. DISCLOSURE OF THE INTENDED USER IN A REPORT

Question: **USPAP requires that each appraisal or appraisal review report state the identity of any other intended user(s) (besides the client) of the assignment results. How can one determine if the intended user statement in a report is adequate?**

Response: USPAP requires disclosure of the intended users in order to ensure that:

1. The client and any other intended users can recognize their relationship to the assignment and report; and
2. Parties other than the intended users will not be misled by putting them on notice that they are neither the client nor an intended user.

Therefore, the statement regarding the intended users must be sufficient to accomplish these objectives. For an Appraisal Report, the appraiser is not obligated to identify an intended user by name. If identification by name is not appropriate or practical, the appraiser may identify an intended user by type. However, for a Restricted Appraisal Report the identification requirements are more stringent. In Restricted Appraisal Reports, if there are any other intended users besides the client, they must be identified by name.

© The Appraisal Foundation

Advisory Opinion 36, *Identification and Disclosure of Client, Intended Use and Intended Users,* provides an example of a statement that may be appropriate for inclusion in an Appraisal Report: *This report is intended for use only by (identify the client) and (identify any other intended users by name or type). Use of this report by others is not intended by the appraiser.*

A statement similar to the following may be appropriate in a Restricted Appraisal Report: *This report is intended for use only by* (*identify the client*) and (*identify any other intended users by name*). *Use of this report by others is not intended by the appraiser.*

318. DISCLOSURE OF THE INTENDED USE IN A REPORT

Question: **USPAP requires that each appraisal or appraisal review report state the intended use of the assignment results. How can one determine if the intended use statement in a report is adequate?**

Response: USPAP requires disclosure of the intended use to avoid misleading parties in possession of an appraisal or appraisal review report. For additional clarity, one might also state that other uses are not intended. The use description provided in the statement must be specific to the assignment.

Advisory Opinion 36, *Identification and Disclosure of Client, Intended Use and Intended Users,* provides an example of a statement that may be appropriate for inclusion in a report:

> *This report is intended only for use in (state the use). This report is not intended for any other use.*

319. MULTIPLE INTENDED USES IN THE SAME APPRAISAL REPORT

Question: **May I perform an appraisal with multiple intended uses and communicate the results in a single report with a single valuation and be in compliance with USPAP?**

Response: Yes. USPAP does not limit the number of intended uses that may be communicated in an appraisal report (however, the report must not be misleading and must contain sufficient information for the intended user(s) to understand it properly). What is required is that the appraiser identify the intended use(s) of the appraiser's opinions and conclusions and state the intended use(s) of the appraisal in the report. Intended use is defined as:

> *The* ***use(s)*** *of an appraiser's reported appraisal or appraisal review assignment results, as identified by the appraiser based on communication with the client at the time of the assignment.* (Bold added for emphasis)

In one example, an appraisal with multiple intended uses may include different types of value (such as market value, liquidation value and insurable value) which require different scopes of work.

In another example, an appraisal with multiple intended uses may be based upon the same type and definition of value and the same scope of work (such as a market value appraisal being prepared both for a private financing and for a possible sale).

© The Appraisal Foundation

320. ORAL REPORTS AND RECORD KEEPING

Question: **An attorney hired me to prepare an appraisal. He asked that I not prepare a report but rather discuss my conclusions with him orally. I have done that, and he concluded that my opinion will not be helpful to his client and therefore does not want a written report. What are my obligations under USPAP in this situation?**

Response: Under the RECORD KEEPING RULE:

An appraiser must prepare a workfile for each appraisal or appraisal review assignment. A workfile must be in existence prior to the issuance of any report or other communication of assignment results. A written summary of an oral report must be added to the workfile within a reasonable time after the issuance of the oral report.

The workfile must include:

- *the name of the client and identity, by name or type, of any intended users;*
- *true copies of all written reports, documented on any type of media;*
- ***summaries of all oral reports or testimony**, or a transcript of testimony, **including the appraiser's signed and dated certification**; and*
- *all other data, information, and documentation necessary to support the appraiser's opinions and conclusions and to show compliance with this Rule and all other applicable Standards, or references to the location(s) of such other data, information, and documentation. (Bold added for emphasis.)*

A workfile in support of a Restricted Appraisal Report or an oral appraisal report must be sufficient for the appraiser to produce an Appraisal Report. A workfile in support of an oral appraisal review report must be sufficient for the appraiser to produce an Appraisal Review Report.

The reporting of the appraisal conclusions to the attorney is an oral report. A summary of such a report, along with the appraiser's signed and dated certification needs to be included in the workfile.

321. ORAL APPRAISAL REPORTING REQUIREMENTS

Question: **A client has asked me to complete an appraisal of a property but does not want me to prepare a written report. Instead, the client has asked that I communicate the results of my appraisal orally. Is this allowed under USPAP? If so, what requirements would I have to follow?**

Response: Yes; USPAP allows an appraiser to provide an oral report. Standards Rules 2-4, 4-4, 8-4, and 10-4 address the reporting requirements for oral reports. However, every appraisal or appraisal review report must be clearly and accurately set forth in a manner that is not misleading and must contain sufficient information to enable intended users to understand the report properly. Thus, the responsibility is on the appraiser to not limit the reporting to such a degree that it would be misleading.

The RECORD KEEPING RULE also has requirements related to oral appraisal reports; specifically, the requirement to include in the appraiser's workfile:

summaries of all oral reports or testimony, or a transcript of testimony, including the appraiser's signed and dated certification.

© The Appraisal Foundation

In addition, the RECORD KEEPING RULE states, in part:

> *A workfile must be in existence prior to the issuance of any report or other communication of assignment results. A written summary of an oral report must be added to the workfile within a reasonable time after the issuance of the oral report.*

322. APPRAISAL REPORT FORM SOFTWARE

Question: **What should I do if my appraisal form software does not address the most recent changes to USPAP?**

Response: Appraisers must take the appropriate steps to ensure that their reports comply with the current version of USPAP.

323. PAPER COPIES OF ELECTRONICALLY TRANSMITTED REPORTS

Question: **Are appraisers required by USPAP to retain a paper copy of electronically transmitted appraisal reports?**

Response: No. The RECORD KEEPING RULE requires appraisers to prepare and retain a workfile for each appraisal and appraisal review assignment.

The workfile must include:

- *true copies of all written reports documented on any type of media (A true copy is a replica of the report transmitted to the client. A photocopy or an electronic copy of the entire report transmitted to the client satisfies the requirement of a true copy.);*
- *A photocopy or an electronic copy of the entire actual written appraisal or appraisal review report sent or delivered to a client satisfies the requirement of a true copy.*

Therefore, a paper copy is not required.

324. APPRAISAL REPORT FORMS COMPLIANCE WITH USPAP

Question: **Fannie Mae, Freddie Mac, and other governmental and private entities issue appraisal report forms. Do these forms comply with USPAP?**

Response: It is the position of the ASB that appraisers, not forms, comply with USPAP. Each assignment is different, and no form could cover all USPAP requirements for all assignments. Appraisal report forms are simply tools to assist in organizing the reporting of assignment results.

It is the responsibility of the appraiser to properly *develop* an appraisal, and to properly *report* the assignment results. A template or form may or may not adequately report the assignment results. It may be necessary for the appraiser to supplement a form with addenda to comply with USPAP requirements.

325. APPLICATION OF APPRAISAL REPORTING REQUIREMENTS

Question: **If an appraiser is bound by USPAP for a particular assignment, when must the appraiser comply with the USPAP appraisal reporting requirements?**

Response: Whenever a value opinion is communicated, compliance with USPAP's appraisal reporting requirements is required.

© The Appraisal Foundation

It may seem obvious in many cases that an appraiser must abide by the appraisal reporting requirements. However, in other cases it is not as obvious, such as the following examples, all of which require compliance with USPAP reporting requirements:

- Selecting and providing a client with comparable sales for a known property is an appraisal assignment as defined by USPAP.
- Informing a property owner that their property tax assessment is too high is an appraisal report as defined in USPAP.
- Providing an opinion of market rent is an appraisal report as defined in USPAP.
- Providing an opinion of the most probable selling price for a homeowner is an appraisal report as defined in USPAP.
- Preparing, analyzing and communicating the results of an automated valuation model (AVM) for a property is an appraisal assignment.

It is important to remember that the applicability of USPAP is not affected by the amount or the lack of a fee.

326. DISCOUNTED CASH FLOW (DCF)

Question: **I am appraising a property that will require a discounted cash flow (DCF) analysis. Are there any special requirements in USPAP for this?**

Response: Standards Rule 1-1, General Development Requirements states, *In developing a real property appraisal, an appraiser must be aware of, understand, and correctly employ those recognized methods and techniques that are necessary to produce credible assignment results.*

Refer to Standards Rule 1-4(c) for the requirements when an income approach is necessary for credible assignment results.

Advisory Opinion 33, Discounted Cash Flow Analysis, contains guidance related to performing a DCF in the appraisal of real property. The following outlines the conclusions at the end of this Advisory Opinion:

> *Use of DCF analysis requires specialized knowledge and experience. Its application requires a high degree of diligence.*
>
> *DCF analysis is a tool available to the appraiser and is often applied in developing value opinions in concert with one or more other approaches.*
>
> *It is the responsibility of the appraiser to ensure that the controlling input is consistent with market evidence and prevailing market attitudes. The appraiser is also responsible for the resulting output.*
>
> *Market value DCF analyses should be supported by market-derived data, and the assumptions should be both market- and property-specific.*
>
> *Appraisal assignments that require the appraiser to employ assumptions that are not based on market data, or to employ assumptions provided by the client, are not market value but rather investment value.*
>
> *If using commercial software, the appraiser should cite the name and version of the software and provide a brief description of the methods and assumptions inherent in the software, if any.*
>
> *DCF accounts for and reflects those items and forces that impact the revenue, expenses, and ultimate earning capacity of an asset and represents a forecast of events that would be considered likely within a specific market.*
>
> *The results of DCF analysis should be tested and checked for errors and reasonableness.*

© The Appraisal Foundation

327. CONTENT OF RESTRICTED APPRAISAL REPORTS

Question: **I have been asked to provide a Restricted Appraisal Report, but I would like to be very descriptive in parts of the report. Does USPAP preclude appraisers from reporting detailed analysis in a Restricted Appraisal Report?**

Response: No. USPAP prescribes the minimum content requirements for the two written report options, Appraisal Report and Restricted Appraisal Report. An appraiser can include more than the minimum required under a Restricted Appraisal Report; however, unless the level of reporting meets the minimum required for an Appraisal Report, the report must be labeled a Restricted Appraisal Report.

328. APPRAISER QUALIFICATIONS IN REPORT

Question: **I've seen several appraisal reports that include a copy of the appraiser's résumé, professional qualifications, or curriculum vitae (CV). Does USPAP require an appraisal report to include the appraiser's qualifications?**

Response: No. Although certain professional appraiser organizations or users of appraisal services might require the report to include the appraiser's qualifications, it is not a USPAP requirement.

329. PROVIDING A DRAFT OF A REPORT

Question: **My client has asked that I provide a draft of my appraisal report prior to issuing the report in final form. Is this permitted under USPAP?**

Response: USPAP does not explicitly define or address drafts of reports. When clients, other intended users, and appraisers use the term draft, they may mean many different things, from a preliminary spreadsheet to a written document that is identical to the final report except that it is labeled a draft and does not contain signatures. Report drafts have traditionally been part of certain types of appraisal practice but have never been considered acceptable in other types of appraisal practice.

State-regulated appraisers should be aware of applicable state laws and regulations. Many laws define a report as "*any communication, written or oral, of an appraisal.*"

Whatever a draft may be in a particular context, it would always be part of appraisal practice because it is a valuation service provided by an appraiser. All services performed as part of appraisal practice must comply with USPAP. The portions of USPAP that apply generally to appraisal practice include the PREAMBLE, the DEFINITIONS, the ETHICS RULE, the COMPETENCY RULE, and the JURISDICTIONAL EXCEPTION RULE.

The second sentence of the PREAMBLE states: *It is essential that appraisers develop and communicate their analyses, opinions, and conclusions to intended users of their services in a manner that is meaningful and not misleading*. Additionally, the Conduct section of the ETHICS RULE states, in part:

An appraiser:

- *must not communicate assignment results with the intent to mislead or to defraud;*
- *must not use or communicate a report or assignment results known by the appraiser to be misleading or fraudulent;*

Therefore, if an appraiser communicates with intended users prior to completion of an assignment, the communication must not be misleading.

© The Appraisal Foundation

The purpose of issuing a draft cannot be to allow the client to improperly influence the appraiser.

Appraisers must also comply with appropriate record keeping requirements. The RECORD KEEPING RULE states, in part:

> *An appraiser must prepare a workfile for each appraisal or appraisal review assignment. A workfile must be in existence prior to the issuance of any report or other communication of assignment results.*

330. DEVELOPING AN UNNECESSARY VALUATION APPROACH

Question: **I have a client that requests the cost approach be included in every appraisal assignment, including those where I feel the cost approach may not yield meaningful results. I am concerned that by complying with the client's request I may be providing a misleading appraisal report. How can I comply with USPAP and satisfy the client at the same time?**

Response: Performing a cost approach that may not yield a meaningful indication of value does not result in a misleading appraisal report if the appraiser properly addresses the applicability and suitability of the approach in the report. Many appraisers address this in the reconciliation by including statements such as, "The cost approach was included solely at the request of the client; it has been given no weight in arriving at the final opinion of value because ...."

See Advisory Opinion 28, *Scope of Work Decision, Performance, and Disclosure,* for further guidance.

331. ALTERING APPRAISAL REPORT PHOTOGRAPHS

Question: **I recently submitted an appraisal report to my client and was subsequently asked to alter the photographs I included in my report. Am I permitted to alter photographs per a client's request?**

Response: As with virtually every appraisal assignment, there are assignment conditions and contractual obligations with which the appraiser is expected to comply (provided the appraiser can produce credible assignment results and produce a report that is not misleading).

Clients sometimes request that photographs do not include certain items or entities that do not affect value. An appraiser may comply with such requests, except when doing so would result in a misleading appraisal report. For example, a photograph may include a person off to the side of the subject of the photo, and the appraiser may be able to crop the photo in a manner that would eliminate the person, but maintain a clear image of the subject of the photo. In this simple example, this would not be misleading and the appraiser could comply with the client's request.

On the other hand, a photograph depicting a relevant physical characteristic (e.g., physical defect) cannot be altered or deleted simply because of a client's request.

© The Appraisal Foundation

332. RESTRICTED APPRAISAL REPORT FOR MULTIPLE PARTIES

Question: **I received an inquiry about performing an appraisal assignment. The caller explained that the assignment would have two intended users: 1) himself (as the client); and 2) his business partner (as an additional intended user). Both parties are very familiar with the property and are frequent users of appraisal services. Therefore, I was asked to produce a Restricted Appraisal Report. Does USPAP permit issuing a Restricted Appraisal Report when there are other intended users besides the client?**

Response: Yes. USPAP permits a Restricted Appraisal Report when there are additional intended users besides the client as long as the other intended users are identified by name in the report.

See Advisory Opinion 36, *Identification and Disclosure of Client, Intended Use, and Intended Users, for additional information.*

333. COMMUNICATING ASSIGNMENT RESULTS WITHOUT AN APPRAISAL REPORT (NEW)

Question: **I was engaged to perform an appraisal of a single-unit residential property for a mortgage lending transaction. After inspecting the property and collecting the necessary data, I concluded that the highest and best use was as a two-unit dwelling. I informed the client of this conclusion prior to completing the appraisal and the client then canceled the assignment. Does USPAP allow an appraiser to convey an opinion of highest and best use prior to transmitting an appraisal report?**

Response: Yes. Nothing in USPAP prohibits communication with the client during an assignment. However, highest and best use opinions are assignment results, and any such communications are subject to specific prohibitions stated in the Conduct section of the ETHICS RULE and are also subject to the workfile requirements of the RECORD KEEPING RULE.

334. IDENTIFYING INTENDED USERS BY NAME IN A RESTRICTED APPRAISAL REPORT (NEW)

Question: **I understand that Standards Rules 2-2(b), 8-2(b), and 10-2(b) permit additional intended users other than the client for appraisals communicated in a Restricted Appraisal Report. Does the reporting requirement to state the identity of these other intended users "by name" not just "by type" mean that each intended user must be a specific individual, or may they be an entity or firm?**

Response: Just as a client may be an individual, group, or entity, other intended users may also be an individual, group or entity. In a Restricted Appraisal Report the identity of other intended users must be stated by name, for example: "Bank of Main Street," or "Smith & Johnson Accounting, LLC," or "Jane Doe, the client's daughter." In a Restricted Appraisal Report it is not permitted to state the identity of the other intended users without a name, for example: "other banks involved in the syndication," or "accounting professionals," or "family members."

© The Appraisal Foundation

335. WHEN DO STANDARDS 3 AND 4 APPLY?

Question: **I am an appraiser and my practice includes requests to comment on a wide range of valuation work performed by others. At various times this work is presented as an Appraisal Report, appraisal review report, market data summary, or even as a broker's price opinion. When do STANDARDS 3 and 4 apply?**

Response: The answer to this question lies in the definition of appraisal review:

> *(noun) the act or process of developing an opinion about the quality of another appraiser's work (i.e., a report, part of a report, a workfile, or some combination of these) that was performed as part of an appraisal or appraisal review assignment; (adjective) of or pertaining to an opinion about the quality of another appraiser's work that was performed as part of an appraisal or appraisal review assignment.*

For this question, the key features of an appraisal review are:

- the work under review was performed by an appraiser, and
- the work under review was performed as part of an appraisal or appraisal review assignment.

Assignments related to market data summaries and broker's price opinions are not appraisal reviews. Even when the work under examination was performed by an appraiser, evaluating these types of work is not part of an appraisal review.

However, even if the service is not an appraisal review, all services performed as part of appraisal practice must comply with USPAP. The portions of USPAP that apply generally to appraisal practice include the PREAMBLE, the DEFINITIONS, the ETHICS RULE, the COMPETENCY RULE, and the JURISDICTIONAL EXCEPTION RULE. These do apply in this instance because you are acting as an appraiser. (See Advisory Opinion 21, *USPAP Compliance*, for further guidance.)

336. GEOGRAPHIC COMPETENCY IN APPRAISAL REVIEWS

Question: **I have a client who has asked me to perform a desk review on an appraisal report for a property located in a different state. I have no knowledge of the real estate market in that state and have never even been there. Can I perform a USPAP-compliant appraisal review on this report?**

Response: Yes. If you are engaged to determine whether or not the appraisal report under review complies with certain guidelines or standards, geographic competence is not typically relevant. Alternatively, review assignments that include evaluating the selection and adjustment of comparable sales typically require geographic competence. As in all assignments, appraisers must identify the scope of work required for the assignment and determine if they have the knowledge and experience to complete the assignment competently.

337. POST-VALUATION DATE INFORMATION IN APPRAISAL REVIEWS

Question: **Can post-valuation date information be used to impeach or impugn appraisals and appraisers?**

Response: No. The Comment to Standards Rule 3-2(g) states:

© The Appraisal Foundation

Information that should have been considered by the original appraiser can be used by the reviewer in developing an opinion as to the quality of the work under review.

Information that was not available to the original appraiser in the normal course of business may also be used by the reviewer; however, the reviewer must not use such information in the reviewer's development of an opinion as to the quality of the work under review.

For additional guidance, see STANDARD 3 and Advisory Opinion 20, *An Appraisal Review Assignment That Includes the Reviewer's Own Opinion of Value.*

338. REVIEWER DISAGREES WITH VALUE CONCLUSION

Question: **In performing an appraisal review, a reviewer disagrees with the value conclusion in the original appraisal. What is the correct action the reviewer should take according to USPAP?**

Response: STANDARD 3 addresses the development of an appraisal review. The Comment to Standards Rule 3-2(c) indicates that reviewers may express their own opinion of value. When the assignment includes the reviewer developing his or her own opinion of value, whether the reviewer's opinion is the same as the appraiser's opinion or different, the reviewer is required to develop the value opinion under the applicable development Standard (STANDARD 1, 3, 5, 7, or 9) and clearly set forth the basis for the reviewer's conclusions. Standards Rule 4-2 addresses the reporting of the reviewer's opinion of value, (i.e., an appraisal) within the appraisal review report.

However, the Comment to Standards Rule 3-3(c) states, in part:

When the assignment includes the reviewer developing his or her own opinion of value or review opinion, the following apply:

- *The reviewer's scope of work in developing his or her own opinion of value or review opinion may be different from that of the work under review.*
- *The effective date of the reviewer's opinion of value may be the same or different from the effective date of the work under review.*
- *The reviewer is not required to replicate the steps completed by the original appraiser. Those items in the work under review that the reviewer concludes are credible can be extended to the reviewer's development process on the basis of an extraordinary assumption. Those items not deemed to be credible must be replaced with information or analysis developed in conformance with STANDARD 1, 3, 5, 7, or 9, as applicable, to produce credible assignment results.*

And, the Comment to Standards Rule 3-2(g) states:

Information that should have been considered by the original appraiser can be used by the reviewer in developing an opinion as to the quality of the work under review.

Information that was not available to the original appraiser in the normal course of business may also be used by the reviewer; however, the reviewer must not use such information in the reviewer's development of an opinion as to the quality of the work under review.

Refer to Advisory Opinion 20, *An Appraisal Review Assignment that Includes the Reviewer's Own Opinion of Value,* for additional guidance.

© The Appraisal Foundation

339. REVIEWER CONCURS WITH VALUE CONCLUSION

Question: **I am performing a review of a real property appraisal and my client has asked me to give my opinion of value, even if I agree with the value in the appraisal. Does my concurrence constitute an appraisal? If so, what do I need to do to comply with USPAP?**

Response: Yes. If you concur with the value in the report, it does constitute an appraisal by the reviewer. Standards Rule 3-3(c) states, in part:

When the assignment includes the reviewer developing his or her own opinion of value or review opinion, the following apply:

(i) The requirements of STANDARDS 1, 5, 7, or 9 apply to the reviewer's opinion of value for the property that is the subject of the appraisal review assignment.
(ii) The requirements of STANDARD 3 apply to the reviewer's opinion of quality for the work that is the subject of the appraisal review assignment

You should be sure that your scope of work clearly includes the requirement to develop your own opinion of value (i.e., develop an appraisal).

The Comment to Standards Rule 3-3(c) shows the steps that must be taken when the assignment includes the reviewers expressing their own opinion of value. One of these requirements is that you must satisfy the applicable development standard. Specifically, whether you concur or disagree with the value in the appraisal being reviewed, you would extend to your development process those items in that appraisal that you conclude are credible and in compliance with STANDARD 1, in this case. This is accomplished on the basis of an extraordinary assumption. Those items not deemed to be credible or in compliance must be replaced with information or analysis by the reviewer.

Additional guidance is contained in Advisory Opinion 20, *An Appraisal Review Assignment that Includes the Reviewer's Own Opinion of Value*.

340. APPRAISAL REVIEW AND STATE APPRAISER BOARDS

Question: **Are reviewers permitted by USPAP to file a complaint with a state appraiser board without the consent of their client?**

Response: It is the opinion of the ASB that reviewers may, absent any higher precedent law or regulation, file a complaint with a state appraiser board without the consent of their client.

The Confidentiality section of the ETHICS RULE states:

An appraiser must protect the confidential nature of the appraiser-client relationship.

The Confidentiality section continues:

An appraiser must not disclose: (1) confidential information or (2) assignment results to anyone other than:

- *the client;*
- *parties specifically authorized by the client;*
- ***state appraiser regulatory agencies;***
- *third parties as may be authorized by due process of law; and*
- *a duly authorized professional peer review committee except when such disclosure to a committee would violate applicable law or regulation.* (Bold added for emphasis)

© The Appraisal Foundation

341. READING APPRAISAL REPORTS

Question: **I recently completed an appraisal and forwarded the report to the client. After receiving the report the client called and stated that they have another appraisal that was recently completed and the values differ significantly. They asked if I would look over the other report and point out the primary differences. Does this assignment constitute an appraisal review?**

Response: No. In this case the client is not asking you to assess the quality of the other appraisal or your opinion of its conclusions. Since you are only noting the differences in the two appraisals you are not performing an appraisal, or appraisal review.

342. REVIEWING TWO APPRAISALS ON THE SAME PROPERTY

Question: **My client has obtained two appraisals of the same real property, and has asked me to perform an appraisal review on each and develop my own opinion of value, which may differ from the value opinions expressed in either appraisal. Can I perform this assignment under USPAP?**

Response: Yes; you can perform this assignment under USPAP. The situation you describe constitutes a real property appraisal review assignment. STANDARD 3 addresses the development and STANDARD 4 the reporting of a real property appraisal review assignment. In this case, you would apply the specific appraisal review requirements of Standards Rule 3-1 and Standards Rule 3-2 to both appraisals being reviewed, and provide your own opinion of value in accordance with Standards Rule 3-3(c) and Standards Rule 4-2(i).

In this situation, it would be appropriate to include the result of your review of both appraisals and your own appraisal opinion within the same appraisal review report. You would provide a single signed certification in accordance with Standards Rule 4-3.

For additional guidance, refer to Advisory Opinion 20, *An Appraisal Review Assignment that Includes the Reviewer's Own Opinion of Value*.

343. REVIEW REPORT ON MULTIPLE APPRAISAL REPORTS

Question: **I have been asked to review multiple appraisal reports and to report my findings in one appraisal review report. Does USPAP permit this?**

Response: Yes. A single appraisal review assignment can include the review of several appraisal reports, with the assignment results presented in one appraisal review report.

344. APPRAISAL REVIEW FOR A STATE APPRAISER BOARD

Question: **I am a state-certified appraiser who serves on the appraisal review panel for our state's appraisal licensure and certification board. The state administrator has asked me to review an appraisal report. The appraiser that prepared the report is the subject of a complaint that was recently filed. The purpose of the review is to develop and state my opinion as to the quality of the work in comparison to the applicable requirements in USPAP, state law, and regulations. My state does not exempt reviewers who are state licensed or certified appraisers from compliance with USPAP when performing such reviews. Do I have to follow STANDARDS 3 and 4 in this assignment?**

Response: Yes. Under the circumstances you describe, you must follow all the applicable requirements of STANDARDS 3 and 4. In this specific situation, just because the intended user and intended use are related to enforcement does not mean such a review assignment would be treated or accomplished any differently.

© The Appraisal Foundation

However, some states have laws or regulations that exempt appraisal review work of this type from USPAP. An appraiser performing such an assignment should discuss the assignment with the client and carefully review the applicable state law and regulation to ensure no misunderstanding about whether the appraiser's compliance with a part or parts of USPAP is, in fact, precluded; or whether a jurisdictional exception results in a part or parts of USPAP, such as STANDARDS 3 and 4, not being applicable.

345. REVIEWING AN APPRAISAL REVIEW REPORT

Question: **An appraiser was recently asked to review another appraiser's appraisal review report. Must the appraiser comply with STANDARDS 3 and 4 in completing this assignment?**

Response: Yes; the appraiser must comply with STANDARDS 3 and 4 in this assignment. STANDARD 3 states:

In developing an appraisal review assignment, an appraiser acting as a reviewer must identify the problem to be solved, determine the scope of work necessary to solve the problem, and correctly complete research and analyses necessary to produce a credible appraisal review.

STANDARD 4 states, in part:

In reporting the results of an appraisal review assignment, an appraiser acting as a reviewer must communicate each analysis, opinion, and conclusion in a manner that is not misleading.

Appraisal review encompasses more than just the review of another appraiser's appraisal. It is *the act or process of developing an opinion about the quality of another appraiser's work.* (See the definition of 'appraisal review')

346. SCOPE OF WORK IN APPRAISAL REVIEW REPORTS

Question: **USPAP requires appraisers to include a description of the scope of work in each appraisal report, the detail of which varies by reporting option. Is there a similar requirement for appraisal review reports?**

Response: Yes. Standards Rule 4-2, states, in part:

The content of an appraisal review report must be appropriate for the intended use of the appraisal review and, at a minimum:

(g) state the scope of work used to develop the appraisal review.

347. REVIEWING A PORTION OF AN APPRAISAL REPORT

Question: **I was recently asked to review an appraisal report and limit my review to the income approach to value. Is such a limitation acceptable?**

Response: Yes. USPAP does not require the reviewer to review the entire report. The Comment to Standards Rule 3-2(d) states:

The subject of an appraisal review assignment may be all or part of a report, a workfile, or a combination of these.

© The Appraisal Foundation

348. CHANGING THE VALUE OPINION WITHOUT THE APPRAISER'S CONSENT

Question: **Is it ethical for an appraiser, acting as a reviewer, to change the reported value opinion in the original appraiser's work without the knowledge or consent of the original appraiser?**

Response: No. Standards Rule 4-1 states, in part:

Each written or oral appraisal review report ***must be separate from the work under review*** (Bold added for emphasis)

In addition, simply changing the original appraisal report, in any way, without the consent of the original appraiser would be a violation of the Conduct section of the ETHICS RULE that states, in part:

An appraiser:

- *must not use or communicate a report or assignment results known* ***by the appraiser*** *to be misleading or fraudulent;*
- *must not knowingly permit an employee or other person to communicate a report or assignment results that are misleading or fraudulent.* (Bold added for emphasis)

349. REVIEWER'S OWN OPINION OF VALUE AND SCOPE OF WORK

Question: **In an appraisal review assignment that includes the reviewer's own opinion of value, is the reviewer required to use the same scope of work as the original appraiser?**

Response: No. The Comment to Standards Rule 3-3(c) states, in part:

When the assignment includes the reviewer developing his or her own opinion of value or review opinion the following apply:

- *The reviewer's scope of work in developing his or her own opinion of value or review opinion may be different from that of the work under review.*
- *The effective date of the reviewer's opinion of value may be the same or different from the effective date of the work under review.*
- *The reviewer is not required to replicate the steps completed by the original appraiser. Those items in the work under review that the reviewer concludes are credible can be extended to the reviewer's development process on the basis of an extraordinary assumption. Those items not deemed to be credible must be replaced with information or analysis developed in conformance with STANDARD 1, 3, 5, 7, or 9, as applicable, to produce credible assignment results.*

For example, the scope of work in the original appraisal may have included an interior and exterior inspection of the subject property, and the scope of work for the appraisal review may include only an exterior inspection or no inspection at all.

350. DISCREDITING THE ORIGINAL APPRAISER'S WORK

Question: **Recently one of my appraisal reports was reviewed. The review report contained information that could not have been available to me at the time I completed my appraisal report. The reviewer used this additional information to discredit my opinion of value. Is this appropriate?**

Response: No. The Comment to Standards Rule 3-2(g) allows a reviewer to use additional information.

© The Appraisal Foundation

Information that was not available to the original appraiser in the normal course of business may also be used by the reviewer; ***however, the reviewer must not use such information in the reviewer's development of an opinion as to the quality of the work under review.*** (Bold added for emphasis)

351. REVIEWER CITATION OF USPAP NON-COMPLIANCE

Question: **If a review appraiser concludes that an appraisal report is unacceptable, does the reviewer need to cite specific requirements in USPAP that were not fulfilled appropriately?**

Response: No, but the review appraisal report must include the reasons for the reviewer's conclusion. When the scope of work requires the review appraiser to evaluate compliance with relevant USPAP requirements, it is appropriate to analyze compliance or non-compliance with USPAP. However, USPAP does not require a reviewer to determine that the subject of an appraisal review complies with USPAP.

352. REVIEW APPRAISER BIAS

Question: **An appraiser receives a request to review an appraisal; however, the reviewer has previously appraised the same property. Does the reviewer's prior experience with the property create a bias that then precludes an objective review?**

Response: No. Prior appraisal experience with the subject of the work under review might be considered an asset and may have contributed to the reviewer being selected for the assignment. Before agreeing to perform any assignment, appraisers must be certain that they will be able to attest in the certification that the assignment results are impartial and unbiased. If the performance of the prior appraisal assignment creates a predisposition regarding appropriate and reasonable assignment results, the appraiser should decline the appraisal review assignment.

In addition, a reviewer with prior experience with the property should be aware that the Conduct section of the ETHICS RULE states:

If known prior to agreeing to perform an assignment, and/or if discovered at any time during the assignment, an appraiser must disclose to the client, and in each subsequent report certification:

- *any current or prospective interest in the subject property or parties involved; and*
- *any services regarding the subject property performed by the appraiser, as an appraiser or in any other capacity, within the three year period immediately preceding the agreement to perform the assignment.*

353. "REBUTTALS" AND APPRAISAL REVIEWS

Question: **I am a state certified appraiser and recently performed an appraisal assignment for a client. The client subsequently had an appraisal review performed on my appraisal and the reviewer brought up some issues that I do not agree with. My client has asked me to provide a written "rebuttal" explaining why I believe I'm correct.**

In "defending" my appraisal, I am concerned that I would be, at least indirectly, offering an "opinion on the quality of another appraiser's work that was performed as part of an ... appraisal review," which could mean that I would be required to comply with STANDARDS 3 and 4. Furthermore, I am concerned that in this "rebuttal" I may not be able to be objective and unbiased, since I have an interest in defending my original appraisal. How can I perform this "rebuttal" without violating USPAP?

© The Appraisal Foundation

Response: USPAP does not prohibit appraisers from "defending" (or explaining) their appraisal. However, there is a fine line between defending one's own appraisal and offering an opinion on the quality of another appraiser's work.

A "rebuttal" where appraisers simply provide additional rationale or support for their analyses, opinions, and conclusions is not a new assignment under USPAP, and there are no Standards that apply. However, if the appraiser agrees to also examine the appraisal review and critique what the reviewer has done, it becomes an appraisal review and the appraiser must comply with STANDARDS 3 and 4.

354. IS COMPLIANCE WITH STANDARDS 3 AND 4 REQUIRED WHEN SUBMITTING A COMPLAINT?

Question: **I am a real property appraiser. I want to submit a complaint regarding an appraisal report to my state appraiser regulatory agency. I would like to express my opinions and comments about the quality of the appraisal report in a cover letter. Am I obligated to comply with STANDARDS 3 and 4 regarding my opinions and comments regarding the appraisal? If so, who is my client?**

Response: No, you are not required to comply with STANDARDS 3 and 4. Because the individual filing the complaint is acting as an appraiser, USPAP applies. However, because there is no client, there is no assignment and so STANDARDS 3 and 4 do not apply. All services performed as part of appraisal practice must comply with USPAP, Therefore, the appraiser making the complaint would be obligated to comply with the portions of USPAP that apply generally to appraisal practice including the PREAMBLE, the DEFINITIONS, the ETHICS RULE, the COMPETENCY RULE, and the JURISDICTIONAL EXCEPTION RULE.

355. UNIFORM ACT AND THE REVIEW OF LOW VALUE ACQUISITION APPRAISAL REPORTS

Question: **I am a review appraiser for a government agency that is subject to the provisions of The Uniform Relocation Assistance and Real Property Acquisitions Act of 1970, as Amended (commonly known as, the Uniform Act), and its implementing regulation, 49 CFR Part 24. There is a provision in this Federal regulation that allows an acquiring agency to adopt an appraisal review reporting process, in cases of low value acquisitions, that may be as simple as the review appraiser stamping such an appraisal report as "Approved," and signing and dating that action.**

This process is intended to be used only in certain acquisitions, such as a partial acquisition for a highway project – and then only in those that are very minor in their impact to the subject properties and which clearly do not result in legally compensable damages to the remainders or any change in highest and best use. Examples of these appraisal reports might be those performed to value easement areas and/or very minor fee simple acquisitions.

In these cases, this federal regulation obviously requires much less than is typically required in STANDARDS 3 and 4 of USPAP.

Does the ASB characterize a review appraiser's simple approval in these instances, as a jurisdictional exception or an assignment condition?

Response: When it applies, 49 CFR Part 24 is an assignment condition. There is no jurisdictional exception because the Uniform Act and its implementing regulation (49 CFR Part 24) allows the use of this simplified review process in cases of low value acquisitions but does not require it. A jurisdictional exception is created only when compliance with USPAP is precluded by a requirement of law or regulation. The Uniform Act does not mandate the use of this simplified review process in cases of low value acquisitions, therefore it is not a requirement of law or regulation, consequently, the simplified review process does not preclude compliance with USPAP.

© The Appraisal Foundation

USPAP STANDARDS 3 and 4 apply to appraisal review assignments and provides for flexibility in the scope of work for the review. Based on the intended use and purpose of the appraisal review, the reviewer can determine an appropriate scope of work necessary to develop credible assignment results.

In the review of low value acquisition appraisal reports under the Uniform Act, the simplified appraisal review process must produce credible assignment results in light of the intended use. If this USPAP requirement is satisfied, the appraisal review process is acceptable.

The USPAP requirements for an appraisal review assignment also allow flexibility in reporting the results of an appraisal review assignment. The format of the appraisal review report is not addressed by USPAP, but Standards Rule 4-1 states:

> *Each written or oral appraisal review report* ***must be separate from the work under review*** *and must:* (Bold added for emphasis)

The application of a stamp to the appraisal report under review does not comply with this reporting requirement. The review appraiser must ensure that the content of the review report complies with the requirements of Standards Rule 4-2.

356. EFFECTIVE DATE THAT DIFFERS FROM THE WORK UNDER REVIEW

Question: **In an appraisal review assignment for which the reviewer develops an opinion of value, is it permissible for the reviewer to use an effective date that differs from the work under review?**

Response: Yes. The Comment to Standards Rule 3-3(c) states, in part:

> *When the assignment includes the reviewer developing his or her own opinion of value or review opinion the following apply:*
>
> - *The reviewer's scope of work in developing his or her own opinion of value or review opinion may be different from that of the work under review.*
> - ***The effective date of the reviewer's opinion of value may be the same or different from the effective date of the work under review.*** (Bold added for emphasis)

357. ADDITIONAL CERTIFICATION IN AN APPRAISAL REVIEW REPORT

Question: **I recently reviewed an appraisal report. As part of the assignment I developed an opinion of value that was different from the value in the appraisal report. I understand that I must provide a signed certification for the review pursuant to Standards Rule 4-3. However, the language in Standards Rule 4-2 seems to suggest that I am also required to prepare an additional certification to comply with Standards Rule 2-3. Are two certifications necessary?**

Response: No, you are not required to provide two certifications in an appraisal review assignment that includes reporting your own value opinion.

This is addressed in the Comment to Standards Rule 4-2(j), which states:

> *The reviewer may include his or her own opinion of value or review opinion related to the work under review within the appraisal review report itself without preparing a separate report. However, data and analyses provided by the reviewer to support a different opinion or conclusion must match, at a minimum,* ***except for the certification requirements****, the reporting requirements for an:*

© The Appraisal Foundation

- *Appraisal Report for a real property appraisal (Standards Rule 2-2(a));*
- *Appraisal Report for a personal property appraisal (Standards Rule 8-2(a));*
- *Appraisal Review Report for an appraisal review (Standards Rule 4-2);*
- *Mass Appraisal Report for mass appraisal (Standards Rule 6-2); and*
- *Appraisal Report for business appraisal (Standards Rule 10-2(a)).* (Bold added for emphasis)

The Comment underscores that whenever a reviewer provides a value conclusion different from the value opinion in the report under review, it is only the data and analyses provided by the reviewer that must be consistent with the applicable reporting Standard.

358. REVIEW FOR AN ETHICS COMMITTEE

Question: **Do STANDARDS 3 and 4 apply to a review of an appraisal report performed by an Ethics Committee or a Board of Examiners of a professional appraisal organization?**

Response: STANDARDS 3 and 4 apply to appraisal review in general, but unlike the other Standards its application is only in the context of an assignment. STANDARD 3 begins:

> *In developing an appraisal review assignment, an appraiser must ...*

So, if the service provided is an appraisal review (as defined in USPAP) and is part of an assignment (as defined in USPAP), STANDARD 3 applies to development and STANDARD 4 to reporting. Even when STANDARDS 3 and 4 do not apply, other parts of USPAP will apply if the service falls within the scope of USPAP's definition of appraisal practice.

Whether compliance with USPAP is required in any given situation is different question. The PREAMBLE states, in part:

> *An appraiser must comply with USPAP when either the service or the appraiser is required by law, regulation, or agreement with the client or intended user.*

Therefore, questions relating to reviews by an Ethics Committee, Board of Examiners, or similar body must be analyzed on a case-by-case basis in the context of the various definitions and the applicable laws, regulations, or agreements.

359. DEFINITION OF VALUE IN APPRAISAL REVIEW REPORTS

Question: **USPAP is clear with regard to the rules reviewers must follow when developing their own opinions of value. In assignments like this, are review appraisers required to provide their own definitions of value in the appraisal review reports?**

A commonly used residential review form neither provides this information, nor has a field for reviewers to provide this information when reviewers are providing their own opinions of value. I recognize that the onus is on the appraiser for USPAP compliance rather than form.

I'm not clear on whether the market value definition used in the original appraisal is implied, should be clarified with an extraordinary assumption, or simply defined in the appraisal review report.

Response: USPAP does not specifically address this issue in STANDARDS 3 and 4. Absent a statement otherwise by the reviewer, it would be assumed that the reviewer's opinion of value would be based upon the definition of value in the appraisal report being reviewed. However, USPAP does not prohibit the reviewer from using another value definition.

© The Appraisal Foundation

When reviewers render their own opinion of value, they must comply with STANDARD 1 (see Standards Rule 1-2 (c)), which states an appraiser must "identify the type and definition of value..."

360. REVIEWER HIGHLIGHTING THE POSITIVE (NEW)

Question: **Should the reviewer try to apply USPAP so that the appraiser whose work is under review is presented in the best light?**

Response: No. USPAP prohibits bias, which is defined as "a preference or inclination that precludes an appraiser's impartiality, independence, or objectivity in an assignment." Furthermore, the reviewer should focus on the work under review, not upon the appraiser.

361. CLIENT REQUIREMENTS AS AN ASSIGNMENT ELEMENT (NEW)

Question: **Are client requirements considered an assignment element that must be taken into account when identifying the appraisal problem and determining the scope of work?**

Response: Yes, sometimes. USPAP DEFINITIONS indicate that "assignment elements" include "assignment conditions," one of which is "...other conditions that affect the scope of work." Sometimes client requirements fit this definition.

362. REVIEWER PROVIDING ADJUSTMENTS (NEW)

Question: **When communicating an opinion that some adjustments applied in the work under review are unreasonable, is the reviewer required to provide better or alternate adjustments?**

Response: No. Unless the appraisal review assignment includes the reviewer's own opinion of value for the subject property, it is not necessary for the reviewer to provide alternate adjustments. An appraisal review report must state "reasons for any disagreement" with the work under review and must provide "sufficient information for the client and intended users to understand the rationale for the reviewer's opinions and conclusions." See Standards Rule 4-2(i).

363. MAY REVIEWER SAY AN APPRAISAL LACKS ANALYSIS? (NEW)

Question: **If no analysis is presented in an Appraisal Report, may a reviewer opine that no analysis was performed in the appraisal?**

Response: Yes. If no analysis is reported, there is a deficiency in the appraisal, the Appraisal Report, or both. An Appraisal Report is required to provide sufficient information to indicate that the appraiser complied with the requirements of (the applicable) STANDARD "by summarizing the information analyzed, the appraisal methods and techniques employed, and the reasoning that supports the analyses, opinions, and conclusions, including reconciliation of the data and approaches." If an Appraisal Report does not provide this required summary, then it is open to question whether the required analysis has been performed in developing the appraisal.

© The Appraisal Foundation

364. DEVELOPING AN OPINION OF REASONABLE EXPOSURE TIME (NEW)

Question: **Is it true that developing an opinion of reasonable exposure time is required only in market value appraisals?**

Response: No. This is not limited to market value appraisals. The appraiser is required to develop an opinion of reasonable exposure time when reasonable exposure time is a component of the value definition being applied. See Standards Rules 1-2(c) and 7-2(c). In addition, if required to develop the opinion, the appraiser must also state the opinion of reasonable exposure time in the Appraisal Report or Restricted Appraisal Report. See Standards Rules 2-2(a)(vi), 2-2(b)(viii), 8-2(a)(vi), and 8-2(b)(viii).

© The Appraisal Foundation

365. VALUATION SERVICE INVOLVING ADVOCACY

Question: **A client feels that her property is over assessed by the county. She's asked me to perform a tax consulting service that involves advocacy for her position and I'd like to charge her on a contingency fee basis. This assignment would not include an appraisal. I have two questions: Is this service allowed under USPAP? If not, can I perform this assignment outside of USPAP?**

Response: You may not perform this assignment under USPAP. An appraiser, in appraisal practice, may not be an advocate. The Conduct section of the ETHICS RULE states:

An appraiser must perform assignments with impartiality, objectivity, and independence, and without accommodation of personal interests.

An appraiser:

- *must not perform an assignment with bias;*
- *must not advocate* ***the cause or interest*** *of any party or issue;* (Bold added for emphasis)

Appraisal practice is defined as:

valuation services performed by an individual acting as an appraiser, including but not limited to appraisal or appraisal review.

Furthermore, none of the certifications in USPAP allow any bias, contingent compensation related to assignment results, or direction in value that favors the cause of the client.

Absent any law or regulation to the contrary, you may complete this assignment outside of USPAP, as long as you are very clear about your role. The ETHICS RULE also states,

An appraiser:

must not misrepresent his or her role when providing valuation services that are outside of appraisal practice.

Refer to Advisory Opinion 21, *USPAP Compliance*, for further guidance.

366. FEASIBILITY STUDIES AND APPRAISAL PRACTICE

Question: **A client recently requested that I perform a feasibility study on a potential retail development. No value conclusions are included in the scope of the work agreed upon with the client, but they have requested that I provide many of the components of what could lead to a value conclusion, such as potential income streams, capitalization rates, cost estimates, and similar information. I have completed numerous appraisal assignments for this client and I am certain that I was chosen, in large part, because I am an appraiser. Does this assignment fall within appraisal practice? And, must I comply with USPAP in completing the assignment?**

Response: Yes. This assignment falls under appraisal practice because it is a valuation service performed by an individual acting as an appraiser.

© The Appraisal Foundation

The appraiser needs to carefully and clearly identify the appropriate valuation services required to complete this assignment competently and ensure that they comply with the applicable sections of USPAP.

Any valuation service that requires an opinion of value requires adherence to both STANDARDS 1 and 2. For example, the portion of the assignment that analyzes "components of what could lead to a value conclusion such as potential income streams" suggests the appraiser might need to provide an opinion of market rent. Market rent represents an opinion of value. So too could the inclusion of recent sales, if analyzed for their comparability to the subject.

For portions of the analysis that are not an appraisal or an appraisal review and do not require an opinion of value, the appraiser must, at a minimum, comply with the ETHICS RULE, the COMPETENCY RULE, and the JURISDICTIONAL EXCEPTION RULE. (The PREAMBLE and the DEFINITIONS apply generally to all appraisal practice.) Refer to Advisory Opinion 21, *USPAP Compliance*, for further guidance.

367. REPLACEMENT COST ESTIMATE

Question: **Is an estimate of replacement cost new (RCN) considered an appraisal?**

Response: No. An appraisal is defined in USPAP as "an opinion of value." USPAP also defines value and cost.

Value is defined as:

> *VALUE: the monetary relationship between properties and those who buy, sell, or use those properties, expressed as an opinion of the worth of a property at a given time.*
>
> Comment: *In appraisal practice, value will always be qualified – for example, market value, liquidation value, or investment value.*

Cost is defined as:

> *COST: the actual or estimated amount required to create, reproduce, replace, or obtain a property.*

Replacement cost may be a major component used in developing an opinion of some types of value, such as insurable value, but an estimate of RCN by itself is not a value, thus this estimate is not an appraisal.

© The Appraisal Foundation

© The Appraisal Foundation

2020-2021 EDITION

INDEX

APPRAISAL STANDARDS BOARD

A

B

© The Appraisal Foundation

© The Appraisal Foundation

© The Appraisal Foundation

J

L

M

N

O

© The Appraisal Foundation

P

Q

R

© The Appraisal Foundation

S

© The Appraisal Foundation

T

U

V

W

Y

Z

© The Appraisal Foundation

© The Appraisal Foundation